THE PRACTICE OF
ENGLISH
LANGUAGE
TEACHING

THIRD EDITION

COMPLETELY REVISED AND UPDATED

Jeremy Harmer

Longman

Pearson Education Limited
Edinburgh Gate
Harlow
Essex CM20 2JE
England
And Associated Companies throughout the World.

www.longman.com

ISBN 0 582 40385 5

Printed in Malaysia, PP
Sixth impression 2004

Acknowledgements

We are grateful to the following for permission to reproduce copyright material:
Cambridge Evening News for the article 'Hero pulls neighbour from blaze' by Dan Grimmer, published in the Cambridge Evening News, 3rd May 1999; Gap Activity Project for an extract by Penny Elvy from *GAP ANNUAL NEWSLETTER* (1996); Granta Publications Ltd for an extract from 'Maximum Security' by R O'Connor in *GRANTA* No 54, 1996, pp220-221; New Statesman Ltd for the 'Lonely Hearts' advertisements in *NEW STATESMAN*, June 12, 2000; Oxford University Press for extracts from *Lifelines Intermediate Student's Book* by Tom Hutchinson © Oxford University Press (1997) and *A Cognitive Approach to Language Learning* by Peter Skehan © Oxford University Press (1998); and Universal Music Publishing Group for the lyrics to IRONIC by Morissette/Ballard © 1999.

We are grateful to the following for permission to reproduce illustrative material:
Cambridge Evening News for page 225; Cambridge University Press for pages 8, 103, 173, 192, and 212, adapted from *The Cambridge Encyclopedia of the English Language* by David Crystal, p. 107 (1995), from *Activate Your English Intermediate Coursebook* by B Sinclair and P Prowse, p. 59 (1996), from *Essential Grammar in Use* by R Murphy, p. 140 (1997), from *Pronunciation Games* by M Hancock, p. 85 (1995), and from *Extensive Reading in the Second Language Classroom*, p. 152 (1998); © The Digital Education Network Ltd for page 149; Getty One Stone for page 239 left; Guardian Unlimited for pages 221 and 222; IH Net Languages for page 148; Life File for page 239 middle; Macmillan Heinemann for page 190 from *Sound Foundations* by A Underhill, p. viii (1994); © Microsoft for page 146 from *Encarta Encyclopedia*; Oxford University Press for pages 120, 172, 193, 239, and 279, from *Roles of Teachers and Learners* by T Wright, p. 130 (1987), from *The English File Student's Book 2* by C Oxenden et al, p. 36 (1997), from *Headway Elementary Pronunciation* by S Cunningham and P Moor, p. 28 (1995), and from *New First Certificate Masterclass Student's Book* by S Haines and B Stewart, p. 162 (1996); Oxford University Press/Gareth Boden for 239 right; and Saffire Press for page 49 quoted with permission from *In Your Hands: NLP in ELT* by J Revell and S Norman, p. 36 (1997).

Illustrations by Liz Roberts; Oxford Illustrators Ltd
Page layout & repro by CPM, Cambridge
Text design by A Ingr
Copy-editing by R Morlin

Contents

PART 3: THEORIES, METHODS, AND TECHNIQUES

PART 4: MANAGING CLASSES

Preface

When the last edition of *The Practice of English Language Teaching* was being written some schools used computers for word processing, and there were a few language games and simulations available on floppy disks. But that was about it. In what seems like a ridiculously short space of time, however, all that has changed. Computers are now, for teachers and students, the gateways to a wealth of information, contacts, and activities. The use of the Internet has mushroomed – indeed some countries have wired up their entire public education systems – and the technology for self study, language laboratories, and computer corpora has developed far beyond what many had anticipated.

Such advances are only the most visible signs of progress in a profession which, thank goodness, refuses to stand still. The teaching of English is in a constant state of flux, with new theories, practices, and materials erupting all over the world on an almost daily basis. We are constantly challenged by new research, provoked by the questioning of long-held beliefs, and amazed by the sheer brilliance and creativity of a diverse population of teachers, methodologists, materials designers – and, of course, students – from all over the globe. In a world where certain values are immutable, and where the qualities that make a good teacher may well be universal, change is nevertheless the lifeblood of our profession. To quote David Crystal in another context, 'we know something is alive when we see it move'.

A book about language teaching methodology has to change too, to take account of all this movement. Since the last edition of *The Practice of English Language Teaching*, there have been many new areas of research and innovation, quite apart from the growth in computer use in teaching and learning. Large corpora have allowed experts to tell us much more about the different grammars for spoken and written English, and now have incontrovertible evidence about the way language chunks itself into phrases of various kinds. Attitudes to language study both in and outside the classroom have been modified too, with serious attempts to put at least one model of language teaching (Presentation, Practice, and Production) firmly in its place. The role of English in our modern world has been the subject of much debate, as has been a growing awareness that language teaching methodology is often as culturally-specific as the cultures it springs from and cannot, therefore, be exported without taking account of where it is headed. At the same time our profession has realised that developing teachers themselves is part of the way they can offer more to their learners whilst at the same time enriching their own lives.

All of these contemporary issues are reflected in this new edition, which also looks (with I hope a fresh eye) at a range of familiar topics, from motivation to the roles of the teacher, from classroom management to feedback and correction. There are completely new chapters on teaching pronunciation, language testing, coursebooks, and learner autonomy/teacher development. The example activities have been taken from up-to-date materials, and the references and bibliography are intended to reflect much of our current states of knowledge and enthusiasm.

This book is aimed at practising teachers and those studying on in-service training programmes and postgraduate courses. In that, it differs significantly from its sister volume, *How to Teach English*, which is designed specifically for those wanting a more gentle introduction to the science and art of teaching English.

Acknowledgements

The first two editions

The first edition of *The Practice of English Language Teaching* all those years ago could not have been written without the input and reaction of teacher colleagues and students at the Instituto Anglo-Mexicano de Cultura both in Mexico City and Guadalajara. They, and the trainees I worked with there, shaped the structure and content of that first edition.

At the very beginning I benefited greatly from help, advice, and reports given by Walter Plumb, Jean Pender, Richard Rossner, Donn Byrne and Jane Willis. Tim Hunt commissioned the book and Judith King edited it.

For the second edition, I was inspired by comments from Richard Rossner, Julian Edge, and Nick Dawson, and spurred on by Damien Tunnacliffe, who together with Helena Gomm and Alyson Lee saw the work through to its completion.

This new edition

Since the publication of the first edition I have had the great good fortune to work with teachers both in the UK and in many other parts of the world. Their responses and concerns, and the enormous amount I have learnt from attending their papers and workshops, led directly to the second edition of the book and have heavily influenced this new version, as have the many teachers around the world whose lessons I have been privileged to observe, and the students I have had the chance to work with.

As this new edition has gone through its various drafts to emerge in this, its final form, a number of people have directly helped the process in many varied and thought-provoking ways.

First among these – and someone to whom I owe a real debt of gratitude – is Martin Parrott, whose advice, encouragement, robust criticism and suggestions have been a feature of the writing process from the very beginning of the project. His unerring ability to spot problems of both style or substance saved me from many mishaps and inspired me to go further than I might otherwise have done.

Sally Blackmore's reports gave a clear, penetrating account of what the manuscript looked like from the point of view of the kind of reader it is especially designed for. She reminded me of what readers like that really need and I am forever in her debt.

Hanna Kijowska's report on part of the manuscript came just at the right time. She was able to bring a unique perspective to her reading of the material, helping me to sort out issues of level and focus. Her influence in the final version of those chapters is strong.

When Katie Head looked at the last third of the book she had little trouble pointing up problems and many roads not taken. Her comments challenged and inspired me, providing just the kind of creative tension that every writer hopes for from his or her reporters.

Thanks are also due to Kip Téllez and David Bowker whose reports helped to guide the book's development in a number of different ways.

Not only have I been blessed with such reporters, but I also got the best editor possible! Brigit Viney's detailed reading of the text and her clear-headed suggestions for how to improve it kept the process going. Without her this book would not be like it is.

Behind all of these people, however, has been my publisher David Lott, who believed in this project from the start, guided it, dealt with all the difficulties I put in his way, read the manuscript many times, and saved me from countless infelicities. Not only that, but he managed to keep me going at times when things got tough. This book exists because of him.

A number of people have generously answered questions, given me their time, or provided me with references I could not find, including Paul Cane, Gillie Cunningham, Chris George, Roger Gower, Kenny Graham, Peter Grundy, Katie Plumb, Michael Rundell, Michael Swan, and Douglas Workman.

When you are writing on your own, you need someone to bounce ideas off, and someone to ask for advice and guidance. As with the previous editions of this book, Anita Harmer has generously provided such counsel, listened to an author's moans and groans, and put up with the whole thing. To her are due heartfelt thanks.

But at the end of everything, the responsibility for what is in this edition of *The Practice of English Language Teaching* is, of course, mine. Where it works all of these people should take the credit, both jointly and severally. If there are places where it does not, it is almost certainly because I did not heed their advice carefully enough.

Jeremy Harmer
Cambridge, UK

1 | The world of English

A The place of English

Although English is not the language with the largest number of native or 'first' language speakers, it has become a **lingua franca**. A lingua franca can be defined as a language widely adopted for communication between two speakers whose native languages are different from each other's and where one or both speakers are using it as a 'second' language. Many people living in the European Union, for example, frequently operate in English as well as their own languages (where these are different), and the economic and cultural influence of the United States has led to increased English use in many areas of the globe. Like Latin in Europe in the Middle Ages, English seems to be one of the main languages of international communication, and even people who are not speakers of English often know words such as *bank, chocolate, computer, hamburger, hospital, hot dog, hotel, piano, radio, restaurant, taxi, telephone, television, university* and *walkman*. Many of these words have themselves been borrowed by English from other languages of course (e.g. *chocolate, hamburger, taxi*, etc.), and speakers of Romance languages are likely to have a number of words in common with English. But there are many 'false friends' too, where similar sounding words actually mean something quite different, for example, Italian *eventualmente* (= in case) contrasts with English *eventually* (= in the end).

A1 The numbers game

Whatever the spread of English across the globe and whatever its overlap with other languages, there has been an intriguing debate over the years as to how many people speak English as either a 'first' or a 'second' language. Estimates of speaker numbers are somewhat variable. For example, Braj Kachru (1985) suggested between 320–380 million people spoke English as a first language, and anywhere between 250–350 million as a second language. On the other hand David Crystal (1995 and 1997) takes 75 territories where English 'holds a special place' (territories which include not only Britain, the USA, Australia, Canada, etc. but also places such as Hong Kong, India, Malaysia and Nigeria) and calculates around 377 million first language speakers of English and only 98 million speakers of English as a second language. However, he points out that it would be easy to get nearer a total of 350 million for second language speakers if we were able to calculate how many speakers of English as a second language there were in, say, Canada or Australia, or in countries like Pakistan or Nigeria. Not only is the calculation of such figures problematic, but a lot, he suggests, also depends on how well we expect people to be able to speak English before we can start including them as second language English speakers. As he points out, 'the more limited command of English we allow to be acceptable, the more this figure can be inflated' (Crystal 1995: 108). It seems to be the case, therefore, that anywhere between 600–700 million people in the world speak English, and of that huge number, a significant minority speak it as a second language.

In 1983, however, Kachru made a prediction which, if correct, means that there are now more second language than first language speakers. He wrote:

> One might hazard a linguistic guess here. If the spread of English continues at the current rate, by the year 2000 its non-native speakers will outnumber its native speakers.
>
> From B Kachru (1983: 3)

David Graddol, writing some fourteen years later, thought it would take until at least 2007 before this position was reached (Graddol 1997).

As we shall observe (in A4), it is not necessarily the case that English will remain dominant among world languages. However, there is no doubt that it is and will remain a vital linguistic tool for many business people, academics, tourists and citizens of the world who wish to communicate easily across nationalities for many years to come.

A2   How English got there

There are a number of interlocking reasons for the popularity of English as a lingua franca. Many of these are historical, but they also include economic and cultural factors which have influenced and sustained the spread of the language:

- **A colonial history:** when the Pilgrim Fathers landed on the Massachusetts coast in 1620 after their eventful journey from Plymouth, England, they brought with them not just a set of religious beliefs, nor only a pioneering spirit and a desire for colonisation, but also their language. Although many years later the Americans broke away from their colonial masters, the language of English remained and it is still the predominant language of the world's greatest economic and political power.

   It was the same in Australia, too. When Commander Philip planted the British flag in Sydney Cove on 26th January 1788, it was not just a bunch of British convicts and their guardians who disembarked (to be rapidly followed by many free settlers of that land), but also a language.

   In other parts of the British Empire, English rapidly became a unifying/ dominating means of control. For example, it became a lingua franca in India, where a plethora of indigenous languages made the use of any one of them as a whole-country system problematic. The imposition of English as the one language of administration helped maintain the coloniser's power.

   Thus, in the same way as Spanish was imposed on much of the new world by the conquistadores from Castile, or Brazil and parts of Africa took on the language of their Portuguese conquerors, English travelled around many parts of the world, until, many years from the colonial reality that introduced it, and long after that colonial power has faded away, it is still widely used as a main or at least an institutional language in countries as far apart as Jamaica and Pakistan, Uganda, and New Zealand.

- **Economics:** a major factor in the spread of English has been the spread of commerce throughout the world, and in particular, the emergence of the United States as a world economic power. Of course other economic blocks are hugely powerful too, but the spread of international commerce has taken English along with it. This is the twentieth-century phenomenon of 'globalisation' described by the journalist John Pilger as '… a term which journalists and politicians have made fashionable and which is often used in a positive sense to denote a "global village" of "free trade", hi-tech marvels and all kinds of possibilities that transcend class, historical experience and ideology' (Pilger 1998: 61). Thus one of the first sights many travellers see arriving in countries as diverse as the Czech Republic and Brazil, for example, is the yellow twin-arched sign of a McDonalds fast food restaurant. Whether we take a benign view of such 'multinational' economic activity or, like John Pilger and many others, view it as a threat to the identities of individual countries and local control, English is the language that frequently rides on its back.

- **Travel:** much travel and tourism is carried on, around the world, in English. Of course this is not always the case, as the multilingualism of many tourism workers in different countries demonstrates, but a visit to most airports on the globe will show signs not only in the language of that country, but also in English, just as many airline announcements are glossed in English too, whatever the language of the country the airport is situated in.

    So far, English is also the preferred language of air traffic control in many countries and is used widely in sea travel communication.

- **Information exchange:** a great deal of academic discourse around the world takes place in English. It is often a lingua franca of conferences, for example, and many journal articles in fields as diverse as astrophysics and zoology have English as a kind of default language.

    The first years of the Internet as a major channel for information exchange have also seen a marked predominance of English (though as we shall see in B3, such a situation may not continue). This probably has something to do with the Internet's roots in the USA and the predominance of its use there in the early days of the World Wide Web (see Chapter 10F for more on the Internet).

- **Popular culture:** in the western world, at least, English is a dominating language in popular culture. Pop music in English saturates the planet's airwaves. Thus many people who are not English speakers can sing words from their favourite English medium songs. Many people who are regular cinemagoers (or TV viewers) frequently hear English in subtitled films coming out of the USA. However, we need to remind ourselves that 'Bollywood' (in

India) produces more films than Hollywood (in the USA) and that many countries, such as France, do their best to fight against the cultural domination of the American movie.

A3 Where English fits

There are many views of the place of English in the world and what it is doing and has done. Is it, for example, an all-conquering language which obliterates everything in its path? Is it a wonderful means of mass communication? Does it carry a lot of cultural baggage with it, and if so how can that be assimilated and/or responded to? And finally, should people from countries all over the world struggle to learn it or would their time be better spent in the study of other languages?

Perhaps the first thing to say is that English is one of the many languages in the world battling it out for position. There are some doubts as to its future status, but even in the present it is worth countering the idea that it is an all-embracing world language.

There are, of course, many more people in the world who do not speak English than there are people who do! But it is not just that. In more and more countries English language films are dubbed into the language of that country, and on the Internet, the growth of non-English information exchange is noticeable; many search engines (like Alta Vista and Hotbot) have, for some time, offered users a choice of languages. According to the company Computer Economics, only 54 per cent of Internet users were English speakers in 1999, and that percentage was due to drop significantly (see A4 below).

Language is an intensely political issue since it is bound up with identity and power. As a consequence of its lingua franca status, English sometimes finds itself in conflict with more local languages, such as Welsh in Wales, or French in parts of French-speaking Canada. It works the other way too, of course. Visitors to Miami airport may well be surprised by the overwhelming use of Spanish in a major American airport because of a numerous Spanish-speaking community in that city. In a large number of countries in the world (of which Britain and the United States have, until now, been prominent exceptions) children regularly grow up speaking more than one language so that English, if it is learnt, becomes a third or fourth means of communication.

Many people worry about what English means for the cultures it comes into contact with, seeing its teaching as a form of 'cultural imperialism' (see, for example, Phillipson 1992 and Pennycook 1994, 1998). Alistair Pennycook draws our attention to the views of many people who have seen English as a way of promoting their own (American, Australian, British, Canadian, etc.) culture, and to the interrelationship of English (in particular) and colonialism. We should also be aware of the supranational power of global companies (see A2 above) which often fall back on English as a means of global communication across the company and largely unthinkingly promote its use.

English can have a negative effect on the languages it comes into contact with, downgrading them so that their use becomes restricted, and in extreme circumstances, bringing about their decline. Nor is it necessarily welcome to those who have been obliged to study it, some of whom see learning English as an unpleasant but sadly necessary occupation (Pennycook 1998: 206–212). However, even Pennycook suggests that a powerful modern paradigm for English as a foreign language may be one of 'appropriation' – where cultures take English and change it in their own way – despite its relentless progress.

The view that learners of English are victims of linguistic and cultural imperialism is not shared by everyone. Joseph Bisong points out that Nigerians, for example, may want to operate with two or more languages in a multilingual setting, choosing which one to use depending upon the situation they are in and the people they wish to communicate with. He suggests that great writers like Achebe, Soyinka, and Ngugi do not write in English as victims, but out of choice – whatever the reasons for this choice might be (Bisong 1995). But this is not a free choice, Phillipson argues (1996). It is determined by their audience not by them. Kanavilil Rajagopalan, on the other hand, suggests that the teaching of English should not be seen as a form of cultural imperialism, '… in a world marked by cultural intermixing and growing multilingualism at a hitherto unprecedented level' (Rajagopalan 1999: 200).

Most English language teaching in the world is not carried out by native speakers, but despite this, as we shall see in Chapter 6, B1, English language teaching methodology – especially that imported directly from English-speaking traditions – may not fit comfortably with the local educational culture in certain parts of the world, just as the contents of language teaching materials need looking at carefully for the cultural messages they may convey (see Chapter 21B).

A4 The future of English

If we accept that English is currently a lingua franca for many people in the world, does this necessarily mean that its pre-eminence is assured? What happens as more and more people appropriate it for their own uses? Will it split into varieties that become less mutually intelligible? Or will it continue to march over the globe, crushing all in its path? Is it conceivable, as David Crystal half-jokingly worries, that in 500 years it will be the only language left? Such an outcome would be, in his words, '… the greatest intellectual disaster that the planet has ever known' (Crystal 1997: 140).

David Graddol does not prophesy a globally destructive English of this kind (Graddol 1997). He considers a number of future possibilities, all of which question the certainty of English as the number one world language. He points out, for example, that the fastest-growing language community in the USA is Hispanic. Taken together with the trade agreements which are springing up in both the North and South American continents, it is highly possible that in the foreseeable future the entire American continent will be an English-Spanish bilingual zone. Looking at the Internet and the World Wide Web he reminds us that whereas English is said to have accounted for 80 per cent of computer-based communication in the 1990s, that proportion is expected to drop to around 40 per cent by 2010. The company Computer Economics predicted the same kind of shift in their 1999 survey (see Figure 1), where the balance between English-speaking users and non-English users of the Internet is set to change dramatically:

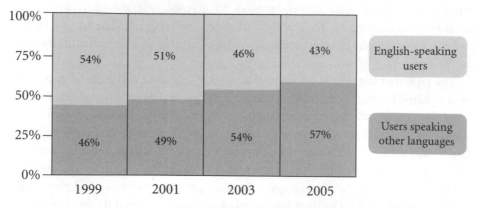

FIGURE 1: Internet usage according to language (based on information at
http://cyberatlas.internet.com/big_picture/demographics/print/0,1323,5901_150171,00.html)

Within the next few decades the number of Internet computer web sites and servers in Asia may well outstrip all other computer hosts put together. Air travel too is set to show the same kind of change. Graddol predicted that Asian air travel would account for half the world's flying by 2010. In such circumstances a form of Mandarin could be the lingua franca of choice in the region.

Whether or not these predictions prove or have proved to be accurate, it is most unlikely that English will ever become the dominant language in the world. On the contrary, its 'top dog' status may have changed in another fifty years so that it becomes just one of a number of other world languages being widely used around the globe.

B Varieties of English

So far in this chapter, we have talked about English as one language, and in our discussion of its position as a lingua franca we have referred to it in the singular. Yet English, much like other languages such as Spanish, Portuguese or Arabic, for example, can take many forms. Depending on who speaks or writes it and where they do this, there can be great differences in pronunciation, vocabulary, and grammar.

B1 Three circles

Most people are familiar with the fact that British and American English, whilst being similar, nevertheless have many differences. It was, after all, Oscar Wilde who wittily described the situation as 'two countries divided by a common language'. Thus, for example, British English speakers regularly use the phrase *have got* in utterances such as *I've got a book about it*, or *Have you got the time?* when American English speakers are more likely to say *I have a book ...* or *Do you have the time?* While British speakers in conversation make use of the present perfect in questions such as *Have you read her latest article yet?* an American English speaker might well say *Did you read her latest article yet?* The sentence *If I would have known I would have come*, is likely to be more acceptable to American than to British ears, and there are many differences in vocabulary use (*lift/elevator, flat/apartment*), pronunciation (/lɔː/ –*law* (British English) vs. /lɑː/ (American English), ad*ve*rtisement (British English) vs. *advertisement* (American English)), and even spelling (*advertise/advertize, colour/color*).

These are not the only varieties of English, of course. For example, there are now two home-grown dictionaries of Australian English; the *Australian Learners Dictionary* (published by the National Centre for English Language Teaching and Research at Macquarie University) is full of specifically Australian vocabulary such as *barby/barbie* (for *barbecue*) or *bottle shop* (for *off-licence*) – though words like this frequently cross over into other varieties such as British English.

There is nothing unique about Australian English in this respect. All varieties, whether South African, Canadian, Sri Lankan or Nigerian will have their own specific words and phrases, their own grammatical mannerisms and pronunciation idiosyncracies. However, calling a variety by the name of a country fails to take account of regional variety. If we consider 'British English', for example, it only takes a moment's thought to realise that there are many varieties of English within the British Isles, each with its own vocabulary, pronunciation, and grammar. While a Londoner might get a *take-away* meal to eat at home, a Scottish person will order a *carry-out*. While an East-end Londoner might talk about having a *barf* /bɑːf/ a Yorkshireman talks about a *bath* /bæθ/. While a speaker of standard southern English says *I did it*, speakers of other varieties say *I done it*.

In addition to geography, factors such as social class, ethnic grouping, and sex affect the language being used – and influence the way in which listeners judge speakers. Until very recently in Britain, it was customary for people to talk about 'BBC English' to describe an accent which derived from the 'Received Pronunciation' (RP) recorded by the phonetician Daniel Jones in the first half of the twentieth century, and which was considered a sign of status. In Britain, while some accents are admired (such as BBC English and some Scottish varieties), others (such as the 'Birmingham' accent) are seen by many as less attractive. Though it is true that such attitudes diminished towards the end of the twentieth century – and some accents, such as 'Cockney' and 'Geordie' became widely admired, particularly in broadcast media – it is still the case that many British people ascribe status, educational background, and social position to a person largely on the basis of accent.

Other countries have their regional and social differences too, as visits to different parts of Boston and Dallas would make instantly clear; there are varieties of American English which show marked differences one from the other so that, as with British English, the concept of one 'American English' is difficult to sustain. And even a city like Boston contains within it a large number of English varieties. There are varieties of Black English, Hispanic English, East Coast English, Chinese English, etc. amongst many others, and future waves of immigrants will appropriate the language for their own uses and in their own ways.

We are faced, then, with a situation where English varies between and within those countries where it is spoken widely. There is, then, a multiplicity of varieties, and this makes it difficult to describe English as any one thing.

Braj Kachru (1985: 12–15) suggests the division of the English-speaking world into three concentric circles. This classification is widely used and may help us to think about English around the globe.

In the first 'inner circle' Kachru puts countries like Ireland, New Zealand, Australia, Canada, Britain, and the United States where English is spoken as a first language. In the second 'outer circle' are all the countries where English is spoken as a second or significant language, such as Singapore, India, Pakistan, Malawi, Malaysia, Nigeria. In the third 'expanding circle' we find countries where English has acquired cultural or commercial importance (China, Sweden, the Czech Republic, Greece, Japan, Israel, etc). See Figure 2:

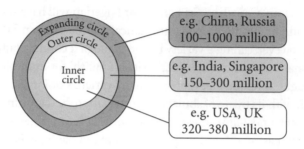

FIGURE 2: A diagrammatic representation of Kachru's circles, based on Kachru (1985)

In a world of so many Englishes, therefore, we have to consider which is the variety we should encourage our learners to aim for.

B2 Appropriate models of English

In Brazil, a country with a population of more than 180 million, many people learn English, not only in school (where it is the foreign language of choice) and at university, but also in many private language schools located the length and breadth of that vast country. Two of the largest of these teaching organisations are the 'Cultura' institutes and the 'Bi-National' centres. The former have evolved from British Council schools and teach essentially British English, while the latter are supported by the United States Information Service and teach American English. Both organisations have centres all over the country from São Paulo to Salvador, from Rio de Janeiro to Recife. In 1999 they catered for some 140,000 and 120,000 students respectively. Do the two varieties, then, have parity? Which variety should the students choose?

Brazil is not alone, of course. In countries all over the world students can choose British or American English to learn. In other countries they can choose Australian English or a more outer circle variety such as Malaysian or Indian English. And if they wish to study abroad should they choose Ireland, Australia or Britain, Canada or New Zealand?

The reason for the students' choice may not be based entirely on the language variety, of course. They might go to one organisation rather than another because their friends do or because of some perceived methodological superiority. Where they travel abroad, their choice of one country over another will also be affected by matters of cost and culture.

But what then of the teachers of English? What variety should they adopt? Of course teachers who are British or Canadian, for example, will probably use their variety of English as a model, but for the majority of non-native speaker teachers the choice may not be so clear cut, and for many programme directors the choice of textbook will be a point at which they have to make up their minds.

Jan Svartvik makes a compelling case for choosing a variety from the inner circle if English is being learnt in an expanding circle country – that is, if English is being studied as a foreign language. Clearly this will not apply if the study is taking place in India or Malaysia (examples of outer circle countries) where home-grown varieties of English are both necessary and desirable. But where students are studying English in Prague or Buenos Aires, in Havana or Istanbul, then an inner circle variety is, in Svartvik's opinion, the only appropriate choice. In a talk in 1998 he argued that the choice of which inner circle variety to learn was not so crucial since the differences between inner circle varieties, while notable, were not nearly so numerous as the underlying similarities. A speaker of Irish English, for example, is intelligible to most other English speakers in the world and will also understand what is said to him or her.

The safest conclusion to draw is that teachers should work with the variety that best reflects their own language use, always provided that this will be understood by most other English speakers in the world – and/or the speakers that the students are most likely to come into contact with.

The fact that teachers and students generally aim at one variety for language production does not mean that they should only ever see or hear that one language variety. Teachers should expose students to different language varieties in listening (and reading) texts so that they do not only hear their teacher's voice. This will prepare students for the times when they come into contact with different language varieties at some later stage (see Chapter 16, A3). Of course, exposing beginner students to too many varieties and accents will be counter-productive since they will already be facing the difficulty of coming to terms with just one variety. But as their level improves (see Chapter 3, B4), they will need to have opportunities to encounter more and different varieties of English.

B3 General and specific

One issue of language variety has little to do with geography and power in the ways we have described in this chapter. As teachers, we have to decide whether the English we teach our students will be general or specific.

A large number of students in the world study 'general' English, that is all-purpose language with no special focus on one area of human experience (e.g. business or academic study) over another. Thus, as we shall see, general English courses usually offer a judicious blend of different language skills and choose their topics from a range of sources, basing their selection of content more on student interest and engagement than on an easily identifiable student need. In schools and institutes all over the world students are taught to communicate on a general social level and to cope with the normal range of texts which educated language users experience outside their professional lives. A decision to teach general English is made, in part, when we do not know how, why or when our students will need the language in the future, and so we give them language with the broadest range of use possible.

In contrast to students of general English, students of English for Specific Purposes (ESP) may have a closely identified goal for learning. Perhaps they are studying (or are about to study) in an English-medium university. They might therefore want a form of ESP referred to as English for Academic Purposes (EAP) in which there is a concentration on writing academic essays, taking notes from oral lectures, perfecting reference skills in English, etc. If they are going to become scientists or engineers, on the other hand, they might be learning English for Science and Technology (EST) in which case their teacher might have them improving on their ability to consult or design manuals amongst other things.

As we shall see in Chapters 14, B2 and 18, B2, different genres of writing and speaking provoke different language use. Scientific articles employ passives more than general ones; academic essays require a style of discourse and particular expressions which would be out of place in normal social interaction. The language of air traffic control has a specific vocabulary which has to be understood and followed if the system is to work; workers in the tourist industry need to be confident about the specific vocabulary and the types of language interactions, such as dealing with dissatisfied customers, that they may encounter.

An enormous growth area in English language teaching has been in the area of Business English because many students perceive a need for the kind of language which will allow them to operate in the world of English-medium commerce. Once again there is specific vocabulary and language events (presenting to colleagues, the language of contracts, etc.) which are unlikely to appear in a general English course, but which are vitally important for business students. And so teachers find themselves training classes in such procedures as the art of negotiating, the correct use of phones and e-mail, or the reading of business reports.

Further reading

- **Native speakers**

  On trying to define a native speaker and his or her status as a language user, see M Rampton (1990).

- **Where English fits**

  On issues of power and the English language, see A Canagarajah (1999).
  R Phillipson (1999) delivers an uncompromising critique of D Crystal (1997) on global issues. Crystal (2000b) answers these points.

- **Appropriate models of English**

  D Crystal (2000a) predicted the coming of a tri-lingual English world with a base (home) level, a national level, and, tantalisingly, an international standard English.

- **ESP**

  For more on ESP (English for Specific Purposes), see T Dudley-Evans and M St John (1998).

2 | Describing language

A Grammar

The grammar of a language is the description of the ways in which words can change their forms and can be combined into sentences in that language. If grammar rules are too carelessly violated, communication may suffer, although, as we shall see in A2, creating a 'good' grammar rule is extremely difficult. Linguists investigating native-speaker speech (and writing) have, over the years, devised various different systems to describe how the language works.

A typical tree diagram will show us one such description and demonstrate how grammar rules provide the scaffolding on which we can create any number of different sentences. If we take a simple sentence like *The mongoose bit the snake*, we can represent it in the following way:

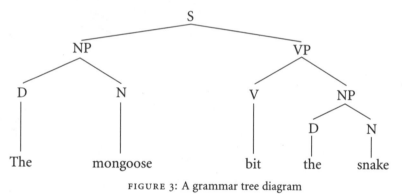

FIGURE 3: A grammar tree diagram

This formulation tells us that the sentence (S) contains a noun phrase (NP) and a verb phrase (VP). The noun phrase contains a determiner (D) and a noun (N) whilst the verb phrase contains a verb (V) and another noun phrase (NP).

What is important is not so much the particular way the grammar is represented here, but the fact that the representation shows us how this simple sentence is structured. It allows us to substitute different words yet retain the same structure, so that *The boy kicked the dog* or *The teacher praised the student* would also qualify as sentences with the same grammatical structure. This type of formulation also allows us to show how sentence structure can be transformed so that the active utterances (e.g. *The mongoose* (NP1) *bit* (VP) *the snake* (NP2)) can be transformed into passive ones (e.g. *The snake* (NP2) *was bitten* (V) *by the mongoose* (NP1)):

$$NP1 + VP + NP2 \implies NP2 + be + V\text{-}ed + by + NP1$$

FIGURE 4: Active → passive transformation

Such descriptions are largely the province of linguists, but they do nevertheless give considerable insight into the structure of a language. And these rules are known, at some subconscious level, by all competent speakers of the language. How else would we be capable of forming sentences? This knowledge is frequently called **competence**, and its realisation (in sentences such as *The mongoose bit the snake* or *The teacher praised the student*) is described as **performance**.

There are, of course, many other rules that go to make up a native speaker's competence. We are all happy to say *It's a big red car*, but find the sentence *It's a red big car* rather uncomfortable. This seems to be because we have a rule which says that when more than one adjective is placed before a noun, an adjective describing size comes before one of colour and not the other way round. When we say *She was elected by a thumping majority* it shows that we know how to change the word *elect* into *elected* by adding the **morpheme** *-ed* to the base form of the verb. Competent speakers know how to use these smallest units of grammar (morphemes) to combine grammatically with words to create new meanings. They know, consciously or subconsciously, that adding the *-ing* morpheme to *thump* turns it into a participle form and that participle forms can be used as adjectives as in *a thumping majority, a singing kettle*, etc.

This knowledge of **morphology** (using morphemes to change the meaning or grammar of a word) and **syntax** (the order that words can be arranged in) is essential to successful communication whether in writing or in speech. Consider the sentence *If he seems impossibly gloomy it may be because he's just heard about his exam results.* Clearly it would be impossible to make such a sentence unless we 'knew' that for the third person singular of the present simple, the base form of the verb (e.g. *seem*) always has the *s* morpheme added onto it. We also need to know that changing the shape of *impossible* to *impossibly* allows us to use it as an intensifying adverb; we need to be aware that we can use the present perfect to refer to something that has recently happened if we add *just*, and that the past participle of *hear* is *heard* – and so on.

A1 Spoken and written grammar

For many years grammars have told us about the written language so that, for example, we confidently state that a sentence needs at least a subject and a verb, which can then be followed by an object (as in *I like biscuits*), by a complement (*He is British*) or by an adverbial (*She lives in Prague*). We know that questions are often formed by inverting the order of subject and verb (*Is he British?*) or (where there is no auxiliary present) bringing in an operator for this function (*Do you like biscuits?*). But the following conversation (in which four people in a kitchen are preparing for a party) seems to call some rules of this type into question:

A: Now I think you'd better start the rice

B: Yeah ... what you got there

    [4 secs]

13

B: Will it all fit in the one

A: No, you'll have to do two separate ones

C: Right . . . what next

[17 secs]

C: Foreign body in there

B: It's the raisins

C: Oh is it oh it's rice with raisins is it

B: [

No

no no it's not supposed to be [laughs] erm

C: There must be a raisin for it being in there

D: Do you want a biscuit

C: Erm

D: Biscuit

C: Er yeah

[9 secs]

D: All right

C: Yeah

[10 secs]

D: Didn't know you used boiling water

B: Pardon

D: Didn't know you used boiling water

B: Don't have to but it's erm ... they reckon it's erm [inaudible]

From R Carter and M McCarthy (1995: 208–209)

This transcript of informal speech is quite difficult to read, but a moment's reflection shows that it is not untypical of a lot of such conversations, containing, as it does, interruptions, non sequiturs, jokes (*There must be a raisin for it*), etc. What is perhaps more interesting is that certain grammatical rules seem to be completely ignored. Look at C's second utterance (*Foreign body in there*). A teacher might tell a student that such a sentence is not well formed and that what it should be is *There's a foreign body in there*. Four lines from the bottom D says *Didn't know you used boiling water*, but a grammar book would suggest that such a sentence should be *I didn't know (that) you used boiling water*. Then there's the biscuit. The first time D makes his or her offer the question is *Do you want a biscuit?*, but the second time all grammar appears to have been done away with and the question is just *Biscuit?* Yet even if this were the first question we would see nothing wrong with it in speech. People in kitchens frequently offer things by saying *Coffee? Sugar? Glass of wine?* **Ellipsis** (where words are 'left out' without destroying the meaning) is a common feature of informal conversation.

The grammar of speech has its own constructional principles (see Biber et al. 1999: 1066–1108); it is organised differently from writing. Spoken English has its own discourse markers too, for example:

- frequent non-clausal units (e.g. *Mmm, No, Uh huh, Yeah*)
- a variety of tags not found in written style, such as question tags (see D2)
- interjections (e.g. *ah, oh, wow, cor* (BrE))
- hesitators (*er, umm, erm*)
- interjections (e.g. *ah, oh wow, cor* (BrE))
- condensed questions (e.g. *More milk?, Any luck?*)
- echo questions (e.g. *Oh did you say San Francisco?, White chocolate hot cocoa?*)
- response forms (e.g. *yeah* or *sure* to acknowledge a request)
- fixed polite speech formulae (e.g. *Happy birthday!, Congratulations!*)

What is clear is that we need different grammar rules for speech and writing as Carter and McCarthy suggest (Carter and McCarthy 1995, McCarthy and Carter 1995). Language corpora (see B1 below and Chapter 12c) are now allowing us to do this as books like the *Longman Grammar of Spoken and Written English* clearly demonstrate (see Biber et al. cited above).

A2 Problems with grammar rules

Once we know the grammatical rules of a language subconsciously, we are in a position to create an infinite number of sentences. However, while some rules are fairly straightforward, others seem to be horribly complex, and some grammatical patterning seems to have escaped perfect description so far.

One of the easiest rules to explain is the use of the *s* morpheme on the third person of the present simple (see above). We always add it with the pronouns *he, she,* and *it*. This is a straightforward rule, but it needs qualifying immediately. We can restate it by saying that we add *s* to all verbs for the third person singular of the present simple unless they are modal verbs (*must, can, will, should,* etc.), thus ruling out **he musts*. So a simple rule has become slightly less simple.

Many rules are considerably more complex than this, and linguists are still researching areas of language which hover teasingly out of reach of cut and dried description. But here a difference has to be made between **descriptive** and **pedagogic** grammars. Whilst the former may attempt to describe everything there is, the latter are designed specifically to be of help to teachers and students of the language who need, as far as possible, clear and easily-digestible summaries of what is and what is not correct. Such pedagogic grammar rules inform much language teaching but if they are carelessly applied, they can sometimes lead to considerable oversimplification – such as the 'rule' which says that *some* is used with affirmative sentences whilst *any* is used with questions and negative sentences. This rule helps students at beginner level to be sure of making correct sentences such as *I've got some sweets, I haven't got any money?,* and *Have you got any petrol?* and as such might be quite useful. But of course it is not true – or rather it is not the whole truth – because we can also say *Would you like some tea?, I refuse to accept any responsibility, I wouldn't mind some beer,* etc.

Michael Swan, an author not only of textbooks but also of one of the most widely-used pedagogic grammars, suggests a number of measures of a good rule (Swan 1994). These include 'simplicity' (though we have seen how this may cause problems), 'truth' (because clearly some rules are more 'true' than others), 'clarity' (because rules that are unclear help nobody) and 'relevance' (because there are some things which a teacher or student probably does not really need to know). In a conference speech in 1998 he quoted the following rule, formulated by Louis Alexander for a magazine article, as an example of a formulation which opted for simplicity above all:

> ### THE PRESENT PERFECT TENSE
>
> We often think that there are endless rules for this tense. In fact these can be boiled down to just two simple precepts:
>
> 1 To describe actions beginning in the past and continuing up to the present moment (and possibly into the future): *I've planted fourteen rose bushes so far this morning.*
>
> 2 To refer to actions occurring or not occurring at an unspecified time in the past with some kind of connection to the present: *Have you passed your driving test?*
>
> Every use of the present perfect (for example with *since, for* and so on) will fit into one of these rules. Proliferating rules without end make this tense sound more difficult than it actually is.
>
> From L Alexander (1988: 59)

Yet Alexander himself devotes three pages to the simple present perfect in his own grammar book (1988: 171–174). Swan needs three and a half pages for an explanation of these and related uses of the present perfect (1995: 418–422) and Raymond Murphy in his intermediate grammar practice book has three separate units to cover the same areas in greater detail (1994: Units 7, 8 and 11). What this shows is that all writers of pedagogic grammar have to strike a balance between the competing measures of good rules which Swan (above) has enumerated. It is clear that Louis Alexander favoured simplicity and clarity above all in his magazine article, whereas both Swan and Murphy (and Alexander himself in a different context) have felt a need for more detailed and complex truth.

B Vocabulary

In this section we will look at what is known about vocabulary as a result, in part, of the computerised analysis of language data. Armed with that knowledge we will discuss word meaning, how words extend their use, how words combine, and the grammar of words.

B1 Language corpora

One of the reasons we are now able to make statements about vocabulary with considerably more confidence than before is because of the work of lexicographers and other researchers who are able to analyse large banks of language data stored on computers. From a **corpus** of millions of words (made up of novels, scientific articles, plays, newspapers, brochures, speeches, recorded conversations, etc.) the computer can now give quick accurate information about how often words are used, and in what linguistic contexts. Compare this to the pioneering work of Michael West (see West 1953) who tried to get the same kind of information through manual sweat and toil and a card index.

Computer corpora have allowed dictionary makers to say how frequently individual words are used, as in the following example:

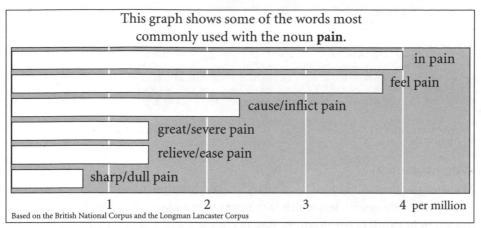

This graph shows some of the words most commonly used with the noun **pain**.

in pain
feel pain
cause/inflict pain
great/severe pain
relieve/ease pain
sharp/dull pain

1   2   3   4 per million

Based on the British National Corpus and the Longman Lancaster Corpus

From the 1995 edition of the *Longman Dictionary of Contemporary English*

Computer corpora can demonstrate that *okay* is far more common in speech than writing . They can also worry us by indicating that although we all know a phrase like *It's raining cats and dogs* this completely fails to appear even in a large corpus of spoken English (Rundell 1995).

Of course we knew some of these things already through a result of study and native speaker intuition, and it is true to say that however many words a corpus contains, it is only as good as the range and balance of material that goes into it. Nevertheless, much of our understanding of words has increased dramatically since the advent of computer databases, once a technological wonder, now commonplace and extremely useful as we will see in more detail in Chapter 12C. Thus, for example, the following computer concordance clearly shows us what adjectives are commonly used with the word we are looking at (in this case *thing* used in a particular journal). We have an easily visible demonstration of vocabulary facts in which we can have some confidence:

```
no matter how much of some other good  thing. And the administration does not really
    make such concessions, that is one  thing. But for the king to be the one to make
     to nurture a child or do the right  thing by our parents. Lee Atwater, stricken
        John Major envisions some vague  thing called a "Citizen's Charter" which
    The proposal "sounds like the same   thing he's been doing all along, using
 U.S. and Japan are trying to do the same thing, he says. Slugs, it seems, have
      about lawyers. A few minutes into the thing, however, and it is clear that these
    Moody's said it's concerned the same  thing may happen to the 33 issues under
"Once martial law is declared, the first  thing (Moscow) will do is stop this kind of
 "Noid" figure of a few years back are a  thing of the past. The ads bear a strong
     "confident" he is doing the right     thing. Schneider, a European power in the
 Scud missile launchers, said the only    thing still holding Israel back is a lack
   also might have played a role. One      thing that certainly had a part in the
       in governing ourselves. The only    thing that is important, and that makes our
  rabbits to pull out of a hat. The only   thing that will save this company is product
 says. "Losing subscribers is the last     thing the newspaper industry needs." At
 he can choose to focus on "the vision     thing. "The old argument -- that recognizing
of the people who go in for this kind of  thing. "They're medieval junkies," she says.
    Crop substitution won't be an easy     thing to accomplish as long as North America
        -- Bookshelf: The Next Best        Thing to Being There? ---- By Lee
```

thing as used in the *Wall Street Journal*, sampled from the *British National Corpus* (BNC)

B2 Word meaning

The least problematic issue of vocabulary, it would seem, is meaning. We know that *table* means a thing with legs which we can write on and eat off and that *book* is a collection of words between covers. But, of course, this is not the end of the story at all. For example, the *Cambridge International Dictionary of English* lists three main meanings for *table* and four main meanings for *book* – let alone the large number of different phrases the words appear in where their meaning is subtly different. You can eat off a *table*, or you can *table* a motion at a conference. You can summarise information in a *table* too. Then again, when you have read your *book* you can ring up a restaurant and *book* a table, but if you drive too fast on the way you might be *booked* for speeding. Some people have been keeping a *book* on whether you will ever manage to persuade your boy/girlfriend to marry you, especially since everyone knows you have been cooking the *books* for years. The point is that the same collection of sounds and letters can have many different meanings. This **polysemy** is only resolved when we see the word in context. It is understanding the **meaning in context** that allows us to say which meaning of the word, in the particular instance, is being used.

What a word means is often defined by its relationship to other words. For example, we explain the meaning of *full* by saying that it is the opposite of *empty*; we understand that *cheap* is the opposite of *expensive*. Such **antonyms** reinforce the meaning of each word in the pair, though, of course, because a word can be polysemous it may have more than one antonym (e.g. *a rich person – a poor person, rich food – plain food*, etc.).

Words have **synonyms** that mean exactly or nearly the same as each other. We say that *bad* and *evil* are nearly synonymous as are *good* and *decent* in certain situations – as in *She's a good/decent pianist*. Once again much will depend on the context the words appear in. Yet in truth it is very difficult to find real synonyms. *Costly* and *expensive* might seem on the surface to mean the same yet they are subtly different: we tend to use the former about larger projects and larger amounts, while *expensive* has a broader range of use. We would be unlikely to say *That pen you've got there looks very costly*, but *The new building programme is proving very costly* sounds perfectly all right.

Another relationship which defines the meaning of words to each other is that of **hyponymy**, where words like *banana, apple, orange, lemon*, etc. are all hyponyms of the **superordinate** *fruit*. And *fruit* itself is a hyponym of other items which are members of the food family. We can express this relationship in the following diagram:

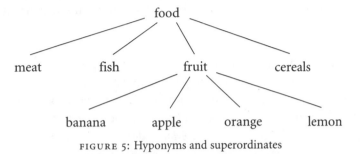

FIGURE 5: Hyponyms and superordinates

Part of a word's meaning, therefore, concerns its relations with other words, not only in terms of antonymy and synonymy, but also in terms of how it fits into the vocabulary hierarchy.

One final point should be made about word meaning, namely that what a word means is not necessarily the same as what it suggests – or rather that words have different **connotations**, often depending on the context they occur in. Thus the word *chubby* has a very positive connotation when it is combined with *baby*, but it suddenly becomes negative in tone if it is combined with *middle-aged English teacher*! And what about a sentence like *He's a very dangerous man* where *dangerous* would appear to have a negative connotation, yet some people have been known to find 'dangerous men' curiously attractive!

B3 Extending word use

Words do not just have different meanings, however. They can also be stretched and twisted to fit different contexts and different uses. We say that someone is in a *black mood* or someone is *yellow*, yet we are not actually describing a colour. In such contexts *black* and *yellow* mean something else.

Jean Aitchison gives many other examples of how the literal meaning of words has been extended (Aitchison 1994: Chapter 13). We say, for example, that *The price of mangoes went up* but *went up* here cannot mean the same as *She went up the stairs*. When we say that *Prices have taken a dramatic tumble* how are we to explain the meanings of *dramatic* and *tumble*?

Such **metaphorical** use of words allows us to move beyond their purely denotational use (where a word only describes a thing rather than the feelings or ideas it suggests). It helps us extend our range of expression and interpretation, allowing us the opportunity to explain our feelings about things in a way that creates readily available images. Poets use such metaphors all the time, of course. Consider, for example, these lines:

19

> The wind clawed through the shrunken trees
> And scratched and bit and roared with rage.

Some metaphors become fixed into phrases which competent speakers recognise at once, even though the meaning of the phrase is not decipherable from any understanding of the individual word. We all know that *She kicked the bucket* means she died and that *He has bitten off more than he can chew* means that he has attempted something that is too difficult for him. If someone says to you *I've got him eating out of my hand* we understand the metaphor, but it is not original; it is a common expression, an accepted **idiom**.

The metaphorical and idiomatic use of words and phrases is not always popular, however. For some years it became commonplace for people to describe someone who had suffered a disappointment being *as sick as a parrot*, and this idiomatic expression became so widely used that it began to irritate everybody, except, perhaps, when used ironically. *As sick as a parrot* had become a **cliché**, what Crystal calls a 'lexical zombie' (Crystal 1995: 186). *Money doesn't grow on trees, you know*, qualifies as a cliché too; as does the phrase *to add insult to injury*.

However, a cliché is not necessarily strongly metaphorical all the time as the following two lines of dialogue from a recent radio soap opera episode show:

Ex-lover: I never meant to hurt you.
Jilted lover: Oh please Richard, not that tired old cliché.

Sometimes words are extended so extremely that their meaning becomes completely impenetrable. The following sentence, Chomsky suggested, is meaningless, despite being grammatically respectable:

Colorless green ideas sleep furiously.

Perhaps there are limits, then, in how far we can bend the meanings and uses of words. But do not bet on it. There are poets everywhere!

B4 Word combinations

Although words can appear as single items which are combined in a sentence (*The mongoose bit the snake*), they can also occur in two-or-more item groups (*The normally **lightning-quick** reactions of the reptile **let it down***). They often combine with each other in ways which competent speakers of the language recognise instantly, but which others often find strange. The kinds of word that go together in one language are often completely different from the kinds of word which live together in another.

Word combinations (also known as **collocations**) have become the subject of intense interest in the recent past, in part spurred on by discoveries from language corpora (see above). Collocation is the way in which words co-occur – combinations which, through custom and practice, have come to be seen as normal and acceptable. It is immediately apparent that while some words can live together, others cannot. We say *fast asleep*, and this is an acceptable collocation, but **fast awake* is not. We can say *clenched fist* and even *clenched teeth*, yet we cannot talk about **clenched ears*.

The way in which words combine collocationally and in larger chunks has led people, most notably Nattinger, to talk about **lexical phrases** (Nattinger 1988). Such phrases are often part of longer memorised strings of speech. We know, for example, what the word *ironic* means, but we can also say that it is typically used in the phrase *It is ironic that … .*

Lexical phrases or 'language chunks' are like prefabricated building units. Apart from phrasal verbs, collocations, and compound words such as *traffic lights*, *walking stick*, and *workshop*, language also chunks itself, according to Maggie Baigent, into 'functional phrases' (*by the way, on the other hand, if you see what I mean*), 'idiomatic' or 'fixed expressions' (*a close shave, an only child, in love*) and 'verbal expressions' (*can't afford to, not supposed to, don't mind*) (Baigent 1999: 51). Michael Lewis demonstrates how a 'lexical unit', like *I'll*, crops up time and time again in what he calls 'archetypal utterances' such as *I'll give you a ring, I'll drop you a line, I'll see what I can do, I'll see you later*, etc. (Lewis 1993: Chapter 5).

The chunking of language in this way suggests that talking about vocabulary exclusively in terms of words is not sufficient to account for the different kinds of meaning unit which language users have at their disposal. A **phrasal verb** is made up of two or more words (if we accept one definition of what a word is) yet it is only one meaning unit. We could argue that *wide awake* and *a close shave* are single meaning units too. Some people refer to such meaning units as 'lexemes' (see Crystal 1995: 118), but whatever we call them, we need to see that words in combination have to be perceived as meaning units in their own right, just as single words such as *book* or *table* do.

What we are saying is that we use words either in prefabricated chunks or insert them into the templates provided by grammar. As Steven Pinker expresses it: '… the mind analyses language as some mixture of memorised chunks and rule-governed assemblies' (1999: 26).

B5 The grammar of words

A key middle ground where words and phrases on the one hand and grammar on the other meet up is through the operation of word classes or parts of speech, such as **noun** or **adjective**. When we say a word is a noun we then know how it can operate in a sentence. The same is true for such word classes as **verbs** or **determiners** or **prepositions**. When we know a word's part of speech, we know what other words it can occur with in a phrase or sentence and where it can be put syntactically, a fact graphically demonstrated by the kind of tree diagram we looked at in A above.

Within word classes there are a number of restrictions. A knowledge of these allows competent speakers to produce well-formed sentences. Speakers of British English, for example, might say *There isn't any furniture in the room*, but would not say * *There aren't any furnitures in the room* because furniture is almost always an **uncountable** noun (sometimes called a 'mass' or a 'non-count' noun). The same is true of words like *pollution* and *sugar* or *cheese*, whereas words like *cup* and *pen* are thought of as **countable** (sometimes called 'count' nouns) because you can pluralise them and therefore use them with plural verbs.

We can say, therefore, that nouns are countable or uncountable and many dictionaries have a [U] or a [C] next to such nouns to show what they are. But since, as we have discussed, the same word can have a number of different meanings, it is not always possible to say that a collection of letters like *sugar* is always uncountable. Change its meaning slightly and it is quite possible to say *Two sugars, please,* and the waiter at your table might well say *So that's two ice creams and two cheeses,* showing that *cheese* has suddenly changed its status from uncountable to countable. We may think we are faced with the same word, but we are actually dealing with two different lexemes or meaning units (see B4 above).

A similar situation occurs with verbs where we often label them either **transitive** (they take an object), **intransitive** (they do not take an object), or both. The verb *herd* (e.g. *to herd sheep*) is a transitive verb. It always takes an object. The verb *open* on the other hand can be either transitive or intransitive. The dentist says *Open your mouth* (transitive), but we can also say that *The dentist's surgery opens at eight o'clock* (intransitive).

Verbs are good examples, too, of the way in which words can trigger the grammatical behaviour of other words around them. *Like* triggers the use of either the *-ing* form in verbs which follow it (*I like listening to music*) or the use of *to* + the infinitive (*I like to listen to music*), but in British English *like* cannot be followed by *that* + a sentence (we cannot say *She likes that she sails*). The verb *tell* triggers the use of a direct object and, if there is a following verb, the construction *to* + infinitive (*She told me to arrive on time*), whereas *say* triggers *that* + a clause construction (*She said that she would arrive on time*).

As we saw on page 13, a word as a part of speech can be changed morphologically; adding the *s* morpheme to the noun *book* makes it plural. Adding the *s* morpheme to the verb *book* is obligatory if we use it with third person singular pronouns. The use of affixes such as *im* and *dis* can change the meaning of words (e.g. *possible* and *impossible, agree* and *disagree*).

Words can also occupy more than one word class, a fact that is frequently (but not always) indicated by morphological change. The word *anger* can be a noun or a verb, but if we want to use the related adjective we change it to *angry*, and if we want it to be used adverbially, we have to change the *y* to an *i* and add *ly*. The table below shows the way in which words can occupy different word classes, sometimes without changing, sometimes by altering their morphological shape:

Verb	Noun	Adjective	Adverb
argue	argument	argumentative	argumentatively
anger	anger	angry	angrily
suggest	suggestion	suggestive	suggestively
calm	calm	calm	calmly

C Language in use

The linguist Peter Grundy reports the following conversation between himself (*me* in the extract) and a student at the University of Durham where he works:

Me:	You're in a no-smoking zone.
Female student:	Am I?
Me:	The whole building's a no-smoking zone.
Female student:	Thanks very much (extinguishing cigarette).

From P Grundy (2000: 60)

We know what the words mean, of course, but why exactly did Peter Grundy give the student the information about the no-smoking zone? He clearly was not just offering information or passing the time. On the contrary, his purpose, as he himself acknowledges proudly, was to stop the student polluting the air! And what are we to make of the student's second utterance? Is she really thanking her lecturer for giving her information that she did not have before? Or does her *Thanks very much* really mean *sorry*? Perhaps its purpose is to indicate to her lecturer that yes, she knows she is smoking in a no-smoking zone and since she has been 'caught' she has no option but to put out her cigarette.

Peter Grundy might have chosen different words for the purpose, especially if, instead of a student, he had found the Dean, his boss, smoking in the corridor. Instead of stating, baldly, that *You're in a no-smoking zone*, he might have said something like *Umm, not sure if I should point this out or not, but didn't we agree that this building would be a no-smoking area?* or maybe he would have employed a different formula of words altogether to get his point across.

The issue that faces us here is that the words we use and what they actually mean in the context we use them are not the same thing at all. We choose words and phrases to have different effects from the surface meanings they appear to express, and we do this on the basis of a number of variables: purpose, appropriacy, language in discourse, and genre.

C1 Purpose

Many years ago, the philosopher J L Austin identified a series of verbs which he called **performatives**, that is verbs which do what those same words mean. Thus, if a speaker says *I promise*, the word *promise* itself performs the function of promising. If a celebrity says *I name this ship 'Ocean 3'* the use of the verb *to name* performs the function of naming.

The idea that language performs certain functions is not restricted to the kind of verbs Austin mentioned, however. We saw above how *This is a no-smoking zone* had the purpose of having the student put out her cigarette, just as a sentence like *It's cold in here* might, in certain circumstances, perform the function of a request to the other person in the room to close the window. We may select language for its denotational (or surface) meaning, in other words, but we also use it to do something else. We have a purpose in mind which we wish to achieve.

One major result of this interest in purpose led applied linguists to propose a category of language **functions** such as 'inviting', 'apologising', 'offering' and 'suggesting'. Thus *Would you like to come for a coffee?* performs the function of inviting where the purpose is to be a good host, whereas *I can't go along with you there* performs the function of disagreeing with the purpose of making your own opinion quite clear. *Why don't you switch it on?* seems to be performing the function of strong suggestion where the purpose is to provoke action, and *I'll do it if you want* is clearly offering help, with the purpose of being helpful.

The study of functions and how they are realised in language has had a profound effect upon the design of language-teaching materials, making language purpose a major factor in the choice of syllabus items and teaching techniques.

C2 Appropriacy

A feature of language functions is that they do not just have one linguistic realisation; the following phrases, for example, show only some of the possible ways of inviting someone to the cinema:

> Would you like to come to the cinema?
> How about coming to the cinema?
> D'you fancy the cinema?
> I was wondering if you might like to come to the cinema tonight?
> What about the cinema?
> Are you on for the cinema?
> Cinema?
> There's a good movie on at the cinema.
> etc.

Thus, when we attempt to achieve a communicative purpose (such as getting someone to agree to an invitation) we have to choose which of these language forms to use. Which form, given our situation, is the most appropriate?

There are a number of variables which govern our choice:

- **Setting:** we speak differently in libraries from the way we do in night clubs. We often use informal and spontaneous language at home, whereas we may use more formal pre-planned speech in an office or work environment.

- **Participants:** the people involved in an exchange – whether in speech or writing – clearly affect the language being chosen. However egalitarian we may want to be we often choose words and phrases in conversation with superiors which are different from the words and phrases we use when talking to friends, members of our families, or colleagues of equal status to us.

- **Gender:** research clearly shows that men and women typically use language differently when addressing either members of the same or the opposite sex. Women have frequently used more concessive language than men for example, and crucially, have often talked less than men in mixed-sex conversations.

- **Channel:** as we saw in A1 above, there are marked differences between spoken and written grammars. But spoken language is not all the same: it is affected by the situation we are in. Are we speaking face to face or on the telephone? Are we speaking through a microphone to an unseen audience or standing up in a lecture hall in front of a crowd? Each different channel will generate different uses of language.

- **Topic:** finally, the topic we are addressing affects our lexical and grammatical choices. The words and phrases that we use when talking or writing about a wedding will be different from those we employ when the conversation turns to particle physics. The vocabulary of childbirth is different from the lexical phrases associated with football.

These, then, are some of the factors that influence our choice of language. When we have our students study the way language is used in speaking or writing, we will want to draw their attention to such issues. We may ask why a speaker uses particular words or expressions. We may have our students prepare for a speaking activity by assembling the necessary topic words and phrases. We may discuss what sort of language is appropriate in an office situation when talking to a superior – and whether the sex of the superior makes any difference.

Language is a social construct as much as it is a mental ability. It is important for students to be just as aware of this in a foreign or second language as they are in their own.

C3 Language as discourse

Our description of language has so far taken in grammar, vocabulary, and language use (translated by applied linguists into a study of language functions and the appropriate use of language in different situations). This has led some researchers to describe conversations in terms such as turn-taking (how people take turns to speak in a conversation), and the patterns and routes which many typical conversations follow. The concern has been not so much to study the bits of language (words and grammar, for example) but to see how they are used in discourse (language used in context over an extended period), since it is at the level of discourse that we can really see how people operate.

We have already seen an example of conversational English discourse in the extract from the work of Carter and McCarthy (see A1). Here the researchers transcribed a conversation carefully, giving details about the pauses between utterances, showing how one speaker's utterance overlaps another's, for example:

C: Oh is it oh it's rice with raisins is it
B: [
    No

From R Carter and M McCarthy (1995: 208)

More detailed transcripts use different symbols for overlapping speech (//), relatively long pauses (…), utterances that are impossible to decipher (( )), not to mention the various symbols for intonation, loudness, etc. (Grundy 2000). With this kind of meticulous observation we can examine discourse under a microscope, to see what is going on.

Apart from the speech details mentioned so far, linguists also describe the organisation of meaning within a text. Nattinger and DeCarrico (1992), for example, describe content in discourse in terms of 'topic markers' (*Let's look at X*, etc.), 'topic shifters' (*By the way*, etc.), 'summarisers' (*to cut a long story short*, etc.), and other markers such as 'exemplifiers', 'relators', 'evaluators' and 'qualifiers'. With such labels it is possible to break any piece of discourse down into small chunks. Then we can see how the chunks are stacked up in a variety of discourse patterns. Now we can say to students, *Look this is how competent speakers put the language together into longer and longer chunks.*

However, we should ask ourselves how useful students will find the study of discourse, especially if it is investigated in the kind of detail we have suggested above. Most teachers and students would say that there is little time for such microscopic analysis. Yet, as the following example shows, a study of a paragraph can yield rich information. Julian Edge, drawing on the work of Michael Hoey (1983), shows how a typical pattern of paragraph organisation (Situation–Problem–Response– Evaluation) is exemplified in a simple story – produced in a teacher's workshop session:

Situation: Once upon a time there was a merchant so rich that he could have paved the streets of his town with silver.

Problem: But his wealth brought him little happiness, because he was allergic to almost everything and had to stay cooped up in a sterile room.

Response: In desperation he offered half his fortune to anyone who could cure his allergies. Doctors came from far and wide but to no avail.

Evaluation: Unless he has died in the meantime he still sits there today, looking at pictures of the world outside.

From *The Foundation Module for the MSc in TESOL* by J Edge published by the University of Aston (1997)

With such a pattern we can say to students that if they wish to understand this type of story-telling – or if they wish to put together their own tales of this kind – the pattern we have drawn their attention to will help them to do so. This kind of approach will be useful, too, for readers and writers in a variety of genres (see below), just as it is here for people who wish to study story-telling.

We use a variety of devices to structure written discourse. Sometimes we repeat words (*Mary Allen, the Mayor of X, is to stand for re-election. Allen says* ...), replace names with pronouns (*Mary Allen, the mayor of X, is to stand for re-election. She* ...). Using such devices to refer to something earlier in the text is called **anaphoric reference**; in the case of reference forwards to something which will occur later, we call such reference **cataphoric**; reference outside the text is **exophoric**.

Contemporary textbooks show that materials writers are fully aware of how important discourse analysis is to our understanding of both spoken and written text. The more our students can identify typical patterns of use, the better they will be able to read, listen, write and speak.

C4 Genre

Discourse analysis allows us to make statements about typical paragraph organisation or the structure of conversations. But we can go even further than this, showing longer stretches of typical discourse which almost always behave in the same way. We can describe different types of film (e.g. *film noir*, *animated cartoon*, *teenage horror movie*) as different genres. In the same way, we can describe different types of writing – in different contexts and for different purposes – as different written genres, and we can look at typical speaking genres too. This then allows us to study different language use in thriller or romantic fiction. We can show the way in which holiday postcards are normally written, or study scientific writing for its general patterning; we can show how typical exchanges take place at post office counters (see page 241), or study the genre of social introductions. Students who have been helped to perceive these patterns will be in a much better position not only to understand what they read and hear, but also to produce their own written and spoken language.

The following examples show how one particular genre, the 'lonely hearts' advertisement, follows clearly identifiable set patterns:

Forty-plus, independent-minded, sensitive lady with a GSOH, would like to meet a genuine man for friendship. Dial 0897 505 100. When asked, dial 5 followed by Phone box no 69984.

Two wonderful women, professional and funny, would like to meet two interesting men over 40, for lunches, outings, music and theatre etc. North London area. Dial 0897 505 100. When asked, dial 5 followed by Phone box no 69984.

Male, 49, intelligent, gentle-natured, pleasant looking and blind seeks partner. Dial 0897 505 100. When asked, dial 5 followed by Phone box no 86846.

Well-travelled, 40s, tall, slim 60s child, changing direction, seeks beautiful woman. West Yorkshire area. 0897 505 100. When asked, dial 5 followed by Phone box no 88749.

Lonely hearts advertisements from the *New Statesman* magazine

It is amusing and instructive for many students to study the 'lonely hearts' genre, even though they may not go on to use their knowledge in any practical way. But the same technique applied to other genres (such as scientific writing, report writing, journalism, or certain kinds of narrative composition) will have more practical applications, allowing students to read or write with a greater understanding of how such texts are constructed.

D The sounds of the language

In writing, we represent words and grammar through orthography. When speaking, on the other hand, we construct words and phrases with individual sounds, and we also use pitch change, intonation, and stress to convey different meanings.

The teaching of pronunciation will be the focus of Chapter 13, where we will also discuss how 'perfect' our students' pronunciation should be (Chapter 13, A1). In this section, however, we will look at five pronunciation issues: pitch, intonation, sounds, sounds and spelling, and stress.

D1 Pitch

One of the ways we recognise people is by the pitch of their voice. We say that one person has a very high voice whereas another has a deep voice. When their voice is very high we talk about them having a 'high-pitched' voice.

While most of us have a pitch range that we normally operate at, in times of tension, for example, the pitch of our voices may change dramatically. We often speak at a higher pitch than normal if we are frightened or excited. When we are tired, bored, or fed up our pitch may be lower than is customary.

A device by which we communicate emotion and meaning, therefore, is through the pitch we use. If we start speaking at a higher pitch than usual, this is noticeable. A low grunt gives some indication of mood too!

D2 Intonation

On its own, pitch is not very subtle, conveying, as we have seen, only the most basic information about mood and emotion. But once we start altering the pitch as we speak, changing the 'tune' we are using, we are able to convey a much subtler range of meanings. The music of speech, that is the **intonation** we use, is a crucial factor in speaking.

Joanne Kenworthy shows how intonation is used to put words and information in the foreground (by using a high or wavering pitch), in the background (by using a lower pitch than normal), to signal ends and beginnings of conversations (we often know when someone has finished speaking because their voice drops in pitch – just as their voice may start at a higher pitch than usual at the beginning of their contribution), or to show whether a situation is 'open' or 'closed' (when we finish what we are saying at a higher pitch than normal we leave other possibilities 'in the air' whereas a falling pitch closes off what we have said from further discussion) (Kenworthy 1987: 88–89).

Intonation is also used to convey emotion, involvement, and empathy. If we use an exaggerated intonation tune in a question like *What's going on?*, starting at quite a high pitch and using large pitch leaps, it shows that we are really surprised or frightened. But if we say the same question at a low pitch with a fairly flat intonation tune it suggests that we are not very concerned at the answer we will get.

Intonation is also a way of modifying the strength or intention of what we are saying. We can perform different functions (see C1 above) by choosing different forms of language. But we can also make the same forms perform different functions. The word *well* can express agreement, acceptance, doubt, or disagreement depending on how we say it. *No* can indicate refusal, questioning of fact, or disagreement.

Finally, we use intonation to show how certain we are about what we are saying and to indicate what response we expect. The most typical example of this is the use of tag questions such as *You're okay, aren't you?* with a falling tone to confirm what we believe to be the case, or with a rising tone to show our uncertainty about what the answer will be.

Intonation, then, is crucial in communicating meaning. Indeed, listeners frequently get the wrong messages from intonation when foreign speakers use it in an idiosyncratic way. That is because intonation tells us what someone means and how they feel about it. We recognise the difference between making a statement and asking a question. We are aware of the fact that someone is surprised, for example, and we gather from their intonation that they are being polite – or rude.

D3 Individual sounds

Words and sentences are made up of sounds (or **phonemes**) which, on their own, may not carry meaning, but which, in combination, make words and phrases. The phonemes /k/ (like the *c* in *can*), /æ/ (like the *a* in *can*) or /t/ (like the *t* in *tooth*) are just sounds, but put them together in a certain order and we get /kæt/ *cat*, a word that is instantly recognisable. If we change just one of these sounds (/b/ for /k/, for example) we will get a different word *bat*; if, on the other hand, we changed /æ/ for /ɒ/ – like the *o* in *hot* – we would get another different word, /kɒt/ *cot*.

'Southern English standard' has forty-four phonemes as the following list shows:

iː	sheep	aʊ	house	θ	think
ɪ	ship	ɔɪ	buoy	ð	then
e	breath	ɪə	cheer	s	cell
æ	back	eə	chair	z	lens
ɑː	arm	ʊə	sure	ʃ	shell
ɒ	what	p	pen	ʒ	measure
ɔː	law	b	board	h	he
ʊ	would	t	little	m	plumb
uː	shoe	d	dance	n	no
ʌ	son	k	cup	ŋ	ring
ɜː	first	g	good	l	let
ə	again	tʃ	chin	r	wring
eɪ	play	dʒ	July	j	yes
əʊ	ago	f	fan	w	when
aɪ	climb	v	van		

The phonemes of 'Southern English standard'

Competent speakers of the language make these sounds by using various parts of the mouth such as the lips, the tongue, the teeth, the alveolar ridge (the ridge behind the upper teeth), the palate, the velum (the flap of soft tissue hanging at the back of the palate – often called the soft palate), and the vocal cords (folds). See Figure 6:

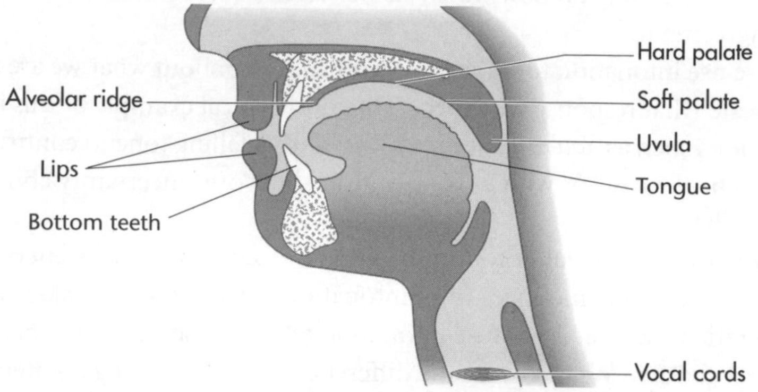

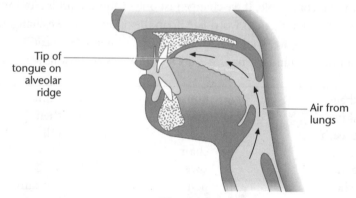

FIGURE 6: Parts of the mouth

As an example we can observe that the consonant /t/ is made when the tip of the tongue is placed on the alveolar ridge above it (the alveolar ridge is the flat surface you can feel immediately behind your top teeth) and when air from the lungs forces the tongue away from the ridge in an explosive burst. That is why /t/ is referred to as an **alveolar plosive**. Figure 7 shows which parts of the mouth are used for alveolar plosives:

FIGURE 7: The alveolar plosive

The consonant /d/ is made in a similar way to /t/ but there are crucial differences. When we say /t/ as in /tʌn/ *ton* the first sound is just air and the air is expelled from the mouth (try saying *t, t, t* to yourself holding your hand in front of your mouth). In the larynx the vocal cords (the two flaps of muscular tissue which, when pressed together, vibrate when air is forced through them) are completely open, so there is no obstruction for the air coming from the lungs. When we say /d/ as in /dʌn/ *done*, however, the vocal cords are closed, the air from the lungs forces them to vibrate, and our voiceless /t/ is now voiced to become /d/. Furthermore there is little **aspiration** (air) as there was with /t/ (again, if you hold your hand in front of your mouth this will become clear). Figure 8 shows the position of the vocal cords for **voiceless** sounds (like /p/, /t/, /k/) and **voiced** sounds (like /b/, /d/, and /g/):

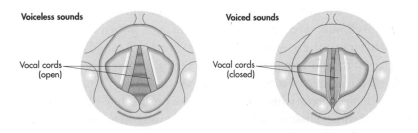

FIGURE 8: Position of the vocal cords (seen from above) for voiceless and voiced sounds

Vowels are all voiced. Two other features create the differences between vowels. The first is the place in the mouth where they are made. The second feature, which is easier to observe, is the position of the lips. For /ɑː/ the lips form something like a circle, whereas for /ɪː/ they are more stretched and spread. Figure 9 shows these two positions:

/ɑː/   /iː/

FIGURE 9: Position of the lips for /ɑː/ and /ɪː/

One sound which does not occur in many phonemic charts but which is nevertheless widely used is the glottal stop, created when a closure of the vocal cords 'stops' air completely, and we say /əpɑːʔmənt/ *apartment*, for example, instead of /əpɑːtmənt/ or /aɪsɔːʔɪt/ *I saw it* instead of /aɪsɔːrɪt/. The glottal stop is often used instead of other stop (or plosive) consonants, in other words.

Speakers of different languages have different sounds. Thus there is no equivalent in English for the 'click' used by Xhosa speakers, so English speakers find it difficult to produce. French people are accustomed to the awkward way in which British speakers mangle French vowels because they are not the same as English ones. Japanese speakers, on the other hand, do not have different phonemes for /l/ and /r/ and so have difficulty differentiating between them, and often find it nearly impossible to make the different sounds.

D4 Sounds and spelling

Whereas in some languages there seems to be a close correlation between sounds and spelling, in English this is often not the case. The sound /ʌ/, for example, can be realised in a number of different spellings (e.g. *won, young, funny, flood*). The letters *ou*, on the other hand, can be pronounced in a number of different ways (e.g. *enough* – /ənʌf/, *through* – /θruː/, *though* – /ðəʊ/, *trough* – /trɒf/, or even *journey* /ˈdʒɜːnɪ/). A lot depends on the sounds that come before and after them, but the fact remains that we spell some sounds in a variety of different ways, and we have a variety of different sounds for some spellings.

Words can change their sound too, and this is not indicated by the way we spell them. Thus we say that *was* sounds like this, /wɒz/. However, when it occurs in a sentence like *I was robbed*, the vowel sound changes from a stressed vowel /ɒ/ to an unstressed vowel /ə/, e.g. /aɪwəzrɒbd/. This unstressed sound /ə/ is called the **schwa**, and is one of the most frequent sounds in English, created by shortening of the vowel and the placing of stress elsewhere (see D5 below).

Other changes occur when sounds get close or slide into each other in connected speech: sometimes **elision** takes place where sounds disappear into each other. Thus /ka:nt/ *can't* finishes with the sound /t/, but when it is placed next to a word beginning with /d/, for example, the /t/ hardly sounds at all (e.g. /aɪka:nda:ns/ – *I can't dance*). Sometimes **assimilation** takes place where the sound at the end of one word changes to be more like the sound at the beginning of the next. Thus the /n/ at the end of /gri:n/ becomes an /m/ when placed next to a word starting with /p/, e.g. /gri:mpen/ *green pen*, but changes to /ŋ/ when placed immediately before /k/ in normal speech, e.g. /pæŋkeɪk/ *pancake*. Sometimes we insert **linking** sounds between vowels, e.g. /r/ in *law and order* /lɔ:rənɔ:də/, or /j/ in *I am* /aɪjæm/. **Juncture** (where two sounds meet) can vary according to such qualities as syllable stress or vowel length, e.g. *ice cream* vs. *I scream*.

D5 Stress

British and American English speakers sometimes differ in where they place the stress in words. Thus *ballet* in British English is stressed on the first syllable (*bal*) whereas in American English the stress usually falls on the second syllable (*let*).

Stress is the term we use to describe the point in a word or phrase where pitch changes, vowels lengthen, and volume increases. In a one-syllable word like *dance* there is no problem, since at least one syllable will need these characteristics, and since there is only one syllable, we know which one it is! A word with more than one syllable is more complex, however. We might stress the word *export* on the second syllable (*exPORT*) if we are using it as a verb. But if, on the contrary, we stress the first syllable (*EXport*) the verb is now a noun.

In multisyllable words there is often more than one stressed syllable (e.g. *singularity, information, claustrophobia*). In such cases we call the strongest force the **primary stress** and the weaker force the **secondary stress**, e.g. ˌsingulˈarity, ˌinforˈmation, ˌclaustroˈphobia. Note that primary stress has a superscript mark whereas secondary stress is marked below the line. Secondary stress is not the same as unstressed syllables, as the presence of the schwa shows, e.g. /ˌɪnfəˈmeɪʃən/.

As was discussed above, words are often not pronounced as one might expect from their spelling. The word *secretary* would appear, on paper, to have four syllables, but when it is spoken there are sometimes only three and the first one is stressed /ˈsekrətrɪ/, or even, in rapid speech, only two, e.g. /ˈsektrɪ/.

It is worth noticing, too, that when a word changes shape, the stressed syllable may shift as well. In English we stress *Japan* on the second syllable (*jaPAN*), but when we turn the word into an adjective the stress moves to the new syllable (*japanESE*). However, this does not always happen (e.g. *amERica, amERican*).

Stress is vitally important in conveying meaning in phrases and sentences. We have already discussed the importance of pitch and intonation, and it is on the stressed part of a phrase that intonation changes are most marked. In British English the stress often falls on the end of the phrase – to give it 'end weight'. So a neutral way of saying *Brad wants to marry my daughter* might have the stress on the *dau* of *daughter*. But if the speaker changes where the stress falls (and thus where the intonation change takes place), then the meaning of the sentence changes too so that an affirmative statement, for example, may well become a question:

> Brad wants to MARRY my daughter? (= I didn't know he was that serious.)
> or
> BRAD wants to marry my daughter? (= Not Brad, surely!)

E Paralinguistic features of language

A number of features of communication take place outside the formal systems of language (sounds, grammar, etc). These **paralinguistic features** fall into two broad categories, those that involve the voice and those that involve the body.

E1 Vocal paralinguistic features

David Crystal gives five examples of 'tones of voice' which, while they are perhaps not central to meaning in the same way as the sound features we noted in Section D above, may nevertheless convey attitude or intention in some way (Crystal 1995: 249). The five are whispering (to indicate the need for secrecy), breathiness (to show deep emotion or sexual desire), huskiness (to show unimportance or disparagement), nasality (to indicate anxiety) and extra lip rounding (to express greater intimacy, especially with babies, for example). Whether or not these characteristics are voluntary or involuntary, they nevertheless convey intention and circumstance.

It is clear that there are a number of ways of altering our tone of voice, and that when we do this consciously, we do it to create different effects.

E2 Physical paralinguistic features

We can convey a number of meanings through the way in which we use our bodies. The expression on our face, the gestures we make, and even proximity or the way we sit, for example, may send powerful messages about how we feel or what we mean. We can look at some of these in more detail.

- **Facial expression:** facial expression is a powerful conveyor of meaning. Smiling is an almost universal signal of pleasure or welcome. Other facial expressions may not be so common, however. Raising eyebrows to suggest surprise or interest may be a part of one culture's normal currency, but may be more extreme for others. Other facial actions such as biting your lip (indicating thought or uncertainty), compressing the lips (to show decision or obstinacy), and a visible clenching of the teeth to show anger are all powerful conveyors of meaning too.

- **Gesture:** we use gesture to indicate a wide range of meanings, although once again the actual gestures we use may be specific to particular cultures. A few examples of British English behaviour show how powerful such gestures can be: shrugging shoulders may indicate indifference, an attitude of *I don't care*, or *I don't know*; crossing your arms may indicate relaxation, but it can also powerfully show boredom. Waving can denote welcome and farewell, whereas scratching your head may indicate puzzlement.

  Each culture group also has its gestures for *go away* both in its polite and ruder forms, and the use of arms, hands, and fingers to make obscene gestures for insults is part and parcel of the currency of society. Other less threatening gestures are also culture-bound as Figure 10 shows:

honesty   *I'm thinking*   *It's a secret*

FIGURE 10: Some gestures and their meanings

Of course some gestures such as head-scratching, hand-clasping, 'cracking' fingers, etc. may not be used to convey meanings, but may rather be unconscious 'ticks' – or be used in some way to displace tension. Such **displacement activities** may convey a person's nervousness or distractedness, but do not send messages in the same way as a clenched fist or a beckoning finger.

- **Proximity, posture, and echoing:** the physical distance between speakers can indicate a number of things and can also be used to consciously send messages about intent. Closeness, for example, indicates intimacy or threat to many speakers whilst distance may denote formality or a lack of interest. Proximity is also both a matter of personal style and is often culture-bound so that what may seem normal to a speaker from one culture may appear unnecessarily close or distant to a speaker from another. And standing close to someone may be quite appropriate in some situations such as an informal party, but completely out of place in others, such as a meeting with a superior.

  Posture can convey meaning too. Hunched shoulders and a hanging head give a powerful indication of mood. A lowered head when speaking to a superior (with or without eye contact) can convey the appropriate relationship in some cultures. Direct level eye contact, on the other hand, changes the nature of the interaction, and can be seen as either open or challenging.

A feature of posture and proximity that has been noted by several observers is that of 'echoing'. An example of this sometimes occurs when two people who are keen to agree with each other find that unconsciously they have adopted the same posture as if in imitation of each other. When used in this way, echoing appears to complement the verbal communication whereas when such imitation is carried out consciously it often indicates some form of mockery.

Paralinguistic features such as tone of voice, gesture, and posture are all part of the way we communicate with each other in face-to-face encounters. When teaching we can draw our students' attention to this, particularly when we are using video material – as we shall see in Chapter 20.

Further reading

- **Spoken grammar**

  For a book which contains transcripts of informal spoken English together with explanations and exercises, see R Carter et al. (1998).

  For an extensive discussion of the grammar of conversation see D Biber et al. (1999) in their substantial grammar which pays equal attention to spoken and written language.

- **Grammar books**

  Of the many pedagogic grammars now available, some of the most widely used are Michael Swan's *Practical English Usage* (M Swan 1995), the *Longman English Grammar* (L Alexander 1988), and R Murphy (1994) whose *English Grammar in Use* is extraordinarily popular with students and teachers for its mixture of simple rules and exercises. M Parrott (2000) has written a grammar especially for teachers with helpful sections on difficulties for students.

- **Vocabulary**

  One of the best books about vocabulary for teachers is still R Gairns and S Redman (1986). See also the excellent M McCarthy (1990).

  For discussions of vocabulary meaning see R Gairns and S Redman (1986: Chapter 2), J Aitchison (1994: Chapter 4), and M Lewis (1993: Chapter 4).

  For more on lexical phrases and the way they operate, see J Nattinger (1988), and J Nattinger and J DeCarrico (1992), and M Lewis (1993).

- **Language corpora**

  For more on language corpora and their uses, see C Tribble and G Jones (1997), J Sinclair (1991), T McEnery and A Wilson (1999), and G Fox (1998). See also the following web sites:

http://web.bham.ac.uk/johnstf/timconc.htm (T Johns' site) and
http://info.ox.ac.uk/bnc/corpora.html (English Language and Corpora Resources).

- **Extending word use**

  On the issue of meaningless grammatical sentences, see S Pinker (1994: 88–89).

- **Language in use**

  The whole issue of performatives first came to prominence in J Austin (1982) –
  a collection of his articles published by his students after his death.

  For a definitive account of language functions and notions, see D Wilkins
  (1976).

  For issues of gender in speech (and in teaching), see J Sunderland (1994) and
  especially D Tannen (1990).

- **Discourse analysis and pragmatics**

  M Coulthard (1985) is still a good introduction to an essentially sociolinguistic
  approach to discourse analysis. See also G Cook (1989) and P Grundy (2000).

  For an example of a detailed transcript for the purposes of discourse/pragmatic
  analysis, see P Grundy (2000: 174–182).

  For the importance of genre in writing, see C Tribble (1997: Chapter 6).

- **Pronunciation**

  On the teaching of pronunciation some of the best books are G Kelly (2000),
  A Underhill (1994), J Kenworthy (1987), P Roach (1991) and C Dalton and
  B Seidlhofer (1995). See also Chapter 13 in this book.

  For a pronunciation dictionary which shows alternative pronunciations and how
  frequently they are used, see J Wells (2000).

- **Physical paralinguistic features**

  For the way we use our bodies and what this means, see D Morris (1977 and
  1985).

3 | Describing learners

A Age

The age of our students is a major factor in our decisions about how and what to teach. People of different ages have different needs, competences, and cognitive skills; we might expect children of primary age to acquire much of a foreign language through play, for example, whereas for adults we can reasonably expect a greater use of abstract thought.

There are a number of commonly held beliefs about age. Some people say that children learn languages faster than adults do. They talk of children who appear to pick up new languages effortlessly. Perhaps this has something to do with the plasticity of a young brain. Something, after all, must account for the fact that with language, according to Steven Pinker, 'acquisition ... is guaranteed for children up to the age of six, is steadily compromised from then until shortly after puberty, and is rare thereafter' (Pinker 1994: 293), and that this applies not only to the acquisition of the first language, but also to second or foreign languages.

Another belief is that adolescents are unmotivated, surly, and uncooperative and that therefore they make poor language learners. And there are those who seem to think that adults have so many barriers to learning (both because of the slowing effects of ageing and because of their past experience), that they only rarely have any success.

There is some truth in many of these beliefs, but they can also be misleading since, like all stereotypes, they suggest that everyone is the same. They also ignore evidence from individuals within these groups (adolescents and adults) which flatly contradicts such assumptions. We should also point out that many of the concerns in this section will have special relevance for the western world where, for example, it is stressed that children should 'learn by doing' and where some generalisations can be made about adolescent behaviour. But as we shall see in Chapter 6B, different educational cultures have very different expectations about teacher and learner behaviour.

In what follows we will consider students at different ages as if all the members of each age group are the same. Yet each student is an individual with different experiences both in and outside the classroom. Comments here about young children, teenagers, and adults can only be generalisations. Much also depends upon individual learner differences and motivation (see B and C below).

A1 **Young children**

Young children, especially those up to the ages of nine or ten, learn differently from older children, adolescents, and adults in the following ways:

- They respond to meaning even if they do not understand individual words.
- They often learn indirectly rather than directly – that is they take in information from all sides, learning from everything around them rather than only focusing on the precise topic they are being taught.
- Their understanding comes not just from explanation, but also from what they see and hear and, crucially, have a chance to touch and interact with.
- They generally display an enthusiasm for learning and a curiosity about the world around them.
- They have a need for individual attention and approval from the teacher.
- They are keen to talk about themselves, and respond well to learning that uses themselves and their own lives as main topics in the classroom.
- They have a limited attention span; unless activities are extremely engaging they can easily get bored, losing interest after ten minutes or so.

In the light of these characteristics, it can be concluded that good teachers at this level need to provide a rich diet of learning experiences which encourages their students to get information from a variety of sources. They need to work with their students individually and in groups developing good relationships. They need to plan a range of activities for a given time period, and be flexible enough to move on to the next exercise when they see their students getting bored.

We can also draw some conclusions about what a classroom for young children should look like and what might be going on in it. First of all we will want the classroom to be bright and colourful, with windows the children can see out of, and with enough room for different activities to be taking place. We might expect them to be working in groups in different parts of the classroom, changing their activity every ten minutes or so. 'We are obviously,' Susan Halliwell writes, 'not talking about classrooms where children spend all their time sitting still in rows or talking only to the teacher' (1992: 18). Because children love discovering things, and because they respond well to being asked to use their imagination, they may well be involved in puzzle-like activities, in making things, in drawing things, in games, in physical movement or in songs.

A2 **Adolescents**

Anyone who has taught secondary school students has had lessons, even days and weeks, when the task seemed difficult, and on especially bad days hopeless. Yet if, as the methodologist Penny Ur suggests, teenage students are in fact overall the best language learners (Ur 1996: 286) this suggests that this is only part of the picture.

When Herbert Puchta and Michael Schratz started to design material for teenagers in Austria they, like many before them, wondered why teenagers seemed to be less lively and humorous than adults. Why were they so much less motivated, they asked, and why did they present outright discipline problems (Puchta and Schratz 1993: 1)?

It is widely accepted that one of the key issues in adolescence, especially perhaps in the west, is the search for individual identity, and that this search provides the key challenge for this age group. Identity has to be forged among classmates and friends; peer approval may be considerably more important for the student than the attention of the teacher which, for younger children, is so crucial.

As we shall see in Chapter 9A there are a number of reasons why students – and teenage students in particular – may be disruptive in class. Apart from the need for self-esteem and the peer approval they may provoke from being disruptive, there are other factors too, such as the boredom they feel – not to mention problems they bring into class from outside school. However, while it is true that adolescents can cause discipline problems, it is usually the case that they would be much happier if such problems did not exist. They may push teachers to the limit, but they are much happier if that challenge is met, if the teacher actually manages to control them, and if this is done in a supportive and constructive way so that he or she 'helps rather than shouts' (Harmer 1998: 2).

However, we should not become too preoccupied with the issue of disruptive behaviour, for while we will all remember unsatisfactory classes, we will also look back with pleasure on those groups and lessons which were successful. Teenagers, if they are engaged, have a great capacity to learn, a great potential for creativity, and a passionate commitment to things which interest them. There is almost nothing more exciting than a class of involved young people at this age pursuing a learning goal with enthusiasm. Our job, therefore, must be to provoke student engagement with material which is relevant and involving. At the same time we need to do what we can to bolster our students' self-esteem, and be conscious, always, of their need for identity.

Herbert Puchta and Michael Schratz see problems with teenagers as resulting, in part, from '… the teacher's failure to build bridges between what they want and have to teach and their students' worlds of thought and experience' (1993: 4). They advocate linking language teaching far more closely to the students' everyday interests through, in particular, the use of 'humanistic' teaching (see Chapter 6, A7). Students must be encouraged to respond to texts and situations with their own thoughts and experience, rather than just by answering questions and doing abstract learning activities. We must give them tasks which they are able to do, rather than risk humiliating them.

We have come some way from the teaching of young children. We can ask teenagers to address learning issues directly in a way that younger learners might not appreciate. We are able to discuss abstract issues with them. Indeed part of our job is to provoke intellectual activity by helping them to be aware of contrasting ideas and concepts which they can resolve for themselves – though still with our guidance. As we shall see in Chapters 5 and 11, there are many ways of studying language, most of which are appropriate for teenagers.

A3 Adult learners

Adult language learners are notable for a number of special characteristics:

- They can engage with abstract thought. Those who succeed at language learning in later life, according to Steven Pinker, '… often depend on the conscious exercise of their considerable intellects, unlike children to whom language acquisition naturally happens' (Pinker 1994: 29). This suggests that we do not have to rely exclusively on activities such as games and songs – though these may be appropriate for some students.
- They have a whole range of life experiences to draw on.
- They have expectations about the learning process, and may already have their own set patterns of learning.
- Adults tend, on the whole, to be more disciplined than some teenagers, and crucially, they are often prepared to struggle on despite boredom.
- They come into classrooms with a rich range of experiences which allow teachers to use a wide range of activities with them.
- Unlike young children and teenagers, they often have a clear understanding of why they are learning and what they want to get out of it. As we shall see in Section c below, motivation is a critical factor in successful learning, and knowing what you want to achieve is an important part of this. Many adults are able to sustain a level of motivation (see Section c3) by holding on to a distant goal in a way that teenagers find more difficult.

However, adults are never entirely problem-free learners, and have a number of characteristics which can sometimes make learning and teaching problematic:

- They can be critical of teaching methods. Their previous learning experiences may have predisposed them to one particular methodological style which makes them uncomfortable with unfamiliar teaching patterns. Conversely, they may be hostile to certain teaching and learning activities which replicate the teaching they received earlier in their educational careers.
- They may have experienced failure or criticism at school which makes them anxious and under-confident about learning a language.
- Many older adults worry that their intellectual powers may be diminishing with age – they are concerned to keep their creative powers alive, to maintain a 'sense of generativity' (Williams and Burden 1997: 32). However, as Alan Rogers points out, this generativity is directly related to how much learning has been going on in adult life before they come to a new learning experience (1996: 54).

Good teachers of adults take all of these factors into account. They are aware that their students will often be prepared to stick with an activity for longer than younger learners (though too much boredom can obviously have a disastrous effect on motivation). As well as involving their students in more indirect learning through reading, listening, and communicative speaking and writing, they also allow them to use their intellects to learn consciously where this is appropriate. They encourage their students to use their own life experience in the learning process too.

As teachers of adults we should recognise the need to minimise the bad effects of past learning experiences. We can diminish the fear of failure by offering activities which are achievable, paying special attention to the level of challenge presented by exercises. We need to listen to students' concerns too and, in many cases, modify what we do to suit their learning tastes (see Chapter 6B).

B Learner differences

In this section we are going to look at a number of approaches to describing the differences between learners, including 'Multiple Intelligence' theory and 'Neuro-linguistic programming' – two ways of looking at learning which have provoked considerable interest among teachers and materials designers.

B1 Aptitude

Some students are better at learning languages than others. At least that is the generally held view, and in the 1950s and 1960s it crystallised around the belief that it was possible to predict a student's future progress on the basis of linguistic aptitude tests. But it soon became clear that such tests were flawed in a number of ways. They did not appear to measure anything other than general intellectual ability even though they ostensibly looked for linguistic talents. Further, they favoured analytic-type learners over their more 'holistic' counterparts, so that the tests were especially suited to people who have little trouble doing grammar-focused tasks. Those with a more 'general' view of things – whose analytical abilities are not so highly developed, and who receive and use language in a more message-oriented way – appeared to be at a disadvantage. In fact, analytic aptitude is probably not the critical factor in success. Peter Skehan, for example, believes that what distinguishes exceptional students from the rest is that they have unusual memories, particularly for the retention of things that they hear (Skehan 1998: 234).

Another damning criticism of traditional aptitude tests is that while they may discriminate between the most and the least 'intelligent' students they are less effective at distinguishing between the majority of students who fall between these two extremes. What they do accomplish is to influence the way in which both teachers and students behave. It has been suggested that students who score badly on aptitude tests will become de-motivated and that this will then contribute to precisely the failure that the test predicted. And teachers who know that particular students have achieved high scores will be tempted to treat those students differently from students whose score was low. Aptitude tests end up being self-fulfilling prophecies whereas it would be much better for both teacher and students to be optimistic about all of the people in the class.

B2 Good learner characteristics

Another line of enquiry has been to try and tease out what a good learner is. If we can narrow down a number of characteristics that all good learners share, then we can, perhaps, cultivate these characteristics in all our students.

Neil Naiman and his colleagues included a tolerance of ambiguity as a feature of good learning together with areas such as positive task orientation (being prepared to approach tasks in a positive fashion), ego involvement (where success is important for a student's self-image), high aspirations, goal orientation, and perseverance (Naiman et al: 1978).

Joan Rubin and Irene Thompson listed no less than fourteen good learner characteristics amongst which learning to live with uncertainty (much like the tolerance of ambiguity mentioned above) is a notable factor (Rubin and Thompson 1982). But the Rubin and Thompson version of a good learner also mentions students who can find their own way (without always having to be guided by the teacher through learning tasks), who are creative, who make intelligent guesses, who make their own opportunities for practice, who make errors work for them not against them, and who use contextual clues.

Much of what various people have said about good learners is based on cultural assumptions which underpin much current teaching practice in countries like Britain, Australia, and America. In these cultures we appreciate self-reliant students, and promote learner autonomy as a main goal (see Chapter 24A). We tend to see the tolerance of ambiguity as a goal of student development, wishing to wean our pupils away from a need for things to be always cut and dried. We encourage students to read texts for general understanding without stopping to look up all the words they do not understand (see Chapter 14, A4); we ask students to speak communicatively even when they have difficulty because of words they do not know or cannot pronounce (see Chapter 19), and we involve students in creative writing (see Chapter 18, B3). In all these endeavours we expect our pupils to aspire beyond their current language level.

Different cultures value different learning behaviours, however. Our insistence upon one kind of good learner profile may encourage us to demand that students should act in class in certain ways, whatever their learning background. When we espouse some of the conclusions mentioned above, we risk imposing a methodology on our students that is inimical to their culture. As we shall see in Chapter 6B and Chapter 9, B1 it is better for us to reach some kind of learning bargain where both our beliefs and the learners' preferences can be satisfied. It is not always just the learners who may have to change.

B3 Learner styles

A preoccupation with learner personalities and styles has been a major factor in psycholinguistic research. Are there different kinds of learner? Are there different kinds of behaviour in a group? How can we tailor our teaching to match the personalities in front of us?

The methodologist Tony Wright describes four different learner styles within a group (1987: 117–118). The 'enthusiast' looks to the teacher as a point of reference and is concerned with the goals of the learning group. The 'oracular' also focuses on the teacher but is more orientated towards the satisfaction of personal goals. The 'participator' tends to concentrate on group goals and group solidarity, whereas the 'rebel' while referring to the learning group for his or her point of reference, is mainly concerned with the satisfaction of his or her own goals.

Other researchers have tried to describe student learning styles in their own words, identifying individual behaviour they have observed. They produce caricatures, of course, which never quite describe any particular student. But they do give us some pointers to the kinds of people we have in our classrooms.

Keith Willing, working with adult students in Australia, produced the following descriptions:

- **Convergers:** these are students who are by nature solitary, prefer to avoid groups, and who are independent and confident in their own abilities. Most importantly they are analytic and can impose their own structures on learning. They tend to be cool and pragmatic.

- **Conformists:** these are students who prefer to emphasise learning 'about language' over learning to use it. They tend to be dependent on those in authority and are perfectly happy to work in non-communicative classrooms, doing what they are told. A classroom of conformists is one which prefers to see well-organised teachers.

- **Concrete learners:** though they are like conformists, they also enjoy the social aspects of learning and like to learn from direct experience. They are interested in language use and language as communication rather than language as a system. They enjoy games and groupwork in class.

- **Communicative learners:** these are language use orientated. They are comfortable out of class and show a degree of confidence and a willingness to take risks which their colleagues may lack. They are much more interested in social interaction with other speakers of the language than they are with analysis of how the language works. They are perfectly happy to operate without the guidance of a teacher.

Learning styles adapted from Willing 1987 quoted in Skehan (1998: 247–250)

However we choose to categorise learner styles, an understanding that there are different individuals in our classes is vitally important if we are to plan the kinds of activity that will be appropriate for them. We need to balance the interests of individuals against what is good for the group and to be aware of certain individual traits when putting students into pairs and groups (see Chapter 8). We need to recognise which students need more personal attention than others, and which need different kinds of explanations and practice of language. As we shall see in Chapters 11 and 12, there are many different styles of language study and student language research. Some students respond better than others to discovery activities, for example (see Chapter 11B), so we will use such exercises with them. Others, however, may prefer a more directed approach to language study and so we will, within reason, adapt our practice accordingly. Yet others may respond with enthusiasm to creative writing or speaking activities (see Chapters 18 and 19), where some of their colleagues may need more structured work.

It is not possible to cater for each preference all of the time, of course. Yet over a period of time the attention we give to different learning styles will ensure that we do our best not only for the whole group but also for the individuals within it.

B4 Language levels

Students are generally described in three levels, **beginner, intermediate**, and **advanced**, and these categories are further qualified by talking about **real beginners** and **false beginners**. Between beginner and intermediate we often class students as **elementary**. The intermediate level itself is often sub-divided into **lower intermediate** and **upper intermediate** and even **mid-intermediate**. One version of different levels, therefore, has the following progression:

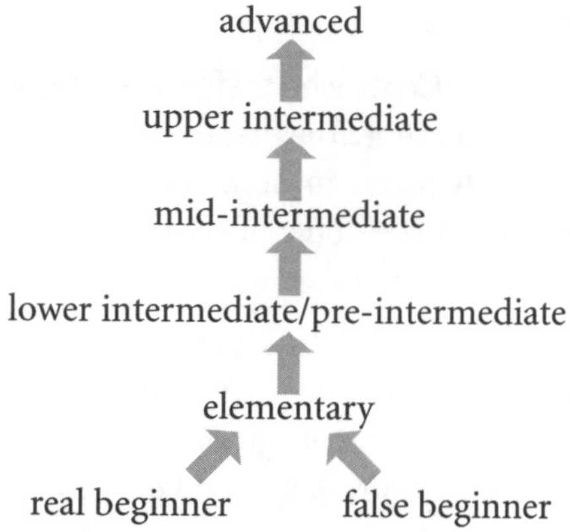

advanced

⬆

upper intermediate

⬆

mid-intermediate

⬆

lower intermediate/pre-intermediate

⬆

elementary

⬈ ⬉

real beginner   false beginner

FIGURE 11: Representing different student levels

The problem with these labels is that they mean different things to different people. What one school or education system calls advanced may be more like intermediate to some other teachers.

Public examinations (see Chapter 23, A1) help us to determine levels and standards, of course. We can judge people by the scores they get on the TOEFL or TOEIC examinations from the USA or the various examinations offered by the University of Cambridge Local Examinations Syndicate (UCLES) and others in the United Kingdom, for example. Coursebooks (see Chapter 21) have a role to play here too, since they generally conform to agreed syllabus requirements and ability. Such information, together with our own experience and intuition, will allow us to use level labels with discrimination.

A number of issues are directly related to the level our students have reached:

- **The plateau effect:** while learners at beginner level find it easy to see progress in their abilities from one week to the next, the same is not so easy for students at higher levels, particularly at intermediate levels, where progress is more subtle, and students do not always find it easy to see where they are going. This seems to cause a plateau effect where students are inclined to accept the level they have reached as adequate for their needs and the limits of their capacity.

Teachers need to be sensitive to the plateau effect, taking special measures to counteract it. Such efforts may include setting goals clearly so that students have a clear learning target to aim at, explaining what still needs to be done, making sure that activities are especially engaging, and sparking the students' interest in the more subtle distinctions of language use.

- **Methodology:** some techniques and exercises that are suitable for beginners look less appropriate for students at higher levels – for example, the use of repetition. Teachers find it quite effective to get beginner students to repeat sentences in chorus, but at higher levels this usually seems strange and patronising. At advanced levels it is easy to organise discussion – whether pre-planned (see Chapter 19, B3) or opportunistic (see Chapter 22, C1), whereas for beginners this option will not be available.

  Teachers of beginners will necessarily use activities whose organisation and content is less complex than those for more advanced learners. And although discovery learning, for example, is seen as desirable at any level (see Chapter 11, B2) it is more widely used at intermediate levels and above than it is at beginner and elementary levels.

- **Language:** we need to adjust the classroom language we use to the level we are working with (see Chapter 4, D3). The language materials we expose students to should be of a completely different level too, not only in terms of complexity, but also in range of genre and length. We would not expect beginners to tackle a national newspaper in English; we would not offer very advanced students a simplified dialogue. However, the issue of how 'authentic' language materials should be is the subject of debate amongst teachers and methodologists, as we shall see in Chapter 14, B1. People have worried about whether simplified language is too insubstantial even for beginner students or, conversely, that 'authentic' English (however that is defined, and whether spoken or written) tends to have a de-motivating effect on even advanced students if it is beyond their level.

- **Topics:** one problem with some beginner coursebook material in particular is the way in which quite complex topics are reduced to banalities because the language available at the level makes it impossible to treat them in any depth. The result is a kind of 'dumbing-down' which sometimes makes English language learning appear almost childish.

  It is important to match topics to the level, reserving complex issues for more advanced classes. But there is a danger here too that by restricting beginners to 'the family', 'the home', etc. the world is being diminished for crude linguistic reasons.

B5 Individual variations

If some people are better at some things than others – better at analysing, for example – this would indicate that there are differences in the ways individual brains work. It also suggests that people respond differently to the same stimuli. How might such variation determine the ways in which individual students learn most readily? How might they affect the ways in which we teach? There are two theories in particular which have tried to account for such perceived individual variation, and which teachers have attempted to use to for the benefit of their learners:

- **Neuro-linguistic programming:** according to practitioners of Neuro-linguistic programming (NLP), we use a number of 'primary representational systems' to experience the world. These systems are described in the acronym 'VAKOG' which stands for Visual (we look and see), Auditory (we hear and listen), Kinaesthetic (we feel externally, internally, or through movement), Olfactory (we smell things), and Gustatory (we taste things).

  Most people, while using all these systems to experience the world, nevertheless have one 'preferred primary system' (Revell and Norman 1997: 31). Some people are particularly stimulated by music when their preferred primary system is auditory, whereas others, who have visual as their primary preferred system, respond most powerfully to images. The extension of this is that a visual person is also likely to 'see' music.

  The VAKOG formulation, while somewhat problematic in the distinctions it attempts to make, offers a framework to analyse different student responses to stimuli and environments. Dede Teeler, for example, suggests that kinaesthetic students behave differently when introduced to the Internet as a language learning tool from predominantly visual learners. The latter need a demonstration of what to do before leaping into Internet tasks, unlike their kinaesthetic colleagues who just get on and do it (Teeler 2000: 60–61). VAKOG also indicates that some students will gain most from the things they hear, whereas others need to see things. This suggests that purely oral presentations of language will be most appropriate for some individuals in a group, while visual material and written text may be more effective for other students. The implications of the olfactory and gustatory systems have not been explored in language teaching so far, however!

- **MI theory:** MI stands for 'Multiple intelligences', a concept introduced by the Harvard psychologist Howard Gardner. In his book *Frames of Mind*, he suggested that as humans we do not possess a single intelligence, but a range of intelligences (Gardner 1983). He listed seven of these: Musical/Rhythmic, Verbal/Linguistic, Visual/Spatial, Bodily/Kinaesthetic, Logical/Mathematical, Intrapersonal and Interpersonal. All people have all of these intelligences, he said, but in each person one (or more) of them is more pronounced. This allowed him to predict that a typical occupation (or 'end state') for people with a strength in logical/mathematical intelligence is that of the scientist, whereas a typical end state for people with strengths in visual/spatial intelligence might well be that of the navigator. The 'athlete' might be the typical end state for people who are strong in bodily/kinaesthetic intelligence, and so on. Gardner has since added an eighth intelligence which he calls

Naturalistic intelligence (Gardner 1993) to account for the ability to recognise and classify patterns in nature. Daniel Goleman has added a ninth 'Emotional intelligence' (Goleman 1996). This includes the ability to empathise, control impulse, and self-motivate.

If we accept that different intelligences predominate in different people, it suggests that the same learning task may not be appropriate for all of our students. While people with a strong logical/mathematical intelligence might respond well to a complex grammar explanation, a different student might need the comfort of diagrams and physical demonstration because their strength is in the visual/spatial area. Other students who have a strong interpersonal intelligence may require a more interactive climate if their learning is to be effective. Murray Loom, a teacher at the Giralang primary school in Canberra, Australia, produced the following chart to show what the original seven intelligences might mean for his students:

TYPE	LIKES TO	IS GOOD AT	LEARNS BEST BY
Linguistic Learner 'The word player'	read, write, tell stories	memorising names, places, dates and trivia	saying, hearing and seeing words
Logical/ Mathematical Learner 'The questioner'	do experiments, figure things out, work things out, work with numbers, ask questions, explore patterns and relationships	maths, reasoning, logic and problem solving	categorising, classifying working with abstract patterns/relationships
Spatial Learner 'The visualiser'	draw, build, design and create things, daydream, look at pictures, watch movies, play with machines	imagining things, sensing changes, mazes/puzzles, reading maps, charts	visualising, dreaming, using the mind's eye, working with colours and pictures
Musical Learner 'The music lover'	sing, hum tunes, listen to music, play an instrument, respond to music	picking up sounds, remembering melodies, noticing pitches/rhythms, keeping time	rhythm, melody, music
Bodily/ Kinaesthetic Learner	move around, touch and talk, use body language	physical activities, (sport/dancing/acting)	touching, moving, interacting with space, processing knowledge through bodily sensations
Interpersonal Learner 'The Socialiser'	have lots of friends, talk to people, join groups	understanding people, leading others, organising, communicating, manipulating, mediating conflicts	sharing, comparing, relating, cooperating, interviewing
Intrapersonal Learner	work alone, pursue own interests	understanding self, focusing inward on feelings/dreams following instincts, pursuing interests/goals, being original	working alone, individualised projects, self-paced instruction, having own space

Taken from 'How to use Gardner's seven intelligences in a class program', presented by M Loom at the Internet site for the University of Canberra in Australia (See note on page 55.)

Armed with this information, teachers can look at the right-hand column and see whether they have given their class a variety of activities to help the various types of learner described here. Although we cannot teach directly to each individual student in our class all of the time, we can ensure that we sometimes give opportunities, during our language programme, for visualisation, for students to work on their own, for sharing and comparing, and for physical movement. By keeping our eye on different individuals, we can direct them to learning activities which are best suited to their own proclivities.

B6 What to do about individual differences

Faced with the different descriptions of learner types and styles which have been described here, it may seem that the teacher's task is overwhelmingly complex. We want to satisfy the many different students in front of us, teaching to their individual strengths with activities designed to produce the best results for each of them, yet we also want to address our teaching to the group as a whole.

We have to start with the recognition of students as individuals as well as being members of a group. Even when classes have been separated into different levels, not everyone in the group will have the same knowledge of English. Some will be better writers than others and some will have greater oral fluency than others.

We need to establish who the different students in our classes are. To ascertain their language level, for example, we can look at their scores on different tests, and we can monitor their progress through both formal and informal observation. This will tell us who needs more or less help in the class. It will inform our decisions about how to group students together (see Chapter 8), and it will guide the type and amount of feedback we give to each student (see Chapter 7). In a general way, we will tailor our teaching methods, the materials we use and the production we expect to the level we are working with.

We want to recognise the other differences we have discussed in this section too. We can do this through observation or, as in the following two examples, through more formal devices. We might ask students what their learning preferences are in questionnaires with items (perhaps in the students' first language) such as the following:

When answering comprehension questions about reading passages I prefer to work:

a on my own ☐

b with another student ☐

c with a group of students ☐

Or we might try to find out which preferred sensory system our students respond to. Revell and Norman suggest the following activity for their teacher readers:

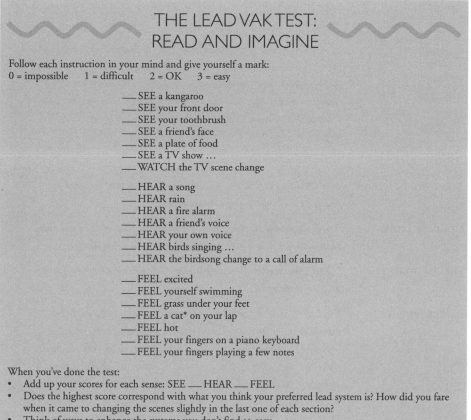

THE LEAD VAK TEST: READ AND IMAGINE

Follow each instruction in your mind and give yourself a mark:
0 = impossible   1 = difficult   2 = OK   3 = easy

—— SEE a kangaroo
—— SEE your front door
—— SEE your toothbrush
—— SEE a friend's face
—— SEE a plate of food
—— SEE a TV show …
—— WATCH the TV scene change

—— HEAR a song
—— HEAR rain
—— HEAR a fire alarm
—— HEAR a friend's voice
—— HEAR your own voice
—— HEAR birds singing …
—— HEAR the birdsong change to a call of alarm

—— FEEL excited
—— FEEL yourself swimming
—— FEEL grass under your feet
—— FEEL a cat* on your lap
—— FEEL hot
—— FEEL your fingers on a piano keyboard
—— FEEL your fingers playing a few notes

When you've done the test:
• Add up your scores for each sense: SEE —— HEAR —— FEEL
• Does the highest score correspond with what you think your preferred lead system is? How did you fare when it came to changing the scenes slightly in the last one of each section?
• Think of ways to enhance the systems you don't find so easy.

'The Lead VAK Test' from *In your Hands* by J Revell and S Norman (Saffire Press)

However we get our information about individuals, we will then be in a position to try and offer activities which offer maximal advantage to the different people in the class. This might involve the way we organise groups in order to satisfy people who prefer working on their own or, conversely, people who benefit most from interaction. We will want to provide different sensory stimuli for the different group members. We will want to offer activities which favour, at different times, students with different learning styles. It is then up to us to keep a record of what works and what does not, either formally or informally. We can also ask our students (either face to face, or, more effectively, through written feedback) how they respond to these activities. The following (unedited) comments, from a multinational group of adult students in Britain, were written in response to a lesson in which they were asked to write an imaginary film scene based on a particular piece of music:

Turkish female: *I liked this subject because everyone could find a connection part of them. After we listened a part of music we could describe what we thing by own sentences. That is why it was very attractive and that type of study was pushing us to talking a lot.*

Italian male:	I didn't like that kind of music. I prefer different kind of music.
Brazilian female:	I think that music is an excellent way to learn. But I think that it will be more interesting if we work with the lyrics of songs. We can learn new expressions, new words and memorize them easily because when we see the words again, we will be able to remember the song, the context the words were used in the songs and consequently your meanings.
Turkish male:	*I love to learn about music.*
Argentinian female:	*It is difficult to express your feelings even in my mother language but finally I could written down something.*
Japanese female:	*I was interested in this theme. Because all students can all enjoy music. But I didn't like making composition from music.*
Turkish male:	I liked this lesson. Because it was funny. And everyone joined at this matters.
Italian female:	This part was interesting as well because we had the opportunity to create something ourself (talking about music listening) using a certain language, immediate, strong and easy at the same time — what I mean is that I never thought that I could, from a piece of music, write down a scene and less of all in English! I liked it and it was not that difficult, well only because we don't have the vocabulary to write something really good.

Apart from demonstrating how individuals respond differently to the same activity, these comments help us to decide whether or not to use a similar kind of activity again, whether to amend it, or whether to abandon such an exercise type.

Such feedback, coupled with questionnaires and our own observation, help us to build a picture of the best kinds of activity for the mix of individuals in a particular class. As we shall see in Chapters 7, B2 and 23, B1, this kind of feedback enables us, over time, to respond to our students with an appropriate blend of tasks and exercises.

This does not mean, of course, that everyone will be happy all of the time (as the feedback above shows). On the contrary, it clearly suggests that some lessons (or parts of lessons) will be more useful for some students than for others. But if we are aware of this and act accordingly, then there is a good chance that most of the class will be engaged with the learning process most of the time.

There is one last issue which should be addressed. We have already referred to the danger of pre-judging student ability through aptitude tests (see B1 above), but we might go further and worry about pigeonholing students with fixed descriptions so that we assume they are always going to behave in the same way. For if this was the case there would be no point in learner training, nor should we waste our time introducing new kinds of activity for the benefit of the group as a whole or the individuals within it. Yet such a position makes no sense. Students do develop as a result of classroom experiences of success or failure. They will almost certainly change in some way as a result of their learning environment and the tasks they perform.

C Motivation

It is accepted for most fields of learning that motivation is essential to success: that we have to want to do something to succeed at it. Without such motivation we will almost certainly fail to make the necessary effort. If motivation is so important, therefore, it makes sense to try and develop our understanding of it. Are all students motivated in the same way? What is the teacher's role in a student's motivation? How can motivation be sustained?

C1 Defining motivation

At its most basic level, motivation is some kind of internal drive which pushes someone to do things in order to achieve something. As H Douglas Brown points out, a cognitve view of motivation includes factors such as the need for exploration, activity, stimulation, new knowledge, and ego enhancement (Brown 2000: 160–166). The adult who starts going to a gym, for example, may hope that a new body image will aid ego enhancement and be stimulated by the active nature of this new undertaking.

Marion Williams and Richard Burden suggest that motivation is a 'state of cognitive arousal' which provokes a 'decision to act' as a result of which there is 'sustained intellectual and/or physical effort' so that the person can achieve some 'previously set goal' (Williams and Burden 1997: 120). They go on to point out that the strength of that motivation will depend on how much value the individual places on the outcome he or she wishes to achieve. Adults may have clearly defined or vague goals. Children's goals, on the other hand, are often more amorphous and less easy to describe, but they can still be very powerful.

In discussions of motivation an accepted distinction is made between extrinsic and intrinsic motivation, that is motivation which comes from outside and from inside. **Extrinsic motivation** is caused by any number of outside factors, for example, the need to pass an exam, the hope of financial reward, or the possibility of future travel. **Intrinsic motivation**, by contrast, comes from within the individual. Thus a person might be motivated by the enjoyment of the learning process itself or by a desire to make themselves feel better.

Most researchers and methodologists have come to the view that intrinsic motivation is especially important for encouraging success. Even where the original reason for taking up a language course, for example, is extrinsic, the chances of success will be greatly enhanced if the students come to love the learning process.

C2 Sources of motivation

The motivation that brings students to the task of learning English can be affected and influenced by the attitude of a number of people. It is worth considering what and who these are since they form part of the world around students' feeling and engagement with the learning process.

- **The society we live in:** outside any classroom there are attitudes to language learning and the English language in particular. How important is the learning of English considered to be in the society? In a school situation, for example, is the language learning part of the curriculum of high or low status? If school students were offered the choice of two languages to learn, which one would they choose and why? Are the cultural images associated with English positive or negative?

  All these views of language learning will affect the student's attitude to the language being studied, and the nature and strength of this attitude will, in its turn, have a profound effect on the degree of motivation the student brings to class and whether or not that motivation continues. Even where adult students have made their own decision to come to a class to study English, they will bring with them attitudes from the society they live in, developed over years, whether these attitudes are thoroughly positive or somewhat negative.

- **Significant others:** apart from the culture of the world around students, their attitude to language learning will be greatly affected by the influence of people who are close to them. The attitude of parents and older siblings will be crucial. Do they approve of language learning, for example, or do they think that maths and reading are what count, and clearly show that they are more concerned with those subjects than with the student's success in English?

  The attitude of a student's peers is also crucial. If they are critical of the subject or activity, the student's own motivation may suffer. If they are enthusiastic learners, however, they may take the student along with them.

- **The teacher:** clearly a major factor in the continuance of a student's motivation is the teacher. Although we will be discussing the role of the teacher in detail in Chapter 4, here it is worth pointing out that his or her attitude to the language and the task of learning will be vital. An obvious enthusiasm for English and English learning, in this case, would seem to be prerequisites for a positive classroom atmosphere.

- **The method:** it is vital that both teacher and students have some confidence in the way teaching and learning take place. When either loses this confidence, motivation can be disastrously affected, but when both are comfortable with the method being used, success is much more likely.

C3 Initiating and sustaining motivation

At the beginning of a course, with students at whatever level and at whatever age, the teacher is faced with a range of motivations. Some students have a clear goal, fed by a strong extrinsic motivation to achieve it. Others have an internal intrinsic drive which has fired them up. Others still may have very weak motivation, whatever type it is. But a student's initial motivation (or lack of it), need not stay the same for ever. As Alan Rogers points out, '… we forget that initial motivation to learn may be weak and die; alternatively it can be increased and directed into new channels' (Rogers 1996: 61).

Increasing and directing student motivation is one of a teacher's responsibilities, though as Dick Allwright argued, we cannot be responsible for all of our students' motivation. In the end it is up to them (Allwright 1977). However, there are three areas where our behaviour can directly influence our students' continuing participation:

- **Goals and goal setting:** we have said that motivation is closely bound up with a person's desire to achieve a goal. A distinction needs to be made here between long- and short-term goals.

   Long-term goals may include the mastery of English, the passing of an exam (at the end of the year), the possibility of a better job in the future, etc. Short-term goals, on the other hand, might be the learning of a small amount of new language, the successful writing of an essay, the ability to partake in a discussion or the passing of the progress test at the end of the week.

   Teachers need to recognise that long-term goals are vitally important but that they can often seem too far away. When English seems to be more difficult than the student had anticipated, the long-term goals can begin to behave like mirages in the desert, appearing and disappearing at random.

   Short-term goals, on the other hand, are by their nature much closer to the student's day-to-day reality. It is much easier to focus on the end of the week than the end of the year. If the teacher can help students in the achievement of short-term goals, this will have a significant effect on their motivation. After all, 'nothing succeeds like success'!

- **Learning environment:** although we may not be able to choose our actual classrooms, we can still do a lot about their physical appearance and the emotional atmosphere of our lessons. Both of these can have a powerful effect on the initial and continuing motivation of students. When students walk into an attractive classroom at the beginning of a course, it may help to get their motivation for the process going. When they come to an unattractive place motivation may not be initiated in this way.

   We can decorate even the most unattractive classrooms with all kinds of visual material to make them more agreeable as learning environments. Even where this is not possible because the classroom is not 'ours', we can still change the atmosphere through such things as the use of music; even the immovability of the furniture (if this is a problem) can be ameliorated by having students get up and walk around the room when this is appropriate.

   All of this is less important, however, than the emotional atmosphere that teachers are able to create and sustain. That is why they have to be careful about how they respond to students, especially in the giving of feedback and correction (see Chapter 7). There is a need for a supportive, cooperative environment to suit the various learner types we discussed in Section B of this chapter. Above all, the teacher's rapport with the students is critical to creating the right conditions for motivated learning.

- **Interesting classes:** if students are to continue to be intrinsically motivated they clearly need to be interested both in the subject they are studying and in the activities and topics they are presented with. We need to provide them with a variety of subjects and exercises to keep them engaged (see Chapter 22A). The choice of material to take into class will be crucial too, but even more important than this will be the ways in which it is used in the lesson.

Our attempts to initiate and sustain our students' motivation are absolutely critical to their learning success (as we shall see with the need for 'engagement' in Chapter 6, A3), for as Alan Rogers writes, 'motivation … is as much a matter of concern for the teacher as it is for the learner; it depends as much on the attitudes of the teacher as on the attitudes of the students' (Rogers 1996: 66).

Chapter notes and further reading

- **Young children**

  On teaching children at and before primary level, see S Reilly and V Ward (1997), W Scott and L Ytreborg (1990), J Brewster et al. (1993), and S Halliwell (1992).

- **Adolescents**

  On the young person's search for identity, see the work of E Erikson (1963) reported in M Williams and R Burden (1997).

  The idea that adolescents present an ideal teaching and learning age is put forward in P Ur (1996: 286) and R Ellis (1994: 484–494).

- **Adult learners**

  On adult learners, see especially J Rogers (1977), A Rogers (1996), and H McKoy and A Tom (2000).

- **Aptitude**

  The best discussion on aptitude I know is in P Skehan (1998: Chapters 8 and 9). See also H D Brown (2000: 98–99).

  The two most widely quoted aptitude test instruments from the 1950s and 1960s were the Modern Language Aptitude Test (MLAT) designed by J Carroll and S Sapon (Carroll and Sapon 1958) and the Pimsleur Language Aptitude Battery (P Pimsleur 1966).

- **Psychology for language teachers**

  The two most approachable books I have come across on the psychology of learning are P Skehan (1998) and M Williams and R Burden (1997).

- **Learning styles**

  For more on learning style, see P Skehan (1998: Chapter 10), A Rogers (1996: 110–112), and H D Brown (2000: Chapter 6).

- **Success and failure**

  On the issue of adults 'dropping out' despite initial motivation, see J Rogers (1977: Chapter 2).

- **Multiple intelligence**

  For more on Multiple intelligence theories, read H Gardner (1983, 1993), D Lazar (1994), and R Christison (1996).

  Murray Loom's web site, which can be found at http://crilt.canberra.edu.au/intranets/examples/giralang/staff/waysoflearning/Mult%20Intel%20Table.html/, seems to have become impossible to access, but those interested in MI theory might want to go to http://www.thomasarmstrong.com/multiple_intelligences.htm/, or for a survey to determine their own 'intelligence' they could visit http://www.surfaquarium.com/MIinvent.htm/.

- **Neuro-linguistic programming (NLP)**

  On NLP, the most enjoyable book I know is J Revell and S Norman (1997). But founded and developed as it was by R Bandler and J Grinder, see also R Bandler and J Grinder (1979) and R Bandler (1985).

- **Motivation**

  On motivation in general, see G Crookes and R Schmidt (1991), Z Dörnyei (1998), and the works referred to in this section of the chapter – in particular M Williams and R Burden (1997: Chapter 6).

4 Describing teachers

A What is a teacher?

Teachers use many metaphors to describe what they do. Sometimes they say they are like actors because 'we are always on the stage'. Others think they are like orchestral conductors 'because I direct conversation and set the pace and tone'. Yet others feel like gardeners, 'because we plant the seeds and then watch them grow'. The range of images – these and others – that teachers use about themselves indicate the range of views that they have about their profession.

Dictionaries also give a variety of messages about teaching. According to the *Cambridge International Dictionary of English*, 'teaching' means 'to give (someone) knowledge or to instruct or train (someone)', whereas the *Longman Dictionary of Contemporary English* suggests that it means to 'show somebody how to do something' or to 'change somebody's ideas'.

It is because views are somewhat mixed as to what teachers are, and because different functions are ascribed to teaching, that we need to examine the teacher's role not only in education generally, but in the classroom itself.

A1 Teachers and learners

Many trainers are fond of quoting from a work called *The Prophet* by Kahlil Gibran. 'If (the teacher) is indeed wise, he does not bid you enter the house of his wisdom, but rather leads you to the threshold of your own mind' (Gibran 1991: 76). Such humanist sentiments expose a dilemma in the minds of many trainers and trainees. Is teaching about the 'transmission' of knowledge from teacher to student, or is it about creating conditions in which, somehow, students learn for themselves? To put it another way, if you were to walk into a classroom, where would you expect to see the teacher – standing at the front controlling affairs, or moving around the classroom quietly helping the students only when needed?

In recent years, under the influence of humanistic and communicative theories (see Chapters 5D and 6, A7), great emphasis has been placed on 'learner-centred' teaching, that is teaching which makes the learners' needs and experience central to the educational process. In this framework, it is students' needs which should drive the syllabus, not some imposed list; it is the students' learning experiences and their responses to them which should be at the heart of a language course. The measure of a good lesson is the student activity taking place, not the performance of the teacher.

The physical manifestation of this trend is to be found in classrooms where learners are given tasks to work on (see Chapter 6, A5), and where, in the process of performing these tasks (with the teacher's help), real learning takes place. In these situations the teacher is no longer the giver of knowledge, the controller, and the authority, but rather a facilitator and a resource for the students to draw on. One writer has suggested that teachers in such learner-centred classrooms need special qualities including maturity, intuition, educational skills (to develop students' awareness of language and learning), an openness to student input, and a greater tolerance of uncertainty. These qualities, he suggests, are in marked contrast to more traditional teacher behaviour (Tudor 1993). Yet they are precisely the characteristics most people would expect of any teacher, traditional or modern, who has their learners' best interests at heart.

Not all methodologists find it easy to accept learner-centredness uncritically, however. Robert O'Neill, an influential materials writer and trainer, wrote an article whose title clearly expressed his disquiet since he called it 'The plausible myth of learner-centredness' (O'Neill 1991). He worried that letting students do the learning on their own with teachers only intervening when and if needed, might amount to a form of neglect. It could be tantamount to an abdication by the teacher of the knowledge-giving role. What is wrong with old-fashioned 'teacher-fronting' he wondered. It seems to work; it has always worked, and many students feel more comfortable with it.

As we shall see in Chapter 6, B1, it is true that in some educational traditions, students, and teachers find learner-centred classrooms quite difficult to come to terms with. It also seems to be the case that there are many occasions when the teacher will want to be at the front of the class to motivate, instruct, or explain something to the whole class. But there are also many activities where encouraging students to solve their own problems on their own or in pairs or groups, will have enormously beneficial effects both on learning, and on the dynamics and atmosphere in the classroom. It is not an 'either ... or' situation, in other words. Instead our behaviour will depend on how we feel about teaching and what we are comfortable with, on the type of activity our students are involved in, and on who the students are and how they feel about what we are asking them to do.

B The roles of a teacher

Within the classroom our role may change from one activity to another, or from one stage of an activity to another. If we are fluent at making these changes our effectiveness as teachers is greatly enhanced.

We have already used the term 'facilitator' in Section A above to suggest the teacher's role in learner-centred lessons – the way in which facilitator is traditionally used by many commentators. Roles such as prompter (B4), resource (B6), or tutor (B7) may well fulfil this concept. Yet in one sense any role which the teacher adopts – and which is designed to help students learn – is to some extent facilitative. All roles, after all, aim to facilitate the students' progress in some way or other, and so it is useful to adopt more precise terms than facilitator as the sections below indicate.

B1 Controller

When teachers act as controllers they are in charge of the class and of the activity taking place in a way that is substantially different from a situation where students are working on their own in groups. Controllers take the roll, tell students things, organise drills, read aloud, and in various other ways exemplify the qualities of a teacher-fronted classroom.

Teachers who view their job as the transmission of knowledge from themselves to their students are usually very comfortable with the image of themselves as controllers. Most people can remember teachers from their past who had a gift for just such a kind of instruction and who inspired their students through their knowledge and their charisma. However, not all teachers possess this ability to inspire, and in less charismatic hands transmission teaching appears to have less obvious advantages. For a start it denies students access to their own experiential learning by focusing everything on the teacher; in the second place it cuts down on opportunities for students to speak because when the class is acting as a whole group, fewer individuals have a chance to say anything at all; and in the third place, over-reliance on transmission teaching can result in a lack of variety in activities and classroom atmosphere.

Of course there are times when acting as a controller makes sense such as when announcements need to be made, when order has to be restored, when explanations are given, or when the teacher is leading a question and answer session. Indeed in many educational contexts this is the most common teacher role. Many teachers fail to go beyond it since controlling is the role they are used to and are most comfortable with. Yet this is a pity because by sticking to one mode of behaviour we deny ourselves and the students many other possibilities and modes of learning which are good not only for learning itself, but also for our students' enjoyment of that learning.

B2 Organiser

One of the most important roles that teachers have to perform is that of organising students to do various activities. This often involves giving the students information, telling them how they are going to do the activity, putting them into pairs or groups, and finally closing things down when it is time to stop.

It is vitally important for teachers to get this role right when it is required. If the students do not understand what they are supposed to do they may well not get full advantage from an activity. If we do not explain clearly the ways pairs or groups should be organised, for example, chaos can ensue. If we have not spent some time engaging the students' interest and ensuring their participation, the activity may be wasted.

The first thing we need to do when organising something is to get students involved, engaged (see Chapter 6, A3) and ready. In most cases this means making it clear that something 'new' is going to happen and that the activity will be enjoyable or interesting or 'good for you'. At this point teachers will often say something like *Now we're going to do this because* ... and offer a rationale for the activity students are to be asked to perform. Thus, instead of just doing something because the teacher says so, they are prepared, hopefully with some enthusiasm, for an activity whose purpose they understand.

Once the students are ready for the activity, we will want to give any necessary instructions, saying what students should do first, what they should do next, etc. Here it is important to get the level of the language right and to try and present instructions in a logical order and in as unconfusing a way as possible. It is frequently a good idea to get students to give the instructions back, in English or in their own language, as a check on whether they have understood it. An important tool in instruction is for the teacher to organise a demonstration of what is to happen. If students are going to use a chart or table to ask other students questions and record their answers, for example, getting a student up to the front to demonstrate the activity with you may be worth any number of complex instructions. Demonstration is almost always appropriate and will almost always ensure that students have a better grasp of what they are supposed to do than instructions can on their own.

Then it is time for us to start or initiate the activity. At this point students probably need to know how much time they have got and exactly when they should start.

Finally we stop the activity when the students have finished and/or when other factors show the teacher and the students that it is time to stop. This might be because they are bored, or because some pairs or groups have already finished before the others (see Chapter 8, B4). Perhaps the lesson is coming to the end and we want to give some summarising comments. At this point it is vital to organise some kind of feedback, whether this is merely a *Did you enjoy that?* type of question (a vitally important question, of course) or whether it is a more detailed discussion of what has taken place.

Teachers should think about 'content feedback' just as much as they concern themselves with the use of language forms in 'form and use feedback'. The latter is concerned with our role as assessor (see below), whereas the former has more to do with the roles of participant and tutor.

When organising feedback we need to do what we say we are going to do, whether this concerns the prompt return of homework (see Chapter 24, A1) or our responses at the end of an oral activity. Students will judge us by the way we fulfil the criteria we offer them.

We can summarise the role of organiser as follows:

engage ➡ instruct (demonstrate) ➡ initiate ➡ organise feedback

B3 Assessor

One of the things that students expect from their teachers is an indication of whether or not they are getting their English right. This is where we have to act as an assessor, offering feedback and correction and grading students in various ways.

We will be dealing with correction in a chapter all of its own (Chapter 7), but where teachers act as assessors, offering feedback on performance, handing out grades, saying whether students can pass to the next level, etc. we can make some important points.

Students need to know how and for what they are being assessed. We should tell them what we are looking for and what success looks like so that they can measure themselves against this. We might say, for example, that *in today's piece of writing I will be looking especially at punctuation* or *in this communication activity I am more interested in your fluency than your accuracy.* Students then have a clear idea of what they need to concentrate on.

Another critical issue is the one of fairness. When students are criticised or score poor grades and they then find that other students have suffered less criticism for an equally good or bad performance, they tend to be extremely unhappy. Most of them want credit for good performance and constructive criticism for poor performance. What they do not want is a feeling that they are being unfairly judged.

When we act as assessors (whether in the matter of 'instant' correction or more drawn-out grade giving) we must always be sensitive to the students' possible reactions. A bad grade is a bad grade, however it is communicated. But it can be made far more acceptable if it is given with sensitivity and support.

B4 Prompter

Sometimes, when students are involved in a role-play activity, for example, they lose the thread of what is going on, or they are 'lost for words' (i.e. they may still have the thread but be unable to proceed productively for lack of vocabulary). They may not be quite sure how to proceed. What should teachers do in these circumstances? Hold back and let them work things out for themselves or, instead, 'nudge' them forward in a discreet and supportive way? If we opt for the latter, we are adopting some kind of a 'prompting' role.

In such situations we want to help but we do not want, at that stage, to take charge because we are keen to encourage the students to think creatively rather than have them hang on our every word. Thus it is that we will occasionally offer words or phrases, suggest that the students say something (e.g. *Well, ask him why he says that*), or suggest what could come next in a paragraph a student is writing, for example. Often we have to prompt students in monolingual groups to speak English rather than using their mother tongue (see Chapter 9D).

When we prompt we need to do it sensitively and encouragingly but, above all, with discretion. If we are too adamant we risk taking initiative away from the student. If, on the other hand, we are too retiring, we may not supply the right amount of encouragement.

B5 Participant

The traditional picture of teachers during student discussions, role-play, or group decision-making activities, is of people who 'stand back' from the activity, letting the learners get on with it and only intervening later to offer feedback and/or correct mistakes. However, there are also times when we might want to join in an activity not as a teacher, but also as a participant in our own right.

There are good reasons why we might want to take part in a discussion. For example, it means that we can enliven things from the inside instead of always having to prompt or organise from outside the group. When it goes well, students enjoy having the teacher with them, and for the teacher, participating is often more instantly enjoyable than acting as a resource.

The danger of teachers as participants, of course, is that we can easily dominate the proceedings. This is hardly surprising since we usually have more English at our disposal than our students do. But it is also due to the fact that even in the most egalitarian classroom, the teacher is still frequently perceived of as 'the teacher' and tends to be listened to with greater attention than his or her students. It takes great skill and sensitivity to avoid this situation.

B6 Resource

In some activities it is inappropriate for us to take on any of the roles we have suggested so far. Suppose that the students are involved in a piece of group writing, or that they are involved in preparation for a presentation they are to make to the class. In such situations having the teacher take part, or try to control them, or even turn up to prompt them might be entirely unwelcome. However, the students may still have need of their teacher as a resource.

Students might ask how to say or write something or what a word or phrase means. They might want to know information in the middle of an activity about that activity or they might want information about where to look for something – a book or a web site for example. This is where we can be one of the most important resources they have.

A few things need to be said about this teacher role. No teacher knows everything about the language! Questions like *What's the difference between X and Y?* or *Why can't I say Z?* are always difficult to deal with because most of us do not carry complex information of this kind in our heads. What we should be able to offer, however, is guidance as to where students can go to look for that information. We could go further, however, and say that one of our really important jobs is to encourage students to use resource material for themselves, and to become more independent in their learning generally. Thus, instead of answering every question about what a word or phrase means, we can instead direct students to a good monolingual dictionary, or in the case of creative work, towards a good production dictionary (see Chapter 12, A1). Alternatively, we need to have the courage to say *I don't know the answer to that right now, but I'll tell you tomorrow.* This means, of course, that we will indeed have to give them the information the next day, otherwise they may begin to lose confidence in us.

When we are acting as a resource we will want to be helpful and available, but at the same time we have to resist the urge to spoon-feed our students so that they become over-reliant on us.

B7 Tutor

When students are working on longer projects, such as pieces of writing or preparations for a talk or a debate, we can act as a tutor, working with individuals or small groups, pointing them in directions they have not yet thought of taking. In such situations we are combining the roles of prompter and resource, acting as a tutor.

It is difficult to be a tutor in a very large group since the term implies a more intimate relationship than that of a controller or organiser. However, when students are working in small groups or in pairs, we can go round the class and, staying briefly with a particular group or individual, offer the sort of general guidance we are describing. Care needs to be taken, however, to ensure that as many individuals or groups as possible are seen, otherwise the students who have not had access to the tutor may begin to feel aggrieved.

It is essential for us to act as tutors from time to time, however difficult this may be. In this more personal contact the learners have a real chance to feel supported and helped, and the general class atmosphere is greatly enhanced as a result. Nevertheless, as with prompting and acting as a resource, we need to make sure that we do not intrude either too much (which will impede learner autonomy) or too little (which will be unhelpful).

B8 Observer

We will want to observe what students do (especially in oral communicative activities) so that we can give them useful group and individual feedback.

When observing students we should be careful not to be too intrusive by hanging on their every word, by getting too close to them, or by officiously writing things down all the time. Above all we should avoid drawing attention to ourselves since to do so may well distract them from the task they are involved in.

It is often useful, when taking notes on students' performance – either as a whole class, or for individual students – to have columns not only for what students get wrong but also what they do right, either in their use of actual language or in their use of conversational strategies. Observing for success often gives us a different feel for how well our students are doing.

But even when we are acting as controllers, giving feedback or organising students, we need to be observing at the same time too, constantly alert to the effect our actions are having, trying to tease out feelings and reactions in the classroom. We need to be able to work and observe simultaneously, listening, watching, and absorbing so that we can create the best kind of rapport between ourselves and our students.

Teachers do not only observe students in order to give feedback. They also watch in order to judge the success of the different materials and activities that they take into lessons so that they can, if necessary, make changes in the future. Indeed, one area of teacher development involves just such observation, built into an action research cycle (see Chapter 24, B1) where we pose questions about what we do in the classroom and use observation to answer such questions.

B9 Which role?

The role that we take on is dependent, as we have seen, on what it is we wish the students to achieve. Where some activities are difficult to organise without the teacher acting as controller, others have no chance of success unless we take a less domineering role. There are times when we will need to act as a prompter where, on other occasions, it would be more appropriate to act as a resource.

What we can say, with certainty, is that we need to be able to switch between the various roles we have described here, judging when it is appropriate to use one or other of them. And then, when we have made that decision, however consciously or subconsciously it is done, we need to be aware of how we carry out that role and how we perform.

C The teacher as performer

In an article published at the end of the 1980s, Christopher Crouch described his experiences of observing his student teachers on teaching practice in Madrid. One of them, who he called W, was obviously full of energy and he writes of how she 'rubbed her hands together' and 'advanced on the front row with a question, almost aggressively …'. Later on, '… seeking students to come out to the front of the class W strode up aisles, literally hauling individuals out of their seats' (Crouch 1989: 107). Yet amazingly, Crouch reports, the students did not seem to mind this at all; on the contrary they were pleased to join in and were clearly fascinated by her behaviour!

W was different from student teacher X who was 'relaxed, at ease, but his non-verbal gestures were exaggerated, larger than life'. He seemed to empathise with his students, gazing into their eyes and generally being more 'laid back' than his colleague. But like W, he too was popular with students. Many of us will be able to remember teachers whose classroom behaviour was exaggerated in a way not unlike W or X – or indeed some mixture of them both.

We can be sure that neither W nor X behave in the same way when they are walking along the street as they did in the classes that Christopher Crouch observed. On the contrary, they clearly went into 'performance' mode when they entered the classroom. When, in a piece of informal research, I asked a number of teachers 'Are you a different person in the classroom than you are out of the classroom?' the responses I got all suggested that the teachers thought of themselves as more energetic, humorous, and creative in class. Frequently, too, they described themselves as 'actors' (Harmer 1995).

If, then, teachers are all performers in the classroom at some level, what does this mean for the learner-centred teacher? Can we 'perform' and still act as a resource? What kind of performance should we adopt when giving feedback? Does 'performance' automatically mean that we must be standing at the front of the class putting on a show? For clearly if this was the case, teacher performance would describe only one kind of teacher role and might be criticised for the very transmissive and teacher-centred behaviour it demonstrated. But as W and X show, different teachers perform differently. Not only that, but any one teacher probably also has many different performance styles depending on the situation. One minute we may be standing at the front commanding or entertaining, but a few minutes later we will be working quietly with a pair while the other students are working in their own pairs.

Knowing that different teachers act differently and that individual teachers vary their behaviour, depending upon what they are doing, gives us insights into classroom behaviour. It suggests that instead of just saying what role teachers should be playing, we can also describe how they should be playing it. Just as stage directions give the actors an insight into what lines mean, so similar descriptions in teaching may give us insights into how activities can best be managed. Thus for an activity where the students are involved in a team game, we will want to behave energetically (because a game needs excitement and energy), encouragingly (if students need a nudge to have a go), clearly (because we do not want the game to fail through misunderstanding) and fairly (because students care about this in a competition situation). If, on the other hand, students are involved in a role-play we should perform clearly (because students need to know exactly what the parameters of the role-play are), encouragingly (because students may need prompting to get them going), but also retiringly (because, once the activity has got going, we do not want to overwhelm the students' performance) and supportively (because students may need help at various points). Figure 12 shows how we might describe these and other activities:

Activity	How the teacher should perform
1 Team game	energetically, encouragingly, clearly, fairly
2 Role-play	clearly, encouragingly, retiringly, supportively
3 Teacher reading aloud	commandingly, dramatically, interestingly
4 Whole-class listening	efficiently, clearly, supportively

FIGURE 12: Describing teacher performance styles

What seems to be clear is that while we certainly need to be aware of the roles we described in Section B (above), and while we also need to be able to use each of these different roles, it is also vitally important to consider how we actually behave during their performance.

D   The teacher as teaching aid

Apart from the roles which we adopt in the classroom – and the way that these roles are performed, we are also a kind of teaching aid ourselves, a piece of teaching equipment in our own right. In particular, we are especially useful when using mime and gesture, as language models, and as providers of comprehensible input.

D1   Mime and gesture

One of the things that we are uniquely able to do on the spot is to use mime, gesture, and expression to convey meaning and atmosphere. It is not difficult to pretend to be drinking, or to pull a sad face. The ability to demonstrate words like *frightened* or *old* is fairly easy for many teachers, just as shrugging shoulders can be used to indicate indifference.

Mime and expression probably work best when they are exaggerated since this makes their meaning explicit. However, gestures do not necessarily have universal meanings (see Chapter 2, E2), and what might seem acceptable in one situation or place will not be appropriate in another. We need, therefore, to use them with care.

We can also use gesture to express or demonstrate meaning. Thus, as we shall see in Chapter 11, A1, fingers can be used to show how verbs are contracted, and arms can be used to 'conduct' choral repetition. Stress can be shown through clapping or clicking fingers, and intonation can be explained through a kind of drawing in the air!

One gesture which is widely used, but which teachers should employ with care, is the act of pointing to students to ask them to participate in a drill or give some other form of response. Though it is quick and efficient, especially when we are having trouble with our students' names, it can seem aggressive and it may make it depressingly obvious to the students that, in having failed to learn their names, we are less than respectful of their identity.

D2 Language model

Students get models of language from textbooks, reading materials of all sorts, and from audio and videotapes. But we can also model language ourselves. This does not only mean the giving of a clear language model as in the PPP procedure described in Chapter 6, A2, but also, for example, the saying of a dialogue or the reading aloud of a text.

One way in which we can model dialogues is to put up two faces on the board and then stand in front of each of them when required to speak their lines. For such activities we should make sure that we can be heard, and we should animate our performance with as much enthusiasm as is appropriate for the conversation we are modelling. We should judge the appropriate speed too, making sure that however slowly we speak, a natural rhythm is maintained and normal intonation patterns preserved as far as possible.

Many of the same requirements apply to reading aloud, a skill which some teachers have tended to ignore. Yet the reading aloud of a particularly exciting or interesting excerpt can be extremely motivating and enjoyable for a class, especially when students have been encouraged to predict what they are going to hear. Poems, too, are very engaging for many students when teachers read them to the class.

Anyone who doubts the power of such activities only has to look at the reading circles in primary classes where children group enthusiastically around the teacher to enjoy the experience of listening to a story. Story-telling and story/poem-reading can work with adults too, though the content and the way it is handled will be significantly different, of course.

Reading passages aloud to students can capture imagination and mood like nothing else, but in order for this to work we need to 'perform' the reading in an interesting and committed way and, as with so many other activities, we must be careful not use this activity too frequently.

D3 Provider of comprehensible input

An issue that confronts many teachers in classrooms is how much they themselves should talk, and what kind of talk this should be. Of course there are times when teachers have to take the roll or ask for quiet, or suggest that students should get into pairs and groups. But there are also times when teachers simply talk to groups, engage in conversation with them, discuss the topic under consideration or ask them about their weekend, etc.

On most training courses a distinction is made between student-talking time (STT) and teacher-talking time (TTT). As we shall see in Chapter 8 it is the concern to maximise the former that leads many teachers to use pair and groupwork; it has been assumed that on the whole we want to see more STT than TTT, since, as trainers frequently point out to their student teachers, *You don't need the language practice, they do*.

It is certainly true that some teachers talk too much and that this is not necessarily advantageous for their students, especially since those teachers are unlikely to be permanently interesting. However, as we shall see in Chapter 5B, it is widely accepted that a vital ingredient in the learning of any language is, of course, exposure to it. The American linguist Stephen Krashen described the best kind of language that students could be exposed to as 'comprehensible input', that is language which students understand the meaning of, but which is nevertheless slightly above their own production level (see Krashen 1985). Yet where can they go for such language input? In the world outside the classroom, English, if they have access to it, will frequently appear incomprehensible, especially when they are at a low level. They need something or someone to provide language which has been 'roughly-tuned' to be comprehensible to them. And there is someone right there in the classroom to give them just that!

As teachers we are ideally placed to provide comprehensible input since we know the students in front of us and can react appropriately to them in a way that a coursebook or a tape, for example, cannot. We know how to talk at just the right level so that even if our students do not understand every word we say, they do understand the meaning of what is being said. At such times the language gains, for the student, are significant.

However, we do need to be aware of how much we ourselves are speaking. If we talk all the time, however 'comprehensible' our language is, the students are denied their own chance to practise production, or get exposure through other means (from reading or listening to tapes, for example). They may also become bored by listening to the teacher all the time.

Basing a lesson on what we can do ourselves as in the examples above clearly has the enormous advantage of not being susceptible to technical malfunction (though that can happen!), power cuts, or unavailability. However, an over-reliance on what we ourselves can offer places excessive demands upon us. It is hard to be permanently motivating and amusing, and it is taxing to have to offer a perpetually varied diet of voices, gestures, and expressions. Nevertheless the ways in which we use our voice, the ways in which we model language and employ gesture and expression are all basic and important teaching skills.

Chapter notes and further reading

- **Metaphors for teaching**
  S Thornbury, in a discussion of the language teachers use to describe what they do, writes that teachers' metaphors 'reveal more than they realise about their beliefs and values' (S Thornbury 1991a: 193).

- **Teachers' roles**
  An important book on teacher roles is T Wright (1987).

- **Teacher-talking time**
  As long ago as 1985 T Lowe was discussing the value of teacher-talking time as roughly-tuned input.

- **Reading aloud**
  On a reassessment of the value of reading aloud, see A Amer (1997).

5 | Some background issues

English language teaching has been influenced by a whole range of theories ranging from scientific studies to opinionated conjecture, from descriptions of what 'seems to work' to philosophical beliefs. Sometimes the connections between such theories and particular teaching methods are easy to perceive, but at other times they are less clear. The five sections in this chapter detail some of the theoretical debates which have enlivened (and continue to inform) the practice of English language teaching.

A Pulling habits out of rats

In an article published in the early part of the twentieth century, two psychologists, Watson and Raynor, reported the results of an experiment they had carried out with a young boy called Albert (Watson and Raynor 1920). When he was nine months old they discovered that the easiest way to frighten him was to make a loud noise by striking a steel bar with a hammer. At various intervals over the next three months they frightened Albert in this way while he was in the presence of various animals (a rat, a rabbit, and a dog). The result was that after three months Albert showed fear when confronted with these animals even when the noise was not made, and furthermore, showed unease when a fur coat was put in front of him. Pleased with their progress, the scientists then proposed to continue their experiment by turning the young baby's fear back to pleasure but they were unable to do so because, unsurprisingly, Albert was withdrawn from the experiment by his parents.

Despite its age Watson and Raynor's experiment is of more than academic interest because the 'conditioning' it demonstrated – and the way that such research into conditioning led on to the theory of **Behaviourism** – had a profound effect upon teaching of all kinds. This is especially true of language teaching where, arguably, Behaviourism still exerts a powerful influence.

To a modern sensibility Watson and Raynor's work with poor little Albert seems extraordinarily unethical, yet they were merely substituting a human being for the various animals who were conditioned to behave in certain ways. Pavlov's dogs, after all, were trained/conditioned to salivate when they heard a bell even if food was not produced.

In Behaviourist theory, conditioning is the result of a three-stage procedure: **stimulus**, **response**, and **reinforcement**. For example, in a classic experiment, when a light goes on (the stimulus) a rat goes up to a bar and presses it (the response) and is rewarded by the dropping of a tasty food pellet at its feet (the reinforcement). If this procedure is repeated often enough, the arrival of the food pellet as a reward reinforces the rat's actions to such an extent that it will always press the bar when the light comes on. It has learnt a new behaviour in other words.

In a book called *Verbal Behaviour* the psychologist Bernard Skinner suggested that much the same process happens in language learning, especially first language learning (Skinner 1957). The baby needs food so it cries and food is produced. Later the infant swaps crying for one- or two-word utterances to produce the same effect, and because words are more precise than cries he or she gradually learns to refine the words to get exactly what is wanted. In this Behaviourist view of learning a similar stimulus–response–reinforcement pattern occurs with humans as with rats or any other animal that can be conditioned in the same kind of way.

Learning a foreign language as an adult may be very different from the baby's acquisition of a mother tongue, but many methodologists supposed that Behaviourist principles could still apply. As we shall see in Chapter 6, A1, Audio-lingual methodology depended quite heavily on stimulus, response, and reinforcement, and much controlled practice that still takes place in classrooms all over the world can trace its heritage back to the influence of Behaviourism.

The almost fatal attack on Behaviourism, when it came, was by the then-little-known linguist Noam Chomsky who wrote a review of Skinner's book (Chomsky 1959). His objection centred on the following conundrum: if all language is learnt behaviour, how come children and adults frequently say things they have never heard before? How on earth would it be possible to create whole new sentences in conversation and poetry, for example, if all language behaviour has been conditioned into us? The fact that we can do these things is the result of having a mental ability to process what we hear, channelling it through the language-processing parts of our brain where rules in some way reside, and where all input adds more information for the better functioning of that processor. This is what stops us from being the mere repeaters, the almost-robots, that Behaviourist principles would seem to describe us as.

Chomsky theorised that all children are born with some kind of language processor – a 'black box' or 'language acquisition device' – which allowed them to formulate rules of language based on the input they received. The mind, in other words, contains 'blueprints for grammatical rules' (Pinker 1994: 43). Once these rules have been activated, the potential for creativity follows. This would suggest that for learners of second languages a methodology based on Behaviourism is not adequate. It is not enough just to teach students 'good' habits: they also need to be given input which will allow their 'processors' to work. They should also be given opportunities for creative language use both in language production and in the processing of written and spoken text.

Despite such reservations about Behaviourism and its influence on language teaching, controlled practice and the use of the Stimulus–Response–Reinforcement model is still widely used and at least one writer was recently prepared to say that:

> We have to admit that some behaviourist principles as applied to foreign language learning were not so far off the mark.
> From A Bruton (1998: 20)

We will see Behaviourist theories applied directly to language teaching in Chapter 6 (A1 and 2).

B 'Language learning will take care of itself'

A major issue in language learning theory has been whether traditional techniques normally associated with language teaching – drills, repetition, controlled practice of specific language items, etc. – actually have any beneficial effect. Indeed, in educational theory generally, there has been some argument about whether teaching 'works' at all.

In his book, *Deschooling Society*, the educational theorist Ivan Illich questioned the whole purpose of formal education. As the title of his book indicates he had a very bleak view of what happens in classrooms. We may think, he suggested, that the more input we are exposed to, the more we learn. We may even go so far as to assume that we can measure knowledge with tests and grades. But all this is a delusion.

> In fact, learning is the human activity which least needs manipulation by others. Most learning is not the result of instruction. It is rather the result of unhampered participation in a meaningful setting.
> From I Illich (1972: 56)

First language learning provides a perfect example of what he is talking about. All children succeed at it to a greater or lesser extent. Although parents and other close adults may help to 'teach' the language in an informal way (for example, through repetition, 'play', or made-up dialogues – where, in the early stages the parent will often take the baby's part when the baby cannot actually speak the words), still the process of learning is unconscious. What the young child does get, of course, is considerable exposure to language which he or she more or less understands the meaning of. And at the end of this process, the language, miraculously, is there as a result of exposure, a clear motivation to communicate – for both physical and emotional reasons – and an opportunity to use what is being acquired.

Perhaps, then, all that anybody needs to learn a new language are those three elements: exposure, motivation, and opportunities for use. This was certainly the view of Dick Allwright and his colleagues who had the task of improving the English language skills of students from overseas who were soon to study on postgraduate courses at the University of Essex in England in the 1970s. The students already had some English knowledge.

The teachers at Essex reasoned that the ways they had been teaching – such as studying grammar, explaining vocabulary, or teaching paragraph organisation – did not seem to have much effect and anyway, they did not 'feel right'. How would it be, they wondered, if they abandoned all that and instead devoted all their efforts to exposing students to English and getting them to use it, particularly given that they were highly motivated to learn. This would satisfy the three criteria we have just detailed. The hypothesis they were working on was, in Allwright's words, that:

... if the language teacher's management activities are directed
exclusively at involving the learners in solving communication problems
in the target language, then language learning will take care of itself...
From R Allwright (1979: 170)

In the course which followed, students were given tasks to do outside the classroom
(such as interviewing people and searching for library books) which involved them
in speaking and reading: real tasks for which the teachers gave no language training,
advice or, crucially, correction. Students also took part in communication games
where the only objective was to complete the task using all and/or any language at
their disposal. A student had to draw the same picture as their partner without
looking at the partner's picture, for example, or they had to arrange objects in the
same order as their partner without looking at their partner's objects – both tasks
relying on verbal communication alone. The results, although not scientifically
assessed, were apparently favourable. Everyone enjoyed the process far more
(especially the teachers) and the students' progress appeared to have been more
impressive than in previous years.

The American applied linguist, Stephen Krashen, writing a short time later,
appeared to be making similar suggestions about language learning too, though by
dividing language 'learning' into **acquisition** and **learning** he was being far more
specific. Language which we acquire subconsciously, he claimed, is language we can
easily use in spontaneous conversation because it is instantly available when we need
it. Language that is learnt, on the other hand, taught and studied as grammar and
vocabulary, is not available for spontaneous use. Indeed, it may be that the only
use for learnt language is to help us to monitor (check) our spontaneous
communication; but then the more we monitor what we are saying, the less
spontaneous we become!

Krashen saw the successful acquisition by students of a second language as being
bound up with the nature of the language input they received. It had to be
comprehensible, even if it was slightly above their productive level, and the students
had to be exposed to it in a relaxed setting. This **roughly-tuned** input is in stark
contrast to the **finely-tuned** input of much language instruction, where specific
graded language has been chosen for conscious learning. Roughly-tuned input aids
acquisition, Krashen argued, whereas finely-tuned input combined with conscious
learning does not.

A further attack on traditional forms of language teaching – especially the use of
repetition and controlled practice – has centred around studies which have
demonstrated that it is impossible to show a direct connection between drilling of
any particular grammatical item, for example, and the acquisition of that item. Dave
Willis describes as a fallacy the idea that controlled practice leads to mastery of
grammar (Willis 1996: 48), and others have made the same point, as we shall see in
Chapter 6, A3.

Despite all these claims, however, language teaching has not been quite so
radicalised as some commentators might have expected. This is partly due to the
theories themselves, whose claims are somewhat weakened when exposed to close

scrutiny. Take Allwright's students at the University of Essex: they all had some knowledge of English, they were all highly motivated (because they would shortly be taking postgraduate degrees at an English university) and, crucially, they were studying in England where their opportunities for exposure to English were greatly increased. Allwright's solution might have been exactly right for such students – the ones it was designed for – but it does not follow, therefore, that the same kind of approach would be appropriate for students at different levels studying in different situations in other parts of the world.

Krashen's claims came under sustained attack partly because they were unverifiable. When someone produces language, how can you tell if this language is 'learnt' or 'acquired'? The speaker will almost certainly be unable to provide you with the answer, and there are no ways, so far, of finding this out. Second, many commentators have questioned his suggestion that learnt language can never pass to the acquired store. This seems observably false. Both roughly-tuned and finely-tuned input (the latter related, of course, to learning) end up becoming acquired language at some point; Rod Ellis suggested that communicative activities might be the switch that took language from the learnt to the acquired store (Ellis 1982). However, no one has suggested that Krashen is wrong about the beneficial qualities of comprehensible input in a relaxed setting.

And what of Willis' criticism of controlled practice, by which he appears to mean both individual and choral repetition? As we shall see in Chapter 6, A3 controlled practice may not fulfil the role originally ascribed to it (the mastery of grammar and vocabulary) but at certain levels it may well have other pay-offs in terms of encouraging motor skills in the spoken production of new language, and in providing the illusion of progress to aid the students' motivation.

Much of the problem in discussing acquisition and learning – in trying to discover whether 'language learning will take care of itself' – occurs when the discussion is divorced from the age of the students (see Chapter 3A), the level they are at (see Chapter 3, B4), their motivation (see Chapter 3C), their educational culture (see Chapter 6B), and the places in which the learning is taking place. Thus we need to balance the fact that all children acquire language against some of the special conditions in which this takes place. Children receive much greater exposure than the average second language student. There is some 'covert teaching' going on as they acquire not only the language itself but the social routines in which it is used. First language acquisition is also closely allied to social growth and general cognitive development.

Most teachers of young learners avoid grammar teaching because experience has shown that it has little effect. Children subconsciously acquire languages with considerable ease. Yet adults find things more difficult, especially when they are learning in classrooms away from target-language communities; for them focused language study is not only useful, it is almost certainly desirable, and most of them want it anyway (see Chapter 3, A1 and 3 for more discussion on this point). Just involving students in communicative tasks may thus be unsatisfactory, provoking 'a general over-emphasis on performance at the expense of progress' (Wicksteed

1998: 3). However, there may be special circumstances (such as those described by Allwright above) where such activities match the motivational drive, level, and situation of the students concerned.

It seems, therefore, that some concentration on language study is helpful for most teenagers and adults learning English whether in the form of finely-tuned input or in some other way, for, as Chapters 6 and 11 will demonstrate, there are many different means of language study. However, many of the theoretical considerations discussed in this section have influenced popular methodology, especially the Communicative approach and its aftermath (see Chapter 6, A4) and Task-based learning (see Chapter 6, A5).

C Noticing

A theme that runs through much discussion of the study of specific graded language is that if controlled practice does not work as well as it should, and if, in Steven Pinker's words, students often depend upon their 'considerable intellects' (1994: 29), then one of the teacher's main tasks is to make students 'aware' of language as an alternative to teaching it. In this approach, often referred to as 'consciousness-raising', the teacher does not expect students to produce new language immediately but instead makes them aware of certain of its features. This awareness will help their acquisition of the language so that when they need to use it, the knowledge thus gained will help them to produce it accurately and fluently.

Richard Schmidt uses the term 'noticing' to describe a condition which is necessary if the language a student is exposed to is to become language that he or she takes in (language intake) (Schmidt 1990). Unless the student notices the new language, he or she is unlikely to process it, and therefore the chances of learning it (and being able to use it) are slim. This suggestion modifies the view of Stephen Krashen (see above) who argued that comprehensible input (with no necessary noticing) was enough for acquisition to take place.

According to Schmidt and based to some extent on his own learning of Portuguese, second language learners notice a language construction if they come across it often enough or if it stands out in some way. One way of coming across it, of course, is through instruction – that is, if teachers draw their attention to it. Of course, whether or not a teacher is present, students need to have already reached a level where they can notice the language feature in question.

This emphasis on noticing and awareness-raising may lead people to suggest that rather than 'teaching' an item of language, the teacher's job is to get students to notice it when it occurs so that it sinks into the brain where it is processed. One way of doing this is to organise tasks where certain language naturally occurs with frequency and where with or without a teacher's help, the student will notice it.

The fact that language has been noticed does not mean it has been acquired/ learnt, nor that students can use it immediately. Rob Batstone suggests that structuring and restructuring of 'noticed' language will be necessary to adjust the hypotheses that the learner has formed (Batstone 1994: 40–43). This means learners trying the language out, often in controlled classroom conditions, to test out its boundaries and characteristics.

Spontaneous production of acquired/learnt language seems to take longer; it happens when the language in question has had enough 'processing' time in the student's memory – through noticing and, perhaps, restructuring – to be available for use. Teachers who expect its instant production in spontaneous conversation are thus often disappointed, but if they wait it will (if students have noticed it) emerge in creative language use in due course.

D The affective variable

One issue that has preoccupied educators in many disciplines is the students' response to their learning experiences and how this makes them feel about themselves. The psychologist Abraham Maslow, for example, suggested that self-esteem was a necessary 'deficiency need' which had to be met before cognitive or aesthetic needs could be engaged with (Maslow 1987). This idea, that the learner's state of mind, his or her personal response to the activity of learning, is central to success or failure in language learning has greatly influenced teaching methods and materials writing. This area of theorising has been called the humanist approach and, as we shall see in Chapter 6, A7, it has given rise to a specific set of teaching methods.

Theorists who are concerned with humanism say that the learner's feelings are as important as their mental or cognitive abilities. If students feel hostile towards the subject of study, the materials, or the teaching methods, they will be unlikely to achieve much success. The American writer Earl Stevick calls these states 'alienations' and suggests that to counter these states, humanist approaches are called for (Stevick 1996). Stephen Krashen, whose ideas were discussed in Section B, would probably agree. His claim for the beneficial value of comprehensible input depends upon the students being relaxed, feeling positive, and unthreatened. If they are not, then their affective filter is raised and blocks the input from being absorbed and processed. But if, on the other hand, the affective filter is lowered – because students are relaxed – then the comprehensible input the students are exposed to will contribute far more effectively to their acquisition of new language.

How then can teachers ensure that their students feel positive about learning – that the **affective filter** is lowered? The psychologist Carl Rogers, whose impact upon this line of thinking has been profound, suggested that learners needed to feel that what they were learning was personally relevant to them, that they had to experience learning (rather than just being 'taught') and that their self-image needed to be enhanced as part of the process (Rogers 1994). Education should speak to the 'whole person', in other words, not just to a small language-learning facility. In a humanist classroom, students are emotionally involved in the learning; they are encouraged to reflect on how learning happens, and their creativity is fostered. The teacher can achieve this by keeping criticism to a minimum and by encouraging them, in plain terms, to feel good about themselves. In a humanist classroom learning a language is as much an issue of personal identity, self-knowledge, feelings and emotions as it is about language.

However, not everyone is happy with this view of the language learning experience. Some humanist activities encourage students to speak from their 'inner' selves, saying, for example, how they feel about their lives, their closeness to different members of their families. John Morgan and Mario Rinvolucri describe such activities as allowing students to 'exteriorise their own internal text' (1986: 9). But critics question whether it is the teacher's job to ask students to reveal things of a private nature, and sometimes even to monitor and nurture the students' inner selves. There is some criticism, too, that there is a strong cultural bias to this view of teaching and learning which would be inappropriate in certain situations. Furthermore a concentration on the inner self may limit the range of language that students can experience, with more emphasis being placed on interpersonal and informal language at the expense of other kinds. Lastly, some doubters suggest, paying too much attention to affective issues in learning may mean that teachers neglect their students' cognitive and intellectual development.

It is certainly true that we want to create an unthreatening environment for our students (just as we will want to foster their cognitive development). We should also be concerned not to do anything which damages their self-esteem. But how far we should act as moral guides and quasi-therapists as well as being teachers of language is a more difficult question, and one which is intimately bound up with our understanding of the role of teachers (see Chapter 4A).

E Discovering language

One school of thought which is widely accepted by many language teachers is that the development of our conceptual understanding and cognitive skills is a main objective of all education. Indeed, this is more important than the acquisition of factual information (Williams and Burden 1997: 24). Such conceptual understanding is arrived at not through 'blind learning', but through a process of exploration which leads to genuine understanding (Lewis 1986: 165). The things we discover for ourselves are absorbed more effectively than things we are taught.

The practical implications of this view are quite clear: instead of explicitly teaching the present perfect tense, for instance, we will expose students to examples of it and then allow them, under our guidance, to work out for themselves how it is used. Instead of telling students which words collocate with *crime*, we can get them to look at a computer concordance of the word (see Chapter 12c) and discover the collocations on their own. Instead of telling them about spoken grammar we can get them to look at transcripts and come to their own conclusions about how it differs from written grammar (see Chapter 2, A2). What we are doing, effectively, is to provoke 'noticing for the learner' (see Batstone 1994: 72 and Section c above).

One powerful reason for encouraging language students to discover things for themselves is the complex nature of language itself. While there may be an argument at lower levels for reducing its complexity into manageable pieces, students who encounter real language outside the classroom will find that it is considerably 'messier' than it may appear in a language lesson. Their response to this may well depend on how prepared they are to observe this messy language and work out, for themselves, how it is put together. Any training in language analysis we have given them will make them more able to do so. In general, encouraging students to be more autonomous learners needs to be a key goal for many teachers particularly of adults and teenagers (see Chapter 24A).

Discovery learning may not be suitable for all students, however, especially if it conflicts with their own learning culture (see Chapter 6, B1). One student in a piece of research by Alan Fortune which compared discovery activities with more traditionally taught grammar said that 'I feel more secure with a rule because my intuition does not tell me a lot' (Fortune 1992: 168). Nor is it clear whether such techniques work equally well with all items of grammar or lexis. If the language students are exposed to is over-complex, they may find it difficult to make any meaningful analysis of it on their own, even if they understand more or less what it means. As we shall see in Chapter 11, B2, however, discovery activities can have an important part to play in the study of language, even when students are initially reluctant to work in this way. In Alan Fortune's study, quoted above, experience of such activities caused a significant number of informants to end up preferring them to more familiar activities.

Chapter notes and further reading

- **Behaviourism**

  I first heard the 'pulling habits out of rats' witticism expressed by Peter Shaw though whether he originated it I do not know!

  For an easily digestible view of Behaviourism, the work of Skinner (for example) and its use in Audio-lingualism and Structuralism, see M Williams and R Burden (1997: 8–13).

- **Acquisition and learning**

  Of all of Krashen's writing on acquisition and learning the most accessible is probably *The Input Hypothesis* (S Krashen 1985).

  R Ellis (1988) suggested that it is impossible to show a direct connection between controlled repetition and the acquisition/learning of some language.

  Krashen's views are effectively challenged in K Gregg (1984). See also J Harmer (1983) and a review of an earlier Krashen book in R Ellis (1983).

- **Controlled practice (repetition)**

  G Cook (1994) argues that repetition is a pleasurable, valuable, and efficent language learning activity which makes learners feel they are involved in authentic and communicative use of language.

- **Noticing**

  For an earlier discussion of consciousness-raising see M Sharwood-Smith (1981).

  On noticing activities, leading on to structuring and re-structuring, see R Batstone (1994: Chapter 7).

- **Humanistic teaching**

  Nearly ten years apart, D Atkinson (1989) and N Gadd (1998) express doubts about humanistic teaching and wonder how far it should be taken. However, humanism is defended passionately in A Underhill (1989) and J Arnold (1998). The most complete modern account of the role of affect in language teaching is J Arnold (ed.) (1999).

- **Discovery learning**

  The way 'real' language is used 'untidily' is demonstrated in D Maule (1988) who looked at the complexity of conditional sentences in real life and G Yule et al. (1992) who showed how people really report speech.

  For examples of discovery material see R Bolitho and B Tomlinson (1995) and N Hall and J Shepheard (1991).

6 | Popular methodology

A Approaches, methods, procedures, and techniques

This chapter looks at how theory has been realised in methodological practice. Within the general area of 'methodology' people talk about approaches, methods, techniques, procedures and models, all of which go into the practice of English teaching. These terms, though somewhat vague, are definable:

- **Approach:** this refers to 'theories about the nature of language and language learning that serve as the source of practices and principles in language teaching' (Richards and Rodgers 1986: 16). An approach describes how language is used and how its constituent parts interlock – in other words it offers a model of language competence. An approach describes how people acquire their knowledge of the language and makes statements about the conditions which will promote successful language learning.

- **Method:** a method is the practical realisation of an approach. The originators of a method have arrived at decisions about types of activities, roles of teachers and learners, the kinds of material which will be helpful, and some model of syllabus organisation (see Chapter 21A). Methods include various procedures and techniques (see below) as part of their standard fare.

  When methods have fixed procedures, informed by a clearly articulated approach, they are easy to describe. The more all-embracing they become, however, the more difficult it is to categorise them as real methods in their own right.

- **Procedure:** a procedure is an ordered sequence of techniques. For example, a popular dictation procedure starts when students are put in small groups. Each group then sends one representative to the front of the class to read (and remember) the first line of a poem which has been placed on a desk there. Each student then goes back to their respective group and dictates that line. Each group then sends a second student up to read the second line. The procedure continues until one group has written the whole poem (see Example 3 on page 264).

  A procedure is a sequence which can be described in terms such as *first you do this, then you do that* …. Smaller than a method it is bigger than a technique.

- **Technique:** a common technique when using video material is called 'silent viewing' (see Chapter 20, B1). This is where the teacher plays the video with no sound. Silent viewing is a single activity rather than a sequence, and as such is a technique rather than a whole procedure. Likewise the 'finger technique' is used by some teachers who hold up their hands and give each of their five fingers a word, e.g. *He is not playing tennis*, and then by bringing the *is* and the *not* fingers together, show how the verb is contracted into *isn't*.

A term that is also used in discussions about teaching is 'model' – used to describe typical procedures or sets of procedures, usually for teachers in training. Such models offer abstractions of these procedures, designed to guide teaching practice. Confusion occurs when these models are elevated to the status of methods, since their purpose is pedagogic in terms of training, rather than inspirational as statements of theoretical belief.

The way in which people announce and develop new teaching practices can make discussions of comparative methodology somewhat confusing. Some methodologists, for example, have new insights and claim a new 'approach' as a result. Others claim the status of method for a technique or procedure. Some methods start as procedures and techniques which seem to work and for which an approach is then developed. Some approaches have to go in search of procedures and techniques with which to form a method. Some methods are explicit about the approach they exemplify and the procedures they employ. Others are not.

What the interested teacher needs to do when confronted with a new method, for example, is to see if and/or how it incorporates theories of language and learning. What procedures does it incorporate? Are they appropriate and effective for the classroom situation that the teacher works with? In the case of techniques and activities, two questions seem worth asking: are they satisfying for both students and teachers, and do they actually achieve what they set out to achieve?

Popular methodology includes ideas at all the various levels we have discussed, and it is these methods, procedures, approaches (and models) which influence the current state of English language teaching.

A1 Audio-lingualism

Audio-lingual methodology owed its existence to the Behaviourist models of learning that were discussed in Chapter 5A. Using the Stimulus–Response–Reinforcement model, it attempted, through a continuous process of such positive reinforcement, to engender good habits in language learners.

Audio-lingualism relied heavily on drills to form these habits; substitution was built into these drills so that, in small steps, the student was constantly learning and, moreover, was shielded from the possibility of making mistakes by the design of the drill.

The following example shows a typical Audio-lingual drill:

Teacher: There's a cup on the table ... repeat
Students: There's a cup on the table

79

Teacher: spoon
Students: There's a spoon on the table
Teacher: Book
Students: There's a book on the table
Teacher: On the chair
Students: There's a book on the chair
etc.

This kind of patterned drilling has some drawbacks quite apart from whether or not it can be shown to lead to grammatical and/or lexical mastery of the structures being focused on (see Chapter 5A). In the first place the language is de-contextualised and carries little communicative function. Second, by doing its best to banish mistakes, so that students only use correct language, such teaching runs counter to a belief among many theorists that making (and learning) from errors is a key part of the process of acquisition. Indeed Audio-lingual methodology seems to banish all forms of language processing that help students sort out new language information in their own minds.

Despite these reservations, however, habit-forming drills have remained popular among teachers and students. The theory behind them still informs some taped materials in language laboratories, for example (see Chapter 10E); teachers who feel insecure with the relative freedoms of some recent methods often feel more confident with the linguistic restriction of such procedures.

A2 Presentation, Practice, and Production

A variation on Audio-lingualism in British-based teaching and elsewhere is the procedure most often referred to as PPP, which stands for **P**resentation, **P**ractice, and **P**roduction. In this procedure the teacher introduces a situation which contextualises the language to be taught. The language, too, is then presented. The students now practise the language using accurate reproduction techniques such as choral repetition (where the students repeat a word, phrase, or sentence all together with the teacher 'conducting'), individual repetition (where individual students repeat a word, phrase, or sentence at the teacher's urging), and cue–response drills (where the teacher gives a cue such as *cinema*, nominates a student by name or by looking or pointing, and the student makes the desired response, e.g. *Would you like to come to the cinema?*). These have similarities with the classic kind of Audio-lingual drill we saw above, but because they are contextualised by the situation that has been presented, they carry more meaning than a simple substitution drill. Later the students, using the new language, make sentences of their own, and this is referred to as production. The following elementary-level example demonstrates this procedure:

- **Presentation:** the teacher shows the students the following picture and asks them whether the people in it are at work or on holiday to elicit the fact that they are on holiday.

The teacher points to the man and attempts to elicit the phrase *He's swimming* by saying *Can anybody tell me … he's … ?* or asking the question *What's he doing … anybody?* The teacher then models the sentence (*He's swimming*) before isolating the grammar she wants to focus on (*he's*), distorting it (*he's … he is … he is*), putting it back together again (*he's … he's*), and then giving the model in a natural way once more (*Listen … He's swimming … he's swimming*). She may accompany this demonstration of form rules by using some physical means such as bringing two hands (for *he* and *is*) together to show how the contraction works or by using the finger technique (see Chapter 11, A1).

- **Practice:** the teacher gets the students to repeat the sentence *He's swimming* in chorus. She may then nominate certain students to repeat the sentence individually, and she corrects any mistakes she hears (see Chapter 7). Now she goes back and models more sentences from the picture (*Mary's reading a book, Paul and Sarah are playing cards*, etc.), getting choral and individual repetition where she thinks this is necessary. Now she is in a position to conduct a slightly freer kind of drill than the Audio-lingual one above:

> *Teacher:* Can anyone tell me? ... Mary? ... Yes, Sergio
> *Student:* She's reading a book.
> *Teacher:* Good. etc.

In this cue–response drill the teacher gives the cue (*Mary*) before nominating a student (*Sergio*) who will give the response (*She's reading a book*). By cueing before nominating she keeps everyone alert. She will avoid nominating students in a predictable order for the same reason.

Usually the teacher puts the students in pairs to practise the sentences a bit more before listening to a few examples just to check that the learning has been effective.

- **Production:** the end point of the PPP cycle is production, which some trainers have called 'immediate creativity'. Here the students are asked to use the new language (in this case the present continuous) in sentences of their own. For example, the teacher may get the students to imagine that they are all in a holiday villa. They must now say what each of them is doing, e.g. *Sergio's reading a book, Juana's sunbathing,* etc. They might write a 'holiday' postcard home, e.g. *It's great here. The sun's shining. Paul and Sarah are playing football … * etc. or, by changing the situation, they may be asked to say what they think their friends and relations are doing at that moment, e.g. *My mother's working at the hospital. My father's driving to London. My sister's studying.* etc.

As we shall see in A3 (below), the PPP procedure has come in for considerable criticism over the last few years, especially as a model for teacher trainees to follow. And even when it was at its most popular teachers knew that what might be appropriate for beginner and elementary students was less likely to find success at higher levels where accurate reproduction and controlled repetition seem out of place.

A3 PPP and alternatives to PPP

The PPP procedure came under a sustained attack the 1990s. It was, critics argued, clearly teacher-centred (at least in the kind of procedure which we have demonstrated above) and therefore sat uneasily in a more humanistic and learner-centred framework. It also seems to assume that students learn 'in straight lines' – that is, starting from no knowledge, through highly restricted sentence-based utterances and on to immediate production. Yet human learning probably is not like that; it is more random, more convoluted. And, by breaking language down into small pieces to learn them, it may be cheating the students of a language which, in Tessa Woodward's phrase, is full of 'interlocking variables and systems' (Woodward 1993: 3). Michael Lewis suggested that PPP was inadequate because it reflected neither the nature of language nor the nature of learning (Lewis 1993: 190), and one trainer, Jim Scrivener, even wrote that 'it is fundamentally disabling, not enabling' (Scrivener 1994a: 15). Later however, Scrivener advanced what is perhaps the most worrying aspect of PPP, the fact that it:

> only describes one kind of lesson; it is inadequate as a general proposal concerning approaches to language in the classroom. It entirely fails to describe the many ways in which teachers can work when, for example, using coursebooks, or when adopting a task-based approach.
>
> From J Scrivener (1996: 79)

This, then, is the problem. Despite writer Andy Hopkins' assertion that 'no language course these days offers an undiluted diet of the dry meaningless PPP-structured lessons that so many commentators like to set up as a straw-man foe' (1995: 11), large numbers of trainers and trainees still use it as the main default model for the teaching of new language forms.

In response to these and earlier criticisms many people have offered variations on PPP and alternatives to it. Keith Johnson offered the 'deep-end strategy' as an alternative (Johnson 1982: Chapter 18), where by encouraging the students into immediate production (throwing them in at the deep end) you turn the procedure on its head. The teacher can now see if and where students are having problems during this production phase and return to either presentation or practice as and when necessary after the production phase is over. A few years later Donn Byrne suggested much the same thing (Byrne 1986: 3), joining the three phases in a circle (see Figure 13). Teachers and students can decide at which stage to enter the procedure.

FIGURE 13: Byrne's 'alternative approach'

However, more recent models, usually designed for training purposes, have gone further than this:

- **ARC:** put forward by Jim Scrivener (1994b), this stands for **A**uthentic use, **R**estricted use, and **C**larification and focus. The basic premise here is that most language in the classroom can be described as either A, R, or C. Thus a communicative activity will demonstrate 'authentic' use, whereas a drill, jazz chant, elicited dialogue or guided writing, for example, will provoke restricted use of language by students. Finally Clarification language is that which the teacher and students use to explain grammar, give examples, analyse errors, elicit or repeat things.

  By labelling different parts of any lesson in this way Scrivener is able to describe lessons differently from the old PPP procedure. An old PPP-type lesson can now be described as **CRA** (where the teacher presents a situation, clarifies the language point, institutes restricted (controlled) practice, before getting 'authentic' use), whereas a different lesson – for example, a task-based lesson – might follow a procedure such as **CACACR**. By introducing new terminology, Scrivener forces us to look at things differently, and by producing a descriptive rather than a prescriptive tool, he is attempting to offer an insight into what he called 'the many ways in which teachers can work'.

- **OHE/III:** Michael Lewis claims that students should be allowed to **O**bserve (read or listen to language) which will then provoke them to **H**ypothesise about how the language works before going on to **E**xperiment on the basis of that hypothesis. Such a description is close to the III of McCarthy and Carter (McCarthy and Carter 1995) where they show students examples of language like the transcripts of conversations (**I**llustration); they then give them discovery activities and questions about the language – for example *How would* *you rewrite this spoken language formally?* (Interaction) as a result of which, through such a noticing routine, students will grasp new facts about language (Induction). We saw an example of the kind of transcript material they might ask students to study in Chapter 2, A1.

- **ESA:** in the ESA model (see Harmer 1998) three components will usually be present in any teaching sequence, whether of five, fifty, or a hundred minutes.

  E stands for **E**ngage. The point here is that unless students are engaged, emotionally, with what is going on, their learning will be less effective.

  S stands for **S**tudy and describes any teaching and learning element where the focus is on how something is constructed, whether it is relative clauses, specific intonation patterns, the construction of a paragraph or text, the way a lexical phrase is made and used, or the collocation possibilities of a particular word.

  A stands for **A**ctivate and this means any stage at which students are encouraged to use all and/or any of the language they know. Communicative activities, for example, are designed to activate the students' language knowledge: so too are reading and listening activities when students are doing it for interest and general understanding such as the extensive reading we discuss in Chapter 15, A1.

  ESA allows for three basic lesson procedures. In the first ('straight arrows') the sequence is **ESA**, much like PPP or CRA (see above). A 'boomerang' procedure, on the other hand, follows a more task-based or deep-end approach. Here the order is **EAS**, so that the teacher gets the students engaged before asking them to do something like a written task, a communication game, or a role-play. Based on what happens there the students will then, after the activity has finished, study some aspect of language which they lacked or which they used incorrectly. 'Patchwork' lessons, on the other hand, may follow a variety of sequences such as ones where engaged students are encouraged to activate their knowledge before studying one and then another language element, and then returning to more active tasks, after which the teacher re-engages them before doing some more study, etc.

What all these models demonstrate is a desire to put PPP firmly in its place as one of a number of teaching procedures for the teacher to employ – rather than the central plank of good teaching. The goal is flexibility, not rigidity.

A4 The Communicative approach

The Communicative approach – or Communicative Language Teaching (CLT) – is the name which was given to a set of beliefs which included not only a re-examination of what aspects of language to teach, but also a shift in emphasis in how to teach.

The 'what to teach' aspect of the Communicative approach stressed the significance of language functions (see Chapter 2, E2) rather than focusing solely on grammar and vocabulary. A guiding principle was to train students to use these language forms appropriately in a variety of contexts and for a variety of purposes.

The 'how to teach aspect' of the Communicative approach is closely related to the idea that 'language learning will take care of itself' (see Chapter 5B), and that plentiful exposure to language in use and plenty of opportunities to use it are vitally important for a student's development of knowledge and skill. Activities in CLT typically involve students in real or realistic communication, where the accuracy of the language they use is less important than successful achievement of the communicative task they are performing. Thus role-play and simulation (see Chapter 19, B6) have become very popular in CLT, where students simulate a television programme or a scene at an airport – or they might put together the simulated front page of a newspaper. Sometimes they have to solve a puzzle and can only do so by sharing information. Sometimes they have to write a poem or construct a story together.

What matters in these activities is that students should have a desire to communicate something. They should have a purpose for communicating (e.g. to make a point, to buy an airline ticket, or write a letter to a newspaper). They should be focused on the content of what they are saying or writing rather than on a particular language form. They should use a variety of language rather than just one language structure. The teacher will not intervene to stop the activity; and the materials he or she relies on will not dictate what specific language forms the students use either. In other words such activities should attempt to replicate real communication. All this is seen as being in marked contrast to the kind of teaching and learning we saw in A1 and A2 above. They are at opposite ends of a 'communication continuum' (see Figure 14).

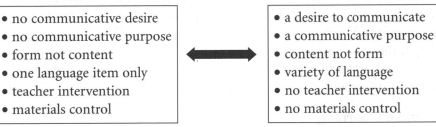

Non-communicative activities

- no communicative desire
- no communicative purpose
- form not content
- one language item only
- teacher intervention
- materials control

Communicative activities

- a desire to communicate
- a communicative purpose
- content not form
- variety of language
- no teacher intervention
- no materials control

FIGURE 14: The communication continuum

Not all activities occur at either extreme of the continuum, however. Some may be further towards the communicative end, whereas some may be more non-communicative. An activity in which students have to go round the class asking questions with a communicative purpose, but with some language restriction, may be nearer the right-hand end of the continuum, whereas a game which forces the use of only one structure (with the teacher intervening occasionally), will come near the non-communicative end.

A key to the enhancement of communicative purpose and the desire to communicate is the information gap. A traditional classroom exchange in which one student asks *Where's the library?* and another student answers *It's on Green Street, opposite the bank* when they can both see it and both know the answer, is not much like real communication. If, however, the first student has a map which does not have the bank listed on it, while the other student has a different map with *post office* written on the correct building – but which the first student cannot see – then there is a gap between the knowledge which the two participants have. In order for the first student to locate the bank on their map, that information gap needs to be closed.

The Communicative approach or Communicative Language Teaching (CLT) have now become generalised 'umbrella' terms to describe learning sequences which aim to improve the students' ability to communicate, in stark contrast to teaching which is aimed more at learning bits of language just because they exist and without focusing on their use in communication. But while it has been widely accepted for some time that communicative activities are a vital part of a teacher's repertoire, it is less clear whether it is possible to pin down exactly what a communicative approach is. After all, most language teaching aims to improve the students' communicative ability, whatever techniques the teacher uses to promote this. And CLT has also included snatches of drilling and focused language work despite the non-communicative nature of such activities.

Communicative Language Teaching has come under attack from teachers for being prejudiced in favour of native-speaker teachers by demanding a relatively uncontrolled range of language use on the part of the student, and thus expecting the teacher to be able to respond to any and every language problem which may come up. In promoting a methodology which is based around group and pairwork, with teacher intervention kept to a minimum during, say, a role-play, CLT may also offend against educational traditions which it aimed to supplant. We will return to such issues in detail in B1 (below). CLT has sometimes been seen as having eroded the explicit teaching of grammar with a consequent loss among students in accuracy in the pursuit of fluency.

Despite these reservations, however, the communicative approach has left an indelible mark on teaching and learning, resulting in the use of communicative activities in classrooms all over the world.

A5 Task-based learning

The idea of Task-based learning (TBL) was greatly popularised by N Prabhu who, working with schools in Bangalore, southern India, speculated that students were just as likely to learn language if they were thinking about a non-linguistic problem as when they were concentrating on particular language forms (see Prabhu 1987). Instead of a language structure, in other words, students are presented with a task they have to perform or a problem they have to solve. For example, after a class performs some pre-task activities which involve questions and vocabulary checking (e.g. *What is this? It's a timetable. What does 'arrival' mean?*), they ask and answer questions to solve a problem such as finding train-timetable information, e.g. *When does the Brindavan express leave Madras/arrive in Bangalore?* (Prabhu 1987: 32). Although the present simple may frequently be used in such an activity, the focus of the lesson is the task, not the structure.

One way of looking at Task-based learning is to see it as a kind of 'deep-end' strategy (see Johnson 1982), or, in the words of Jane Willis, 'like a sort of PPP upside down' (Willis 1994: 19). In other words students are given a task to perform and only when the task has been completed does the teacher discuss the language that was used, making corrections and adjustments which the students' performance of the task has shown to be desirable. However, as Willis herself makes clear, Task-based methodology is in fact considerably more complicated than this. She suggests three basic stages: the Pre-task, the Task cycle, and Language focus (see Figure 15).

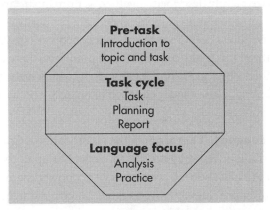

FIGURE 15: The Willis TBL framework (Willis 1996: 52)

In the Pre-task the teacher explores the topic with the class and may highlight useful words and phrases, helping students to understand the task instructions. The students may hear a recording of other people doing the same task. During the Task cycle, the students perform the task in pairs or small groups while the teacher monitors from a distance. The students then plan how they will tell the rest of the class what they did and how it went, and they then report on the task either orally or in writing, and/or compare notes on what has happened. In the Language focus stage the students examine and discuss specific features of any listening or reading text which they have looked at for the task and/or the teacher may conduct some form of practice of specific language features which the task has provoked.

TBL implies a shift away from some traditional teacher roles (see Chapter 4B). We cannot always be acting as a controller if we want students to 'manipulate, comprehend and interact' with a task (Nunan 1989a: 10). It suggests different attitudes to accuracy on the part of the teacher from the Audio-lingual approach and the PPP procedure too. The emphasis on language study will decrease in proportion to the amount of time spent on the tasks themselves.

Critics of TBL have worried about its applicability to lower learning levels – though in fact there are many tasks that are suitable for beginners and/or younger learners. They have also asserted that while it may be highly appropriate to base some learning on tasks, it would be 'unsound' to make tasks 'the basis for an entire pedagogical methodology' (Seedhouse 1999: 155). Seedhouse points out that the kind of interaction which typical tasks promote leads to the use of specific 'task-solving' linguistic forms. These fail to include the kind of language we might expect from discussion, debate, or social interactions of other kinds. There is also a problem with how to grade tasks in a syllabus, as we shall see in Chapter 21, A2.

Despite these caveats, however, tasks are now widely used in language teaching, either as the basis of a language course or as one of its component parts.

A6 Four methods

Four methods, developed in the 1970s and 1980s, have had a considerable impact upon language teaching even if they are rarely used exclusively in 'mainstream' teaching. They are frequently described, together, as humanistic approaches because in three out of the four cases at least, the designers are primarily concerned to lower the students' affective filters (see Chapter 5D), and so remove a psychological barrier to learning. Nevertheless, as many commentators point out, there are elements in the Silent Way or Total Physical Response (see below) which seem entirely teacher-centred and may, indeed, cause exactly the kind of anxiety which humanist theorising aims to prevent.

- **Community Language Learning:** in the classic form of Community Language Learning (CLL) students sit in a circle. It is up to them to decide what they want to talk about. A counsellor or a 'knower' stands outside the circle. The knower provides or corrects target language statements so that if, for instance, a student says something in their own language, the knower can then give them the English equivalent for them to use.

  A student says what he or she wants to say either in English or in his or her first language. In the latter case the knower translates it into English, in effect 'teaching' the student how to make the utterance. The student can now say what he or she wants to the circle. Later, when students are more confident with the language, they can be put in lines facing each other for pairwork discussion.

  In some CLL lessons the students' utterance – helped or provided by the knower – are recorded onto tape to be analysed later. There is often a period for reflection during which students comment frankly on how they felt about the activity. In all of these cases teachers help students achieve what they want, offering help and counsel to the 'community' of the class. The job is to 'facilitate' rather than to 'teach'.

  The influence of CLL in mainstream teaching has been fairly pronounced. The idea that students should reflect upon their learning experiences is now widely accepted as we shall see in Chapter 24, A1. We have already seen in Chapter 4 how teachers need to be conscious of the variety of roles they can adopt in the classroom, and the idea that they should use English to communicate things that they want to say is not disputed.

- **The Silent Way:** one of the most notable features of the Silent Way is the behaviour of the teacher who, rather than entering into conversation with the students, says as little as possible. This is because the founder of the method, Caleb Cattegno, believed that learning is best facilitated if the learner discovers and creates language rather than just remembering and repeating what has been taught. The learner should be in the driving seat, in other words, not the teacher.

In the Silent Way learners interact with physical objects too, especially Cuisenaire rods – which we will describe in more detail in Chapter 10D. There is a problem-solving element involved too, since students have to resolve language construction problems for themselves.

In a classic Silent Way procedure, a teacher models sounds while pointing to a phonemic chart – or to an arrangement of Cuisenaire rods. A student imitates the teacher and the teacher indicates (silently) if he or she is correct. If not, another student is prompted to help the first student. A third or fourth student is prompted if necessary until a correct version of the phoneme is produced. The class continues with the teacher pointing to different phonemes while the students work out what they are – and then how to combine them. Later, students can point to elements on the chart or arrange the Cuisenaire rods in such a way that they have provided a stimulus for the language in the same way as the teacher did. They and their colleagues have to work out what the correct language is.

Through all this procedure the teacher indicates by gesture or expression what the students should do and whether or not they are correct. Examples and corrections are only given verbally if no student can do it first time round. Thus it is up to the students – under the controlling but indirect influence of the teacher – to solve problems and learn the language.

To some, the Silent Way has seemed somewhat inhuman, with the teacher's silence acting as a barrier rather than an incentive. But to others, the reliance students are forced to place upon themselves and upon each other is exciting and liberating. It is students who should take responsibility for their learning; it is the teacher's job to organise this.

The Silent Way has had a direct influence on mainstream teaching by promoting the use of phonemic charts and pointing to objects and sounds (see Example 2 in Chapter 13, B1), and Cuisenaire rods (see Chapter 10D), and an indirect one in the use of discovery techniques (Chapter 11, B2).

- **Suggestopaedia:** developed by Georgi Lozanov, Suggestopaedia sees the physical surroundings and atmosphere of the classroom as of vital importance. By ensuring that the students are comfortable, confident and relaxed, the affective filter is lowered, thus enhancing learning.

    A feature of Suggestopaedia is referred to as 'infantilisation'; that is the teacher and students exist in a parent-children relationship where, to remove barriers to learning, students are given different names from their outside real ones. Traumatic themes are avoided, and the sympathy with which the teacher treats the students is vitally important.

    A Suggestopaedic lesson has three main parts. There is an oral review section in which previously learnt material is used for discussion. This is followed by the presentation and discussion of new dialogue material and its native language equivalent. Finally, in the 'séance' or 'concert' session, students listen to relaxing music (slow movements from the Baroque period at about sixty beats per minute are preferred) while the teacher reads the new dialogue material in a way which synchronises with the taped music. During this phase there are also 'several minutes of solemn silence' (Lozanov 1978: 272) and the students leave the room silently.

The emphasis on lowering the affective filter is now accepted as an important part of all teaching. Music is frequently used in classes too, though not necessarily in the ways and of the type that Lozanov recommended (see Chapters 3, B5, and 16c).

- **Total Physical Response (TPR):** the originator of TPR, James Asher, worked from the premise that adult second language learning could have similar developmental patterns to that of child language acquisition. If children learn much of their language from speech directed at them in the form of commands to perform actions, then adults will learn best in that way too. Accordingly, TPR asks students to respond physically to the language they hear. Language processing is thus matched with physical action.

  Like many other methodology devisers, Asher sees the need to lower the affective filter and finds that organising physical actions in the classroom helps to do this. A typical TPR class might involve the teacher telling students to 'pick up the triangle from the table and give it to me' or 'walk quickly to the door and hit it' (Asher 1977: 54–56). When the students can all respond to commands correctly, one of them can then start giving instructions to other classmates.

  Critics of TPR point out that this kind of teaching may only be appropriate for beginner learners and question how TPR ties in with any real-world needs. Asher himself says it should be included together with other methods. Yet certain features of TPR have had an influence. In TPR students do not have to give instructions themselves until they are ready. This kind of pre-speaking phase was considered of vital importance by Stephen Krashen and Tracey Terrell in their book *The Natural Approach* (Krashen and Terrell 1982). And in responding to commands students get a lot of comprehensible input (see Chapter 5B), and in performing physical actions they seem to echo the claims of Neuro-linguistic programming that certain people benefit greatly from kinaesthetic activity (see Chapter 3, B5).

A7 Humanistic teaching

Concerns about the affective variable (see Chapter 5D) influenced the designers of methods such as Community Language Learning and Suggestopaedia. But humanistic teaching has also found a greater acceptance at the level of procedures and activities, in which students are encouraged to make use of their own lives and feelings in the classroom. Such exercises have a long history and owe much to a work from the 1970s called *Caring and Sharing in the Foreign Language Classroom* by Gertrude Moscowitz (Moscowitz 1978) in which many activities are designed to make students feel good and remember happy times whilst at the same time practising grammar items. Students might be asked to make sentences with *was* and *were* about their favourite things, for example *When I was a child my favourite food was hamburgers* or *When I was a child my favourite relative was my uncle.*

A more recent example of the same kind of thinking is the following 'choosing the passive' activity. Students are asked to read paired active and passive sentences and to underline the sentence from each pair which best fits their personal story. They can change words too (e.g. from *loved* to *ignored*) if they want.

PASSIVE AND ACTIVE LIST

I was born.	I pushed out of my mother's womb.
I was taught to yawn.	I gave my first yawn.
I was shown how to crawl.	I crawled all over the floor.
I was loved by my Dad.	I loved my Dad.

From *More Grammar Games* by M Rinvolucri and P Davis (Cambridge University Press)

Students then explain their choices to each other and, later, write their own passive and active sentences. By the end of the activity they will have said a lot about themselves, reflected on their lives, and will have come to understand a lot about the relationship between active and passive verb forms.

The decision to use humanistic-style activities will depend on how comfortable teachers and students are about working with real lives and feelings. In one sense it seems crazy not to. Nevertheless, as we saw in Chapter 5D, this has not stopped people from worrying about how appropriate it is to have the teacher encouraging personal disclosure on the part of the students; how well are teachers able to deal with such disclosure(s)? How culturally appropriate is the idea of talking about personal experiences and feelings? However, those who enjoy taking such exercises into class feel that using the students themselves as the topic may help them to 'absorb grammar, as it were, through peripheral vision' (Rinvolucri and Davies 1995: xii).

A8 The Lexical approach

The Lexical approach, discussed by Dave Willis (Willis 1990) and popularised by the writer Michael Lewis (1993, 1997), is based on the assertion that 'language consists not of traditional grammar and vocabulary but often of multi-word prefabricated chunks' (Lewis 1997: 3). These are the 'lexical phrases' that were discussed in Chapter 2, B4, the collocations, idioms, fixed and semi-fixed phrases which form such an important part of the language. Lewis proposes that fluency is the result of the acquisition of a large store of fixed and semi-fixed prefabricated items which are 'available as the foundation for any linguistic novelty or creativity' (1997: 15).

This highlighting of an area of language that was, perhaps, previously undervalued has played a valuable role in provoking debate about what students should study. A lexical approach would steer us away from an over-concentration on syntax and tense usage (with vocabulary slotted into these grammar patterns) towards the teaching of phrases which show words in combination, and which are generative in a different way from traditional grammar substitution tables. Thus, instead of teaching *will* for the future, we might instead have students focus on its use in a series of 'archetypical utterances' (Lewis 1993: 97), such as *I'll give you a ring, I'll be in touch, I'll see what I can do, I'll be back in a minute*, etc.

In the area of methodology Lewis' account of a Lexical approach is fairly straightforward. Typical activities include asking students to add intensifiers to semi-fixed expressions, e.g. *It's obvious something's gone wrong (quite)* (Lewis 1997: 96), and getting students, once they have read a text, to underline all the nouns they can find and then to underline any verbs that collocate with those nouns (1997: 109). Word-order exercises can be adapted to focus on particular phrase components, as in this example for expressions with *get*:

Rearrange these to make fixed expressions with the verb *(get)*.

1. Things much can't worse get.
2. What we to there are supposed time get?
3. I you the very weren't happy impression got.
4. We've we as as the for can far moment got.
5. We be to don't anywhere seem getting.
6. What you I can get?

Which of these suggests:

flying   offering a drink   frustration   despair

'Sentence anagrams' from *Implementing the Lexical Approach* by M Lewis (Language Teaching Publications)

Elsewhere, however, Lewis suggests that exposure to enough suitable input, not formal teaching, is the 'key to increasing the learner's lexicon', and that 'most vocabulary is acquired, not taught' (1997: 197).

Suggesting that language should be taught in such a Lexical approach is not without problems, however. In the first place, no one has yet explained how the learning of fixed and semi-fixed phrases can be incorporated into the understanding of a language system. Indeed it can be argued that learning the system is a vital prerequisite of the ability to string phrases together into a coherent whole. Otherwise we are left with the danger of having to learn an endless succession of phrase-book utterances, 'all chunks but no pineapple' (Thornbury 1998: 12).

Another problem is the way in which we might order such phrases for teaching and learning purposes or, if we believe that exposure to enough suitable input is the key, what kind of input that should be.

Finally we need to ask in what way a Lexical approach differs from other accounts of language teaching since there are as yet no sets of procedures to exemplify an approach to language learning.

Despite these reservations, however, the Lexical approach has certainly drawn our attention to facts about the composition of language; what it has not yet done is make the leap from that stage to a set of pedagogic principles or syllabus specifications which could be incorporated into a method.

B What methodology?

With so many different approaches and methods available, many teachers are unsure of which to choose and how to go about making that choice. In this section we will look at some of the cultural implications of the methods we use, and come to some conclusions about the bases on which we can decide on our approach to teaching.

B1 Methods and culture

In the following transcript from a class at the University of Alabama in Tuscaloosa, USA, two students, a Japanese male (S3) and a Malaysian female (S4) are taking part in a role-play about buying a wedding dress. Hovering over them to help and/or correct is the teacher (T2).

> *S4:* The price ...
> *S3:* A little costly ...
> *T2:* (*helping out*) Too expensive.
> *S3:* No ... not ... a little costly?
> *T2:* OK, so you won't choose that because it is too expensive ...
> *S3:* I think it is costly.
> *T2:* Yeah, in English we say too expensive.
> *S3:* I can't say costly?
> *T2:* Well ... (*long pause*). Costly is OK, yeah, but more often ... probably we say expensive ...
> *S3:* OK, you are my teacher ... (*laughs*)
> *T2:* No, you don't have to agree with me ...
> *S3:* I don't have to ... ?
>
> From B Kumaravadivelu (1991: 107)

This exchange is interesting for a number of reasons: in the first place S3 has come across the word *costly* before and is sure it is right, so sure, in fact, that he does not want to let it go. In the second place the teacher's attempts to help, well-meaning as they are, run into an essential problem which so many teachers face in the hurly-burly of the classroom. What <u>is</u> the difference between *costly* and *expensive*? The teacher is left to fall back on the common explanation (since he is unable, on the spot, to summon up the necessary information about why the meanings are different) that *more often ... we say expensive.* But it is what happens next that is most interesting. In a sense S3 gives up the fight, and, accepting that the teacher is ultimately the authority figure in an educational exchange (OK, *you are my teacher*), agrees to change the word he has fought so hard to keep. The teacher is not very sure of his authority, however, believing perhaps that his role is facilitative, that teachers and students are essentially equal as they work towards a common learning goal. *No*, he says, *you don't have to agree with me ...* at which point the student gets really confused, and his (derisory? amused? puzzled?) comment is the question *I don't have to ... ?*

What has happened in this short incident is that two educational cultures seem to have come sharply into conflict, that there is, in Kumaravadivelu's words, a mismatch between 'teacher intention and learner interpretation'. In the same way Greg Ellis points to similar mismatches when 'communicative' teachers who have a facilitative view of the teacher's role in communicative activities try and impose this view of the teacher–student relationship in cultures where students expect the teacher to behave in a more authoritative way (Ellis 1996: 213–218).

As Alistair Pennycook has said, 'we need to see English language teaching as located in the domain of popular culture as much as in the domain of applied linguistics' (Pennycook 1998: 162). Our attitudes to the language, and to the way it is taught, reflect cultural biases and beliefs about how we should communicate and how we should educate each other. And where, as in the example above, there are differing beliefs or expectations, the teaching-learning exchange can become problematic. Dilys Thorp goes further and suggests that where these mismatches are concerned, it is the students – not the teachers – who tend to get judged negatively. What, she wonders, are we to make of the following comment by a British lecturer about an Indonesian student; 'his work shows that he's very bright, but he's quiet in class' (Thorp 1991: 112)? If the comment was made about a British student, she suggests, it might indeed indicate that the student was of a quiet and shy disposition, whereas for the Indonesian student the judgement might not be about that student's personality at all, but rather about norms of classroom behaviour that the student feels are culturally appropriate. 'It is far too easy', she writes, ' to think that our own ideas as to what constitute "good" learning are universal, and forget their cultural specificity' (Thorp 1991: 117).

The fact is that many of the approaches and teaching methods we have discussed in this chapter are based on a very western idea of what constitutes 'good' learning. For example, we have expected active participation in class, and we have encouraged adventurous students who are prepared to 'have a go' even when they are not completely sure of the language they are trying to use. We sometimes ask students to talk about themselves and their lives in a potentially revealing way. We tell students that they should take charge of their learning, that the teacher is a helper and guide rather than the source of knowledge and authority. Yet all of these tenets fly in the face of the educational traditions of some different cultures. Thus British and American teachers working in other countries, for example, sometimes complain that their students have 'nothing to say' when in fact it is not an issue of the students' intelligence, knowledge, or creativity which makes them reluctant to communicate in a British or American way, but their educational culture.

The situation is no easier for the students themselves who are being subjected to methods which they find extremely uncomfortable, or for which they are simply unprepared. Nor is this problem restricted to teachers from one culture teaching students from another. In 1998 an Argentinian teacher, Pablo Toledo, posted a message to a discussion list on the Internet for teachers from South America which he called 'Howl' after the celebrated poem by the American Allan Ginsberg (Toledo 1998). In his posting he lamented the fact that teachers who try 'affective learning' and humanistic teaching, who try drama and role-play and other communicative techniques, fall flat on their faces in secondary classes where the students are not interested and who merely wish to get good grades. He argues passionately for a new kind of methodology to suit that kind of reality since the ideas developed in 'comfy little schools with highly motivated students' just are not right for less 'privileged' contexts, 'not', he writes, 'because there is something wrong with the ideas, but they just were not made for our teaching reality, and do not deal with our problems'.

These are some of the realities of the classroom which methodological theories sometimes ignore. Where teachers blindly follow one or other method or procedure even in the face of student resistance or incomprehension, we get the kind of problems which we have discussed so far. What then is to be done?

Teaching and learning is a contract between two parties for which they both need to agree the terms. It is not a one-sided affair. Teachers need to understand student wants and expectations just as much as they are determined to push their own methodological beliefs. However, this does not necessarily mean that they have to abandon their own theories because the students are not used to what their teacher wants to do. It means, instead, that some accommodation has to be reached between what the two parties want and expect. It means, perhaps, initiating gradual rather than immediate change. If students are not used to giving instant opinions in class, for example, teachers can introduce the procedure gradually. Perhaps, instead of trying to get students to say, in front of their classmates, what they think is beautiful (a question which might meet with an uncomfortable silence) the teacher could dictate this sentence to her students: *One of the most beautiful things I have ever seen is .... .* She can then ask them, individually, to complete the sentence in writing in any way they want (e.g. seriously, humorously, profoundly) with one word or a whole phrase. When they have done this they can read their sentences out. Two sentences, from Japanese students, that stick in my mind are: *One of the most beautiful things I have ever seen is sunrise over Mount Fuji,* and *One of the most beautiful things I have ever seen is my daughter's smile.* If the teacher perceives that students are very worried about making mistakes in their sentence completion, she can check the sentences first before the students read them aloud. There is nothing special about this procedure, of course, but it is possible that activities like this will gradually move students, over time, to a position where they are more prepared to speak spontaneously in class. They bridge the gap between original teacher intention and initial student discomfort.

Dilys Thorp, whose article was cited above, had the same kind of problem with her students in China when they were confronted with listening tasks. An important skill for students is listening for gist (general understanding) without getting hung up on the meaning of every single word (see Chapter 14, A4). Yet Thorp's students were not used to this idea; they wanted to be able to listen to tapes again and again, translating word for word. It is worth quoting her response to this situation in full:

> In listening, where they needed the skill of listening for gist and not
> every word, and where they wanted to listen time and time again, we
> gradually weaned them away from this by initially allowing them to listen
> as often as they liked; but in return – and this was their part of the

bargain – they were to concentrate on the gist and answer guided questions. These guided questions moved them away from a sentence-by-sentence analysis towards inferential interpretation of the text. Then, we gradually reduced the number of times they were allowed to listen. This seemed to work: it was a system with which they were happy, and which enabled them to see real improvements in their listening skills.
From D Thorp (1991: 115)

Teaching and learning is about making the kind of bargain that Thorp describes. Even where teachers and students come from the same town, village, or social group they are likely to live in different cultures – that of teacher and student. Reaching an accommodation between those two cultures (which may involve moderating beliefs, and making compromises – for example, where teacher and students have different views on how often the textbook should be used) is part of what all teachers do to a greater or lesser extent. It is one of the things which makes teaching consistently challenging.

B2 Making choices

It is extremely difficult to come to conclusions about which approaches and methods are best and/or most appropriate for our own teaching situations. As previous chapters have suggested, both theorists and practitioners argue constantly about how languages are learnt and the best ways to encourage this. Yet certain conclusions can be drawn:

- **Exposure to language:** students need constant exposure to language since this is a key component of language acquisition.

- **Input:** students need comprehensible input but this is not enough in itself, unless there is some language study or some opportunity for noticing or consciousness-raising to help students remember language facts.

- **CLT:** communicative activities and task-based teaching offer real learning benefits, though neither tasks nor communicative activities on their own are sufficient for a whole language programme.

- **The affective variable:** anxiety needs to be lowered for learning to take place.

- **Discovery:** where culturally appropriate, students should be encouraged to discover things for themselves, as this is likely to lead to better retention in the long run.

- **Grammar and lexis:** lexis is as important as grammar. Showing how words combine together and behave both semantically and grammatically is an important part of any language learning programme.

- **Methodology and culture:** teaching methodology is rooted in popular culture. Assumptions that methodologists and teachers make are not necessarily shared by students from different traditions. Compromise may be necessary.

All this amounts to a pragmatic eclecticism where decisions about what and how to teach are based, essentially, on what seems to work. The alternative models to PPP discussed in A3 offer coherent frameworks for the operation of such an eclecticism. What seems to work will depend upon the age and character-type of learners, their cultural backgrounds, and the level they are studying at – not to mention the teacher's own beliefs and preferences. Course designers and materials writers have a large part to play here since any coursebook that is used embodies approaches and methods. Writers of current coursebooks tend to mix work on language skills with various kinds of study, providing communicative activities alongside more traditional grammar practice, and mixing in elements of learner training (see Chapter 24, A1) and activities designed to encourage humanistic engagement.

What really matters, for teachers who wish to grow and develop as they teach (and for the students whom they work with), is that practices should be constantly scrutinised to see if they are working and why or why not. That is why action research is so important, as we shall see in Chapter 24, B1. If we and our students constantly monitor our classes and adjust what we do accordingly, there is a really good chance that the methods and techniques we use will be the best for the classes we teach.

Pragmatic eclecticism does not just mean that 'anything goes'. On the contrary, students have a right to expect that they are being asked to do things for a reason, and that their teacher has some aim in mind which he or she can, if asked, articulate clearly. Teaching plans should always be designed to meet an aim or aims (see page 314).

Chapter notes and further reading

- **Approaches and methods**
  For a discussion of approach vs. method, etc. see J Richards and T Rodgers (1986: Chapter 2).

- **Audio-lingualism**
  For a concise description of Audio-lingualism, see Williams and Burden (1997: 10–13). Chapters 2 and 3 of Richards and Rodgers (1986) put Audio-lingual methodology into its context.

- **PPP and teaching models**
  For a classic description of PPP, see D Byrne (1986: Chapter 1). Some of the books and articles which influenced the PPP debate of the 1990s are Lewis (1993, 1996) whose critiques became increasingly pronounced, articles in Sections 1 and 2 of J and D Willis (eds.) (1996), T Woodward (1993), and J Harmer (1996).

- **Communicative approaches**

  For a discussion of what a communicative activity really is, see J Harmer (1982).

  The appropriacy of the Communicative approach both in and outside inner circle countries (see Chapter 1, B1) has come under attack from P Medgyes (1986) and G Ellis (1996).

  The whole value of the Communicative approach was the subject of a bitter clash in the mid-1980s between M Swan (Swan 1985) and H Widdowson (Widdowson 1985).

- **Task-based learning**

  On TBL in general, see C Crookes and S Gass (1993a and b) and D Willis (1990). J Willis (1996) suggests a specific approach to TBL.

  On teacher and learner roles in TBL it is well worth reading D Nunan (1989a: Chapter 4).

- **Four methods**

  H Douglas Brown (2000: 103–108) calls these 'Designer methods'. See also M Celce Murcia (1981). J Richards and T Rodgers (1986) have excellent separate chapters for each.

  On Community Language Learning, see C Curran (1976) and L La Forge (1983).

  On the Silent Way, see C Gattegno (1976) and R Rossner (1982).

  On Suggestopaedia, read G Lozanov (1978). More easily accessible examples can be found in J Cureau (1982) and M Lawlor (1986). On Total Physical Response, see J Asher (1977).

- **The Lexical approach**

  A major populariser of the Lexical approach has been M Lewis (1993, 1997). D Willis (1990) wrote about a lexical syllabus.

  An impressive critique of Lewis' work is S Thornbury (1998). An enthusiast for the Lexical approach is M Baigent (1999).

- **Methodology and culture**

  C Kramsch and P Sullivan (1996) write about appropriate pedagogy from their experiences of teaching and researching in Vietnam.

  We should avoid making assumptions about what students from different methodological cultures appreciate. J Flowerdew, for example, shows how groupwork is appropriate in a Hong Kong setting (Flowerdew 1998). W Littlewood (2000) urgently reminds us that not all the individuals in a culture share the same educational beliefs or respond in the same way.

7 | Mistakes and feedback

Feedback encompasses not only correcting students, but also offering them an assessment of how well they have done, whether during a drill or after a longer language production exercise. The way we assess and correct students will depend not only upon the kind of mistakes being made (and the reasons for them), but also on the type of activity the students are taking part in.

A Students make mistakes

One of the things that puzzles many teachers is why students go on making the same mistakes even when such mistakes have been repeatedly pointed out to them. Yet not all mistakes are the same; sometimes they seem to be deeply ingrained, yet at other times students correct themselves with apparent ease.

In his book on mistakes and correction Julian Edge suggests that we can divide mistakes into three broad categories: 'slips' (that is mistakes which students can correct themselves once the mistake has been pointed out to them), 'errors' (mistakes which they cannot correct themselves – and which therefore need explanation), and 'attempts' (that is when a student tries to say something but does not yet know the correct way of saying it) (Edge 1989: Chapter 2). Of these, it is the category of errors that most concerns teachers, though the students' attempts will tell us a lot about their current knowledge – and may well provide chances for opportunistic teaching (see Chapter 11, A2).

It is now widely accepted that there are two distinct causes for the errors which most if not all students make at various stages:

- **L1 interference:** students who learn English as a second language already have a deep knowledge of at least one other language, and where L1 and English come into contact with each other there are often confusions which provoke errors in a learner's use of English. This can be at the level of sounds: Arabic, for example, does not have a phonemic distinction between /f/ and /v/, and Arabic speakers may well say *ferry* when they mean *very*. It can be at the level of grammar where a student's first language has a subtly different system: French students often have trouble with the present perfect because there is a similar form in French but the same time concept is expressed slightly differently; Japanese students have problems with article usage because Japanese does not use the same system of reference, and so on. It may, finally, be at the level of word usage where similar sounding words have slightly different meanings:

librería in Spanish means 'bookshop', not 'library', *embarazada* means 'pregnant', not 'embarrassed' (such so-called 'false friends' are common between Romance languages).

- **Developmental errors:** for a long time now researchers in child language development have been aware of the phenomenon of 'over-generalisation'. This is best described as a situation where a child who starts by saying *Daddy went, They came*, etc. perfectly correctly suddenly starts saying **Daddy goed* and **They comed*. What seems to be happening is that the child starts to 'over-generalise' a new rule that has been (subconsciously) learnt, and as a result even makes mistakes with things that he or she knew before. Later, however, it all gets sorted out, as the child begins to have a more sophisticated understanding, and he or she goes back to saying *went* and *came* whilst, at the same time, handling regular past tense endings.

  Foreign language students make the same kind of 'developmental' errors as well. This accounts for mistakes like **She is more nicer than him* where the acquisition of *more* for comparatives is over-generalised and then mixed up with the rule that the student has learnt – that comparative adjectives are formed of an adjective + *-er*. Errors of this kind are part of a natural acquisition process. When second language learners make errors, they are demonstrating part of the natural process of language learning.

Errors are part of the students' **interlanguage**, that is the version of the language which a learner has at any one stage of development, and which is continually reshaped as he or she aims towards full mastery. When responding to errors teachers should be seen as providing feedback, helping that reshaping process rather than telling students off because they are wrong.

B Assessing student performance

Assessment of student performance can come from the teacher or from the students themselves.

B1 Teachers assessing students

Assessment of performance can be explicit when we say *That was really good*, or implicit when, during a language drill for example, we pass on to the next student without making any comment or correction (there is always the danger, however, that the student may misconstrue our silence as something else).

Because the assessment we give is either largely positive or somewhat negative students are likely to receive it in terms of praise or criticism. Indeed, one of our roles is to encourage students by praising them for work that is well done, just as it is one of our duties to say when things have not been successful (see Chapter 4, B3). Yet the value of this praise and blame is not quite as clear-cut as such a bald statement might imply.

While it is true that students respond well to praise, over-complimenting them on their work – particularly where their own self-evaluation tells them they have not done well – is likely to prove counter-productive. Williams and Burden (1997: 134–136) show that to be effective, praise has to be combined, in the students' eyes, with the teacher's genuine interest in their work. They report on research (Caffyn 1984) in which secondary students reported their need to understand the reasons for the teacher's approval or disapproval. Such students were likely to respond better to private assessment which leads to successful future action than to public recognition. Punishment was seen as completely counter-productive.

What this suggests is that assessment has to be handled with subtlety. Indiscriminate praise or blame will have little positive effect – indeed it will be negatively received – but measured approval and disapproval which demonstrates a teacher's interest in and attention to a student's work may well result in continuing or even increased motivation (see Chapter 3C).

It is sometimes tempting to concentrate all our feedback on the language which students use such as incorrect verb tenses, pronunciation, or spelling for example, and to ignore the content of what they are saying or writing. Yet especially when we involve them in language production activities (see Chapters 17–19) this is a mistake. Whenever we ask students to give opinions or write creatively, whenever we set up a role-play or involve them in putting together a school newspaper, or in the writing of a report, what they choose to say is just as valuable as they how they choose to say it.

Apart from tests and exams (which we will consider in Chapter 23) there are a number of ways in which we can assess our students' work:

- **Comments:** commenting on student performance happens at various stages both in and outside the class. Thus we may say *good*, or nod approvingly, and these comments (or actions) are a clear sign of a positive assessment. When we wish to give a negative assessment we might do so by indicating that something has gone wrong (see C2 below), or by saying things such as *That's not quite right* or *Your invitation language was a bit mixed up.* When we make comments about our students' written work we can write speaking-like comments at the end of a piece of writing such as *You've written a very interesting composition,* or *Paragraph 2 is confusing because the sequence of events is not clear.* We can write our comments in note form in the margins, or use comment symbols (see D1 below).

- **Marks and grades:** when students are graded on their work they are always keen to know what grades they have achieved. Awarding a mark of 9/10 for a piece of writing or giving a B+ assessment for a speaking activity are clear indicators that students have done well.

  When students get good grades their motivation is often positively affected – provided that the level of challenge for the task was appropriate. Bad grades can be extremely disheartening. Nor is grading always easy and clear cut. If we want to give grades, therefore, we need to decide on what basis we are going to do this and be able to describe this to the students (see Chapter 23, C2 on marking tests).

  When we grade a homework exercise (or a test item) which depends on multiple choice, sentence fill-ins, or other controlled exercise types, it will be relatively easy for students to understand how and why they achieved the marks or grades which we have given them. The same is less obviously true with more creative activities where we ask students to produce spoken or written language to perform a task. In such cases our awarding of grades will necessarily be somewhat more subjective. It is possible that despite this our students will have enough confidence in us to accept our judgement, especially where it coincides with their own assessment of their work. But where this is not the case – or where they compare their mark or grade with other students and do not agree with what they find – it will be helpful if we can demonstrate clear criteria for the grading we have given, either offering some kind of marking scale (see Chapter 23, C2), or some other written or spoken explanation of the basis on which we will make our judgement.

Awarding letter grades is potentially awkward if people misunderstand what letters mean. In some cultures success is only achieved if the grade is 'A', whereas for people in other education systems a 'B' indicates a good result. If, therefore, we wish to rely on grades like this our students need to be absolutely clear about what such grades mean – especially if we wish to add plus and minus signs to (e.g. C++ or A−).

Though grades are popular with students and teachers, some practitioners prefer not to award them, because they find the difference between an A and a B difficult to quantify, or because they cannot see the dividing line between a 'pass' and a 'distinction' clearly. Such teachers prefer to rely on the kind of comments mentioned above.

If we do use marks and grades, however, we can give them after an oral activity, for a piece of homework, or at the end of a period of time (a week or a semester).

- **Reports:** at the end of a term or year some teachers write reports on their students' performance either for the student, the school, or the parents of that student. Such reports should give a clear indication of how well the student has done in the recent past and a reasonable assessment of their future prospects.

  It is important when writing reports to achieve a judicious balance between positive and negative feedback, where this is possible. Like all feedback students have a right (and a desire) to know not only what their weaknesses may be, but also what strengths they have been able to demonstrate.

Reports of this kind may lead to future improvement and progress. The chances for this is greatly increased if they are taken together with the students' own assessment of their performance.

B2 Students assessing themselves

Although, as teachers, we are ideally placed to provide accurate assessments of student performance, students can also be extremely effective at monitoring and judging their own language production. They frequently have a very clear idea of how well they are doing or have done, and if we help them to develop this awareness, we may greatly enhance learning.

Student self-assessment is bound up with the whole matter of learner autonomy since if we can encourage them to reflect upon their own learning through learner training (Chapter 24, A1) or when on their own away from any classroom (see Chapter 24, A3), we are equipping them with a powerful tool for future development.

Involving students in assessment of themselves and their peers occurs when we ask a class *Do you think that's right?* after writing something we heard someone say up on the board, or asking the class the same question when one of their number gives a response. We can also ask them at the end of an activity how well they think they have got on – or tell them to add a written comment to a piece of written work they have completed, giving their own assessment of that work. We might ask them to give themselves marks or a grade and then see how this tallies with our own.

Self-assessment can be made more formal in a number of ways. Students can be given material to guide them in making their own judgements, as in the following example from a coursebook review unit for intermediate students:

B
Checklist

Use this checklist to record how you feel about your progress. Tick if you are satisfied with your progress. Put a cross if you are not satisfied.

I can	Yes/no	I know	Yes/no
deal with misunderstandings		how to get my meaning across in a conversation	
use questions tags correctly		some American colloquial expressions	
express my opinions		how to listen actively	
take part in meetings		more about effective communication	
agree and disagree politely		how to interrupt politely in meetings	
give compliments		more about using connectors and conjunctions	
use prepositions of time		some different ways of learning vocabulary	
recognise and pronounce weak forms of prepositions		more about my learning preferences	
use the simple present passive		how well I'm doing	

From *Activate your English Intermediate* by B Sinclair and P Prowse (Cambridge University Press)

A final way of formalising an assessment dialogue between teacher and student is through a 'record of achievement' (ROA). Here students are asked to write their own assessment of their successes and difficulties and say how they think they can proceed. The teacher then adds their own assessment of the students' progress (including grades), and replies to the points the student has made.

A typical ROA form might look like this:

Student comment	Signed: ....
Teacher comment	Signed: ....

Such ROAs, unlike the more informal journal and letter writing which students and teachers can engage in (see Chapter 24, A1), force both parties to think carefully about strengths and weaknesses and can help them decide on future courses of action. They are especially revealing for other people who might be interested in a student's progress, such as parents.

Where students are involved in their own assessment there is a good chance that their understanding of the feedback which their teacher gives them will be greatly enhanced as their own awareness of the learning process increases.

C Feedback during oral work

Though feedback – both assessment and correction – can be very helpful during oral work teachers should not deal with all oral production in the same way. Decisions about how to react to performance will depend upon the stage of the lesson, the activity, the type of mistake made, and the particular student who is making that mistake.

C1 Accuracy and fluency

A distinction is often made between accuracy and fluency. We need to decide whether a particular activity in the classroom is designed to expect the students' complete accuracy – as in the study of a piece of grammar, a pronunciation exercise, or some vocabulary work for example – or whether we are asking the students to use the language as fluently as possible. We need to make a clear difference between 'non-communicative' and 'communicative' activities (see Chapter 6, A4); whereas the former are generally intended to ensure correctness, the latter are designed to improve language fluency.

Most students want and expect us to give them feedback on their performance. For example, in one celebrated correspondence a non-native speaker teacher was upset when, on a teacher training course in Great Britain, her English trainers refused to correct any of her English because they thought it was inappropriate in a training situation. 'We find that there is practically no correcting at all,' the teacher wrote, 'and this comes to us as a big disappointment' (Lavezzo and Dunford 1993: 62). Her trainers were not guilty of neglect, however. There was a principle at stake: 'The immediate and constant correction of all errors is not necessarily an effective way of helping course participants improve their English', the trainer replied on the same page of the journal.

This exchange of views exemplifies current attitudes to correction and some of the uncertainties around it. The received view has been that when students are involved in accuracy work it is part of the teacher's function to point out and correct the mistakes the students are making. In Chapter 6, A4 we called this 'teacher intervention' – a stage where the teacher stops the activity to make the correction.

During communicative activities, however, it is generally felt that teachers should not interrupt students in mid-flow to point out a grammatical, lexical, or pronunciation error, since to do so interrupts the communication and drags an activity back to the study of language form or precise meaning. Indeed, according to one view of teaching and learning, speaking activities in the classroom, especially activities at the extreme communicative end of our continuum (see Chapter 6, A4), act as a switch to help learners transfer 'learnt' language to the 'acquired' store (Ellis 1982) or a trigger, forcing students to think carefully about how best to express the meanings they wish to convey (Swain 1985: 249). Part of the value of such activities lies in the various attempts that students have to make to get their meanings across; processing language for communication is, in this view, the best way of processing language for acquisition. Teacher intervention in such circumstances can raise stress levels and stop the acquisition process in its tracks.

If that is the case, the methodologist Tony Lynch argues, then students have a lot to gain from coming up against communication problems. Provided that they have some of the words and phrases necessary to help them negotiate a way out of their communicative impasses, they will learn a lot from so doing. When teachers intervene, not only to correct but also to supply alternative modes of expression to help students, they remove that need to negotiate meaning, and thus they may deny students a learning opportunity. In such situations teacher intervention may sometimes be necessary, but it is nevertheless unfortunate – even when we are using 'gentle correction' (see C3 below). In Tony Lynch's words, '… the best answer to the question of when to intervene in learner talk is: as late as possible' (Lynch 1997: 324).

Nothing in language teaching is quite that simple, of course. There are times during communicative activities when teachers may want to offer correction or suggest alternatives because the students' communication is at risk, or because this might be just the right moment to draw the students' attention to a problem. Furthermore, intensive correction can be just as unpleasant during accuracy work too. It often depends on how it is done, and, just as importantly, who it is done to. Correction is a highly personal business and draws, more than many other classroom interactions, on the rapport between teacher and students. As one student once told me, a good teacher 'should be able to correct people without offending them' (Harmer 1998: 2). This means, for example, not reacting to absolutely every mistake that a student makes if this will de-motivate that student. It means judging just the right moment to correct. In communicative or fluency activities it means deciding if and when to intervene at all.

C2 Feedback during accuracy work

As suggested at the beginning of this chapter, correction is usually made up of two distinct stages. In the first, teachers show students that a mistake has been made, and in the second, if necessary, they help the students to do something about it. The first set of techniques we need to be aware of, then, is devoted to showing incorrectness. These techniques are only really beneficial for what we are assuming to be language slips rather than embedded errors. The students are being expected to be able to correct themselves once the problem has been pointed out. If they cannot do this, however, we need to move on to alternative techniques.

- **Showing incorrectness:** this can be done in a number of different ways.
  1 Repeating: here we can ask the student to repeat what they have said, perhaps by saying *Again?* which, coupled with intonation and expression, will indicate that something is not clear.
  2 Echoing: this can be a precise way of pin-pointing an error. We repeat what the student has said emphasising the part of the utterance that was wrong, e.g. *Flight 309 GO to Paris?* (said with a questioning intonation). It is an extremely efficient way of showing incorrectness during accuracy work.
  3 Statement and question: we can, of course, simply say *That's not quite right,* or *Do people think that's correct?* to indicate that something has not quite worked.
  4 Expression: when we know our classes well, a simple facial expression or a gesture (for example a wobbling hand), may be enough to indicate that something does not quite work. This needs to be done with care as the wrong expression or gesture can, in some circumstances, appear to be mocking or cruel.
  5 Hinting: a quick way of helping students to activate rules they already know (but which they have temporarily 'disobeyed') is to give a quiet hint. We might just say the word 'tense' to make them think that perhaps they should have used the past simple rather than the present perfect. We could say 'countable' to make them think about a concord mistake they have made. This kind of hinting depends upon the students and the teacher sharing **metalanguage** (linguistic terms) which, when whispered to students, will help them to correct themselves.
  6 Reformulation: an underrated correction technique is for the teacher to repeat what the student has said correctly, reformulating the sentence, but without making a big issue of it, for example:

  Student: I would not have arrived late if I heard the alarm clock.
  Teacher: If I had heard ...
  Student: ... if I had heard the alarm clock.

In all the procedures above, teachers hope that students will be able to correct themselves once the teacher has indicated that something was wrong. However, where students do not know or understand what the problem is because we are dealing with an error or an attempt that is beyond the students' knowledge or capability, the teacher will want to help the students to get it right.

- **Getting it right:** if the student is unable to correct herself, or respond to reformulation, we need to focus on the correct version in more detail. We can say the correct version emphasising the part where there is a problem (e.g. *Flight 309 GOES to Paris*) before saying the sentence normally (e.g. *Flight 309 goes to Paris*), or we can say the incorrect part correctly (e.g. *Not 'go'. Listen, 'goes'*). If necessary we can explain the grammar (e.g. *We say 'I go', 'you go', 'we go', but for 'he', 'she' or 'it' we say 'goes', for example 'He goes to Paris', or 'Flight 309 goes to Paris'*), or a lexical issue (e.g. *We use 'juvenile crime' when we talk about crime committed by children; a 'childish crime' is an act that is silly because it's like the sort of thing a child would do*). We will then ask the student to repeat the utterance correctly.

  Sometimes we ask students to correct each other. We might say *Can anyone help Jarek/Krystyna?* and hope that other students know the correct version of the utterance – after which the student who made the mistake should be able to say the sentence, question, or phrase accurately.

  Student-to-student correction works well in classes where there is a genuinely cooperative atmosphere; the idea of the group helping all of its members is a powerful concept. Nevertheless it can go horribly wrong where the error-making individual feels belittled by the process, thinking that they are the only one who does not know the grammar or vocabulary. We need to be exceptionally sensitive here, only encouraging the technique where it does not undermine such students.

C3 Feedback during fluency work

The way in which we respond to students when they speak in a fluency activity will have a significant bearing not only on how well they perform at the time but also on how they behave in fluency activities in the future (see Chapter 17c on how to counter negative expectations in productive skill activities). We need to respond to the content not just the language form; we need to be able to untangle problems which our students have encountered or are encountering, but these are things we may well do after the event, not during it. Our tolerance of error in fluency sessions will be much greater than it is during more controlled sessions. Nevertheless, there are times when we may wish to intervene during fluency activities, just as there are ways we can respond to our students once such activities are over.

- **Gentle correction:** if communication breaks down completely during a fluency activity, we may well have to intervene. If our students cannot think of what to say, we may want to prompt them forwards. If this is just the right moment to point out a language feature we may offer a form of correction.

Provided we offer this help with tact and discretion there is no reason why such interventions should not be helpful.

Gentle correction can be offered in a number of ways. We might simply reformulate what the student has said in the expectation that they will pick up our reformulation (see C2 above), even though it hardly interrupts their speech, for example:

> *Student:* I am not agree with you ...
> *Teacher:* I don't agree ...
> *Student:* I don't agree with you because I think ...

It is even possible that students can learn something new in this way when they are making an attempt at some language they are not quite sure of.

We can use a number of other accuracy techniques of showing incorrectness too, such as echoing and expression, or even say *I shouldn't say X, say Y,* etc. But because we do it gently and because we do not move on to a 'getting it right' stage – our intervention is less disruptive than a more accuracy-based procedure would be.

Over-use of even gentle correction will, however, be counter-productive. By constantly interrupting the flow of the activity, we may bring it to a standstill. What we have to judge, therefore, is whether a quick reformulation or prompt may help the conversation move along without intruding too much or whether, on the contrary, it is not especially necessary and has the potential to get in the way of the conversation.

- **Recording mistakes:** as we saw in Chapter 4, B8, we frequently act as observers, watching and listening to students so that we can give feedback afterwards. Such observation allows us to give good feedback to our students on how well they have performed, always remembering that we want to give positive as well as negative feedback.

  One of the problems of giving feedback after the event is that it is easy to forget what students have said. Most teachers, therefore, write down points they want to refer to later, and some like to use charts or other forms of categorisation to help them do this, as in the following example:

Grammar	Words and phrases	Pronunciation	Appropriacy

In each column we can note down things we heard, whether they are particularly good or especially incorrect or inappropriate. We might write down errors such as *according to my opinion* in the words and phrases column, or *I haven't been yesterday* in the grammar column; we might record phoneme problems or stress issues in the pronunciation column and make a note of places where students disagreed too tentatively or bluntly in the appropriacy column.

We can also record students' language performance on audio or videotape. In this situation the students might be asked to design their own charts like the one above so that when they listen or watch they too will be recording more and less successful language performance in categories which make remembering what they heard easier. Another alternative is to divide students into groups and have each group watch for something different – for example, one group focuses on pronunciation, one group listens for the use of appropriate or inappropriate phrases, while a third looks at the effect of the physical paralinguistic features that are used. If teachers want to involve students more – especially if they have been listening to audiotape or watching the video – they can ask them to write up any mistakes they think they heard on the board. This can lead to a discussion in which the class votes on whether they think the mistakes really are mistakes.

Another possibility is for the teacher to transcribe parts of the recording for future study. However, this takes up a lot of time!

- **After the event:** when we have recorded student performance we will want to give feedback to the class. We can do this in a number of ways. We might want to give an assessment of an activity, saying how well we thought the students did in it, getting the students to tell us what they found easiest or most difficult. We can put some of the mistakes we have recorded up on the board and ask students firstly if they can recognise the problem, and then whether they can put it right. Or, as in the example above, we can write both correct and incorrect words, phrases, or sentences on the board and have the students decide which is which.

  When we write examples of what we heard on the board, it is not generally a good idea to say who made the mistakes since this may expose them in front of their classmates. Indeed, we will probably want to concentrate most on those mistakes which were made by more than one person. These can then lead on to quick teaching and re-teaching sequences which arrive opportunistically in this way (see Chapter 11, A2).

  Another possibility is for teachers to write individual notes to students, recording mistakes they heard from those particular students with suggestions about where they might look for information about the language – in dictionaries, grammar books, or on the Internet.

D Feedback on written work

The way we give feedback on writing will depend on the kind of writing task the students have undertaken, and the effect we wish to create. When students do workbook exercises based on controlled testing activities, we will mark their efforts right or wrong, possibly pencilling in the correct answer for them to study. However, when we give feedback on more creative or communicative writing (such as letters, reports, stories, or poems) we will approach the task with circumspection and clearly demonstrate our interest in the content of the students' work.

D1   Written feedback techniques

When handing back students' written work (on paper), or using a computer 'reviewing program' to give feedback on word-processed documents (see Chapter 10F), we can use a number of devices to help them write more successfully in the future:

- **Responding:** one way of considering feedback is to think of it as 'responding' to students' work rather than assessing or evaluating what they have done. When we respond, we say how the text appears to us and how successful we think it has been – and, sometimes, how it could be improved. Such responses are vital at various stages of the writing process cycle (see Chapter 18, B1). Thus students may show us a first draft of their work; our response will be to say how it is progressing and how we think they might improve it in subsequent drafts. The comments we offer them need to appear helpful and not censorious. Sometimes they will be in the margin of the student's work (or, on a computer, written as viewable 'comments'), or if more extensive may need a separate piece of paper – or separate computer document. Consider this example in which the teacher is responding in the form of a letter to a student's first draft of a composition about New Year's Eve:

Dear Gabrielle,

I really enjoyed reading your draft. You have some good expressions, e.g.

... you look to the dark sky and it seems like a special party.

Why don't you begin with that sentence? e.g.

I looked up at the dark sky and it seemed a special party. It was like an explosion everywhere. People were throwing fireworks into the sky, and everywhere there were lights.

Now at this point you can tell the reader what night it is:

It was New Year's Eve and everyone was celebrating.

Then you can explain what New Year's Eve means in Uruguay, how families and friends come together and how everyone has hopes for the future. You can end by coming back to the idea of fireworks.

You can organise your essay to have two times:

Past	*I looked up ...* *it seemed*	Introduction
General present	*Family celebrations in Uruguay are very important.* *People usually send greetings to each other ...*	
Past	????	Conclusion

From *Process Writing* by Ron White and Valerie Arndt (Pearson Education Ltd)

This type of feedback takes time, of course, but it can be more useful to the student than a draft covered in correction marks. However, it is designed specifically for situations in which the student will go back and review the draft before producing a new version.

When we respond to a final written product (an essay or a finished project) we can say what we liked, how we felt about the text, and what they might do next time if the students are going to write something similar.

Another constructive way of responding to students' written work is to show alternative ways of writing through reformulation (see C2 above). Instead of providing the kind of comments in the example above, we might say *I would express this paragraph slightly differently from you*, and then rewrite it, keeping the original intention as far as possible but avoiding any of the language or construction problems which the student's original contained. Such reformulation is extremely useful for students since by comparing their version with yours they discover a lot about the language. However it has to be done sympathetically, since we might end up 'steamrollering' our own view of things, forcing the student to adopt a different voice from the one they wanted to use.

- **Coding:** some teachers use codes, and can then put these codes either in the body of the writing itself, or in a corresponding margin. This makes correction much neater, less threatening, and considerably more helpful than random marks and comments. Frequently used symbols of this kind refer to issues such as word order, spelling, or verb tense as in the following table:

SYMBOL	MEANING	EXAMPLE
S	Incorrect spelling	I recieved jour letter.
W.O.	Wrong word order	We know well this city. Always I am happy here.
T	Wrong tense	If he will come, it will be too late.
C	Concord. Subject and verb do not agree	Two policemen has come. The news are bad today.
WF	Wrong form	We want that you come. That table is our.
S/P	Singular or plural form wrong	We need more informations.
⋀	Something has been left out	They said⋀was wrong. He hit me on ⋀ shoulder.
[ ]	Something is not necessary	It was too much difficult
?M	Meaning is not clear	Come and rest with us for a week. The view from here is very suggestive.
NA	The usage is not appropriate	He requested me to sit down.
P	Punctuation wrong	Whats your name He asked me what I wanted?

From *Teaching Writing Skills* by D Byrne (Pearson Education Ltd)

When we use these codes we mark the place where a mistake has been made and use one of the symbols in the margin to show what the problem is. The student is now in a position to correct the mistake.

We can decide on the particular codes and symbols we use with our students, making sure that they are quite clear about what our symbols mean through demonstration and example. We might also consider having a two-stage approach with simple and more complex codes for students at different levels (Cox and Eyre 1999).

It is worth remembering, however, that one of the marks that students respond to best is ticks when they have used language well, or made a particularly telling point.

A way of avoiding the over-correction of scripts, which also has the advantage of helping students to concentrate on particular features of written English, is **focusing**. In this mode we restrict feedback to a particular aspect of language. We can tell students that we will only give feedback on, say, spelling for the next piece of writing. On other occasions we can say that we are going to focus only on punctuation or tense usage or linking words or paragraph construction – or any other written feature we consider important for our students at that stage. Because we tell students this before they write, we guarantee their close attention to the features we have singled out.

D2 Finishing the feedback process

Except where students are taking achievement or proficiency tests (see Chapter 23, A1), written feedback is designed not just to give an assessment of the students' work, but also to help and teach. We give feedback because we want to affect our students' language use in the future as well as commenting upon its use in the past (see 'homework' in Chapter 24, A1).

When we respond to first and second written drafts of a written assignment we expect a new version to be produced which will show how the students have responded to our comments. In this way feedback is part of a learning process, and we will not have wasted our time. Our reasons for using codes and symbols is the same: if students can identify the mistakes they have made they are then in a position to correct them. The feedback process is only really finished once they have made these changes. If students consult grammar books or dictionaries as a way of resolving some of the mistakes we have signalled for them, the feedback we have given has had a positive outcome.

Chapter notes and further reading

- **Feedback and correction in general**

  See P Ur (1996: Module 17), and J Edge (1989). M Rinvolucri (1998) and R Bolitho et al. (1994) discuss many of the issues surrounding feedback and correction.

- **Written feedback**

  See J Muncie (2000) on the kind of feedback teachers should give.

- **Analysing errors**

  On interlanguage and analysing errors, see H D Brown (2000: Chapter 8).

- **Student self-assessment**

  M Harris (1997) shows how self-assessment is useful both for autonomous learners, but also for students in a more formal educational setting.

- **Teachers' attitudes to feedback and correction**

  In a fascinating teacher-training activity R Tanner (1992) shows how teachers do not necessarily enjoy the feedback methods which they use in class when they themselves are being corrected.

8 | Grouping students

A Different groups

There is no real limit to the way in which teachers can group students in a classroom, though certain factors such as over-crowding, fixed furniture, and entrenched student attitudes may make things problematic. Nevertheless, teaching a class as a whole group, getting students to work on their own, or having them perform tasks in pairs or groups all have their own advantages and disadvantages; each is more or less appropriate for different activities.

A1 Whole-class teaching

When people think of teaching and learning they frequently conjure up a picture of students sitting in rows listening to a teacher who stands in front of them. For many, this is what teaching means, and it is still the most common teacher–student interaction in many cultures. Though it has many limitations, whole-class grouping like this has both practical advantages and disadvantages:

- **Advantages of whole-class grouping:**
  - It reinforces a sense of belonging among the group members, something which we as teachers need to foster (Williams and Burden 1997: 79). If everyone is involved in the same activity, then we are all 'in it together'. Such experiences give us points of common reference to talk about and can be used as reasons to bond with each other. It is much easier for students to share an emotion such as happiness or amusement in a whole-class setting. Twenty people laughing is often more enjoyable than just two; forty people holding their breath in anticipation create a much more engaging atmosphere than just the person sitting next to you.
  - It is suitable for activities where the teacher is acting as a controller (see Chapter 4, B1). It is especially good for giving explanations and instructions, where smaller groups would mean having to do these things more than once. It is an ideal way of showing material whether in pictures, texts, or on audio or videotape. It is also more cost-efficient, both in terms of material production and organisation, than other groupings can be.
  - It allows teachers to 'gauge the mood' of the class in general (rather than on an individual basis); it is a good way for us to get a general understanding of student progress.

– It is the preferred class style in many educational settings where students and teachers feel secure when the whole class is working in lockstep, and under the direct authority of the teacher.

- **Disadvantages of whole-class grouping:**
  – It favours the group rather than the individual. Everyone is forced to do the same thing at the same time and at the same pace.
  – Individual students do not have much of a chance to say anything on their own.
  – Many students are disinclined to participate in front of the whole class since to do so brings with it the risk of public failure.
  – It may not encourage students to take responsibility for their own learning (see A2 below and Chapter 24A). Whole-class teaching favours the transmission of knowledge from teacher to student rather than having students discover things (see Chapter 11, B2) or research things for themselves (see Chapter 12).
  – It is not the best way to organise communicative language teaching (see Chapter 6, A4) or specifically task-based sequences (see Chapter 6, A5). Communication between individuals is more difficult in a group of twenty or thirty than it is in groups of four or five. In smaller groups it is easier to share material, speak quietly and less formally, and make good eye contact. All of these contribute to successful task resolution.

A2 Students on their own

At the opposite end of the spectrum from whole-class grouping is the idea of students on their own, working in a pattern of individualised learning. This can range from students doing exercises on their own in class, to situations in which teachers are able to spend time working with individual students, or when students take charge of their own learning in self-access centres or other out-of-class environments (see Chapter 24A). Such individualised learning is a vital step in the development of learner autonomy.

If we wish students to work on their own in class we can, for example, allow them to read privately and then answer questions individually; we can ask them to complete worksheets or writing tasks by themselves. We can give them worksheets with different tasks and allow individuals to make their own decisions about which tasks to do. We can hand out different worksheets to different individuals depending upon their tastes and abilities. We can allow students to research on their own or even choose what they want to read or listen to – especially where this concerns extensive reading (or 'learner literature' – see Chapter 15, A1).

- **Advantages of individualised learning:**
  – It allows teachers to respond to individual student differences in terms of pace of learning, learning styles, and preferences (see Chapter 3, B3).
  – It is likely to be less stressful for students than performing in a whole-class setting or talking in pairs or groups.

- It can develop learner autonomy and promote skills of self-reliance and investigation over teacher-dependence.
- It can be a way of restoring peace and tranquillity to a noisy and chaotic situation.

- **Disadvantages of individualised learning:**
  - It does not help a class develop a sense of belonging. It does not encourage cooperation in which students may be able to help and motivate each other.
  - When combined with giving individual students different tasks, it means a great deal more thought and materials preparation than whole-class teaching involves. When we work with individual students as a resource or tutor (see Chapter 4, B6 and B7), it takes much more time than interacting with the whole class.

A3 Pairwork

In pairwork students can practise language together, study a text, research language or take part in information-gap activities (see Example 5 in Chapter 19C). They can write dialogues, predict the content of reading texts, or compare notes on what they have listened to or seen.

- **Advantages of pairwork:**
  - It dramatically increases the amount of speaking time any one student gets in the class.
  - It allows students to work and interact independently without the necessary guidance of the teacher, thus promoting learner independence.
  - It allows teachers time to work with one or two pairs while the other students continue working.
  - It recognises the old maxim that 'two heads are better than one', and in promoting cooperation helps the classroom to become a more relaxed and friendly place. If we get students to make decisions in pairs (such as deciding on the correct answers to questions about a reading text), we allow them to share responsibility rather than having to bear the whole weight themselves.
  - It is relatively quick and easy to organise.

- **Disadvantages of pairwork:**
  - Pairwork is frequently very noisy and some teachers and students dislike this. Teachers in particular worry that they will lose control of their class.
  - Students in pairs can often veer away from the point of an exercise, talking about something else completely, often in their first language (see Chapter 9D). The chances of 'misbehaviour' are greater with pairwork than in a whole-class setting.
  - It is not always popular with students, many of whom feel they would rather relate to the teacher as individuals than interact with another learner who may be just as linguistically weak as they are.

– The actual choice of paired partner can be problematic (see B2 below), especially if students frequently find themselves working with someone they are not keen on.

A4 Groupwork

We can put students in larger groups too, since this will allow them to do a range of tasks for which pairwork is not sufficient or appropriate. Thus students can write a group story or role-play a situation which involves five people. They can prepare a presentation or discuss an issue and come to a group decision. They can watch, write, or perform a video sequence (see Chapter 20); we can give individual students in a group different lines from a poem which the group has to reassemble.

In general it is possible to say that small groups of around five students provoke greater involvement and participation than larger groups. They are small enough for real interpersonal interaction, yet not so small that members are over-reliant upon each individual. Because five is an odd number it means that a majority view can usually prevail. However, there are occasions when larger groups are necessary. The activity may demand it (see the poem activity above where the number of students depends on the number of lines in the poem), or we may want to divide the class into teams for some game or preparation phase.

- **Advantages of groupwork:**
  - Like pairwork, it dramatically increases the amount of talking for individual students.
  - Unlike pairwork, because there are more than two people in the group, personal relationships are usually less problematic; there is also a greater chance of different opinions and varied contributions than in pairwork.
  - It encourages broader skills of cooperation and negotiation than pairwork, and yet is more private than work in front of the whole class. Lynne Flowerdew (1998) found that it was especially appropriate in Hong Kong where its use accorded with Confucian principles which her Cantonese-speaking students were comfortable with. Furthermore, her students were prepared to evaluate each other's performance both positively and negatively whereas in a bigger group a natural tendency for self-effacement made this less likely.
  - It promotes learner autonomy by allowing students to make their own decisions in the group without being told what to do by the teacher.
  - Although we do not wish any individuals in groups to be completely passive, nevertheless some students can choose their level of participation more readily than in a whole-class or pairwork situation.

- **Disadvantages of groupwork:**
  - It is likely to be noisy (though not necessarily as loud as pairwork can be). Some teachers feel that they lose control, and the whole-class feeling which has been painstakingly built up may dissipate when the class is split into smaller entities.

– Not all students enjoy it since they would prefer to be the focus of the teacher's attention rather than working with their peers. Sometimes students find themselves in uncongenial groups and wish they could be somewhere else.

– Individuals may fall into group roles that become fossilised, so that some are passive whereas others may dominate (see B2 and B3 below).

– Groups can take longer to organise than pairs; beginning and ending groupwork activities – especially where people move around the class – can take time and be chaotic.

A5 Ringing the changes

Deciding when to put students in groups or pairs, when to teach the whole class, or when to let individuals get on with it on their own will depend upon a number of factors:

- **The task:** if we want to give students a quick chance to think about an issue which we will be focusing on later we may put them in buzz groups (see Chapter 19, B3) where they have a chance to discuss or 'buzz' the topic amongst themselves before working with it in a whole-class grouping. However, small groups will be inappropriate for many explanations and demonstrations, where working with the class as one group will be more appropriate.

    When students have listened to a tape we may let them compare answers in quickly organised pairs. If we want our students to practise an oral dialogue quickly pairwork may the best grouping too.

    If the task we wish our students to be involved in necessitates oral interaction we will probably put students in groups, especially in a large class, so that they all have a chance to make a contribution. If we want students to write sentences which demonstrate their understanding of new vocabulary, on the other hand, we may choose to have them do it individually.

    Although many tasks suggest obvious student groupings, however, we can usually adapt them for use with other groupings. Dialogue practice can be done in pairs, but it can also be organised with two different halves of the whole class. Similarly, answering questions about a listening extract can be an individual activity, or we can organise students to discuss the answers in pairs, or we can have different students listen to different bits of a 'jigsaw' (see Example 4 on page 237) so that they can reassemble the whole text in groups.

- **Variety in a sequence:** a lot depends on how the activity fits into the lesson sequences we have been following and are likely to follow next (see Chapter 22, B4). If much of our recent teaching has involved whole-class grouping there may be a pressing need for pairwork or groupwork. If much of our recent work has been boisterous and active, based on interaction between various pairs and groups, we may think it sensible to allow students time to work individually to give them some breathing space. The advantage of having different student groupings is that they help to provide variety, thus sustaining motivation.

- **The mood:** crucial to our decision about what groupings to use is the mood of our students. Changing the grouping of a class can be a good way to change its mood when required. If students are becoming restless with a whole-class activity – and if they appear to have little to say or contribute in such a setting – we can put them in groups to give them a chance to re-engage with the lesson. If, on the other hand, groups appear to be losing their way or not working constructively, we can call the class back into plenary session and redefine the task, discuss problems that different groups have encountered, or change the activity.

B Organising pairwork and groupwork

Sometimes we may have to persuade reluctant students that pairwork and groupwork are worth doing. They are more likely to believe this if pair and group activities are seen to be a success. Ensuring that pair and group activities work well will be helped if we have a clear idea about how to resolve any problems that might occur.

B1 Making it work

Because some students are unused to working in pairs and groups, or because they may have mixed feelings about working with a partner or about not having the teacher's attention at all times, it may be necessary to invest some time in discussion of learning routines. Just as we may want to create a joint code of conduct (see Chapter 9, B1), so we can come to agreement about when and how to use different student groupings.

One way to discuss pairwork or groupwork is to do a group activity with students and then, when it is over, ask them to write or say how they felt about it (either in English or their own language). Alternatively we can initiate a discussion about different groupings as a prelude to the use of groupwork and pairwork. This could be done by having students complete sentences such as:

> I like/don't like working on my own because ....
> ....
> I like/don't like working in pairs because..
> ....
> I like/don't like speaking in front of the whole class because ....
> ....

They can then compare their sentences with other students to see if everyone agrees. We can also ask them to list their favourite activities and compare these lists with their classmates.

When we know how our students feel about pairwork and groupwork we can then decide, as with all action research (see Chapter 24, B1), what changes of method, if any, we need to make.

We might decide that we need to spend more time explaining what we are doing; we might concentrate on choosing better tasks, or we might even, in extreme cases, decide to use pairwork and groupwork less often if our students object strongly to them. However, even where students show a marked initial reluctance to working in groups we might hope, through organising a successful activity demonstration and/or discussion, to strike the kind of bargain we discussed in Chapter 6, B1.

B2 Creating pairs and groups

We have to decide how to put individual students into pairs and groups, and with which of their classmates. We can base such decisions on any one of the following principles:

- **Friendship:** a key consideration when putting students in pairs or groups is to make sure that we put friends with friends, rather than risking the possibility of people working with others whom they find difficult or unpleasant. Through observation, therefore, we can see which students get on with which of their classmates and make use of this observation later. The problem, of course, is that our observations may not always be accurate, and friendships can change over time.

  Perhaps, then, we should leave it to the students, and ask them to get into pairs or groups with whom they want to. In such a situation we can be sure that members of our class will gravitate towards people they like, admire, or want to be liked by. Such a procedure is likely to be just as reliable as one based on our own observation. However, letting students choose in this way can be very chaotic and may exclude less popular students altogether so that they find themselves standing on their own when the pairs or groups are formed.

  A more informed way of grouping students is to use a sociogram. In this procedure students are asked to write their name on a piece of paper and then write, in order of preference, the students they like best in the class. They know that only the teacher will look at what they have written. On the other side of the piece of paper they should list the people they do not like. We can now use the information they have written to make sociograms like this imaginary one (⟶ = likes, ┈┈▶ = doesn't like):

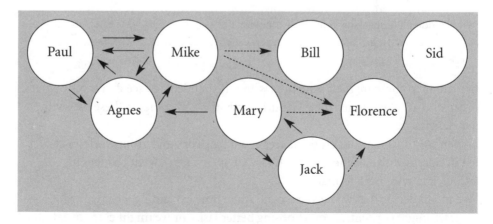

From *Roles of Teachers and Learners* by T Wright (Oxford University Press)

This will then allow us to make informed choices about how we should pair and group individuals. However, sociograms are time consuming, and fail to answer the problem of what to do with unpopular students. In the end, we will still have to put them in some pair or group, and will therefore have to fall back upon our own judgement in order to do so appropriately.

- **Streaming:** much discussion centres round whether students should be streamed according to their ability. One suggestion is that pairs and groups should have a mixture of weaker and stronger students. In such groups the more able students can help their less fluent or knowledgeable colleagues; the process of helping will help such strong students to understand more about the language themselves. The weaker students will benefit from the help they get.

  If we are going to get students at different levels within a class to do different tasks, it makes sense to create groups where all the students in that group are at the same level (a level that will be different from some of the other groups in the class). This gives us the opportunity to go to a group of weaker students and give them the special help they need but which stronger students might find irksome. It allows us to give groups of stronger students more challenging tasks to perform. However, some of the value of cooperative work – all students helping each other regardless of level – may be lost.

  Apart from streaming groups by ability we might also decide to stream them on the basis of participation. If we see that some students participate less than others, we might make a group of weak participators. Now they will find it less easy to hide behind their more talkative colleagues. We can also make groups of especially talkative students too.

  Streaming is a complex task, since it forces teachers to divide students by level or behaviour. It demands constant monitoring to make sure that students are not in inappropriate groups, especially since they may change both language level and the nature of their participation as a course develops.

- **Chance:** we can also group students by 'chance' – that is for no special reasons of friendship, ability, or level of participation. This is by far the easiest way of doing things since it demands little pre-planning, and, by its very arbitrariness, stresses the cooperative nature of working together.

  One way of grouping people is to have students who are sitting next or near to each other work in pairs or groups. A problem can occur, though, with students who always sit in the same place since it means that they will always be in the same pairs or groups which could give rise to boredom over a prolonged period.

  A way of organising pairwork is the 'wheels' scenario (Scrivener 1994b: 95). Here half of the class stand in a circle facing outwards, and the other half of the class stand in an outer circle facing inwards. The outer circle revolves in a clockwise direction and the inner circle revolves in an anti-clockwise direction. When they stop, students work with the person facing them.

We can organise groups by giving each student in the class (in the order they are sitting) a letter from A to E. We now ask all the As to form a group together, all the Bs to be a group, all the Cs to be a group and so on. Depending upon the size of the class we end up with groups of more than five, but this may not be a problem if the task is appropriate (see A5 above). We can also arrange random groups by asking people to get out of their chairs and stand in the order of their birthdays (with January at one end of the line and December at the other). We can then group the first five, the second five, and so on. We can make groups of people wearing black or green, of people with or without glasses, or of people in different occupations (if we are in an adult class).

It is interesting to note that modern computer language laboratories often have a 'random' pairing and grouping program so that the teacher does not have to decide who should work with whom (see Chapter 10E).

- **Changing groups:** just because we put students in groups at the beginning of an activity does not mean that they have to stay in these groups until the end. The group may change while an activity continues, as described in Chapter 15, A3, where students start by listing vocabulary and then discuss it first in pairs, then in groups of four, then in groups of eight – or even sixteen. In an interview activity students can start working in two main groups and then break into smaller groups for a role-play. If groups are planning something or discussing, members from other groups can come and visit them to share information and take different information back to their original group. A longer sequence may start with the teacher and the whole class before moving between pairwork, individual work, and groupwork until it returns back to the whole-class grouping.

We make our pairing and grouping decisions based on a variety of factors. If we are concerned about the atmosphere of the whole class and some of the tensions in it, we may try and make friendship groups. If our activity is based on fun (such as Example 4, 'Julia's story', on page 265), we may leave our grouping to chance. If, on the other hand, we are dealing with a non-homogeneous class (in terms of level) or if we have some students who are falling behind, we may stream groups so that we can help the weaker students while keeping the more advanced ones engaged in a different activity. We might, for example, stream pairs to do research tasks (see Chapter 12D), so that students with differing needs can work on different aspects of language.

B3 Procedures for pairwork and groupwork

Our role in pairwork and groupwork does not end when we have decided which students should work together, of course. We have other matters to address too, not only before the activity starts but also during and after it:

- **Before:** when we want students to work together in pairs or groups we will follow the 'engage–instruct–initiate' sequence we detailed in Chapter 4, B2.

This is because students need to feel enthusiastic about what they are going to do. They need to understand what they are going to do, and they need to be given an idea of when they will have finished the task they are going to get involved in.

Sometimes our instructions will involve a demonstration – when, for example, students are going to use a new information-gap activity or when we want them to use cards (see Chapter 10A). On other occasions, where an activity is familiar, we may simply give them an instruction to practise language they are studying in pairs, or to use their dictionaries to find specific bits of information.

The success of a pairwork or groupwork task is often helped by giving students a time when the activity should finish – and then sticking to it. This helps to give them a clear framework to work within. Alternatively in lighter-hearted activities such as a poem dictation (see Example 3 on page 264), we can encourage groups to see who finishes first. Though language learning is not a contest (except, perhaps a personal one), in game-like activities 'a slight sense of competition between groups does no harm' (Nuttall 1996: 164).

The important thing about instructions is that the students should understand and agree on what the task is. To check that they do we may ask them to repeat the instructions, or, in monolingual classes, to translate them into their first language.

- **During:** while students are working in pairs or groups we have a number of options. We could, for instance, stand at the front or the side of the class (or at the back or anywhere else in the room) and keep an eye on what is happening, noting who appears to be stuck or disengaged, or about to finish. In this position we can 'tune in' to a particular pair or group from some distance away. We can then decide whether to go over and help that pair or group.

  An alternative procedure is to go round the class watching and listening to specific pairs and groups. We can stay (with their agreement) for a period of time and then intervene if we think it is appropriate or necessary, always bearing in mind what we have said about the difference between accuracy and fluency work (see Chapter 7, C1). If students are involved in a discussion, for example, we will correct gently (see Chapter 7, C3); if we are helping students with suggestions about something they are planning, or trying to move a discussion forwards, we will be acting as prompter, resource, or tutor (see Chapter 4B). Where students succumb to the temptation to use their first language, we will do our best to encourage or persuade them back into English (see Chapter 9D).

  When students are working in pairs or groups we have an ideal opportunity to work with individual students whom we feel would benefit from our attention. We also have a great chance to act as observer, picking up information about students' progress (see Chapter 4, B8) – and seeing if we will have to 'troubleshoot' (see below). But however we intervene or take part in the work of a pair or group it is vital that we bear in mind the most appropriate way to do so.

- **After:** when pairs and groups stop working together we need to organise feedback (see Chapter 7). We want to let them discuss what occurred during the groupwork session and, where necessary, add our own assessments and make corrections.

  Where pairwork or groupwork has formed part of a practice session (see Chapter 11, B3), our feedback may take the form of having a few pairs or groups quickly demonstrate the language they have been using. We can then correct it, if and when necessary, and this procedure will give both those students and the rest of the class good information for future learning and action.

  Where pairs or groups have been working on a task with definite right or wrong answers, we need to ensure that they have completed it successfully. Where they have been discussing an issue or predicting the content of a reading text, we will encourage them to talk about their conclusions with us and the rest of the class. By comparing different solutions, ideas, and problems, everyone gets a greater understanding of the topic.

  Where students have produced a piece of work, we can give them a chance to demonstrate this to other students in the class. They can stick written material on notice boards; they can read out dialogues they have written or play audio or videotapes they have made.

  Finally, it is vital to remember that constructive feedback on the content of student work can greatly enhance students' future motivation. The feedback we give on language mistakes (see Chapter 7C and D) is only one part of that process.

B4 Troubleshooting

When we monitor pairs and groups during a groupwork activity we are seeing how well they are doing, and deciding whether or not to go over and intervene. But we are also keeping our eyes open for problems which we can resolve either on the spot or in the future:

- **Finishing first:** a problem that frequently occurs when students are working in pairs or groups is that some of them finish earlier than others and/or show clearly that they have had enough of the activity and want to do something else. We need to be ready for this and have some way of dealing with the situation. Saying to them *Okay, you can relax for a bit while the others finish* may be appropriate for tired students but can also make some students feel that they are being ignored.

  When we see the first pairs or groups finish the task we might stop the activity for the whole class. That removes the problem of boredom, but it may be very de-motivating for the students who have not yet finished, especially where they are nearly there and have invested some considerable effort in the procedure.

  One way of avoiding the problems we have mentioned here is to have a series of spare activities handy so that where a group has finished early, we can give them a short little task to complete while they are waiting. This will show the students that they are not just being left to do nothing. When planning groupwork it is a good idea for teachers to make a list of the extras that first-finishing groups and pairs can be involved in.

Even where we have set a time limit on pair and groupwork we need to keep an eye open to see how the students are progressing. We can then make the decision about when to stop the activity based on the observable (dis)engagement of the students and how near they all are to completing the task.

- **Awkward groups:** when students are working in pairs or groups we need to observe how well they interact together. Even where we have made our best judgements – based on friendship or streaming – it is possible that apparently satisfactory combinations of students are not ideal. Some pairs may find it impossible to concentrate on the task in hand and instead encourage each other to talk about something else, usually in their first language. In some groups (in some educational cultures) members may defer to the oldest person there, or to the man in an otherwise female group. People with loud voices can dominate proceedings; less extrovert people may not participate fully enough. Some weak students may be lost when paired or grouped with better classmates.

  In such situations we may need to change the pairs or groups. We can separate best friends for pairwork; we can put all the high-status figures in one group so that students in other groups do not have to defer to them. We can stream groups or in other ways reorganise them, so that all group members gain the most from the activity.

  One way of finding out about groups, in particular, is to simply observe, noting down how often each student speaks. If two or three observations of this kind reveal a continuing pattern we can take the kind of action suggested above.

Chapter notes and further reading

- **Pairwork and groupwork**

  On the advantages and disadvantages of pairwork, see S Haines (1995).

  M Courtney (1996) looks at both pairwork and groupwork for oral tasks. J Reid (1987) found that students have definite views about class grouping, and T Woodward (1995) worries about issues related to pair and groupwork.

- **Group dynamics**

  On group dynamics, see J Hadfield (1992).

- **Sociograms**

  The use of a sociogram for organising groups was described many years ago in M Long (1977).

9 | Problem behaviour and what to do about it

Most teachers, in many different learning cultures, have moments when their students fail to cooperate in some way, thus disrupting the learning which should be taking place, sometimes getting significantly 'out of control'. Such moments of disruption can be unsettling not just for teachers but also for students.

Problem behaviour can take many forms; Paul Waddon and Sean McGovern list disruptive talking, inaudible responses, sleeping in class, tardiness and poor attendance, failure to do homework, cheating in tests and unwillingness to speak in the target language (Wadden and McGovern 1991). Of course their list may reflect the educational culture where they were teaching rather than being universal. In other contexts we might add behaviours such as insolence to the teacher, insulting or bullying other students, damaging school property, and refusing to accept sanctions or punishment. However, what is characterised as indiscipline '… depends on what counts as a well-ordered or disciplined classroom for the individual teacher' (Brown and McIntyre 1993: 44).

Whatever form problem behaviour takes, though, we need to know why it occurs, how we can prevent it, and what to do if it arises.

A Why problems occur

There are many reasons for problem behaviour. It can stem from a student's reactions to their teacher's behaviour, from other factors inside the classroom, or from outside factors:

- **The family:** students' experiences in their families have a profound influence on their attitudes to learning and to authority. Sometimes indiscipline can be traced back to a difficult home situation. Sometimes home attitudes to English, to learning in general, or even to teachers themselves can predispose students to behave problematically.

- **Education:** previous learning experiences of all kinds affect students' behaviour. Even at the level of *the last teacher let me …*, students are influenced by what went before, and their expectations of the learning experience can be coloured either by unpleasant memories (see Chapter 3, A3), or by what they were once allowed to get away with.

- **Self-esteem:** a student's self-esteem is vitally important if effective learning is to take place. Self-esteem may result partly from teacher approval (especially for children), from a student's peers (especially for adolescents), or as a result of success (see Chapter 3, C3). A lack of respect from teacher or peers – or being asked to do something where they are almost certainly bound to fail – can make students feel frustrated and upset. In such a situation disruptive behaviour is an attractive option. It can impress peers, and does, at least, force the teacher to take them seriously.

- **Boredom:** when students are engaged with a task or a topic they are unlikely to behave disruptively. But if they lose that engagement they may misbehave. When pairs or groups finish early and are left unattended, boredom may lead to disruption (see Chapter 8, B4); when the chosen topic or activity is inappropriate, students sometimes show their lack of interest by behaving badly.

- **External factors:** some external factors may affect students' behaviour too. If they are tired they will not be able to concentrate. If the classroom is too hot or too cold this may result in students being too relaxed or too nervy. Discomfort then leads to disengagement. Noise from outside the classroom can impact badly upon students' concentration.

  Teachers at primary level, especially, notice significant behaviour changes in different weathers, so that a high wind, in particular, tends to make their children 'go wild'.

- **What the teacher does:** a lot will depend on how we behave in class, especially when problem behaviour first takes place. Students who feel their self-esteem to have been damaged by the way we discipline them – especially if we appear unfair – are more likely to be badly behaved in the future (see B2 below).

B Preventing problem behaviour

There are a number of strategies that teachers can make use of to avoid problems occurring in the first place, because prevention is always better than the disciplining cure.

B1 Creating a code of conduct

An important part of effective classroom management is for the students to 'know where they stand'. This is often done, with younger learners especially, by establishing a code of conduct – although in fact, such a code can be equally valid for use with unenthusiastic adult classes.

An effective way of establishing a code of conduct is to include the students' own opinions in the code; these will frequently be as responsible and forthright as anything a teacher might come up with. With a class of adults, for example, the teacher and students together can talk about a range of issues such as how often homework is expected, what a good learner is, attitudes to mistakes and feedback, and the use of their mother tongue (see D below). When a teacher and students have divergent views about what is acceptable and what is not, the teacher should take their opinions into account, but ultimately he or she will have to be firm about what he or she is prepared to accept. With low-level classes teachers may need to hold the discussion in the students' first language. Where this is not possible – as in a multilingual class – they will need to show quickly and calmly, through example, what is expected and what is not acceptable.

Some teachers adopt a formula where teacher and students produce a chart which says *As your teacher/a learner I expect …* , *As your teacher/a learner, I will …* . This document can be put on the class noticeboard for all to see. Then, when students are disruptive or uncooperative, they can be referred to the code of conduct and expected to abide by rules and norms which they themselves agreed to.

When a code has been thus democratically arrived at – with everyone having a say and coming to an agreement – it has considerable power.

B2 Teachers and students

Just as a teacher's behaviour may itself sometimes be the cause of disruptive events, so the way we teach, and the relationship we have with students, can help to prevent problem behaviour from ever occurring. In particular, maintaining our students' interest and relating to them in appropriate ways holds the key to this.

- **Interest and enthusiasm:** students who are interested and enthusiastic do not generally exhibit problem behaviour. When we plan our classes, therefore, we need to bear in mind the need for such qualities as flexibility and variety (see Chapter 22). We also need, for example, to think how we can engage students in a reading or listening text before starting detailed work on it (see Chapter 14, B2 and B3); we need to do our best to introduce topics that are relevant to our students' experience.

  Interest can be also be generated by a teacher's performance. There is no doubt that students can be engaged by the energy and enthusiasm of their teachers (see Chapter 4C).

- **Professionalism:** students generally respect teachers who show that they know what they are doing. This can be demonstrated not only by our knowledge of our subject, but also by evidence that we have invested time in thinking about and planning our lessons.

  Professionalism also means practising what we preach. If we insist on students handing their homework in promptly, then marking it and giving it back promptly are also obligatory (see Chapter 24, A1). If we berate students for coming to class late, we will have to be seen to arrive punctually ourselves.

  We must not be seen to issue idle threats. It is no good saying *If you do this again I will …* if we cannot or will not take the action we have promised.

- **Rapport between teachers and students:** a critical aspect in the prevention of problem behaviour is the rapport we have with our students. This can be greatly enhanced by making sure that we listen to what they say with interest (see Chapter 7), and that we look at them when we talk to them; we need to ensure that we do not only respond to the students at the front – or the more extrovert ones – but that we try and work with all of the people in our class.

C Reacting to problem behaviour

Whatever the reason for problem behaviour, it should not be ignored when it happens. How a teacher reacts to it should depend upon the particular type of disruption and the person exhibiting the behaviour. Nevertheless it is advisable to have some general guidelines in mind for such situations:

- **Act immediately:** it is vital to act immediately when there is a problem since the longer a type of behaviour is left unchecked, the more difficult it is to deal with. Immediate action sometimes means no more than stopping talking, pausing, and looking at the student in question (Brown and McIntyre 1993: 42). Sometimes, however, it may demand stronger action.

- **Focus on the behaviour not the pupil:** we should take care not to humiliate an uncooperative pupil. It is the behaviour that matters, not the pupil's character. Though it may sometimes be tempting to make aggressive or deprecatory remarks, or to compare the student adversely to other people, such reactions are almost certainly counter-productive: not only are they likely to foster hostility on the part of the student and/or damage their self-esteem, they may also be ineffective in managing the situation.

  The way in which we deal with problem behaviour has an effect not just on the 'problem student' but also on the class. We need to treat all students the same (something that adults as well as younger students are conscious of, though it is especially at younger ages that favouritism is resented – by the favourite as well as everybody else); we must treat the individual fairly, not overreacting, nor making light of disruption, particularly if we and the class had agreed earlier it was unacceptable.

- **Take things forward:** where a simple look or brief comment is not sufficient, we need to think carefully about how we respond. It is always better to be positive rather than negative. It is usually more effective for a teacher to say *Let's do this*, rather than saying *Don't do that*. Taking things forward is better than stopping them in other words. Our objective will be to move on to the next stage of an activity or to get a new response rather than focusing on the old one. In extreme cases we may decide to change the activity in order to take the steam out of the situation and allow students to refocus. However, we should be careful not to base such decisions only on the inappropriate behaviour of one or two students.

  Other ways of going forward are to reseat students, especially where two or more of them have encouraged each other. Once separated in an effective (but not humiliating) way, students often calm down and the problem behaviour dies away.

- **Reprimand in private:** it is appropriate to discuss a student's behaviour in private, and talk about how to improve it. This is not always possible, of course, but disciplining a student in front of his or her classmates will not help that student's self-esteem at all. When we deal with individuals during class time eye contact is important; a personal, though formal, relationship has to be established if and when we are required to assert our authority. Ideally, however, we will try and deal with problem behaviour with the student after the class.

  One way in which we can attempt to change students' behaviours, is by writing to them – a general letter to each member of the class expressing a problem and asking students to reply in confidence. In this way students have a chance to make contact with us without other people listening, or the student having to face us directly. However, this kind of correspondence takes up a lot of time, and there are dangers of over-intimacy too. Nevertheless, the use of letters may help to break the ice where teachers have found other ways of controlling misbehaviour to be unsuccessful.

  Dealing with indiscipline is often a matter of 'pastoral' care, helping students to recognise the problem behaviour and start to find a way towards changing it. This is far less likely to happen in class with everybody listening, than in private ongoing communication with the student outside the class.

- **Keep calm:** in many students' eyes teachers who have to shout to assert their authority appear to be losing control. Shouting by the teacher raises the overall level of noise in the classroom too. It is usually more effective to approach the student who is being disruptive and speak more quietly. Many teachers have also reported the benefits of restoring order and/or silence by either speaking very quietly to the class as a whole – so that students have to stop talking in order to hear what is going on – or by raising a hand, having previously agreed with students that they are expected then to raise their hands in reply and go quiet. As more and more hands go up, all the students realise that it is time to quieten down.

- **Use colleagues and the institution:** it is no shame to have disruptive students in our classroom. It happens to everyone. So when there is a problem we should consult our colleagues, asking them for guidance. When the problem is threatening to get beyond our control (for example, a pattern of disruption which continues for a series of lessons), we would be well advised to talk to coordinators, directors of studies and/or principals. They should all have considerable experience of the kind of problems being faced and will be in a position to offer the benefit of their experience.

However much we worry about discipline, it is important to realise that, like almost all of our colleagues, we will suffer disruptive or uncooperative behaviour from our students at some time. Usually the problem is minor and can be easily dealt with, especially if we can refer to a previously established code of conduct, and if our responses to indiscipline are based on the principles and strategies we have outlined above.

D 'Please speak English!'

One thing that can drive teachers wild is when their students are apparently unwilling to use English in the classroom, especially during communicative activities. This is often seen as an example of student/teacher failure. After all, if students are not using English everyone is wasting their time. However, there are many understandable reasons why students revert to their own language in certain activities.

D1 Why students use the mother tongue in class

A principal cause of this L1 use is the language required by the activity. If we ask beginners to have a free and fluent discussion about global warming, for example, we are asking them to do something which they are linguistically incapable of. Their only possible course of action, if they really want to say anything about the topic, is to use their own language. In other words the choice of task has made the use of L1 almost inevitable: students can hardly be blamed for this.

Another reason why students use their own language in the classroom is because it is an entirely natural thing to do; when we learn a foreign language we use translation almost without thinking about it, particularly at elementary and intermediate levels. This is because we try to make sense of a new linguistic (and conceptual) world through the linguistic world we are already familiar with. Code-switching between L1 and L2 is naturally developmental (Eldridge 1996: 310), and not some example of misguided behaviour.

Students use their L1 when performing pedagogical tasks, especially when one student is explaining something to another. This is a habit 'that in most cases will occur without encouragement from the teacher' (Harbord 1992: 354).

Another cause of mother tongue use can be teachers themselves. If, they frequently use the students' language (whether or not they themselves are native speakers of that language), then the students will feel comfortable doing it too. Teachers need, therefore, to be aware of the kind of example they themselves are providing (see D2 below).

Finally, it is worth pointing out that the amount of L1 use by particular students may well have a lot to do with differing learner styles and abilities. Some use mostly English from the very beginning, whereas others seem to need to use their L1 more frequently.

D2 Attitudes to mother tongue use in the classroom

The idea that all use of the mother tongue in the language classroom should be avoided stems from the advent of the Direct Method at the beginning of the twentieth century (where the language itself was talked and taught rather than being talked about in the students' L1), and from the training of native-English speaker teachers who either had to deal with multilingual classes and/or teach in countries before they were themselves competent in the language of their students.

More recently, however, attitudes to the use of the students' mother tongue have undergone a significant change. David Atkinson argued that 'it is not difficult to think of several general advantages of judicious use of the mother tongue' (Atkinson 1987: 242), suggesting that such activities as grammar explanations, checking comprehension, giving instructions, discussing classroom methodology and checking for sense fell into this category. If teachers can use the students' language, he claims, these tasks will be expedited more efficiently.

This view is not shared, however, by Peter Harbord who points out that the giving of instructions and many other teacher–student interactions are 'an ideal source of language for student acquisition' (Harbord 1992: 353).

No one is in any doubt that students will use their L1 in class, whatever teachers say or do; the question is whether we should try and stop it. John Eldridge thinks not, suggesting that there is no evidence to suggest that this would improve learning efficiency. He claims that most of the code-switching he has observed is 'highly purposeful, and related to purposeful goals' (Eldridge 1996: 303).

Two issues seem to arise here. In the first place since students are likely to use their L1 anyway, there is little point in trying to stamp it out completely. Such an approach will not work, and may only discourage the students who feel the need for it at some stages. However, a lot will depend on when students use their L1. If they are working in pairs studying a reading text, for example, the use of their L1 may be quite acceptable since they are using it to further their understanding of English. If, on the other hand, they are doing an oral fluency activity, the use of a language other than English makes the activity essentially pointless. Furthermore, as teachers we will want to promote as much English use as possible. So we will try and insist on the use of English in language study and oral production activities, but be more relaxed about it in other pedagogic situations, though we will continue to encourage students to try to use it as often as possible.

As for teachers, they are a principal source of comprehensible input (see Chapter 5B); teacher-talking time (TTT) has an important part to play in language acquisition (see Chapter 4, D3). It therefore makes sense for us to speak English as much as possible in the class, especially since if we do not, students will not see the need to speak too much English either. However there are times, especially at lower levels, where the use of L1 may help both teacher and students such as in an explanation or discussion of methodology, or the giving of announcements which would be impossibly difficult in English.

D3 What to do about it

There are a number of actions which teachers can take to promote the use of English and explain clearly what is expected of students:

- **Set clear guidelines:** students need to know when mother tongue use is permissible and when it is not. Part of the agreed code of conduct with a class will be just this understanding of when it is more or less 'okay' and when it is seriously counter-productive. Students need to be aware of when English is absolutely essential.

  As with other issues in the code, our own adherence to it will be vital if it is to succeed.

- **Choose appropriate tasks:** we should choose tasks which the students, at their level, are capable of doing in English. While there is nothing wrong in 'stretching' them with challenging activities which engage them, it is clearly counter-productive to set them tasks they are unable to perform.

- **Create an English atmosphere:** if we create an English environment, making English the classroom language as well as the language to be learnt, and perhaps even anglicising our students' names (see Suggestopaedia in Chapter 6, A6), then there will be more chance of the students making the classroom truly English themselves.

- **Use persuasion and other inducements:** teachers all over the world spend a lot of their time going round to students, especially during speaking activities, saying things like, *Please speak English!* or *Stop using Turkish/Arabic/Portuguese/ Greek,* etc. and it often works! If it does not, we can stop the activity and tell students there is a problem. This sometimes changes the atmosphere so that they go back to the activity with a new determination.

  One teacher I knew used to make students pay a fine if they used the mother tongue in speaking activities, a course of action not recommended for the faint-hearted! But however it is done – the art of persuading students to have a go in English depends on the guidelines that were set, the agreement we made with them, and the friendly encouragement and persuasion we use while activities are taking place. This, together with other measures that have been suggested, generally ensures that most students are speaking English most of the time.

Chapter notes and further reading

- **Code of conduct**
  C Kyriacou (1992: Chapter 8), calls the establishing of a code of conduct 'pre-empting misbehaviour'. J Harmer (1998: 174) has a chart-based code.

- **Self-esteem**
  Teacher approval is not just important for children. T Lowe (1987) quotes diaries from English teachers who became students of Chinese. In their Chinese classes they were very keen for approval from their teacher.

- **Writing (letters) to students**
  See M Rinvolucri (1983, 1995) and Chapter 24, A1.

- **Mother tongue**
  P Ur (1996: 122) suggests appointing class monitors to remind students to keep using English.

10 | Educational technology and other teaching equipment

As language teachers we use a variety of teaching aids to explain language meaning and construction, engage students in a topic, or as the basis of a whole activity. In this section we will look at a variety of items that can be helpful both for practical and for motivational reasons. Some teaching aids will be dealt with elsewhere, however. We will look at the use of coursebooks in Chapter 21. We will be detailing examples of using audio material in Chapter 16, and video material in Chapter 20. The dictionary, perhaps the most useful aid a student can ever have, is discussed in Chapter 12A.

A Pictures and images

Teachers have always used pictures or graphics – whether drawn, taken from books, newspapers and magazines, or photographs – to facilitate learning. Pictures can be in the form of flashcards (smallish cards which we can hold up for our students to see), large wall pictures (big enough for everyone to see details), cue cards (small cards which students use in pair or groupwork), photographs, or illustrations (typically in a textbook). Some teachers also use projected slides, images from an overhead projector (see B below), or projected computer images (see F below). Teachers also draw pictures on the board to help with explanation and language work (see C below).

Pictures of all kinds can be used in a multiplicity of ways, as the following examples show:

- **Drills:** with lower-level students a traditional use for pictures – especially flashcards – is in cue–response drills (see Chapter 6, A2). We hold one up (the cue) before nominating a student and getting a response. Then we hold up another one, and nominate a different student and so on. Flashcards are particularly useful for 'drilling' grammar items, for cueing different sentences, or practising vocabulary.

  Sometimes teachers use larger wall pictures, where pointing to a detail of a picture will elicit a response such as *There's some milk in the fridge* or *John's swimming in the pool*, etc.

Sometimes teachers put students in pairs or groups and give them some cue cards so that when a student picks up the top cue card in a pile he or she has to say a sentence that the card suggests. Thus the student picks up a picture of a piece of cheese and has to make the question *How much cheese have you got?*; the next student picks up a picture of eggs and has to ask *How many eggs have you got?* and so on.

- **(Communication) games:** pictures are extremely useful for a variety of communication activities, especially where they have a game-like feel, such as describe and draw activities (see Chapter 19, B2) where one student describes a picture and a paired classmate has to draw the same picture without looking at the original. We can also divide a class into four groups (A, B, C, D) and give each group a different picture that shows a separate stage in a story. Once the members of the group have studied their picture, we take it away. New groups are formed with four members each – one from group A, one from group B, one from group C, and one from group D. By sharing the information they saw in their pictures, they have to work out what story the pictures together are telling.

  Teachers sometimes use pictures for creative writing. They might tell students to invent a story using at least three of the images in front of them (on cue cards, for example). They can tell them to have a conversation about a specified topic, and at various stages during the conversation, they have to pick a card and bring whatever that card shows into the conversation.

- **Understanding:** one of the most appropriate uses for pictures is for the presenting and checking of meaning. An easy way of explaining the meaning of the word *aeroplane*, for example, is to have a picture of one. In the same way it is easy to check students' understanding of a piece of writing or listening by asking them to select the picture (out of, say, four) which best corresponds to the reading text or the listening passage.

- **Ornamentation:** pictures of various kinds are often used to make work more appealing. In many modern coursebooks, for example, a reading text will be adorned by a photograph which is not strictly necessary, in the same way as in newspaper and magazine articles. The rationale for this is clearly that pictures enhance the text, giving readers (or students) a view of the outside world.

  Some teachers and materials designers object to this use of pictures because they consider it gratuitous. But it should be remembered that if the pictures are interesting they will appeal to at least some members of the class strongly. They have the power (at least for the more visually oriented) to engage students (for more on the issue of engagement, see Chapter 6, A3).

- **Prediction:** pictures are useful for getting students to predict what is coming next in a lesson. Thus students might look at a picture and try to guess what it shows (are the people in it brother and sister, husband or wife, and what are they arguing about – or are they arguing? etc). They then listen to a tape or read a text to see if it matches what they expected on the basis of the picture. This use of pictures is very powerful and has the advantage of engaging students in the task to follow.

- **Discussion:** pictures can stimulate questions such as: *What is it showing? How does it make you feel? What was the artist's/photographer's purpose in designing it in that way? Would you like to have this picture in your house? Why? Why not? How much would you pay for the picture? Is the picture a work of art?*

  Pictures can also be used for creative language use, whether they are in a book or on cue cards, flashcards, or wall pictures. We might ask students to write a description of a picture; we might ask them to invent the conversation taking place between two people in a picture, or in a particular role-play activity, ask them to answer questions as if they were the characters in a famous painting.

We can make wall pictures, flashcards, and cue cards in a number of ways. We can take pictures from magazines and stick them on card. We can draw them. We can buy reproductions, photographs, and posters from shops or we can photocopy them from a variety of sources (though we should check copyright law before doing this).

The choice and use of pictures is very much a matter of personal taste, but we should bear in mind three qualities they need to possess if they are to engage students and be linguistically useful. In the first place they need to be appropriate not only for the purpose in hand but also for the classes they are being used for. If they are too childish students may not like them, and if they are culturally inappropriate they can offend people.

The most important thing for pictures in the end is that they should be visible. They have to be big enough so that all our students – taking into account where they will be sitting – can see the necessary detail.

Lastly, we will not want to spend hours collecting pictures only to have them destroyed the first time they are used! Thought should be given about how to make them durable. Perhaps they can be stuck to cards and protected with transparent coverings.

B The overhead projector

Overhead projectors (OHPs) are extremely useful pieces of equipment since they allow us to prepare visual or demonstration material. They require little technical knowledge, and usually are easy to carry around. It is not surprising they are so widely used.

Just about anything can go on overhead transparencies (OHTs): we can show whole texts or grammar exercises, pictures or diagrams, or students' writing. Because transparencies can be put through a photocopier or get printed from any computer, they can be of very high quality. Especially where teachers are unimpressed by their own handwriting, the overhead transparency offers the possibility of attractive well-printed script.

One of the major advantages of the overhead projector is that we do not have to show everything on an OHT all at once. By covering some of the transparency with a piece of card or paper we can blank out what we do not want the students to see. So, for example, we might show the first two lines of a story and ask students what is going to happen next, before revealing the next two lines and then the next, gradually moving the paper or card downwards. We might have questions on one side of the transparency and answers on the other. We start the teaching sequence with the answers covered, and use the same 'gradual revelation' technique to maintain interest.

Because transparencies are, as their name suggests, transparent, they can be put on top of each other so that we gradually build up a complex picture, diagram, or text. This is done by putting down the first transparency, say of a room, and asking students what kind of a room it is and what happens there. Then a new transparency can be laid over that one with pictures of one person in that room who the students can speculate about, before we lay down another transparency on top of that with more people. A diagram can start with one simple feature and have extra elements added to it in the same way. We can put up a gapped text and have students say what they think goes in the blanks before putting a new transparency with some or all of the filled-in items on top of the gapped one.

Sometimes we can put a text with blanks on the OHP and then lay a blank transparency on top of it so that students, using OHP pens can come up and write in what they think should go there. Alternatively, students working in groups can list the points they want to make after they have discussed a topic (e.g. whether or not children under twelve should have a curfew from ten o'clock every evening) and show their transparency to the class while they make their presentation.

Overhead projectors are extremely versatile, but they can pose some problems too. They need electricity of course, and bulbs do fail from time to time. Some models are quite bulky too. They are not that powerful either, especially when they are up against natural light coming in from windows and doors. When projected onto shiny surfaces such as boards they can be uncomfortable to look at, and when projected onto some other surfaces it can be very difficult to make out what is on them.

A lot depends on how big or small the projector 'square' is on the wall or screen and whether the image is in focus. A mistake that some users make is to put too much on the transparency so that when they ask *Can people see this at the back?* the answer they get is a frustrated shaking of the head. However, if all these potential problems are taken into account and resolved, the OHP is an extremely useful resource.

C The board

The most versatile piece of teaching equipment is the board – whether this is of the more traditional chalk-dust variety or the whiteboard, written on with marker pens. Boards provide a motivating focal point during whole-class grouping (see Chapter 8, A1).

We can use boards for a variety of different purposes, including:

- **Note pad:** teachers frequently write things up on the board as these come up during the lesson. They might be words that they want students to remember, phrases which students have not understood or seen before, or topics and phrases which they have elicited from students when trying to build up a composition plan, for example.

Where we write up words we can show how that word is stressed so that students can see and 'hear' the word at the same time (see Figure 16). We can sketch in intonation tunes or underline features of spelling too. We can group words according to their meaning or grammatical function. Some teachers use different colours for different aspects of language.

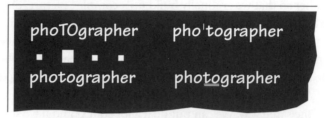

FIGURE 16: Different ways of recording word stress

- **Explanation aid:** boards can be used for explanation too, where, for example, we show the relationship between an affirmative sentence and a question by drawing connecting arrows (see Figure 17). We can show where words go in a sentence by indicating the best positions diagrammatically, or we can write up phonemic symbols (or draw diagrams of the mouth, for example) to show how a word or sound is pronounced. The board is ideal for such uses.

FIGURE 17: Using the board to show sentence/question relationships (elementary)

- **Picture frame:** boards can be used for drawing pictures of course, the only limitation being our 'artistic ability'. But even those who are not artistically gifted can usually draw a sad face and a happy face. They can produce stick men sitting down and running, or make an attempt at a bus or a car. What is more, this can be done whenever it is required because the board is always there, helping students to understand concepts and words.

- **Public workbook:** a typical procedure is to write up fill-in sentences or sentence transformation items, for example, and have individual students come up to the board and write a fill-in item, or a transformed sentence. That way the whole class becomes involved in seeing what the correct version is.

Teachers sometimes write mistakes they have observed in a creative language activity on the board. They can ask class members who think they know how to correct them to come up and have a go.

By focusing everyone's attention in the one place such activities are very useful.

- **Game board:** there are a number of games that can be played using the board. With noughts and crosses, for example, teachers can draw nine box frames and write different words or categories in each box (see below). Teams have to make sentences or questions with the words and if they get them right they can put their symbol (0 or X) on the square to draw their winning straight line.

  A popular spelling game involves two teams who start off with the same word. Each team has half the board. They have to fill up their side with as many words as possible, but each new word has to start with the last letter of the word before. At the end of a given period of time the team with the biggest number of correct words is the winner.

can't	won't	like
must	enjoy	want
dislike	hate	has to

FIGURE 18: Noughts and crosses (tic-tac-toe)

- **Noticeboard:** teachers and students can stick things on boards – pictures, posters, announcements, charts, etc. This is especially useful if they are metallic boards so that magnets can be used.

Handwriting on the board should be clear and easy to decipher; we should organise our material in some way too so that the board does not just get covered in scrawls in a random and distracting fashion. We could, for example, draw a column on one side of the board and reserve that for new words. We can then put the day's or the lesson's programme in the left-hand column, and use the middle of the board for grammar explanations or games.

It is probably not a good idea to turn our back to the class while we write on the board, especially if this goes on for some time. This tends to be de-motivating and may cause the class to become restless. Indeed it is better to involve the students with board work as much as possible, either getting them to tell us what to write, or using them to actually do the writing themselves.

When the class is over, courteous teachers clean the board and leave it ready for their colleagues to use.

D Bits and pieces

Of course there is no limit to the various bits and pieces which we can bring into the classroom. It might be photographs of our family, letters we have received (see Burbidge et al. 1996), or even a pet. Just as children in primary school are often asked to 'show and tell' about objects they hold dear, so we can base lesson sequences on objects that we think our students might find interesting – though of course this has to be done with discretion and a large dose of common sense about what will be appropriate in terms of age and culture.

Three particular items are worth considering in this category:

- **Realia:** with beginners and particularly children, 'real' or lifelike items are useful for teaching the meanings of words; teachers sometimes appear in the classroom with plastic fruit, cardboard clock faces, or two telephones to help simulate phone conversations.

  Objects that are intrinsically interesting can provide a good starting-point for a variety of language work and communication activities. We can find an object with an obscure use and ask students to speculate what it is for (*it might be/could be/probably is*) and/or design various explanations to account for it (*it is used for-ing*). The class could vote on the best idea. Where we bring in more than one object, especially where they are not obviously connected, students can speculate on what they have in common or they can invent stories and scenarios using the various objects. They can choose from a collection of objects which three they will put in a time capsule, or which would be most useful on a desert island, etc.

  Some teachers use a soft ball to make learning more enjoyable. When they want a student to say something, ask a question, or give an answer, they throw a ball to the student who then has to give the answer. The student can then throw the ball to a classmate who, in his or her turn, produces the required response before throwing the ball to someone else. Not all students find this appealing however, and there is a limit to how often the ball can be thrown before people get fed up with it.

  The only limitations on the objects which we bring to class are the size and quantity of the objects themselves and the students' tolerance, especially with adults who may think they are being treated childishly. As with so many other things, this is something we will have to assess on the basis of our students' reactions.

- **Language cards:** many teachers put a variety of cards and posters around the classroom. Such posters can have notes about language items on them, or be a collection of ways of apologising or inviting, for example. Sometimes, with new groups, teachers get students to write about themselves on a card and put their photograph next to what they have written so that the class all know who everyone is. Students can also make presentation posters of projects they have worked on. In multinational classes, for example, many students enjoy providing short guides to their countries.

  Cards are also useful for matching activities, where students have to find another student in the class with a similar card or one that has the answer to the question on his or her card. They can be asked to place cards in the correct column for sounds, or with the correct lexical group on a board or on a poster. Students can each be given word cards to hold in front of them and then be asked to move around until they form a line where all the cards together form a question or a sentence.

- **Cuisenaire rods:** these are small blocks of wood of different lengths (see Figure 19). Each length is a different colour. The rods are featureless, and are only differentiated by their size and colour. Simple they may be, but they are useful for a wide range of activities. For example, we can say that a particular rod is a pen or a telephone, a dog or a key so that by holding them up or putting them together a story can be told. All it takes is a little imagination.

   The rods can be used to demonstrate word stress too: if one is bigger than the others (in a sequence representing syllables in a word or words in a sentence) it shows where the stress should be (see Chapter 13, B2).

   We can also assign a word or phrase to each of, say, five rods and the students then have to put them in the right order (e.g. *I usually get up at six o'clock*). By moving the *usually* rod around and showing where it can and cannot occur in the sentence the students get a clear visual display of something they are attempting to fix in their minds.

   Rods can be used to teach prepositions. Teachers can model with the rods sentences like: *The red one is on top of/beside/under/over/behind (etc.) the green one.* They can show rods in different relative positions and ask students to describe them. Students can then position the rods for other students to describe (in ever more complex arrangements)!

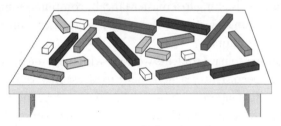

FIGURE 19: Cuisenaire rods

Cuisenaire rods are also useful for demonstrating colours (of course), comparatives, superlatives, and a whole range of other semantic and syntactic areas, particularly with people who respond well to visual or kinaesthetic activities.

E The language laboratory

The modern language laboratory has between ten or twenty booths, each equipped with a tape deck, headphones, microphone, and now computers. The technology is organised in such a way that students can work on their own, can be paired or grouped with other students, or can interact (though their headphones and microphones) on a one-to-one basis with the teacher. The teacher can broadcast the same taped (or filmed) material to each booth, or can have different students or groups of students work with different material. Students can interact with each other, and written texts can be sent to each computer screen.

Language laboratories have three special characteristics which mark them out from other learning resources:

- **Double track:** the design of tapes and machines means that students can listen to one track on their tapes and record on another. They can then listen back not only to the original recording on the tape, but also to what they themselves said into the microphone which is attached to their headset.

- **Teacher access:** apart from the separate language booths, laboratories also have a console and/or computer terminal manned by a teacher who can not only listen in to individual students, but can also talk, with the use of microphones and headsets, with one student at a time. Modern systems allow teachers to join booths in pairs or groups, irrespective of their position in the laboratory, by selecting them on the screen. This can be done on the same basis as we create pairs and groups in classrooms (see Chapter 8, B2), or, by selecting the right computer command, randomly.

  Laboratories equipped with computers for each booth allow teachers to read what students are writing and make corrections individually either by talking to the student or by using the editing facility attached to their word-processing package.

- **Different modes:** from the console the teacher can decide whether or not to have all the students working at the same time and speed – in 'lockstep' – because they are all listening to a master tape. In computer-equipped laboratories, they can all watch a video which the teacher is broadcasting to their individual monitors.

  An alternative is to have students working with the same material, but at their own individual speed. Thus teachers may broadcast an audiotape which records onto each individual tape at each booth. Each student can now work at their leisure. In computer-equipped laboratories the teacher can send the same text to each machine for them to read and/or manipulate according to their own needs.

  Finally, since teachers can group students mechanically, each pair or group can be given different material to work with.

E1 Advantages of the language laboratory

In many self-access centres or SACs (see Chapter 24, A2) there are audiotape machines, videos, and computers which perform some of the functions of a language laboratory, giving students opportunities for both extensive and intensive listening and reading. The sound quality for audio and videotapes is likely to be significantly better than that for individuals in classrooms, since in SACs and laboratories tapes are listened to through headphones.

Language laboratories offer the same potential as SACs, but also have other special advantages which make them a welcome addition to any school's resources:

- **Comparing:** the double track allows students to compare the way they say things with the correct pronunciation on a source tape. In this way they can monitor and get feedback on their own performance, even without the intervention of a teacher.

- **Privacy:** students can talk to each other (through their microphones), record onto the tape, wind and rewind tapes or type on computer keyboards without disturbing their colleagues. Since every student is cocooned by their headphones, they are guaranteed some privacy, and are free from the intrusion that the work of others would cause in a normal classroom setting.

- **Individual attention:** when teachers want to speak to individual students in a laboratory they can do so from the console. Unlike the situation in the classroom where this is often difficult because it stops them from working with the rest of the class – who may resent such private conversation – in a laboratory all the other students are working away on their own. The attention that teachers give to one student does not distract the others.

- **Learner training:** the language laboratory helps to train some students to really listen to what they say and how they say it. When they compare their pronunciation with the correct version on the tape, they begin to notice the differences, and this awareness, over a period, helps them to hear and pronounce English better.

  Not all students find comparisons easy, however. Different students are better or worse at hearing sounds (see Chapter 13, A2). It will be up to the teacher, from the console, to guide individual students who are experiencing difficulties into noticing differences and similarities.

- **Learner motivation:** a worry about learner autonomy in general, and self-access centres in particular, is that some students are better at working on their own than others. The language laboratory (where teachers take the whole group into the laboratory) offers a good half-way house between teacher control and learner autonomy since, although students work at their own pace, they are more open to the guidance of the teacher.

E2 Activities in language laboratories

- **Repetition:** the simplest use of a double-track laboratory is repetition. Students hear a word, phrase, or sentence on the tape. A space (indicated by a bleep or buzz signal) is left for them to repeat what they have heard, and the word, phrase, or sentence is then said again, so that they get instant feedback on whether they have spoken correctly. A basic pronunciation item might, therefore, look like this:

  Tape voice: information
  Buzz signal: ... (Pause of 3 seconds)
  Tape voice: information

- **Drills:** based on Audio-lingual methodology (see Chapter 6, A1), language laboratories have often been used for substitution drills, using the same basic model as the repetition example above. The difference is that the student has to work out what to say (based on a cue) before the tape voice then gives the correct response, as in the following example practising the present perfect:

Tape voice:	Do you watch television every night?
Cue:	Three nights.
Buzz signal:	(Pause)
Tape voice:	No, I haven't watched television for three nights.
Tape voice:	Do you listen to the radio every day?
Cue:	Last Monday.
Buzz signal:	(Pause)
Tape voice:	No I haven't listened to the radio since last Monday.

From Adrian-Vallance (1986: 211)

- **Speaking:** language laboratories can give students the opportunity of speaking (apart from repetition and drilling) in a number of ways. They can record their own talks and speeches and then listen back to them and make adjustments in the same way as they draft and redraft written text in a process-writing approach (see Chapter 18, B1). But the tape can also ask them a series of questions which encourages them to practise language which they have recently been focusing on as in the following example for beginners:

Tape voice:	What's your last name?
Buzz signal:	(Pause)
Tape voice:	What's your first name?
Buzz signal:	(Pause)
Tape voice:	Where do you live?
Buzz signal:	(Pause)

In a language laboratory individual students can play and replay questions until they are sure what they are being asked. From the console, teachers can listen in and give focused individual feedback too.

- **Pairing, double-plugging, and telephoning:** almost any interactive speaking activity can be performed by students at different booths who are paired together (or two of whom plug their headphones into the same machine). They can describe objects or people for others to identify. They can give directions for their pair to follow on a map and they can make decisions, or role-play dialogues. Together they can plan and tell stories.

  In modern laboratories students can also dial the number of different booths and have telephone conversations with the person who answers.

- **Parallel speaking:** Adrian Underhill (1994: 181, 186–187) gives two examples of parallel speaking, where students are encouraged to imitate the way the teacher says something and, because of the double-track system, do so at the same time as the teacher is speaking.

From the console the teacher can record a rhyme or story (first in separate phrases, but later as a whole) onto all the individual student machines. At first, as the material is being recorded the students just listen. But then, once they have the recording of (all or part of) the rhyme or story, they speak along with the teacher's taped voice, doing their best to imitate the teacher's pronunciation and the speed at which he or she speaks. The aim is 'to try and do the same as you, not because you are right, but as an exercise in attention and noticing, and to gain insight from experience' (Underhill 1994: 187). Later, they record the material independently onto their machines, at which point the teacher can listen in and give feedback where appropriate.

- **Listening:** listening of all kinds can be practised in the language laboratory. Activities such as note-taking, dictation, finding differences between a written text and a taped account of the same events, and answering comprehension questions can all be performed successfully in the laboratory setting. Tapes can be accompanied by written worksheets and/or students can be asked questions on the tape which they have to record their answers to on the student track. In computer-equipped laboratories, questions and texts can be provided on the computer screen.

  Because teachers can group students differently, the laboratory is an ideal location for jigsaw listening (see Example 4 on page 237).

  Students at their separate booths can also do a variety of video-watching activities.

- **Reading:** students can read texts and then record their answers on tape. In computer-equipped laboratories both text and answers can be supplied on the computer screen itself. The teacher can also have all students reading material from the same Internet web site.

- **Writing and correcting writing:** language laboratories allow teachers to give individual, private spoken feedback on students' written work. In computer-equipped laboratories students can write at their individual machines and the teacher can then correct their work either orally or in writing since he or she can look at each student's work from the console.

F What computers are for

Although computer use is still restricted to a fraction of the world's population, the use of computers (and the Internet) in education generally, and in the teaching of English in particular, continues to increase at an extraordinary speed – quite apart from its use in language laboratories (see above). As with any technological advance such as the language laboratory, video, and even the tape recorder, the proper place for the various riches which computers have to offer is still under discussion. All we know is that at any moment there are exciting new developments just round the corner. Currently, the main uses for computers in language teaching include the following:

- **Reference:** one of the chief uses of computers, either through the Internet or on CD/DVD-ROMS, is as a reference tool. This can be connected to teaching, the English language or general facts about the world (see Figure 20). There are already a number of popular encyclopedias available on CD-ROM (for example, Encarta, Grollier, Hutchinson, etc.) and all sorts of other information is also available, whether it is about plant life, animals, aircraft design or music history. One of the great advantages of computers is that with the right equipment, we can do all this research at home or in self-access centres (see Chapter 24, A2).

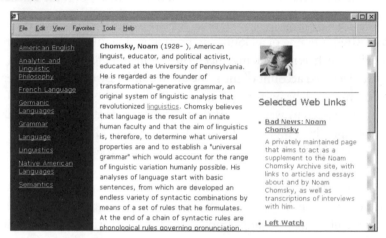

FIGURE 20: A screen from the Encarta encyclopedia

The availability of research material such as this means that we can send students to the computer to prepare for all sorts of task and project work, following up references in coursebooks, or finding out about topics they are interested in. Many of the programs have excellent visuals and sound which make the material very attractive.

There are now a number of ELT dictionaries available on CD-ROM too, which offer, apart from definitions, spoken pronunciation of words and practice exercises and activities. Increasingly, publishers are also making dictionaries available online. And whether on CD-ROM or through the Internet, students can now access language corpora to search for facts about English (see Chapters 2, B1 and 12C).

The greatest potential for the computer as a reference tool is, of course, the Internet, where, by accessing directories and search engines (such as 'Alta Vista', 'Google', and 'Hotbot'), users can look for information on just about any subject under the sun. However, as any regular 'surfers' will attest, these searches often throw up a huge amount of irrelevant material so that a simple search can become a protracted trawl through a number of useless web sites. When we encourage students to use search engines to find information on the Internet, we should prepare the ground beforehand – by suggesting search methods and/or narrowing down the focus of the enquiry – so that students do not waste a whole class period searching. We also need to keep an eye on proceedings to avoid a situation in which students just surf the net, becoming distracted by what they find there, and thus lose sight of the original task. However, if these drawbacks are taken into account, the Internet is an extraordinary resource which has changed the face of information gathering both in and outside the classroom (see also web sites below).

- **Teaching and testing programs:** language teaching software packages, often supplied on CD-ROM, offer students the chance to study conversations and texts, to do grammar and vocabulary exercises, and even to listen to texts and record their own voices.

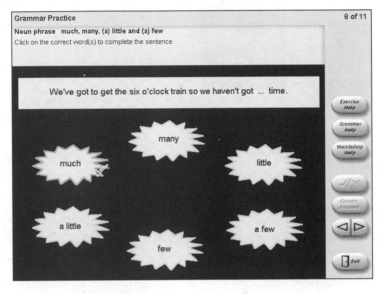

FIGURE 21: A screen from *The FCE Grammar ROM* (Pearson Education Ltd)

Although some teachers have criticised computer-based programs of this kind as being only dressed-up workbook exercises, it would be unwise to underestimate their usefulness for variety and motivation. Students who have been sitting behind their desks for hours might well find going over to a computer to 'play' with some language exercises a welcome relief. Such programs now include extensive reference resources as well.

A trend which will almost certainly gather pace is the attachment of CD-ROM-based packages to accompany coursebooks, full of extra input material and exercises. Some of these will be available, too, on the Internet. However, there are also web sites where students can sign up for complete self-study courses, which include all the regular features of a coursebook together with the possibility of sending work to a tutor who will monitor progress. The following example (for lower intermediate students) written and designed at International House, Barcelona, is a reading text which is then followed by comprehension questions which users answer on screen and can then check to see if they were right. They can also click on words in the text for a quick definition.

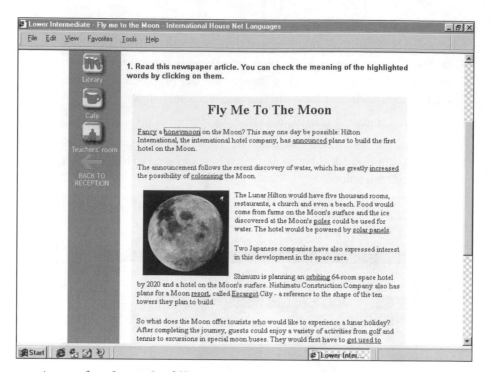

1. Read this newspaper article. You can check the meaning of the highlighted words by clicking on them.

Fly Me To The Moon

Fancy a honeymoon on the Moon? This may one day be possible: Hilton International, the international hotel company, has announced plans to build the first hotel on the Moon.

The announcement follows the recent discovery of water, which has greatly increased the possibility of colonising the Moon.

The Lunar Hilton would have five thousand rooms, restaurants, a church and even a beach. Food would come from farms on the Moon's surface and the ice discovered at the Moon's poles could be used for water. The hotel would be powered by solar panels.

Two Japanese companies have also expressed interest in this development in the space race.

Shimuzu is planning an orbiting 64-room space hotel by 2020 and a hotel on the Moon's surface. Nishimatu Construction Company also has plans for a Moon resort, called Escargot City - a reference to the shape of the ten towers they plan to build.

So what does the Moon offer tourists who would like to experience a lunar holiday? After completing the journey, guests could enjoy a variety of activities from golf and tennis to excursions in special moon buses. They would first have to get used to

A screen from International House Net Languages at http://www.netlanguages.com/

A number of language tests have gone or are in the process of going electronic as well. Students can send their answers straight from the computer screen to the examinations centre (see page 333 for listings of tests).

- **E-mail exchange:** one of the main uses for computers which are hooked up to the Internet is as senders and receivers of e-mail, allowing easy access to people all over the world. This makes the idea of pen-pals (or mouse-pals – see the references on page 268 for pen-pal sites) and/or contact between different schools much more plausible than the 'snailmail' equivalent. Getting students from different countries to write to each other has greatly increased both their English development and especially their motivation.

It should be remembered, however, that e-mails are often written in a special speaking-like informal style (see Chapter 17, A3). There is less of an obligation for grammatical correctness or even correct spelling. So while e-mailing may promote written fluency, and while it may give students a real chance to communicate, it may not enhance accuracy or help students to write in more than one or two genres.

Of particular interest to teachers and students is the fact that documents can be attached to e-mail and sent along with them, so that students can send word-processed work to their teachers who can then send back feedback in the same way (see 'the word processor' below).

- **Web sites:** almost any web site has potential for students of English. They can go and visit a virtual museum for a project on history or science. They can go to a web site which offers information and song lyrics from their favourite rock group and they can access timetables, geographical information, and weather facts. There are also a number of sites designed specially for students of English as a foreign language where they can exchange e-mails, do exercises, and browse around reading different texts, playing games, or doing exercises. The following web site, for example, provides practice in relative clauses:

Relative clause practice from Edunet Ltd at
http: www.edunet.com/english/practice/rside/Home.html

One of the real advantages of the Internet is that now, for the first time, teachers and students have access to 'authentic' English wherever they happen to be working. There is reading material available and, increasingly, there are audio and video sites too where music, news, and film can be listened to, though the downloading and/or classroom use of any such material will depend upon the copyright restrictions attached to it.

Some teachers plan whole lessons around the Internet. In her book on Internet use Dede Teeler gives a number of such sequences including designing a lesson around students visiting a teenage advice web site, or getting students to make their own newspapers and using a web site for that purpose (Teeler 2000: Chapter 5). We could also ask students to look at a number of different newspaper web sites from Britain or the USA (for example) to compare which stories they think are the most important and how those stories are told. We might get them to look up film reviews to make a class choice about which one to see, or download song lyrics which they can then put blanks in to 'test' their colleagues. The potential is almost literally endless; training students to use that potential sensibly will be of great benefit to them, especially if and when they wish to continue studying on their own (see Chapter 24, A3).

- **The word processor:** in an article published in 1987, Alison Piper suggested that the most successful educational use of the computer at that time was as a word processor, with students grouped around a screen drafting and redrafting collaboratively (Piper 1987). Unlike pen and paper, word processors allow students to compose as they think, and change their minds in the course of writing. Because the writing takes place on a screen all the students in a small group can see what is happening and contribute in a cooperative way.

  There is no reason to revise Alison Piper's judgement even though many years have elapsed since it was made. Though computers are ideal for students working on their own, they also have enormous potential for students working together, either operating a program or offering suggestions about what to do next. Word processing is the simplest and most obviously cost-effective way of tapping into this potential. However, as we have already seen in Section E (above), there is also scope for individually word-processed work which the teacher can give feedback on (see Chapter 7D) using the editing program which comes with the word processor. Students can now send such work as attached documents via e-mail so that teachers can give feedback at their leisure and 'hand back' the work the moment they have finished.

The widespread use of the computer – indeed the digital revolution generally – changed late twentieth-century life as surely as the industrial revolution impacted on the world over a century before. In language teaching, too, things will never be the same again with computer-based materials finding their way into coursebook packages, self-access centres, and classrooms everywhere. Such developments will be of inestimable value.

Yet we need to remind ourselves that there are still huge areas of the world where access to a computer is impossible or very difficult. Though there are wonders and marvels a-plenty on the Internet, there is a lot of rubbish too, and worse. We might also observe our students in class and conclude that groups of people talking and working together are still (and always will be) vitally important in language learning. Finally, we should remain conscious of the fact that different people learn and respond in different ways. The American writer Theodore Roszak argues that putting computers in schools is a bad use of money, pushing our expenditures on other vitally important items such as materials and teachers to one side. His views may be somewhat extreme, but it is difficult to argue with the opinion that:

> There are about as many kids born computer-proficient as there are born piano-proficient or poetry-proficient. It is mere folklore that all children born since 1980 have mutated into brilliant computer-users.

From T Roszak (1996: 14)

G Homegrown materials production

Many of the pictures, cards, OHTs or realia items which we bring into class will have been made or designed by teachers themselves. We may also want to record our own audiotapes (see Chapter 16, A2) or produce our own videos (see Chapter 20).

Homegrown materials range from grammar worksheets to word/sentence cards (see Section D above), from OHTs with words or exercises to photocopied texts (or texts taken from the Internet) that we design our own exploitation for. 'Do-it-yourself' teachers who choose not to use coursebooks end up producing a lot of such material themselves (see Chapter 21, C1), but even where we are using ready-made material that we are happy with, we will still want to supplement it from time to time with material that we have prepared especially for our own groups (see Chapter 21, C2).

When we make our own materials for classroom use (having taken care that our materials are legible, clear, attractive – and durable so that we can use them more then once) we can follow a simple five-stage procedure:

- **Planning:** homegrown materials start with planning. We need to decide what our aims and objectives are, what activity we want to involve the students in, how we want them to be grouped, and what the content of our materials should be. Once this is done we can move on to producing the materials, bearing in mind the characteristics we mentioned above.

- **Trialling:** it is absolutely vital to try out our material before taking it into the lesson. Ideally we will get a colleague or colleagues to comment on what we have made and/or do the exercises we have written. If this is not possible we can get a friend or another student to go through it. In this way we can avoid problems, and hope that other eyes will spot spelling mistakes or ambiguities which we missed.

- **Evaluating:** when we have produced and trialled our material we take it into the lesson and use it. This is where we need to observe carefully in order to evaluate its appropriacy. That way we can redesign it for future use and/or come to conclusions about how or when to use it in the future. Evaluating material we have produced will also help us to make decisions about what material to make in the future.

- **Classifying:** when we have used material in the classroom we need to find some way of storing it and classifying it so that we can lay our hands on it quickly the next time we want to use it. We might want to do this alphabetically by topic, by vocabulary area, or by grammar point. As with any other filing system we use, the way we organise our categorisation is a matter of personal preference and style.

- **Record-keeping:** we need to keep a record of what material we have used together with evaluations of how well it has worked. This will prevent us from using the same material twice with the same class, and it will help us with our long-term planning (see Chapter 22).

Chapter notes and further reading

- ### Pictures

  One of the best books on pictures is still A Wright (1984). See also A Wright and S Haleem (1991).

  N Cundale (1999) shows different uses of news pictures. M Early (1991) discusses the advantages of wordless picture books for language production with young students.

- ### Picture/card-based communication games

  Some of the best collections of card-based communication games for pairs and groups are Jill Hadfield's elementary, intermediate, and advanced games (Hadfield 1984, 1990, and 1987).

- ### Cuisenaire rods

  For a straightforward introduction to Cuisenaire rods, see J Scrivener (1994b: 169–172).

- ### The Internet

  An excellent book on the Internet and what it has to offer teachers and students of EFL is D Teeler (2000). See also S Windeatt et al. (1999) and D Sperling (1998).

  S Mace (1998) wrote an information-packed short article on designing tasks using the Internet.

  P Sweeney (1998) found that getting young learners to access the Internet was far more time consuming, teacher intensive, and generally chaotic than he and his colleague had anticipated! For excellent advice on training people to use the Internet in the classroom see D Teeler (2000: Chapter 4).

- ### Internet sites

  There are literally millions of Internet sites for students and teachers of English. However, a good place to start for advice on various sites is in book form, as in D Teeler (2000: Appendix D) and D Sperling (1998).

  One of the best web sites with materials for students and teachers, and links to EFL sites of all kinds is Dave Sperling's Internet café at http://www.eslcafe.com/.

  Any teacher educator can set up their own site, so teachers and students will just have to try out the ones that look interesting. At the time of writing, Wolfgang Rothfritz in Germany, for example, has an EFL business site at http://econscience.unipaderborn.de/WiWi/English/home.htm/, while Karin Cintron in California runs Karin's ESL 'partyland' at http://www.eslpartyland.com/default.htm/.

In the end Internet users may want to type in requests for grammar exercises, news sites, teacher resource sites, etc. on search engines such as the following:

All the web at www.alltheweb.com

Alta Vista at www.altavista.com

Google at www.google.com

Hotbot at www.hotbot.com

- **The language laboratory**

Very little is currently being written about language laboratories, but see P Ely (1984) and D Horner (1987).

- **Computer-based material**

All the major publishers have CD-ROM-based dictionaries. Pearson Education also have the *Longman Web Dictionary* which allows users to look up any word that appears on the Internet at http://www.longmanwebdict.com. It is also possible to access Cambridge University Press's *CIDE* dictionary on the Internet.

For an overview on the use of computers in language learning, see M Warschauer and D Healey (1998) and H Jarvis (2000).

- **E-mail exchange**

Michael Legukte offered an inspiring example of this (students in Germany corresponding with students in the Bronx) in his plenary to the IATEFL conference in Manchester, UK, April 1998.

H Hennigan (1999) shows how the idea of pen-pals can be adapted to become 'keypals'. D Teeler (2000: 75–76) has a good discussion of things to watch out for when organising keypals.

B Skinner and R Austin (1999) discuss the use of computer conferencing as a motivating activity.

- **Homegrown materials**

P Ahrens (1993b) designed her own rod system which used clothes pegs and loops of string to hang pictures from in her classroom. With one string of pictures at the front wall and one at the back, classes could do information-gap activities even though there were too many of them for pairwork.

D Block (1991) and A Maley (1998) discuss DIY ('do-it-yourself') materials production.

11 | Studying language

Language study refers to any stage in a lesson where students and teachers focus in on (the construction of) a specific feature of the language in order to understand it better. The immediate goal of language study is to increase knowledge of the language system so that the longer-term aim of improving productive and receptive skills can be achieved. As we shall see in Chapter 12, students should not only study language in the classroom under the direction of a teacher, but should also research language on their own. We need to have as one of our goals the training of autonomous learners (see Chapter 24A). However, the activities in this chapter are designed for the vast majority of students who benefit from a teacher-led focus on specific language forms.

 ## A Studying structure and use

The language study described in this chapter focuses on the structure and use of language forms, particularly in the following areas:

- the morphology of forms (e.g. the fact that *is* and *am* are forms of *be*, but **amn't* is not)
- the syntax of phrases, clauses, and sentences (e.g. the rules of question formation or the construction of *if*-sentences)
- vocabulary, including the meanings of words, their lexical grammar (e.g. the fact that *enjoy* can be followed by an *-ing* form but not by an infinitive), and collocation rules (e.g. we say *even-handed* and not **even-footed*)
- the meanings and functions that phrases and sentences can convey
- pronunciation
- spelling

There are of course other ways in which students can study language, such as genre analysis and the study of written and spoken text construction (see Chapters 15 and 16). In both these cases, however, students are asked to notice a number of different aspects of the texts in front of them rather than focusing on a specific language item or items as they will be asked to do in the examples below. Pronunciation is part of this, but it will also be dealt with separately in Chapter 13.

A1 Language study techniques

There are a number of study techniques which we can use to ensure that students not only understand the meaning of a language form and how it is used in exchanges or texts, but are also clear about its construction:

154

- **Demonstration:** we can demonstrate the language forms which we want students to study by offering them a situation which shows the language in action and then modelling the language ourselves (see Chapter 4, D2). The language can be used in a text which clearly shows what it means; we can also use pictures or various items of realia to demonstrate meaning (as described in Chapter 10).

  Demonstration on its own may not be enough; some students will need a mixture of demonstration and explanation, and the other techniques described below to be sure of understanding the new form(s) correctly.

- **Explanation:** we can explain the construction of language in diagrams using the board or overhead projector. We can make use of equipment such as Cuisenaire rods to show syntactic relationships or stress patterns (see Chapter 10D). We can use finger-pointing to show how contractions are made, e.g:

Uncontracted form   Contracted form

At higher levels we can offer grammatical explanations by saying things such as *We don't use words or phrases which refer to a specific time in the past (like 'yesterday' or 'last week') with the present perfect* or *The choice of which verb we use to talk about the future depends on our precise intention – how definite we wish to be about future plans and arrangements.* We can explain rules in the students' own language, but this can detract from the English atmosphere of the class.

In the traditional PPP model, explanation is frequently given by isolating and distorting bits of the language which the teacher is modelling (see Chapter 6, A2).

The way we offer explanation to our students will depend upon the language form we are focusing on and the age, level, and preferences of the class.

- **Discovery:** students can be encouraged to understand new language forms either by discovering them for themselves in a text, or by looking at grammatical evidence in order to work out a grammar rule.

  In order for us to have confidence that discovery leads to real understanding, we need to be available for students to check with us whether they have worked things out correctly. In the words of one Swedish student 'You can't be 100 per cent sure that you've found the rule. You must have the possibility to get the right rule from the teacher' (Fortune 1992: 168).

- **Accurate reproduction:** one of the ways students learn new language forms best is through an accurate reproduction stage. Here we ask students to repeat new words, phrases, or sentences in a controlled way, correcting them when they get things wrong and showing approval when they use the form correctly. Not only does this allow them to try out the new language, but the teacher's feedback also serves as further demonstration and explanation of the new forms.

Accurate reproduction – or controlled practice – is the 'practice' stage of the PPP model (see Chapter 6, A2). However, where students show an immediate grasp of the language forms such controlled repetition may not be necessary. This is especially the case at higher levels.

- **Immediate creativity:** where students show an understanding of the meaning, use, and construction of the language form we are focusing on, we can ask them to create their own sentences using the language form. Such early language production will give a good indication, to both students and the teacher, of how well the language form has been understood.

  Immediate creativity is the 'production' phase of the traditional PPP model. As an early activation of language it is not strictly a study activity, though most study sequences will allow for it at some stage. It can also be used after any explanation, or after a discovery activity.

- **Check questions:** we can use check questions to see if students have understood meaning and use. If students are learning to use past continuous sentences such as *At eight o'clock she was watching television* we can measure their comprehension by asking *Did she start watching television at exactly eight o'clock or before?* If they are working with *as … as* comparisons in sentences such as *Denise isn't as tall as Chris*, we can ask *Who's taller?* to check their understanding of the language.

A2 ## Language study in lesson sequences

The status of language study depends on why and when it occurs. It may form the main focus of a lesson: we might say, for example, that a chief part of today's lesson will be the teaching of relative clauses (or the future continuous, or ways of suggesting) and design the lesson around this central purpose.

Many study activities (especially in coursebooks) have tended to follow the PPP model. Yet, this may be entirely inappropriate for certain types of students and with certain areas of language (see Chapter 6, A3). We may also wish to preface a study exercise with activities which show us how much of the language in question is already known, or we may interleave the study with other elements. Rather than always following 'straight arrow' sequences, in other words, we will often find that 'boomerang' or 'patchwork' lessons are more suitable (see page 84).

Language study may not be the main focus of a lesson sequence, however, but may be only one element in a grander design, in which case a decision will have to be taken about where the study activity should be placed in a sequence. Should the focus on any necessary language forms take place before, during, or after the performance of a communicative task or a receptive skills activity?

One approach (often taken by materials writers) is for students to study language in a variety of ways, then explore a topic, and then use what they have learnt to perform a task (see, for example, Cunningham and Moor 1998). Alternatively, the study of language forms may happen during a task-based sequence. We might focus on one or two past tense forms in the middle of an extended narrative-writing task; we might have our students study vocabulary to describe the weather in the middle of a sequence on holiday planning. Students can also research language as part of a task (see Chapter 12).

Sometimes we study forms after the students have performed the task. This usually happens as a form of language repair when the task has shown up language problems – or when students might have found the task easier if they had been able to produce certain language forms which they did not use at all. Studying language after the task has been completed is a feature of the Task-based model followed by Jane Willis (1996).

However, even where we have not planned to include language study in a particular lesson sequence we sometimes find opportunities presenting themselves which we find impossible to ignore, and, as a result, we get students to focus on language items which we had not anticipated including. Such 'opportunistic' study may happen because a student wants to know how or why some language is constructed; it might take place because completely unforeseen problems present themselves; we might suddenly become aware of the chance to offer students some language which they cannot use but which – if they are now exposed to it – will significantly raise the level at which they are performing the task.

Opportunistic teaching – studying language which suddenly 'comes up' – exposes the tension between planning lessons in advance but yet responding to what actually happens in class (see Chapter 22, C1). When used appropriately, the relevance and immediacy of opportunistic language study may make it the most memorable and effective kind of language study there is.

A3 Known or unknown language?

Apart from real beginners each individual student has some degree of linguistic knowledge and ability in English. In addition to this, individual students learn at different speeds and in different ways. These two facts taken together explain why so many classes can rightly be described as 'mixed ability' – though this is more extreme in some cases than in others.

The fact of mixed ability throws up a problem for the study of language forms since it will frequently be impossible to know whether such forms really are new or not for the individual students in a class. And even if most of our students have experienced the language before, it is not necessarily the case that they can all use it.

If – for the reasons stated above – we cannot be sure whether or not our students know the language we are about to ask them to study, we will need to find this information out. If we do not, we risk teaching them things they already know, or assuming knowledge they do not have.

One way of avoiding teaching already known language is to have students perform tasks and see how well they use the language forms in question before deciding whether we need to introduce those forms as if they were new. A less elaborate technique is to attempt to elicit the new language forms we wish them to study. If we find that students can produce them satisfactorily we will not want to demonstrate or explain them all over again, and accurate reproduction will be a waste of time. If elicitation is unsuccessful, however, we have good grounds for treating the language forms as new and proceeding accordingly.

A4 **Choosing study activities**

We will frequently decide how and when to have students study language form and use on the basis of the syllabus and/or the coursebook since it may offer an explanation and an exercise that we are happy to use almost unchanged. However, many of these sequences may not suit the particular styles and progress of our learners, and may thus need adjusting or replacing in some way (see Chapter 21, c2). We may want to try out new activities, or be concerned not to go on using the same kind of activity day after day. How then do we make such decisions?

- **Following planning principles:** when deciding how to have students study language form we need to bear general planning principles in mind (see Chapter 22A). This means that we have to think about activities which the students do before and after this study session so that we do not simply repeat the same kind of activity again and again. We need to offer a varied diet of exercises when studying language forms both because all our students have different learning styles (see Chapter 3, b3 and b5) and also to help sustain student motivation.

- **Assessing a language study activity for use in class:** when assessing an activity designed for the study of language form we need to decide how effective it will be when we take it into class. It should justify the time we will need to spend on it both before and during the lesson. We need to believe that the activity demonstrates meaning and use clearly and that it allows opportunities for a focus on (and practice of) the construction of the language form. We have to think that it will engage our learners successfully.

  Scott Thornbury, in his book on grammar teaching, suggests measuring activities according to 'efficiency' and 'appropriacy' factors. In the first category he wants us to work out the economy, ease, and efficacy of the activity (Is it do-able economically? How easy is it for the teacher? Does it work?). In terms of appropriacy we need to judge whether the activity is suitable for our particular group of students at their level, for that time of day, for those classroom conditions, and so on (Thornbury 1999a: 25–27).

  We often take activities and exercises into class that we have used before with other groups. We will have, therefore, a good idea of how effective they will be. Nevertheless we need to remember that groups are different, and that what was appropriate for one class may not work as well with other students.

- **Evaluating a study activity after use in class:** we need to evaluate the success of an activity which focuses on language form, whether we do this formally or informally. That is one reason why we should keep records of our classes (see Chapter 22, C2) and why we should conduct our own action research (see Chapter 24, B1).

Evaluation of an activity answers questions such as whether or not the exercise helped students to learn the new language, whether it was clear, whether it took more or less time than anticipated, whether students were engaged by it, and whether or not we want to use it again. Part of this evaluation involves us in thinking about how we might modify the activity the next time we use it.

B Examples of language study activities

The activities in this section demonstrate both the teacher-led introduction of new language, and material designed to enable students to work things out for themselves with the teacher's help.

B1 Introducing new language

The following example shows how a situation can be used to provide the context for the introduction of new language (though elicitation will show if the language really is new).

Example 1: Light in space	Language:	*should/shouldn't have done*
	Age:	any
	Level:	intermediate/upper intermediate

The sequence starts when the students are asked if they ever read science fiction, making sure that they understand what genre of fiction we are talking about. This might develop into a quick discussion of what they read and why. The point is to get them engaged and interested in what is coming. Students can be prompted to say what they would expect to find in a science-fiction text.

We now ask the students to read the following text. While they do this they must find out information such as how many people are in the space station at the beginning and end of the text, whether they are men or women, and how long they have been there.

They had been up here for five years. Five years for five people, cut off from earth since World War IV. True the Moonshuttle came every six months with a supply of food, but it was pilotless. They had not been able to make contact with Moonbase for two years. Cathy said it was weird.

'You say that three times a day,' Rosie answered.

'Well it's true. It's weird and I don't think I can stand it much longer.'

'Oh for Jupiter's sake shut up! Go and play eight-dimensional death-chess and leave me alone. You drive me crazy!'

'Thanks!' Cathy said quietly, 'I can see I'm not wanted.' She left the cabin.

The door hissed behind her.

When she got to the exit chamber she didn't look at the record book where Mitch had written '9 – motor malfunction. Do not use'. She got into suit number nine and pressed the exit key. The outside door hissed open and she sailed out into space. She hadn't told the others where she was going (space station rule 345/2/z3). It gave her a good sense of freedom.

Back in the station Rosie saw the red warning light above the exit control but she ignored it. They'd had trouble with the lights recently. Nothing serious. Captain Clarke saw it, though. She got on her personal people communicator and called Tim Hotzenfop the station engineer.

'I think we've got a problem. You'd better come up quick.' But Tim was deep in conversation with Leila so he said 'Sure. I'll be up,' and then switched off the radio. Leila was nicer to listen to than old Clarke.

Mitch was in the repair shop next to the exit chamber when the audio-alarm went off. But he was wearing his spacewalk-man. He didn't hear a thing.

200 metres away from the station Cathy suddenly realised that she had forgotten to close the station exit door. She must go back. She pressed the motor control on the front of her suit. There was no response. She pressed it again. Nothing. At that moment, looking back, she saw the space station she had just left roll over and she thought she heard a scream echoing out into the darkness. Her eyes widened in horror. And then she saw the light.

When the students have read the text and shown that they have understood it by answering comprehension questions we can then ask them to say what they think happens next: '*What is the light? What has happened to the space station and why?*' The object is to get them to be creative with language and with their response to the text.

We now ask the students to list things that people did that were 'bad' or 'not sensible' and write them on the board, for example:

> a Rosie was rude to Cathy.
> b Cathy didn't look at the record book.
> c Cathy didn't tell the others where she was going.
> d Rosie ignored the red warning light.
> e Tim switched off his radio.
> f Tim didn't do anything about the captain's call.
> g Mitch was wearing his spacewalk-man.
> h Cathy didn't close the station exit door.

We then ask the students if they can make a sentence about event (a) using *should not* to elicit the sentence *Rosie shouldn't have been rude to Cathy*. We may write *should (not) have DONE* on the board. We then encourage students to make sentences about the other 'silly' actions using the same construction. We may get students to come up to the board and write the sentences so that the board ends up looking like this:

> a Rosie was rude to Cathy.
>   She shouldn't have been rude to Cathy.
> b Cathy didn't look at the record book.
>   She should have looked at the record book.
> c Cathy didn't tell the others where she was going.
>   She should have told the others where she was going.
> d Rosie ignored the red warning light.
>   She shouldn't have ignored the warning light.
> e Tim switched off his radio.
>   He shouldn't have switched off his radio.
> f Tim didn't do anything about it.
>   He should have done something about it.
> g Mitch was wearing his spacewalk-man.
>   He shouldn't have been wearing his spacewalk-man.
> h Cathy didn't close the station exit door.
>   She should have closed the station exit door.

If students are having trouble pronouncing any of the parts of the sentences we may model those parts and possibly have students repeat either chorally or individually. For example, we may focus on /ˈʃədəv/ and /ˈʃədntəv/, showing how the phrases are stressed and contracted.

Students are now in a position to tell stories of things in the past which they should/shouldn't have done (*I should have done my homework on time/I shouldn't have left the car unlocked*) after the teacher has told stories, perhaps, about himself to demonstrate what is expected.

Other situation-based contexts for introducing new language might include (for vocabulary) asking students to label items in a house with 'new' words we give them or (for a functional lesson) getting them to try and match problems and suggestions as a lead-in to the introduction of suggestion language.

B2 Discovery activities

In the following examples, students are encouraged to work out for themselves how language forms are constructed and used.

Example 2: Comparative adjectives	Language:	word formation – comparative adjectives
	Age:	any
	Level:	elementary/pre-intermediate

In this example students have listened to a dialogue in which people have been comparing things. Before moving on to make their own sentences, the teacher wants to draw their attention to the way that we make adjectives comparative. She could have done this by giving rules, or perhaps just by ignoring such technical information and hoping that students will 'notice' the various possibilities for themselves. Instead she chooses to put them in pairs and give them the following exercise:

Look at this!

old	→ older
new	→ newer
light	→ lighter
big	→ bigger
thin	→ thinner
noisy	→ noisier
silly	→ sillier
expensive	→ more expensive
beautiful	→ more beautiful

Now work these out!

a How do we make one-syllable adjectives into comparative adjectives?

b Why are 'big' and 'thin' different?

c What has to change when we make words like 'noisy' and 'silly' into comparative adjectives?

d What is different about 'expensive' and 'beautiful'? Why?

When the pairs have finished she checks through the answers making sure they understand that one-syllable words which end with a vowel and a consonant double the last letter, that -*y* becomes -*i*-, and that longer words are preceded by *more* but otherwise stay the same. She now moves on to a practice exercise.

There are two potential problems with this approach. First, it is not always easy to give a complete grammatical picture. This exercise does not give all the necessary information about comparatives. There are no irregular ones here (like *good* – *better*), nor are there examples of words that are made comparative by either taking -*er* or being preceded by *more* (e.g. *clever* in many spoken varieties of the language). Second, it is not necessarily the case that all students enjoy this kind of detective work. But as a way of encouraging them to think about how language works such exercises are extremely useful, especially when, as here, the language rules they are investigating are fairly easy to discern.

Example 3: Rules and freedom	Language:	functions – expressing obligation (*can't/have to/ must/allowed to*)
	Age:	adult
	Level:	intermediate

In this example from an intermediate coursebook, the students are going to look at obligation language, some of which they may have already come across separately.

The teaching sequence starts when students discuss how many rules and regulations they can think of for either the school they are studying in, or related to different ages (e.g. before people are eighteen), or for when there is a political election, or for when you travel to a foreign country. The object of this discussion is to interest the students in the topic and to elicit some of the language which will be the focus of study.

The teacher now gets students to look at the following illustration. They are asked how many signs they can see and what they mean:

From *Cutting Edge Intermediate*, by S Cunningham and P Moor (Pearson Education Ltd)

At this stage the teacher will be happy to accept sentences like *Don't smoke* or *Smoking is okay*. The main thing is that students should understand the meaning of the signs.

Students are now asked to put a tick next to the following sentences if they mean the same as the signs in the picture and a cross if they do not:

a You <u>can</u> use a credit card in the duty-free shop. ☑
   You <u>have to</u> use a credit card in the duty-free shop. ☒
b You <u>have to</u> have a visa to leave the transit lounge. ☐
   You<u>'ve got to</u> have a visa to leave the transit lounge. ☐
c You <u>can't</u> smoke in the area at the back. ☐
   You<u>'re allowed to</u> smoke in the area at the back. ☐
d The public <u>mustn't</u> go through the door that says 'staff only'. ☐
   The public <u>aren't allowed to</u> go through the door that says 'staff only'. ☐
e You <u>mustn't</u> smoke in the area at the front. ☐
   You <u>don't have to</u> smoke in the area at the front. ☐

This is an ideal opportunity for the students to do an exercise in pairs or groups. By discussing each sentence and sharing their knowledge they help each other understand things they did not previously know.

The teacher checks through the answers with the whole class and then asks them to go through the following 'Analysis' box where they have to work out the grammar and meaning of the underlined verbs:

Analysis

1 Look at the underlined verbs in the sentences above. Complete the following lists showing how the verbs are used.

a *it is necessary have to*	b *it is okay / permitted can*	c *it is a good idea / the correct thing*
d *it is not necessary*	e *it is not okay / it is prohibited*	f *it is not a good idea / not the correct thing*

2 What is the difference (if any) in the use of *must* and *have to* in the following pairs of sentences?
   a • *You must finish all the medicine – it's really important.*
      • *The doctor says I have to finish all the medicine – it's really important.*
   b • *You mustn't walk home alone in the dark – it's dangerous.*
      • *You don't have to walk home – we'll give you a lift.*

Now read Language summary A on page 150.

Once the teacher has checked that the students have been able to complete the analysis chart, she can get them to do a fill-in exercise where they have to discriminate between *have to, don't have to, should, shouldn't,* and *are/aren't allowed.* They then make their own sentences about what the rules are in places which they know and visit, or they can give rules and the other students have to guess what place is being talked about (e.g. *You have to be quiet. You can't take books unless you sign them out at the desk. You can't take food into this place.* etc).

We can also have students discover grammar with any reading text (where we might ask them to find *if*-sentences, for example, and work out the different constructions they find), or get them to study the transcript of a conversation to see how people agree and disagree.

B3 Remembering

At various stages of learning teachers will want students to revisit language forms which they have been exposed to previously. This may be part of an overt correction stage, part of a sequence which the teacher has slotted in because students have had trouble with that language in a task, or part of a straightforward revision process where language forms are recycled from time to time to help students remember them better.

Remembering activities usually fall towards the middle of the 'communication continuum' (see page 85); they encourage students to bridge the gap between language study and language activation (see Chapter 6, A3). In more communicative activities we hope that students will activate previously learnt language forms subconsciously, but in remembering exercises students will be aware of an overt focus on particular forms, which they will then be expected to use.

The following examples of remembering activities all presuppose that the students have already worked on the language areas which they will be using.

Example 4: Perfect one-liners	Language: structure – past perfect continuous
	Age: any
	Level: intermediate/advanced

In this activity students practise the past perfect continuous tense based on prompts from the teacher. They are required to use their imagination and/or sense of humour and the exercise is given added enjoyment by being designed as a team game.

The teacher divides the class into small teams of two to four people. She tells them that she will be reading sentences for which they have to find appropriate responses, using the past perfect continuous. She starts by giving them a sentence such as *When I got home last night my flatmate was asleep in the car.* She asks the class, in general, what kind of reason they can think of, and hopes to elicit sentences like *Well, she had been listening to a programme on the radio and fallen asleep,* or *Yes, well that's because she had been talking to a hypnotist on her mobile phone,* etc.

Now that the students understand the idea of the exercise she reads out the following sentences:

a	When I came to see you yesterday your cat was in the fridge.
b	Can you explain why you bit my dog?
c	That was my new Rolls Royce your son pushed over the cliff.
d	You had blood all over your wedding clothes after the ceremony.
e	You were the only one in the room before the theft.
f	You had different coloured socks on the other day.
g	Why did Henry VIII have his wife Anne Boleyn beheaded?

From *The Anti-Grammar Grammar Book* by N Hall and J Shepheard (Pearson Education Ltd)

For each sentence the teams are given a short time to come up with good sentences. If they are correct and/or appropriate the teacher awards a point, but no team can offer a sentence that has been used previously.

This game-like practice does nothing more or less than force students to make sentences using a particular verb tense. Yet by adding the element of surreal humour it can cause great enjoyment. Of course students may find it difficult, and teachers may want to use different sentence prompts from those given here for any number of reasons. But the idea of a teacher giving prompts in this way has considerable attraction since it requires no material or technology and can be slotted into a lesson at various stages.

Example 5: In the queue	Language: vocabulary – physical description
	Age: adult
	Level: beginners

In this practice activity designed to get students using the language of description (e.g. *He's quite tall. She has blond hair. He has a beard*), an artificial 'information gap' is created by getting the students to look at different pictures.

The teacher starts by putting a picture of people in a queue on the board and giving the students a list of names. They can then ask him, e.g. *What's John like?* to which the teacher replies *He's quite tall with glasses. He has a beard.* A student then comes up and points to the correct person in the picture.

The teacher now puts students in pairs. In each pair one student is A and the other is B. Each A student looks at the following two pictures – which are in colour in the original – and is told (a) to find out which of the following names apply to which of the people in the cinema queue (picture A1):

Cathy   Jim   Karly   Kit   Mick   Monica   Philip   Susan

and (b) to answer B's questions about the people in picture A2. Thus, for picture A1, A will ask *What's Cathy like?* and B will reply *She's quite young. She's tall and thin and her hair is quite long.*

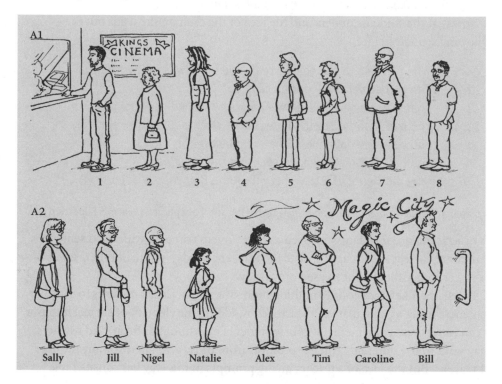

Each student B, on the other hand, looks at the following two pictures and is told (a) to find out which of the following names apply to which of the people in the queue to 'Magic City' (picture B2):

Alex   Bill   Caroline   Jill   Natalie   Nigel   Sally   Tim

and (b) to answer A's questions about the people in picture B1. Thus, for picture B2, B will ask *What's Alex like?* and A will reply *She's medium height and quite well-built. She has dark hair.*

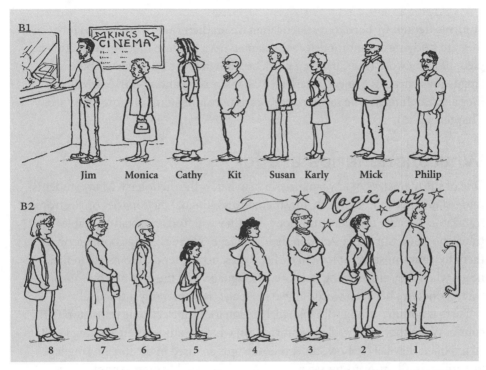

When the activity is over the teacher has different students describe the various characters (Alex, Cathy, Susan, etc.) to check that they are happy using the description language.

Chapter notes and further reading

- **Situations for introducing new language**

  In his ground-breaking book *English in Situations* Robert O'Neill was one of the first to create situations which provoked a number of examples of the target language (O'Neill 1972).

- **Mixed-ability classes**

  On mixed-ability classes, see L Prodromou (1992), B Bowler and S Parminter (1997 and 2000) and J Rose (1997).

12 | Researching language

Students frequently need to research language on their own, whether this is because they are studying autonomously (see Chapter 24A), because they are correcting a piece of homework (see Chapter 24, A1), because they are finding out about language as part of a project or task (see Chapters 6, A5 and 17–19), or because they are searching for the meanings of words in reading and listening texts (see Chapters 14–16).

A What dictionaries are for

One of the mainstays of any language 'researcher' is the dictionary. Many students understand this and, as a result, buy themselves bilingual dictionaries or electronic translators because they fervently hope that they will find an instantly usable translation of a word they know in their language. There is every good reason for them to want this since, at least in earlier stages, people tend to translate in their heads when they are learning in a foreign language, and the idea of a one-to-one correspondence between words in two languages is immensely attractive.

There is nothing wrong with bilingual dictionaries (or electronic translators) of course. When they work well they provide just what the students are looking for. But all too often they fail to show students how words are used in the foreign language, providing simple answers for what is, in effect, considerably more complex. Sometimes, for example, a word in the L1 may have six or seven equivalencies in the L2; if these equivalencies are just offered as a list of words they provide the student with no information about which one to choose – and when. Sometimes there are restrictions on the use of a word in L1 which do not apply in the L2. Unless these are given, the information is not complete. Many bilingual dictionaries also fail to give sufficient information about grammatical context, appropriacy, and connotation.

This does not mean that all bilingual dictionaries are bad or that students should never use them. There are some excellent examples available now and whether we like it or not, students will always use them, especially at lower levels. What we can do is show them something different which is just as good – and in many ways better: the monolingual dictionary (MLD).

MLDs, whether in book form, on CDs or available on the Internet, are those written in only one language (in this case English). Although most 'general' dictionaries are, of course, monolingual in this sense, the acronym tends to be used to describe dictionaries written especially for language learners, and that is the sense in which we use it here. Current examples include the *Longman Dictionary of Contemporary English*, the *Cambridge International Dictionary of English*, the *Oxford Advanced Learner's Dictionary*, and the *COBUILD Dictionary*. In them users will find information such as the different meanings that words have, how they are pronounced, what other words they collocate with, and when they can be used. They also give examples of the words in phrases and sentences so that students get a very good idea of how they themselves can use this word. One of the more important features of many of the current generation of MLDs is that their definitions are written in a language which is itself simplified, thus avoiding the possibility that the definition is more difficult to understand than the word itself: it makes a lot more sense to say that a *dog* is *a very common animal that people keep as a pet or to guard a building* (*Longman Dictionary of Contemporary English*) than that it is a *canine quadruped*!

Students at beginner level will usually find MLDs too difficult to use because the language in the definitions will be way above their heads however careful the lexicographers have been. Such people may well rely on their bilingual dictionaries. But from somewhere around the intermediate level, students will find the information that MLDs contain invaluable, as we shall see in the following examples in this section.

A1 Reference and production dictionaries

Reference dictionaries – the kind that we most frequently use – need to be distinguished from production dictionaries, a type of dictionary which has emerged comparatively recently.

A reference dictionary is one where a student looks up a word to see what meanings it has, how it is used, and the way it is spelt and pronounced, e.g:

re.search[1] /rɪˈsɜːtʃ, ˈriːsɜːtʃ‖-ɜːr-/ *n* [U] also **researches** [plural] **1** serious study of a subject, that is intended to discover new facts or test new ideas: [+**into/on**] *research into the causes of cancer* | **research project / student /grant etc** *Alison is a research student in our lab.* **2** the activity of finding information about something that you are interested in or need to know about: **do research** *I'm doing some research for an article about student life.* | *I've done some research – it looks as if the train will be fastest.* – see also MARKET RESEARCH, R AND D
re.search[2] /rɪˈsɜːtʃ‖-ɜːr-/ *v* [T] **1** to study a subject in detail, especially in order to discover new facts or test new ideas: *He's researching the effects of aerosols on the environment.* **2** to supply all the necessary facts and information for something: *This book has been very well researched.* – **researcher** *n* [C]

Entries for *research* in the *Longman Dictionary of Contemporary English* (Pearson Education Ltd)

Depending on the particular word being defined (and exemplified) some or all of the following information may also be given:

- differences between British and American usage, for example *Monday to Friday inclusive* (British), and *Monday through Friday* (American)
- similar words, for example the difference between *gaze, stare,* and *gape*
- frequency in different media, for example the fact that *certainly* is more common in speech than in writing

— levels of formality, for example the fact that *indolent* is a formal word
— connotation, for example the fact that *vagabond* is 'especially literary' and that certain words are 'taboo'

Dictionaries are generally used when students have already come across a word and then look it up to check that they know how to use it. Sometimes they will find a word in their bilingual dictionaries and then check with the MLD to see if they have understood correctly.

Production dictionaries, on the other hand, are designed for students to use the other way round, starting with a meaning they wish to express and in order to look for the word that expresses it. Suppose, for example, that they wish to express the idea of someone secretly listening to someone else while standing near him, perhaps on the other side of a door. A native speaker would immediately choose the word *eavesdrop* to describe the situation. The foreign student might find this in a bilingual dictionary, but would have more trouble with a reference MLD since, not knowing the word in the first place, he or she would not, of course, be able to look it up.

In a production dictionary students look for a general word that they already know, and which is a bit like the concept they wish to be able to express in English. In the case of *eavesdrop*, for example, that word might be *listen*. Opening the production dictionary (in this case the *Longman Essential Activator*) the student finds the following:

LISTEN
see also HEAR

> ⚠ Don't confuse listen and hear. If you listen to something, you pay attention so that you can hear it well.

Listen /ˈlɪsən/ [v I] to pay attention to what someone is saying or to a sound that you hear: *I didn't hear the answer because I wasn't listening when she read it out.*
+ to *Gordon was lying on his bed, listening to his music.*
listen carefully *They all listened carefully while she was telling them the story.*
Listen! SPOKEN (say this when you want to get someone's attention) *Listen! I've just had a brilliant idea.*

> ⚠ Don't say 'I listen music'. Say **I listen to music.**

pay attention /ˌpeɪ əˈtenʃən/ to listen carefully to what someone is saying: *I have some important information about travel arrangements, so please pay attention.*
+ to *She went on talking, but I wasn't really paying attention to what she was saying.*
eavesdrop /ˈiːvzdrɒp‖-draːp/ [v I] to secretly listen to someone else's conversation by standing near them, hiding behind a door etc: *"How does Jake know that?" "He must have been eavesdropping."*

+ **on** *We talked very quietly so that no-one could eavesdrop on us.*
listen in /ˌlɪsən ˈɪn/ [*phrasal verb* I] to listen to someone else's telephone
conversation when they do not know you are listening.
+ **on** *The police were listening in on their conversation.*

From the *Longman Essential Activator* (Pearson Education Ltd)

Going down the column they come across a word which, through its definition and
the examples given, is exactly what they are looking for. They can now use it with
confidence.

Reference MLDs are packed full of information which is invaluable to students
checking word use. Production dictionaries, in contrast, allow students to find
new words.

A2 Training students to use dictionaries

If we want students to use dictionaries it will probably not be sufficient just to
recommend a dictionary and tell them how useful it is. Even though huge
improvements have been made in dictionary design over the last few years – and even
though there are now a number of Internet, CD-ROM, and DVD-based dictionaries –
still the wealth of information can be extremely daunting to some users. Indeed the
frequently dense design of some dictionaries may be enough to put them off
altogether.

In order to avoid this problem many teachers and materials designers put
dictionary training into lesson sequences, so that students will see how to use them
and what the benefits of such use are. Thus we can make sure, for example, that
students recognise the metaphorical meanings that are given, and that they identify
typical lexical phrases which the word they are looking for occurs in – and which
good dictionaries list clearly.

The following two examples show dictionary training in action:

Example 1: The bilingual dictionary   Level: pre-intermediate

The following example from a textbook for elementary/pre-intermediate learners is
based on the assumption that students will be using a bilingual dictionary and
therefore points out to them some of the things they can find out from it:

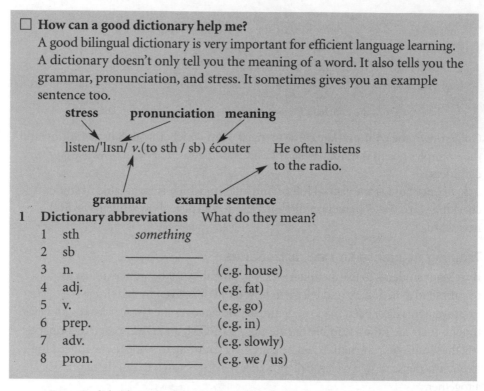

From *English File Student's Book* 2 by C Oxenden et al. (Oxford University Press)

At the very least such a good piece of advice shows students that dictionaries are a 'good thing' and that they contain a variety of useful information. The next example goes further, however, taking entries from MLDs and asking students some exacting questions which they answer as they learn how to use the MLD.

Example 2: Dictionary codes	Level: intermediate

One thing that students need to discover is what the various abbreviations and definitions in a dictionary mean, and how meanings are given and explained. The following exercise is designed for this purpose:

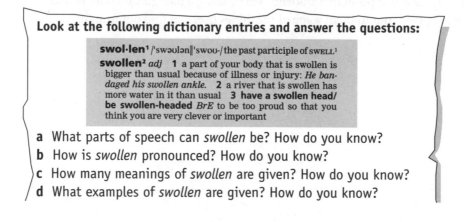

e Are any of the uses of swollen particular to any special national or regional language variety? How do you know?

Such questions point the students towards the grammar labels (for example, adj), towards the phonetic transcriptions that are given, towards the way the dictionary lists different meanings, to the fact that examples are usually in italics, and to labels like *BrE* to denote special usage in one particular language variety.

B What grammar books are for

Grammar books come in many shapes and sizes. The most popular ones tend to offer quick digestible explanations of grammar points and provide opportunities for practice of these specific points, for example:

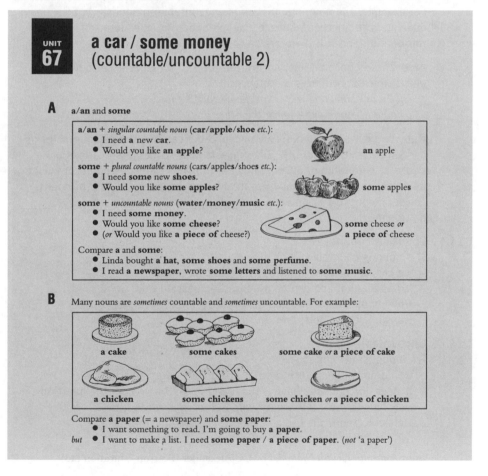

UNIT
67

a car / some money
(countable/uncountable 2)

A a/an and some

a/an + *singular countable noun* (**car/apple/shoe** *etc.*):
- I need **a** new **car**.
- Would you like **an apple**?

an apple

some + *plural countable nouns* (cars/apples/shoes *etc.*):
- I need **some** new **shoes**.
- Would you like **some apples**?

some apples

some + *uncountable nouns* (**water/money/music** *etc.*):
- I need **some money**.
- Would you like **some cheese**?
- (*or* Would you like **a piece of** cheese?)

some cheese *or*
a piece of cheese

Compare **a** and **some**:
- Linda bought **a hat**, **some shoes** and **some perfume**.
- I read **a newspaper**, wrote **some letters** and listened to **some music**.

B Many nouns are *sometimes* countable and *sometimes* uncountable. For example:

a cake   **some cakes**   **some cake** *or* **a piece of cake**

a chicken   **some chickens**   **some chicken** *or* **a piece of chicken**

Compare **a paper** (= a newspaper) and **some paper**:
- I want something to read. I'm going to buy **a paper**.

but - I want to make a list. I need **some paper** / **a piece of paper**. (*not* 'a paper')

From *Essential Grammar in Use* by R Murphy (Cambridge University Press)

At intermediate and higher levels, however, it is possible to give more complex explanations, as in the following example:

2.14 How to identify countable and uncountable nouns

All common nouns fall into one of two sub-classes: they may be either **countable nouns** (sometimes known as **unit** or **count** nouns) or **uncountable nouns** (sometimes known as **mass** or **non-count** nouns). The distinction between countable and uncountable nouns is fundamental in English, for only by distinguishing between the two can we understand when to use singular or plural forms and when to use indefinite, definite and zero articles: *a/an*, *the* and Ø [> 3.2–3], or the appropriate quantifier: a *few, much, many*, etc. [>3.1, 5.1].

Unfortunately, we cannot always rely on common sense (using the idea of counting as a guide) to tell us when a noun is countable or uncountable. For example, the noun *information* is uncountable in English, but its equivalent in another language may refer to an item or items of information and will therefore be countable [> 2.17].

Experience is uncountable, but we can refer to *an experience* to mean an event which contributes to *experience:*
   *They want someone with **experience** for this job.*
   *I had **a strange experience** the other day.*

Many nouns which are normally uncountable can be used as countables in certain contexts [>2.16.3]. This suggests that strict classifications of nouns as countable or uncountable are in many cases unreliable. It would be better to think in terms of countable and uncountable *uses* of nouns. For detailed information about individual nouns, consult a good dictionary.

2.14.1 Countable nouns
If a noun is countable:
- we can use *a/an* in front of it: **a** *book,* **an** *envelope.*
- it has a plural and can be used in the question *How many?:*
  ***How many** stamps/envelopes? – Four stamps/envelopes.*
- we can use numbers: ***one** stamp,* **two** *stamps.*

2.14.2 Uncountable nouns
If a noun is uncountable:
- we do not normally use *a/an* in front of it: ***Sugar** is expensive.*
- it does not normally have a plural and it can be used in the question *How much?:* ***How much** meat/oil? – A lot of meat/A little oil.*
- we cannot normally use a number (*one, two*) in front of it.

From *Longman English Grammar* by L G Alexander (Pearson Education Ltd)

Both students and teachers may consult grammar books for a number of reasons. For example, students may be drafting or redrafting a piece of written work and may want to check that they are using some grammar correctly. Alternatively, a teacher, having noticed that a student is making a lot of mistakes in one particular area, might tell that student to look up the language in a grammar book in order to understand it better. Perhaps a student gets back a piece of written homework which has correction marks on it highlighting grammatical problems; when the student is rewriting the homework he or she can consult a reference grammar (such as the *Longman English Grammar* above). But students can also work through the explanations and exercises in self-study grammars such as *Essential Grammar in Use* either on their own or because a teacher sets exercises for homework (see Chapter 24, A1) or classwork. Finally, teachers often use grammar books (e.g. Alexander (1988), Swan (1995), Parrott (2000)) to check grammar concepts, especially where students ask difficult questions which we cannot answer on the spot, or where an area is complex so that we need to revisit it from time to time to remind ourselves of the full picture. Grammar books are also vital for the preparation of materials.

C What language corpora are for

With a very few notable exceptions (see, for example, Tribble and Jones 1997), it has always been assumed that language corpora (huge collections of language from sources such as books, magazines, newspapers, and speech, stored on computers) are only useful for language researchers. The complexity of the software needed to use them and the unfriendly look of the evidence which they produce has deterred many teachers and students from going anywhere near them. Another problem has been the source of the texts that have gone into the corpora. How can students be expected to understand language evidence that, perhaps, comes from scientific journals or from highly idiosyncratic language varieties which they are not used to?

Things are changing, however, and the development of new programs and more user-friendly interfaces has started to bring corpora into more common use. Materials writers are also thinking of compiling the kind of language corpora which students might find usable – removing texts which they would conceivably have significant problems with.

At their simplest, software programs used with language corpora show how particular words are used. These 'key words in context' (KWICs) appear on the screen embedded in the sentences or phrases where they occur. Each line of the concordance is taken from the different texts stored on the corpus (though you may, of course, have different examples from the same text too).

People who use concordancing software packages often ask their computer to give them a 'sample' of the word. This is because on a large corpus of 200 million words or more, asking the computer to give every example of a high frequency word (such as *crime*) would produce screen after screen of lines. Instead we can get a representative sample of the word, so that if we asked for a 25-line sample of a word like *handsome* we might get the following:

is back. The third cell (82d) contains a	handsome	young man clad in (very dated) Estalian clothing
and wait. His patient was on for fifty, a	handsome,	tall woman, very well-dressed. Her
do look a trifle … stale. You make a	handsome	couple." "Thank you, Herr Direktor
message and show the rest of the readership what a	handsome	chap you are. May I also pass on my thanks to
week of digging up roads, try presenting them with a	handsome	bound volume of Gaelic poetry. Please
Guppy was his best man. Smooth, dark and	handsome	in morning dress and blue cravat, he took his
could see now that he was a big fellow, sleek and	handsome.	His fur shone and his claws and teeth
Actually Hamilton himself, so smart and	handsome	when he travels; soon looked as grimy and
Carly still looked on with awe. Brian had been	handsome	before alcohol thickened his face, and she
lifted her face – the features somewhat masculine but	handsome	– to the constable's. The sleep was
sheet and tucked it around him. Looking at his	handsome	face, she felt a pang for what might have been
the light craft through the water effortlessly, his	handsome	mouth formed into a smile, his back held straight
Drew, and Randy Sherwood, who was laughing his	handsome	head off, had jumped into the pool and were trying
The frown gave a ruthless edge to his	handsome	face, as though the leashed danger in him had
impossibly blue eyes, the golden hair, the laughing	handsome	face; and the awful thing was that, if he came
in the sunlight, and silver dishes were laid out on	handsome	chests and cabinets. In the great hall
raucously at each other, but they really are quite	handsome	birds. Everywhere there was luxurious
The Dean gazed affectionately at her: a tall,	handsome	woman whose company he'd enjoyed immensely
emerged behind the bodyguard. He was a tall,	handsome	man who had an air of confidence about him.
did extremely well to beat Redbridge and Ilford by the	handsome	score of 4 – 1 in the semi-final, but the rugged
economy aligned him with the new Liberals: hence the	handsome	tribute he paid to J.A. Hobson, spite of the
was very proud of. Nutmeg thought himself very	handsome.	He lived in a big house which had a
My husband was an accountant. He was very	handsome	and he was very good to me. But one
after my grandfather. He was wonderfully	handsome,	incredibly dashing, astoundingly brave and
Oh, but he was so handsome! Yet,	handsome?	No, no. Not to be trusted

handsome sampled from the *British National Corpus* (BNC)

Although this may look confusing to the unaccustomed eye, people (such as researchers, teachers, and more advanced students) who are used to reading concordances will quickly spot examples not only of *very handsome*, but also of *quite handsome*, and even *wonderfully handsome*.

Because, too, we have asked the computer program to 'left-sort' the word immediately before the KWIC (in alphabetical order), we can quickly see three examples of the pattern *[adjective] and handsome* before a noun (*dark and handsome, sleek and handsome, smart and handsome*), and even an example of *[adjective] but handsome* (*masculine but handsome*). It is also clear that a common pattern is indefinite article + *handsome* + noun. We will also notice that the word is used to describe both men and women. It is interesting, too, to see that *handsome* (when used to describe people) often has the concept of 'tall' included with it. The concordance – even sampled down to only 25 KWIC sentences – has already yielded a wealth of information.

If we 'right-sorted' the concordance (in alphabetical order of the words immediately following the KWIC) it would instantly become clear that we can talk about *handsome men* and *women*, but also about *handsome birds/chests/couples/faces* (three times)/*heads/mouths/scores/tributes*. Because *face* occurs three times in such a small number of examples it is reasonable to suppose that this is a common collocation. Notice too that both occurrences of the word with *woman* use the word *tall*, suggesting that we would be unlikely to use the word for a short woman.

Left- and right-sorting give us convincing evidence that would take longer to find if we did not use these tools. We can also refine our search by asking the software to sort the lines by two or three words to the left or right, or in various other ways. Each time different facts about words and how they are used emerge from the mass of data in front of us.

Apart from left- and right-sorting we can also get examples of a word from only the spoken corpus or from the written corpus – so that we can see if a word is used differently in speech and writing. We can ask it to give us only KWIC sentences from fiction or from newspapers to learn more about language use in certain genres (see Chapter 2, C4). We can ask the software to give us examples of the word only when used as a noun. We can also find out how common a word is, too, and may be able to do a number of more complex tasks as well.

C1 Typical or divergent?

Students who consult a language corpus get the thrill of being their own language researchers and of seeing evidence that is immediately persuasive. This is language 'in the raw', and its authenticity makes it instantly attractive. Although much of this information is available in dictionaries, it is predigested there, and even in the most user-friendly examples, surrounded by signs and symbols which some students find off-putting – and which they need to be trained to use. Here, on the contrary, students are looking at compelling language evidence which they can evaluate themselves.

However, language corpora can be problematic too, both because of the texts that are put into them, and because of the KWIC sentences they produce.

- **What goes in:** a language corpus depends upon the texts that have gone into it. If every text in a corpus came from Shakespeare then we would get a strange idea of what modern English was like; if every text came from contemporary teenage magazines we would only have information about teenage magazine language, whereas if we fill our computer corpus with *The Times* newspaper we will get only a partial view of language use. We need, therefore, to know how a corpus was assembled, so that we can be sure it is appropriate for us and for our students.

- **What comes out:** if students accept all uses of a word in a concordance as equally valid they may have problems since at least some uses which the program throws up will be idiosyncratic or, in some cases, just plain wrong. We need to train students, therefore, to recognise when certain uses are divergent. A simple rule is that the more often a pattern occurs, the more confident the student can be that this is a common usage. Where it only occurs once they might want to check with a dictionary or a teacher.

D Examples of language research

In the following examples students become language researchers: by finding out information for themselves, they increasingly become more independent and self-reliant, and develop as autonomous learners (see Chapter 24A).

Example 3: Body movements	Language: body movement collocations
	Age: any
	Level: intermediate

In this example the teacher wants the students to discuss different body movements and what they mean/are used for. In a multicultural class this can cause great amusement as people discover that the same gesture can mean different things in different cultures. Where teachers are working with monolingual groups, however, the same effect can be created by discussing what gestures English people use and how this compares with other people – or by discussing how different people use gesture to give clear messages.

The teaching sequence starts when the teacher gets students to discuss how they should behave if they meet the president, the king/queen, the prime minister, a religious leader, a film star or a national beauty queen (in other words bowing, if this is appropriate, or shaking hands perhaps). After this activity, which is intended to introduce the topic of physical gesture and engage the students' interest, they are given the following exercise to perform individually or in pairs:

Which of the following parts of the body can go with these verbs?
arm(s) ears eyebrow(s) fist finger hand(s) head hips leg(s) shoulders teeth

wave		hunch	
fold		shrug	
clench		nod	
point		raise	
wiggle		cross	
wag		shake	

What special meaning (if any) does each gesture or action have?

What actions or gestures do you use to do the following?

Meaning	Gesture
say hello	
say goodbye	
express anger	
express surprise	
express indifference	
express agreement	
express disagreement	

In order to complete the task students work with each other and, crucially, they consult their dictionaries and/or the computer corpus when they are not sure which words collocate. If they look up *clench*, for example, they will find:

> **clench** /klentʃ/v [T] **clench your fists/teeth/jaw etc** to hold your hands, teeth etc together tightly, usually because you feel angry or determined: *She muttered "Go away" through clenched teeth.*

From the *Longman Dictionary of Contemporary English* (Pearson Education Ltd)

It is immediately clear that the main words which collocate with *clench* are *fists*, *teeth*, and *jaw*. The students can now use these collocations with confidence.

If students have access to a language corpus and they ask for a concordance of *shrug*, they might find:

nightmare or perk of budding stardom? His	shrug	seems to say, "Hell, why not?"
those circumstances potential customers will simply	shrug	their shoulders, walk away and do without
shared experience, giving her the confidence to	shrug	her shoulders when she feels like it.
if somebody's got to benefit from inequality, her	shrug	suggests, it might as well be her.
the garage just pursed his lips and said with a	shrug,	"Madame, there are no parts.
a furious damp face on Rossendale who could only	shrug	mute agreement. Lord John though
He stared, then, with an enormous	shrug	of reluctance, he walked to the door,
"Use your own," replied the Mason with a	shrug.	"Isn't that the way of it?
he mean by that? Then she gave a tiny	shrug.	The man was more than just a mystery
people like them?" She felt Fitzalan	shrug.	"Sometimes there's trouble."
killed him." Our eyes meet. I	shrug	and look away, as if it doesn't matter.
if they throw me out ..." he trailed off with a	shrug.	"Those are my terms, Sabrina.
She lifted her shoulders in a dismissive	shrug,	wishing heartily that someone else would
to the ether from where he'd been summoned; to	shrug	off the body which Sartori had congealed
stopped by a blizzard? The she gave a tiny	shrug.	She couldn't back out now – Kelly
shamefaced grin but probably looks like a careless	shrug.	"You're right," I tell him.
It's ingrained. We can't	shrug	it off." "I'm not worried about
Jezrael raised her eyebrows in a facial	shrug,	gave a faint nod: I think I might live.
McKimm has fought a losing battle to	shrug	off injury and is replaced by another
Newcastle line-up, but Paul Bracewell is likely to	shrug	off a toe injury. Keegan
flights are always crowded," he told her with a	shrug.	"But I'm hoping to catch the
point of view. "Anyway," she added with a	shrug,	"the jacket might not be there now.
hat?" The stiff shoulders moved in a	shrug	that almost failed to happen. What
"And had there been?" Again a	shrug,	this time dismissive. "No, not to
got to move fast, though." He tried to	shrug	her off, but Cally held on to him.

shrug sampled from the *British National Corpus* (BNC)

From this concordance it is immediately apparent that *shrug* can be a verb, a noun, or a part of the phrasal verb *shrug off*. Where *shrug* collocates with a part of the body, that is always *shoulder* and, once again, the student can now use this collocation with confidence.

Researching words in this way allows students to complete the task; they can then go on to use some or all of the collocations they have found in scenarios where people show how they are feeling and what they mean with the body movements they use.

Example 4: Films	Language: film vocabulary
	Age: teenage and above
	Level: elementary

If students are doing a project on films and film-going, they need to find appropriate words and phrases for the topic. They could rely on the teacher or the textbook, of course; both or either of these could give them everything they needed. But they might be working on their own, in which case they need to consult some other source of information.

Students who consult a production dictionary will be able to research words they have perhaps never heard or seen before. Thus, within the topic of films/ movies they might search for words for films and going to see them (e.g. *film, movie, cinema, go to the cinema,* etc.), types of film (*horror, comedy, war film, road movie,* etc.), people in films (*actor, actress, star*), people who make films (*director, producer, film crew,* etc.) – and various other categories, including what happens in a film.

7 what happens in a film

plot/story /plɒt, 'stɔːri‖plɑːt-/ [n C] the things that happen in a film: *Tom Hanks was great, but I thought the plot was really boring.* | *It's basically a love story.*

scene /siːn/ [n C] one part of a film: *The first scene takes place on a beach.* | *a love scene* | *I love the scene where the alien comes out through John Hurt's chest.*

special effect /ˌspeʃəl ɪˈfekt/ [n C] an unusual image or sound that is produced artificially, in order to make something that is impossible look as if it is really happening: *The special effects were amazing – the dinosaurs looked as if they were alive.*

ending /'endɪŋ/ [n C] the way that the story in a film ends: *I like movies with a happy ending best.*

twist /twɪst/ [n C] something surprising that happens in a film, which you did not expect: *The film has a twist at the end, when we discover that the detective is the murderer.*

From the *Longman Essential Activator* (Pearson Education Ltd)

Provided that the dictionary designers have managed to predict the words which the students are likely to need, such production material is an ideal tool for language research. The students can now use the words for the project or task they are involved in.

Example 5: *Say* and *tell*	Language:	verb complementation (*say* and *tell*)
	Age:	any
	Level:	intermediate and above

A student has got a corrected piece of homework back from the teacher. The teacher has underlined the sentence *He was tired of people saying him what to do*. In the margin he has written *There is a problem here with the verb 'say'. Look at Practical English Usage, page 489, and rewrite the sentence before the next class.*

When the student looks at the correct page she reads that both verbs can be used with direct and indirect speech and that *say* refers to any kind of speech whereas *tell* is only used to mean *instruct* or *inform*. She then goes on to read the following:

2 objects

After *tell*, we usually say who is told.
> She **told me** that she would be late. (NOT ~~She **told that**~~ ...)

Say is most often used without a personal object.
> She **said** that she would be late. (NOT ~~She **said me**~~ ...)

If we want to put a personal object after *say*, we use *to*.
> And I **say to all the people** of this great country ...

Tell is not used before objects like *a word, a name, a sentence, a phrase*.
> Alice **said** a naughty word this morning. (NOT ~~Alice **told**~~ ...)

We do not usually use *it* after *tell* to refer to a fact.
> 'What time's the meeting?' 'I'll tell you tomorrow.'
> (NOT '~~I'll tell you **it** tomorrow.~~')

3 Infinitives

Tell can be used before **object + infinitive**, in the sense of 'order' or 'instruct'. *Say* cannot be used like this.
> I **told the children to go away**. (NOT ~~I **said the children go away**.~~)

4 *tell* without a personal object

Tell is used without a personal object in a few expressions. Common examples: *tell the truth, tell a lie, tell a story/joke*.
> I don't think she's **telling the truth**. (NOT ... ~~**saying the truth**.~~)

Note also the use of tell to mean 'distinguish', 'understand', as in *tell the difference, tell the time*.

5 Indirect questions

Neither *tell* nor *say* can introduce indirect questions.
> Bill **asked** whether I wanted to see a film.
> (NOT ~~Bill **said whether I wanted to see a film**.~~)
> (NOT ~~Bill **told me whether**~~ ...)

But *say* and *tell* can introduce the answers to questions.
> Has she **said who's coming**?
> He only **told** one person **where the money was**.

From *Practical English Usage* by Michael Swan (Oxford University Press)

Now she can rewrite the homework sentence as *He was tired of people telling him what to do* and know that she has got it right. Research has offered a powerful alternative to teacher explanation.

Chapter notes and further reading

- **Bilingual dictionaries**

  Kernerman Publishing in Israel, for example, produces a 'semi-bilingual' dictionary (*Oxford Student's Dictionary for Hebrew Speakers*) which mixes the benefits of a monolingual dictionary with Hebrew translations.

  Cambridge University Press publishes a series of bilingual books called *Word Routes* and *Word Selector* for five languages (Catalan, French, Greek, Italian, Spanish). Because they are organised by topic and concept, they have strong production potential.

- **MLDs**

  For an excellently clear history of MLD dictionary development, see M Rundell (1998).

  Many dictionaries are available on CD-ROM and some are also available on the Internet (see references on pages 152–153).

- **Concordancing**

  Concordancing packages are gradually becoming available (and usable) for teachers and students. See especially the *WordSmith Tools* software designed by Mike Scott and published by Oxford University Press and the sampler CD from the *British National Corpus* distributed by the Humanities Computing Unit of Oxford University on behalf of the BNC consortium. More information about the BNC, including details of its free online browse facility, is available at http://info.ox.ac.uk/bnc. See also the corpus references on pages 35–36.

- **Typical or divergent**

  C Owen (1996) has doubts about how useful language concordancing may be for resolving issues of correctness. He is also interesting about the limitation of computer concordances in dictionary design (Owen 1993) – though these doubts were answered by G Francis and J Sinclair (1994).

13 | Teaching pronunciation

A Pronunciation issues

Almost all English language teachers get students to study grammar and vocabulary, practise functional dialogues, take part in productive skill activities, and become competent in listening and reading. Yet some of these same teachers make little attempt to teach pronunciation in any overt way and only give attention to it in passing. It is possible that they are nervous of dealing with sounds and intonation; perhaps they feel they have too much to do already and pronunciation teaching will only make things worse. They may claim that even without a formal pronunciation syllabus, and without specific pronunciation teaching, many students seem to acquire serviceable pronunciation in the course of their studies.

However, the fact that some students are able to acquire reasonable pronunciation without overt pronunciation teaching should not blind us to the benefits of a focus on pronunciation in our lessons. Pronunciation teaching not only makes students aware of different sounds and sound features (and what these mean), but can also improve their speaking immeasurably. Concentrating on sounds, showing where they are made in the mouth, making students aware of where words should be stressed – all these things give them extra information about spoken English and help them achieve the goal of improved comprehension and intelligibility.

In some particular cases pronunciation help allows students to get over serious intelligibility problems. Joan Kerr, a speech pathologist, described (in a paper at the 1998 ELICOS conference in Melbourne, Australia) how she was able to help a Cantonese speaker of English achieve considerably greater intelligibility by working on his point of articulation – changing his focus of resonance. Whereas many Cantonese vowels happen towards the back of the mouth, English ones are frequently articulated nearer the front or in the centre of the mouth. The moment you can get Cantonese speakers, she suggested, to bring their vowels further forward, increased intelligibility occurs. With other language groups it may be a problem of nasality (e.g. Vietnamese) or the degree to which speakers do or do not open their mouths. Other language groups may have trouble with intonation or stress patterns in phrases and sentences (see Chapter 2, D2 and D5), and there are many individual sounds which cause difficulty for different first language speakers.

For all these people, being made aware of pronunciation issues will be of immense benefit not only to their own production, but also to their own understanding of spoken English.

A1   Perfection versus intelligibility

A question we need to answer is how good our students' pronunciation ought to be. Should they sound like native speakers, so perfect that just by listening to them we would assume that they were British or American or Australian? Or is this asking too much? Perhaps we should be happy if they can at least make themselves understood.

The degree to which students acquire 'perfect' pronunciation seems to depend very much on their attitude to how they speak and how well they hear. In the case of attitude there are a number of psychological issues which may well affect how 'foreign' a person sounds when they speak. For example, many students do not especially want to sound like native speakers; frequently they wish to be speakers of English as an international language and this does not necessarily imply trying to sound exactly like someone from Britain or Canada, for example. Frequently foreign language speakers want to retain their own accent when they speak the foreign language because that is part of their identity. Thus speaking English with, say, a Mexican accent is fine for the speaker who wishes to retain his or her 'Mexican-ness' in the foreign language.

Under the pressure of such cultural considerations it has become customary for language teachers to consider intelligibility as the prime goal of pronunciation teaching. This implies that the students should be able to use pronunciation which is good enough for them to be always understood. If their pronunciation is not up to this standard, it is thought, then there is a serious danger that they will fail to communicate effectively.

If intelligibility is the goal then it suggests that some pronunciation features are more important than others. Some sounds, for example, have to be right if the speaker is to get their message across (for example /n/ as in /sɪnɪŋ/ versus /ŋ/ as in /sɪŋɪŋ/) though others (for example /ð/ and /θ/) may not cause a lack of intelligibility if they are confused. Stressing words and phrases correctly is vital if emphasis is to be given to the important parts of messages and if words are to be understood correctly. Intonation – the ability to vary the pitch and tune of speech – is an important meaning carrier too.

The fact that we may want our students to work towards an intelligible pronunciation rather than achieve a native-speaker quality may not appeal to all, however. Despite what we have said about identity, some may wish to sound exactly like a native speaker. In such circumstances it would be churlish to deny them such an objective.

A2   Problems

Two particular problems occur in much pronunciation teaching and learning:

- **What students can hear:** some students have great difficulty hearing pronunciation features which we want them to reproduce. Frequently speakers of different first languages have problems with different sounds, especially where, as with /b/ and /v/ for Spanish speakers, there are not the same two sounds in their language. If they cannot distinguish between them, they will find it almost impossible to produce the two different English phonemes.

There are two ways of dealing with this: in the first place we can show students how sounds are made through demonstration, diagrams, and explanation. But we can also draw the sounds to their attention every time they appear on a tape or in our own conversation. In this way we gradually train the students' ears. When they can hear correctly they are on the way to being able to speak correctly.

- **The intonation problem:** for many teachers the most problematic area of pronunciation is intonation. Some of us (and many of our students) find it extremely difficult to hear 'tunes' or to identify the different patterns of rising and falling tones. In such situations it would be foolish to try and teach them.

  However, the fact that we may have difficulty recognising specific intonation tunes does not mean that we should abandon intonation teaching altogether. Most of us can hear when someone is being enthusiastic or bored, when they are surprised, or when they are really asking a question rather than just confirming something they already know. One of our tasks, then, is to give students opportunities to recognise such moods and intentions either on tape or through the way we ourselves model them (see Chapter 4, D2). We can then get students to imitate the way these moods are articulated, even though we may not (be able to) discuss the technicalities of the different intonation patterns themselves.

The key to successful pronunciation teaching, however, is not so much getting students to produce correct sounds or intonation tunes, but rather to have them listen and notice how English is spoken – either on audio or videotape or from the teachers themselves. The more aware they are the greater the chance that their own intelligibility levels will rise.

A3 The phonemic alphabet: to use or not to use?

It is perfectly possible to work on the sounds of English without ever using any phonemic symbols. We can get students to hear the difference, say, between *sheep* and *cheap* or between *ship* and *sheep* just by saying the words enough times. There is no reason why this should not be effective. We can also describe how the sounds are made (by demonstrating, drawing pictures of the mouth and lips, or explaining where the sounds are made).

However, since English is bedevilled, for many students (and even first language speakers), by problems of sound and spelling correspondence, it may make sense for them to be aware of the different phonemes, and the clearest way of promoting this awareness is to introduce the various symbols.

There are other reasons for using phonemic symbols too. Dictionaries usually give the pronunciation of their words in phonemic symbols. If students can read these symbols they can know how the word is said even without having to hear it. When both teacher and students know the symbols it is easier to explain what mistake has occurred and why it has happened; we can also use the symbols for pronunciation tasks and games.

Some teachers complain that learning the symbols places an unnecessary burden on students. For certain groups this may be true, and the level of strain is greatly increased if they are asked to write in phonemic script (Newton 1999). But if they are only asked to recognise rather than produce the different symbols, then the strain is not so great, especially if they are introduced to the various symbols gradually rather than all at once.

In this chapter we assume that the knowledge of phonemic script is of benefit to students.

A4 When to teach pronunciation

Just as with any aspect of language – grammar, vocabulary, etc. – teachers have to decide when to include pronunciation teaching into lesson sequences. There are a number of alternatives to choose from:

- **Whole lessons:** some teachers devote whole lesson sequences to pronunciation, and some schools timetable pronunciation lessons at various stages during the week.

   Though it would be difficult to spend a whole class period working on one or two sounds, it can make sense to work on connected speech concentrating on stress and intonation over some forty-five minutes, provided that we follow normal planning principles (see Chapter 22A). Thus we could have students do recognition work on intonation patterns, work on the stress in certain key phrases, and then move on to the rehearsing and performing of a short play extract which exemplified some of the issues we worked on.

   Making pronunciation the main focus of a lesson does not mean that every minute of that lesson has to be spent on pronunciation work. Sometimes students may also listen to a longer tape, working on listening skills before moving to the pronunciation part of the sequence. Sometimes students may work on aspects of vocabulary before going on to work on word stress, sounds, and spelling.

- **Discrete slots:** some teachers insert short, separate bits of pronunciation work into lesson sequences. Over a period of weeks they work on all the individual phonemes either separately or in contrasting pairs. At other times they spend a few minutes on a particular aspect of intonation, say, or on the contrast between two or more sounds.

   Such separate pronunciation slots can be extremely useful, and provide a welcome change of pace and activity during a lesson. Many students enjoy them, and they succeed precisely because we do not spend too long on any one issue. However, pronunciation is not a separate skill; it is part of the way we speak. Even if we want to keep our separate pronunciation phases for the reasons we have suggested, we will also need times when we integrate pronunciation work into longer lesson sequences.

- **Integrated phases:** many teachers get students to focus on pronunciation issues as an integral part of a lesson. When students listen to a tape, for example, one of the things which we can do is draw their attention to pronunciation features on the tape, if necessary having students work on sounds that are especially prominent, or getting them to imitate intonation patterns for questions, for example.

  Pronunciation teaching forms a part of many sequences where students study language form (see Chapter 11). When we model words and phrases we draw our students' attention to the way they are said; one of the things we want to concentrate on during an accurate reproduction stage (see Chapter 11, A1) is the students' correct pronunciation.

- **Opportunistic teaching:** just as teachers may stray from their original plan when lesson realities make this inevitable, and teach vocabulary or grammar opportunistically because it has 'come up' (see Chapter 11, A2), so there are good reasons why we may want to stop what we are doing and spend a minute or two on some pronunciation issue that has arisen in the course of an activity. A lot will depend on what kind of activity the students are involved in since we will be reluctant to interrupt fluency work inappropriately (see Chapter 7, C3), but tackling a problem at the moment when it occurs can be a successful way of dealing with pronunciation.

Although whole pronunciation lessons may be an unaffordable luxury for classes under syllabus and timetable pressure, many teachers tackle pronunciation in a mixture of the ways suggested above.

B Examples of pronunciation teaching

The areas of pronunciation which we need to draw our students' attention to include individual sounds they are having difficulty with, word and phrase/sentence stress, and intonation. But students will also need help with connected speech for fluency and the correspondence between sounds and spelling. All of these areas are touched on in the examples below.

B1 Working with sounds

We often ask students to focus on one particular sound. This allows us to demonstrate how it is made and show how it can be spelt – a major concern with English since there is far less one-to-one correspondence between sound and spelling than there is in some other languages – especially Romance languages.

We could follow the approach taken in the *Lifelines Intermediate* books and have students identify which words in a list (including *bird, word, worm, worth, curl, heard, first, lurch,* etc.) have the sound /ɜː/ (Hutchinson 1998: 45). They are then asked to identify the one consonant (r) which is always present in the spelling of words with this sound. We could also show or demonstrate the position of the lips when this sound is made and get students to make the sound and say words which include it.

Two more examples show specific approaches to the teaching and practising of sounds:

Example 1: *Ship* and *chip*	Sounds: /ʃ/ and /tʃ/
	Level: intermediate

Contrasting two sounds which are very similar and often confused is a popular way of getting students to concentrate on specific aspects of pronunciation.

The sequence starts with students listening to pairs of words and practising the difference between /ʃ/ and /tʃ/, for example:

ship	chip	washing	watching
sherry	cherry	cash	catch
shoes	choose	mash	match
sheep	cheap	wish	which, witch

From *Sounds English* by J O'Connor and C Fletcher (Pearson Education Ltd).
The teaching sequence described here comes directly from this book.

If they have no problem with these sounds the teacher may well move on to other sounds and/or merely do a short practice exercise as a reminder of the difference between them. But if the students have difficulty discriminating between /ʃ/ and /tʃ/ the teacher asks them to listen to a tape and, in a series of exercises, they have to work out which word they hear, for example:

1 Small shops/chops are often expensive.
2 The dishes/ditches need cleaning.
3 I couldn't mash/match these things up.
4 She enjoys washing/watching the children.

They now move on to exercises which practise each sound separately, for example:

It's very cheap.
a grey chair
a cheese sandwich
You cheat!
no chance
a pretty child

before doing a communication task which has words with the target sounds built into it, for example:

How much do you enjoy the things in the chart below?
1 very much   **2** not much   **3** not at all
Fill in the chart for yourself, and then ask three other people.

	You		
playing chess watching TV washing up going to a football match cooking chips eating chips lying in the sunshine shopping			

If, during this teaching sequence, students seem to be having trouble with either of the sounds, the teacher may well refer to a diagram of the mouth to help students see where the sounds are made, for example:

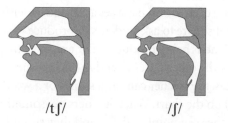

/t ʃ/   /ʃ/

Contrasting sounds in this way has a lot to recommend it. It helps students concentrate on detail, especially when they are listening to hear the small difference between the sounds. It identifies sounds that are frequently confused by various nationalities. It is manageable for the teacher (rather than taking on a whole range of sounds at the same time), and it can be good fun for the students.

This kind of exercise can be done whether or not the teacher and students work with phonemic symbols.

Example 2: The phonemic chart   Sounds: all
                                         Level: any

The writer Adrian Underhill is unambiguous about the use of phonemic symbols (see A3 above) and has produced a 'phonemic chart', which he recommends integrating into English lessons at various points.

The phonemic chart is laid out in relation to where in the mouth the forty-four sounds of southern British English are produced. In its top right-hand corner little boxes are used to describe stress patterns, and arrows are used to describe the five basic intonation patterns (i.e. fall, rise, fall–rise, rise–fall, and level):

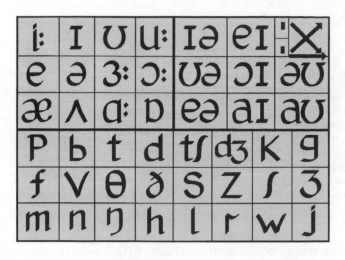

The phonemic chart from *Sound Foundations* by A Underhill (Macmillan Heinemann)

What makes this chart special are the ways in which Adrian Underhill suggests that it should be used. Because each sound has a separate square, either the teacher or the students can point to that square to ask students to produce that sound or to show they recognise which sound is being produced. For example, the teacher might point to three sounds one after the other (/ʃ/, /ɑ/, and /p/) to get the students to say *shop*. Among other possibilities, the teacher can say a sound or a word and the student has to point to the sound(s) on the chart. When learners say something and produce an incorrect sound, the teacher can point to the sound they should have made. When the teacher first models a sound he can point to it on the chart to identify it for the students (Underhill 1994: 101).

The phonemic chart can be carried around by the teacher or left on the classroom wall. If it is permanently there and easily accessible, the teacher can use it at any stage when it becomes appropriate. Such a usable resource is a wonderful teaching aid as a visit to many classrooms where the chart is in evidence will demonstrate.

There are many other techniques and activities for teaching sounds apart from the ones we have shown here. Some teachers play sound bingo where the squares on the bingo card have sounds, or phonemically 'spelt' words instead of ordinary orthographic words. When the teacher says the sound or the word the student can cross off that square of their board. When all their squares are covered they shout 'bingo'. Noughts and crosses can be played in the same way, where each square has a sound and the students have to say a word with that sound in it to get that square, for example:

/æ/	/dʒ/	/t/
/iː/	/ə/	/d/
/ə/	/ɔː/	/z/

Teachers can get students to say 'tongue-twisters' sometimes too (e.g. *She sells sea shells by the sea shore*) or to find rhymes for poetry/limerick lines. When students are familiar with the phonemic alphabet they can play 'odd man out' (five vocabulary items where one does not fit in with the others), but the words are written in phonemic script rather than ordinary orthography.

B2 Working with stress

Stress is important in individual words, in phrases, and in sentences. By shifting it around in a phrase or a sentence we can change emphasis or meaning.

As we saw in Figure 16 in Chapter 10C, it is assumed that when students meet new words in class (and if the new words end up on the board) the teacher will mark the stress of those words (using a consistent system of stress marking). Another common way of drawing our students' attention to stress issues is to show where the weak vowel sounds occur in words (rather than focusing on the stressed syllables themselves). We can draw attention to the **schwa** /ə/ in words like /fəˈtɒgrəfə/ (*photographer*), or /ˌɒpəˈtjuːnɪtɪ/ (*opportunity*).

However, we can also focus on stress issues in longer phrases and in sentences, as the following two examples demonstrate.

| **Example 3:** Fishing | Sounds: phrase stress patterns |
| | Level: pre-intermediate upwards |

The following activity (in which students are asked to recognise stress patterns in phrases) comes from a book of pronunciation games which are designed to '… engage learners in a challenge and, at the same time, highlight an aspect of pronunciation' (Hancock 1995: 1).

The sequence starts when the teacher chooses some short phrases which the students are familiar with and writes them on the board. She then reads the phrases aloud and, as she does so, draws a large circle under each stressed syllable (which will be in the content words like *belˈieve* and *ˈlater*, as opposed to grammatical words like *to*, *of*, and *by*) and small circles under the unstressed syllables.

Now that students are clued in to the big and small circles the teacher gives them a copy of the following game board:

From *Pronunciation Games* by M Hancock (Cambridge University Press)

Using the 'circles' stress patterns they have to join pairs of phrases with the same stress patterns, e.g. *Look – wait!*, *Begin! – she talked*, *Who cares? – Don't stop!* The object of the game is to discover which fish is caught (a fish is caught when it is completely surrounded by lines). If students get the exercise right they will have encircled fish B.

Students can now say the phrases and teachers can ask them to come up with their own phrases to follow the various stress patterns – or teachers can make their own game along similar lines.

Example 4: Special stress

Sounds: variable stress
Level: elementary

The stress in phrases changes depending upon what we want to say. The following exercise draws students' attention to this fact and gets them to ask why it happens.

Students listen to the following conversations:

3 Special stress

1 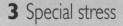 Walter is a waiter in a busy snack bar.
Listen to some of his conversations with the customers.

a W So that's two coffees, a beef sandwich, and a tomato soup …
   C *No, a chicken sandwich.*
   W Sorry, sir …

b W Yes, sir?
   C A small mushroom pizza, please.
   W Okay …
   C *No, make that a large mushroom pizza.*
   W Certainly, sir …

c W Okay, so you want one coffee, six colas, four strawberry ice-creams, two chocolate ice-creams and a piece of apple pie …
   C *No, four chocolate ice-creams and two strawberry …*
   W Anything else?

From *Headway Elementary Pronunciation* by S Cunningham and P Moor (Oxford University Press)

They are now asked to listen again and look at the lines in italics. They should underline the words that are specially stressed and then say why they think this happens in this particular conversation (because the customer is correcting a mistake). Students can then practise saying the dialogues.

We might also give students a straightforward sentence like *I lent my sister ten pounds for a train ticket last week* and ask them what it would mean if different words took the main stress, e.g. *I LENT my sister ten pounds …* (= I didn't give it to her), or *I lent my sister ten pounds for a train ticket last WEEK* (= Can you believe it? She still hasn't paid me back!).

There are many other ways of teaching and demonstrating stress. Some teachers like to choose appropriate texts and have students read them aloud after they have done some work on which bits of phrases and sentences take the main stress. Some teachers like to train students in the performance of dialogues, much as a theatre director might do with actors. This will involve identifying the main stress in phrases and seeing this in relation to the intonation patterns (see B3 below).

Cuisenaire rods (see Chapter 10D) are also useful in that they can provide graphic illustrations of how words and phrases are stressed. These rods of different lengths and colours can be set up to demonstrate the stress patterns of phrases and sentences as in the following example *I'll ring you next WEEK*:

Whereas if we want to say *I'll RING you next week* (= I won't come and see you), we can organise the rods like this:

For stress in words, we can ask students to put words in correct columns depending upon their stress patterns, for example:

■ ■ ■ ■	■ ■ ■ ■
information	discovery
consultation	recovery
aggravation	acknowledgement
insulation	catastrophe
agoraphobic	photographer

B3 Working with intonation

We need to draw our students' attention to the way we use changes in pitch to convey meaning, to reflect the thematic structure of what we are saying, and to convey mood.

One simple way of doing this is to show how many different meanings can be squeezed out of just one word such as *yes*. To do this we can get students to ask us any 'yes/no' question (e.g. *Are you happy?*) and answer *Yes* to it in a neutral way. Now we get them to ask the question again. This time, through changing our intonation, we use *Yes* to mean something different, e.g. *I'm not sure* or *How wonderful of you to ask that question* or *How dare you ask that question*. Students can be asked to identify what we mean each time by using words for emotions or matching our intonation to pictures of faces with different expressions. We can now get them to ask each other similar 'yes/no' questions and, when they answer, use intonation to convey particular meanings which their classmates have to identify.

The point of exercises like this is not so much to identify specific intonation patterns, but rather to raise the students' awareness of the power of intonation and to encourage them to vary their own speech. It also trains them to listen more carefully to understand what messages are being given to them.

Example 5: Falling and rising tones Sounds: falling and rising tones
Level: pre-intermediate

In the following exercise students listen to identify nuclear stress (that is the main stress where there is a change of pitch) in phrases and to hear falling and rising intonation:

1 Listen to these examples. Prominent words are in capital letters. Notice how the voice FALLS at the end.

It's MINE.   She's from ROME.   Is it YOURS?
I MET him at a DISCO.

Now listen to these examples. Notice how the voice RISES at the end.

I THINK so.   PROBABLY.   Are they HERE yet?
Is THIS the PARIS train?

From *Pronunciation Tasks* by M Hewings (Cambridge University Press)

When they have done this the teacher may ask them to repeat the phrases with the right intonation before moving on to Exercise 2 where they have to listen to a tape and identify whether the voice falls or rises:

2 Listen to these sentence halves. Write (↘) in the space if the voice falls at the end and write (↗) if it goes up. Two are done for you.

1 a) I went to London ... (↘)	b) ... on Saturday. (↗)
2 a) David ... ( )	b) ... works in a bookshop. ( )
3 a) There's some cake ... ( )	b) ... in the kitchen. ( )
4 a) In Hong Kong ... ( )	b) ... last year. ( )
5 a) I'm fairly sure ... ( )	b) ... it's upstairs. ( )
6 a) Yes, ... ( )	b) ... of course. ( )
7 a) Turn left here ...	b) ... then go straight on. ( )
8 a) Oh dear, ... ( )	b) ... I *am* sorry. ( )
9 a) I like it ... ( )	b) ... very much. ( )
10 a) I don't smoke ... ( )	b) ... thank you. ( )

They then join the sentence halves together before working in pairs to answer questions with their new complete sentences, e.g. *What does your son do now? David works in a bookshop*, etc. Later they make their own conversations after noticing how a character uses a rising tone for a subject which is already being talked about and a falling tone to give new information.

This exercise not only gets students to listen carefully to intonation patterns, but by dividing sentences in two before joining them up again it allows them to identify basic fall–rise patterns. We can also get students to listen to the way speakers react to see whether words like *okay* or *really* indicate enthusiasm, boredom, or indifference.

There are other ways to teach intonation too: some teachers like to get their students to make dialogues without words – humming the 'tune' of what they want to say in such a way that other students can understand them. Many teachers also use a variety of devices such as arrows on the board and arm movements which 'draw' patterns in the air to demonstrate intonation. Some teachers exaggerate (and get their students to exaggerate) intonation patterns which can be extremely amusing and which also makes patterns very clear.

B4   Sounds and spelling

Although there are many regularities in English spelling (such as word roots and grammatical endings) the fact that there is no complete one-to-one correspondence between letters and phonemes causes many problems for learners. The following two exercises are designed to teach sound–spelling correspondence for particular spellings.

Example 6: Sounds of *ou*	Level: elementary

Students are asked to listen to a tape and see how many different pronunciations they can find for the *ou* spelling in words like the following:

could	rough	country
sound	foul	thought
ground	though	house
through	out	unconscious
round	young	

They can record the different sounds in their vocabulary books (see Chapter 24, A1).

Teachers can also help students by giving them typical spellings for sounds every time they work on them. In a class on /ʃ/ and /tʃ/, for example, they can be given the following information:

S P E L L I N G

/ʃ/ Shop		/tʃ/ chin
Common:	*Less common:*	MOST **ch** chin,
ALL **sh** shop,	**ch** *in words of*	rich
wish,	*French origin:*	ALL **tch** match,
bishop	machine,	butcher,
Endings with	champagne	kitchen
ti + *vowel or*	**s** insurance	
ci + *vowel*		ALL **t** + ure
education,		future,
initial,		nature,
musician,		picture
delicious		

From *Sounds English* by J O'Connor and C Fletcher (Pearson Education Ltd)

Example 7: Looking for rules   Level: intermediate and above

In this exercise students are asked to read the following two lists of words aloud. When they have agreed that the letter *c* can be pronounced in two ways, we can ask them if they can see what the rule is which decides which pronunciation will be used. We might have to prompt them by suggesting that they look at the letter which follows the *c*.

These are the lists they see:

A		B	
cell	certain	cat	catch
place	dance	cup	coffee
city	cycle	cry	coin
policy	cent	call	cake
decide	cinema	came	cost
		custom	could

From *Teaching English Pronunciation* by J Kenworthy (Pearson Education Ltd)

This kind of discovery approach (see Chapter 11, B2) to sound and spelling rules allows students to become aware that English spelling is not quite so random as they might think.

B5   Connected speech and fluency

Good pronunciation does not just mean saying individual words or even individual sounds correctly. The sounds of words change when they come into contact with each other. This is something we need to draw students' attention to in our pronunciation teaching.

We can adopt a three-stage procedure for teaching students about features such as elision and assimilation (see Chapter 2, D4):

- **Stage 1/comparing:** we can start by showing students sentences and phrases and having them pronounce the words correctly in isolation, e.g. *I am going to see him tomorrow* /aɪ/ /æm/ /gəʊɪŋ/ /tuː/ /sɪ/ /hɪm/ /təmɒrəʊ/. We then play them a tape of someone saying the sentences in normal connected speech (or we say them ourselves), e.g. /aɪmgɒnəsɪjɪmtəmɒrəʊ/. We ask students what differences they can hear.

- **Stage 2/identifying:** we have students listen to recordings of connected speech (or we say the phrases ourselves), and the students have to write out a full grammatical equivalent of what they heard. Thus we could say /dʒəwɒnəkɒfɪ/ and expect the students to write *Do you want a coffee?*, or we could play them a tape with someone saying /aɪdəvkʌmbɪfɔː/ and expect them to write *I would have come before.*

- **Stage 3/production:** in our modelling and teaching of phrases and sentences we will give students the connected version, including contractions where necessary, and get them to say the phrases and sentences in this way.

Fluency is also helped by having students say phrases and sentences (such as the ones used in stages 1–3 above) as quickly as possible, starting slowly and then speeding up. Getting students to perform dialogues and play extracts – if we spend some time coaching them – will also make them aware of speaking customs and help them to improve their overall fluency.

Chapter notes and further reading

- **Meaning and perfection**

  For a discussion about what pronunciation norms and models we should get our students to aim for, see J Jenkins (1998). See also C Dalton and B Seidlhofer (1995: Chapter 1).

- **Different languages**

  For the pronunciation difficulties experienced by different first language speakers, see J Kenworthy (1987: Part 2). G Kelly (2000: Appendix B) lists English sounds that cause problems for different speakers.

- **Phonemic chart**

  G Kelly (2000: Appendix A) has created a different pronunciation chart for students which categorises sounds in terms of their place of articulation, and whether they are voiced or voiceless – in the case of consonants.

- **Sounds and spelling**

  See J Kenworthy (1987: Chapter 5) and G Kelly (2000: Appendix C).

14 | Teaching receptive skills

Receptive skills are the ways in which people extract meaning from the discourse they see or hear. There are generalities about this kind of processing which apply to both reading and listening – and which will be addressed in this chapter – but there are also significant differences between reading (Chapter 15) and listening (Chapter 16) processes too, and in the ways we can teach these skills in the classroom.

A How we read and listen

When we read a story or a newspaper, listen to the news, or take part in conversation we employ our previous knowledge as we approach the process of comprehension, and we deploy a range of receptive skills; which ones we use will be determined by our reading or listening purpose.

A1 What we bring to the task

If a British reader walks past a newspaper stand and sees the headline 'England in six-wicket collapse' he or she will almost certainly guess that the England cricket team has been beaten in an international match. This guess will be based on the reader's pre-existing knowledge of newspapers, their experience of how headlines are constructed, their understanding that *wicket* is a cricketing term, and their knowledge that England has not been doing too well in the sport lately. If the reader then goes on to buy the newspaper he or she will use all this pre-existing knowledge to predict the relevant article's contents both before and during the reading of it. However, a reader who did not have such pre-existing knowledge (because he or she did not know anything about cricket, for example), would find the reading task more difficult.

What the above example suggests is that understanding a piece of discourse involves much more than just knowing the language. In order to make sense of any text we need to have 'pre-existent knowledge of the world' (Cook 1989: 69). Such knowledge is often referred to as **schema** (plural **schemata**). Each of us carries in our heads mental representations of typical situations that we come across. When we are stimulated by particular words, discourse patterns, or contexts, such schematic knowledge is activated and we are able to recognise what we see or hear because it fits into patterns that we already know. As Chris Tribble points out, we recognise a letter of rejection or a letter offering a job within the first couple of lines (Tribble 1997: 35).

When we see a written text our schematic knowledge may first tell us what kind of text **genre** we are dealing with (see Chapter 2, c4). Thus if we recognise an extract as coming from a novel we will have expectations about the kind of text we are going to read. These will be different from the expectations aroused if we recognise a piece of text as coming from an instruction manual. Knowing what kind of a text we are dealing with allows us to predict the form it may take at the text, paragraph, and sentence level. Key words and phrases alert us to the subject of a text, and this again allows us, as we read, to predict what is coming next.

In conversation a knowledge of typical interactions helps participants to communicate efficiently. As the conversation continues, the speakers and listeners draw upon various schemata – including genre, topic, discourse patterning, and the use of specific language features – to help them make sense of what they are hearing. As with readers, such schemata arouse expectations which allow listeners to predict what will happen in the conversation. Such predictions give the interaction a far greater chance of success than if the participants did not have such pre-existing knowledge to draw upon.

Shared schemata make spoken and written communication efficient. Without the right kind of pre-existing knowledge, comprehension becomes much more difficult. And that is the problem for some foreign language learners who, because they have a different shared knowledge of cultural reference and discourse patterning in their own language and culture from that in the English variety they are dealing with, have to work doubly hard to understand what they see or hear.

A2 Reasons for reading and listening

When we read a sign on the motorway our motives are different from when we read a detective novel; when we take an audiotape guide round a museum we have a different purpose in mind from when we listen to a stranger giving us directions on a street corner. We can divide reasons for reading and listening into two broad categories:

- **Instrumental:** a large amount of reading and listening takes place because it will help us to achieve some clear aim. Thus, for example, we read a road sign so that we know where to go. We read the instructions on a ticket machine because we need to know how to operate it. When we ring up a technical support company because we cannot make our computer or washing machine work, we listen to a customer advisor because we are desperate to know what to do next.

   One type of reading or listening, in other words, takes place because we have some kind of utilitarian or instrumental purpose in mind.

- **Pleasurable:** another kind of reading and listening takes place largely for pleasure. Thus people read magazines or spend hours buried in the Sunday paper. Others go to poetry readings or listen to Talk Radio. Some people read illustrated cartoon or photo-stories while others listen to comedy tapes or programmes.

Instrumental reading and listening can be pleasurable too; reading history textbooks or going to history lectures (or any other subject we are studying or which interests us) may be done for fun as well as for some utilitarian purpose. There is a great deal of 'crossover' between the two categories. But a consideration of the two types does at least allow us to consider different receptive skill styles, and helps us to ensure that we do not ignore genres which students need to be able to handle.

A3 Top–down and bottom–up

A frequent distinction is made – especially in the analysis of reading – between top–down and bottom–up processing. In metaphorical terms this can be likened to the difference between looking down on something from above – getting an overview – and, on the contrary, being in the middle of something and understanding where we are by concentrating on all the individual features. It is the difference between looking at a forest, or studying the individual trees within it.

It has been said that in top–down processing the reader or listener gets a general view of the reading or listening passage by, in some way, absorbing the overall picture. This is greatly helped if the reader or listener's schemata allow them to have appropriate expectations of what they are going to come across. In bottom–up processing, on the other hand, the reader or listener focuses on individual words and phrases, and achieves understanding by stringing these detailed elements together to build up a whole.

It is probably most useful to see acts of reading and listening as interactions between top–down and bottom–up processing. Sometimes it is the individual details that help us understand the whole; sometimes it is our overview that allows us to process the details. Without a good understanding of a reasonable proportion of the details gained through some bottom–up processing we will be unable to get any clear general picture of what the text is about. A non-scientist attempting to read a specialist science journal finds this to be the case almost immediately. A person listening to a conversation in a foreign language with many words he or she does not know finds bottom–up and top–down processing almost impossible.

A4 Different skills

The processes we go through when reading a novel or listening to a poem are likely to be different from those we use when we are looking for someone's number in a telephone directory, or when we are listening to a spoken 'alert' message on a computer. Our use of these different skills will frequently depend on what we are reading or listening for.

- **Identifying the topic:** good readers and listeners are able to pick up the topic of a written or spoken text very quickly. With the help of their own schemata they quickly get an idea of what is being talked about. This ability allows them to process the text more effectively as it progresses.

- **Predicting and guessing:** both readers and listeners sometimes guess in order to try and understand what is being written or talked about, especially if they have first identified the topic. Sometimes they look forward, trying to predict what is coming; sometimes they make assumptions or guess the content from their initial glance or half-hearing – as they try and apply their schemata to what is in front of them. Their subsequent reading and listening helps them to confirm their expectations of what they have predicted or to readjust what they thought was going to happen in the light of experience.

- **Reading and listening for general understanding:** good readers and listeners are able to take in a stream of discourse and understand the **gist** of it without worrying too much about the details. Reading and listening for such 'general' comprehension means not stopping for every word, not analysing everything that the writer or speaker includes in the text.

  A term commonly used in discussions about reading is **skimming** (which means running your eyes over a text to get a quick idea of the gist of a text). By encouraging students to have a quick look at the text before plunging into it for detail, we help them to get a general understanding of what it is all about. This will help them when and if they read for more specific information.

  Gist reading and listening are not 'lazy' options. The reader or listener has made a choice not to attend to every detail, but to use their processing powers to get more of a top–down view of what is going on.

- **Reading and listening for specific information:** in contrast to reading and listening for gist, we frequently go to written and spoken text because we want specific details. We may listen to the news, only concentrating when the particular item that interests us comes up. We may quickly look through a film review to find the name of the director or the star. In both cases we almost ignore all the other information until we come to the specific item we are looking for. In discussions about reading this skill is frequently referred to as **scanning**.

- **Reading and listening for detailed information:** sometimes we read and listen in order to understand everything we are reading in detail. This is usually the case with written instructions or directions, or with the description of scientific procedures; it happens when someone gives us their address and telephone number and we write down all the details. If we are in an airport and an announcement starts with *Here is an announcement for passengers on flight AA671 to Lima* (and if that is where we are going), we listen in a concentrated way to everything that is said.

- **Interpreting text:** readers and listeners are able to see beyond the literal meaning of words in a passage, using a variety of clues to understand what the writer or speaker is implying or suggesting. Successful interpretation of this kind depends to a large extent on shared schemata as in the example of the lecturer who, by saying to a student *You're in a non-smoking zone* was understood to be asking the student to put her cigarette out (see page 23).

  We get a lot more from a reading or listening text than the words alone suggest because, as active participants, we use our schemata together with our knowledge of the world to expand the pictures we have been given, and to fill in the gaps which the writer or speaker seems to have left.

B Problems and solutions

The teaching and learning of receptive skills presents a number of particular problems which will need to be addressed. These are to do with language, topic, the tasks students are asked to perform, and the expectations they have of reading and listening, as we shall discuss below.

B1 Language

What is it that makes a text difficult? In the case of written text some researchers look at word and sentence-length (Wallace 1992: 77), on the premise that texts with longer sentences and longer words will be more difficult to understand than those with shorter ones. Others, however, claim that the critical issue is quite simply the number of unfamiliar words which the text contains. If readers and listeners do not know half the words in a text, they will have great difficulty in understanding the text as a whole. To be successful they have to recognise a high proportion of the vocabulary without consciously thinking about it (Paran 1996). It is clear that both sentence length and the percentage of unknown words both play their part in a text's comprehensibility.

When students who are engaged in listening encounter unknown lexis it can be 'like a dropped barrier causing them to stop and think about the meaning of a word and thus making them miss the next part of the speech' (Underwood 1989: 17). Unlike reading, there may be no opportunity to go back and listen to the lexis again. Comprehension is gradually degraded, therefore, and unless the listener is able to latch on to a new element to help them back into the flow of what is being said the danger is that they will lose heart and gradually disengage from the receptive task since it is just too difficult.

If, as Stephen Krashen suggests, comprehensible input aids language acquisition (see Chapter 5B), then it follows that 'incomprehensible' input will not. We can try and get students to read or listen to such texts, but the only effect this will probably have is to de-motivate them.

Apart from the obvious point that the more language we expose students to the more they will learn, there are specific ways of addressing the problem of language difficulty: pre-teaching vocabulary, using extensive reading/listening, and considering alternatives to authentic language.

- **Pre-teaching vocabulary:** one way of helping students is to pre-teach vocabulary that is in the reading or listening text. This removes at least some of the barriers to understanding which they are likely to encounter.

    However, if we want to give students practice in what it is like to tackle authentic reading and listening texts for general understanding then getting past words they do not understand is one of the skills they need to develop. By giving them some or all of those words we deny them that chance.

    We need a common-sense solution to this dilemma: where students are likely to be held back unnecessarily because of three or four words, it makes sense to teach them first. Where they should be able to comprehend the text despite some unknown words, we can leave vocabulary work till later (see Chapter 15, A3).

An appropriate compromise is to use some (possibly unknown) words from a reading or listening text as part of our procedure to create interest and activate the students' schemata, since the words may suggest topic, genre, or construction – or all three. The students can first research the meanings of words and phrases (see Chapter 12) and then predict what a text with such words is likely to be about (see Example 1 in Chapter 15, B1).

- **Extensive reading and listening:** most researchers like to make a difference between 'extensive' and 'intensive' reading and listening. Whereas the former suggests reading or listening at length, often for pleasure and in a leisurely way, intensive reading or listening tends to be more concentrated, less relaxed, and often dedicated not so much to pleasure as to the achievement of a study goal.

  Extensive reading and listening frequently take place when students are on their own, whereas intensive reading or listening is often done with the help and/or intervention of the teacher.

  Extensive reading – especially where students are reading material written specially at their level – has a number of benefits for the development of a student's language (see Chapter 15, A1). Colin Davis suggests that any classroom will be the poorer for the lack of an extensive reading programme, and will be 'unable to promote its pupils' language development in all aspects as effectively as if such a programme were present' (1995: 335). He also claims that such a programme will make students more positive about reading, improve their overall comprehension skills, and give them a wider passive and active vocabulary. Richard Day and Julian Bamford agree, citing as two of the many goals for extensive reading, enabling students to read without constantly stopping and providing an increased word recognition (Day and Bamford 1998).

  What these commentators and others are claiming is that extensive reading is the best possible way for students to develop automaticity – that is the automatic recognition of words when they see them. It is by far the best way to improve their English reading (and writing) overall.

  The benefits of extensive reading are echoed by the benefits for extensive listening: the more students listen, the more language they acquire, and the better they get at listening activities in general. Whether they choose passages from textbooks, recordings of simplified readers, listening material designed for their level, or recordings of radio programmes which they are capable of following, the effect will be the same. Provided the input is comprehensible they will gradually acquire more words and greater schematic knowledge which will, in turn, resolve many of the language difficulties they started out with.

- **Authenticity:** because it is vital for students to get practice in dealing with written text and speech where they miss quite a few words but are still able to extract the general meaning, an argument can be made for using mainly authentic reading and listening texts in class. After all, it is when students come into contact with 'real' language that they have to work hardest to understand.

Authentic material is language where no concessions are made to foreign speakers. It is normal, natural language used by native – or competent – speakers of a language. This is what our students encounter (or will encounter) in real life if they come into contact with target-language speakers, and, precisely because it is authentic, it is unlikely to be simplified, spoken slowly, or to be full of simplistic content (as some textbook language has a tendency to be).

Authentic material which has been carelessly chosen can be extremely de-motivating for students (see Chapter 3, C2) since they will not understand it. Instead of encouraging such failure, therefore, we should let students read and listen to things they can understand. For beginners this may mean roughly-tuned language from the teacher and specially designed reading and listening texts from materials writers. However, it is essential that such listening texts approximate to authentic language use. The language may be simplified, but it must not be unnatural. As Ronald Carter and his colleagues suggest, 'concocted, made-up language can be perfectly viable but it should be modelled on naturalistic samples' (Carter et al. 1998: 86).

Authentic material can be used by students at fairly low levels, however, if the tasks that go with it are well designed and help students understand it better, rather than showing them how little they know. A gently paced sequence of activities with small tasks leading to bigger ones, for example, can enable students to watch television soap operas in English and end up understanding far more than they might have thought possible (Farrell 1998).

It is worth pointing out that deciding what is or is not authentic is not easy. A stage play, written for native speakers, is a playwright's representation of spontaneous speech rather than the real thing, so it is, in a sense, both authentic and inauthentic. A father talking to his baby daughter may be employing 'baby talk' – rough-tuning the language so that it can be comprehensible – but there is nothing inauthentic about it. The language which students are exposed to has just as strong claims to authenticity as the play or the parent, provided that it is not altered in such a way as to make it unrecognisable in style and construction from the language which native speakers encounter in many walks of life.

B2 Topic and genre

Many receptive skill activities prove less successful than anticipated because the topic is not appropriate or because students are not familiar with the genre they are dealing with. If students are not interested in a topic, or if they are unfamiliar with the text genre we are asking them to work on, they may be reluctant to engage fully with the activity. Their lack of engagement or schematic knowledge may be a major hindrance to successful reading or listening.

To resolve such problems we need to think about how we choose and use topics, and how we approach different reading and speaking genres:

- **Choose the right topics:** we should try and choose topics which our students will be interested in. We can find this out by questionnaires, interviews, or by the reactions of students in both current and previous classes to various activities and topics we have used (see Chapter 24, B1). However, individual students have individual interests, so that it is unlikely that all members of a class will be interested in the same things (see Chapter 3, B5). For this reason we need to include a variety of topics across a series of lessons so that all our students' interests will be catered for in the end.

- **Create interest:** if we can get the students engaged in the task (see Chapter 6, A3) there is a much better chance that they will read or listen with commitment and concentration, whether or not they were interested in the topic to start with.

    We can get students engaged by talking about the topic, by showing a picture for prediction, by asking them to guess what they are going to see or hear on the basis of a few words or phrases from the text, or by having them look at headlines or captions before they read the whole thing. Perhaps we will show them a picture of someone famous and get them to say if they know anything about that person before they read a text about them or hear them talking. Perhaps students can be asked to say which sport they might find most frightening (as a lead-in to a listening about ski-jumping or mountaineering).

- **Activate schemata:** in the same way we create interest by giving students predictive tasks and interesting activities, we want to activate their knowledge before they read or listen so that they bring their schemata to the text. If they are going to read 'lonely hearts' advertisements (see Chapter 2, C4) we can discuss how they expect them to be constructed as a way of directing their reading. We can ask them what they know about the way speeches are structured if they are going to listen to someone proposing the health of a couple at a wedding, or talk about the kinds of questions an interviewer might use with a celebrity if they were going to listen to an interview with a sports star.

- **Vary topics and genres:** a way of countering student unfamiliarity with certain written and spoken genres is to make sure we expose them to a variety of different text types, from written instructions and taped announcements to stories in books and live, spontaneous conversation, from Internet pages to business letters, from pre-recorded messages on phone lines to radio dramas.

    In good general English coursebooks a number of different genres are represented in both reading and listening activities. If the teacher is not following a coursebook, however, then it is a good idea to make a list of text genres which are relevant to the students' needs and interests in order to be sure that they will experience an appropriate range of texts. Ensuring students' confidence with more than one genre becomes vitally important, too, in the teaching of productive skills (see Chapter 17, A3).

B3 **Comprehension tasks**

A key feature in the successful teaching of receptive skills concerns the choice of comprehension tasks. Sometimes such tasks appear to be testing the students rather than helping them to understand. Although reading and listening are perfectly proper mediums for language and skill testing (see Chapter 23, B3), nevertheless, if we are trying to encourage students to improve their receptive skills, testing them will not be an appropriate way of accomplishing this. Sometimes texts and/or the tasks which accompany them are far too easy or far too difficult.

In order to resolve these problems we need to use comprehension tasks which promote understanding and we need to match text and task appropriately.

- **Testing and teaching:** the best kinds of tasks are those which raise students' expectations, help them tease out meanings, and provoke an examination of the reading or listening passage. Unlike reading and listening tests, these tasks bring them to a greater understanding of language and text construction. By having students perform activities such as looking up information on the Internet, filling in forms on the basis of a listening tape, or solving reading puzzles, we are helping them become better readers and listeners.

  Some tasks seem to fall half way between testing and teaching, however, since by appearing to demand a right answer (for example, by asking if certain statements about the text are true or false, or by asking questions about the text with *what, when, how many,* and *how often*) they could, in theory, be used to assess student performance. Indeed when they are done under test conditions, their purpose is obviously to explore student strengths and weaknesses. Yet such comprehension items can also be an indispensable part of a teacher's receptive skills armoury too. By the simple expedient of having students work in pairs to agree on whether a statement about part of a text is true or false – or as a result of a discussion between the teacher and the class – the comprehension items help each individual (through conversation and comparison) to understand something, rather than challenging them to give right answers under test-like conditions. If students predict the answers to such questions before they read or listen, expectations are created in their minds to help them focus their reading or listening. In both cases we have turned a potential test task into a creative tool for receptive skill training.

  Whatever the reading task, in other words, a lot will depend on the conditions in which students are asked to perform that task. Even the most formal test-like items can be used to help students rather than frighten them!

- **Appropriate challenge:** when asking students to read and listen we want to avoid texts and tasks that are either far too easy or far too difficult. As with many other language tasks we want to get the level of challenge right, to make the tasks 'difficult but achievable' (Scrivener 1994b: 149).

  Getting the level right depends on the right match between text and task. Thus, where a text is difficult, we may still be able to use it, but only if the task is appropriate. We could theoretically, for example, have beginners listen to the famous soliloquy from Shakespeare's Hamlet (*To be or not to be?/That is the question./Whether 'tis nobler ...*, etc.) and ask them how many people are speaking. We could ask students to read *Ulysses* by James Joyce and ask them how many full stops they can find. Despite the difficulty of the texts, both of these tasks are achievable. Yet we might feel that neither is appropriate or useful. On the other hand, having students listen to a news broadcast where the language level is very challenging, may be entirely appropriate if the task only asks them – at first – to try and identify the five main topics in the broadcast.

B4 Negative expectations

Students sometimes have low expectations of reading and listening. They can feel that they are not going to understand the passage in the book or on tape because it is bound to be too difficult, and they predict that the whole experience will be frustrating and de-motivating.

Such attitudes, where they exist, are often due to previous unhappy or unsuccessful experiences. If, in the past, students have been given reading and listening texts which are too difficult for them, that will colour their view of the process. If they have been given reading or listening passages in which they have no interest (and where teachers failed to excite their interest) then they are likely to expect future procedures to be boring – so they probably will be.

Where students have low expectations of reading and listening (and of course not all students do) it will be our job to persuade them, through our actions, to change these negative expectations into realistic optimism.

- **Manufacturing success:** by getting the level of challenge right (in terms of language, text, and tasks) we can ensure that students are successful. By giving students a clear and achievable purpose, we can help them to achieve that purpose. Each time we offer them a challenging text which we help them to read or listen to successfully, we dilute the negative effect of past experiences, and create ideal conditions for future engagement.

- **Agreeing on a purpose:** it is important for teacher and students to agree on both general and specific purposes for their reading or listening. Are the students trying to discover detailed information or just get a general understanding of what something is about? Perhaps they are listening to find out the time of the next train; maybe they are reading in order to discern only whether a writer approves of the person they are describing.

  If students know why they are reading or listening they can choose how to approach the text. If they understand the purpose they will have a better chance of knowing how well they have achieved it.

Chapter notes and further reading

- **Schema**

  For more (and slightly differing) accounts of schema theory see G Cook (1989: 68–74), C Wallace (1992: 33–38), and C Tribble (1997: 33–35).

- **Pre-teaching vocabulary**

  J Field (1998b) thinks that pre-teaching vocabulary for listening may be unhelpful in the development of listening skills.

Reading

A Extensive and intensive reading

To get maximum benefit from their reading, students need to be involved in both extensive and intensive reading. Whereas with the former a teacher encourages students to choose for themselves what they read and to do so for pleasure and general language improvement, the latter is often (but not exclusively) teacher chosen and directed, and is designed to enable students to develop specific receptive skills (see Chapter 14, A4).

A1 Extensive reading

We have discussed the importance of extensive reading for the development of our students' word recognition – and for their improvement as readers overall (see Chapter 14, B1). But it is not enough to tell students to 'read a lot'; we need to offer them a programme which includes appropriate materials, guidance, tasks, and facilities such as permanent or portable libraries of books.

- **Extensive reading materials:** one of the fundamental conditions of a successful extensive reading programme is that students should be reading material which they can understand. If they are struggling to understand every word, they can hardly be reading for pleasure – the main goal of this activity. This means that we need to provide books which either by chance, or because they have been specially written, are readily accessible to our students.

  Specially written materials for extensive reading – what Richard Day and Julian Bamford call 'language learner literature' (1998: 61) – are often referred to as 'readers' or 'simplified readers'. They can take the form of original fiction and non-fiction books as well as simplifications of established works of literature. Such books succeed because the writers or adaptors work within specific lists of allowed words and grammar. This means that students at the appropriate level can read them with ease and confidence. At their best such books, despite the limitations on language, can speak to the reader through the creation of atmosphere and/or compelling plot lines. Consider, for example, the following short extract from the second chapter of a level 1 (elementary) murder mystery for adults. In the first chapter a man in a hospital bed appears to be suffering from amnesia. In the second chapter that same man speaks to us directly:

There is a man near my bed. His clothes are white. No. Some of his clothes are white. He has a white coat, but his trousers are brown. He also has brown hair. The man in the white coat says he's a doctor. He says his name is Doctor Cox. He tells me to call him Philip. He says he is going to help me.

But he's not going to help me. They think I don't remember. They think I don't know anything. They know nothing, the doctors. Or the police. Nobody knows who I am. I sit in the bed and answer questions. They ask lots of questions.

'Do you know what amnesia is, John?' Doctor Cox asks me.

Doctor Cox. Doctor Philip Cox. He thinks he's somebody. He's nobody. I know what amnesia is.

From *John Doe* by A Moses (Cambridge University Press)

The language is simple and controlled, but the atmosphere – in true murder-mystery style – is satisfyingly creepy. A student who likes this kind of story and whose level of English is fairly low should enjoy it enormously.

- **Setting up a library:** in order to set up an extensive reading programme, we need to build up a library of suitable books. Although this may appear costly, it will be money well spent. If necessary, we should persuade our schools and institutions to provide such funds, or raise money through other sources.

  If possible, we should organise static libraries in the classroom or in some other part of a school. If this is not possible we need to work out some way of carrying the books around with us – in boxes or on trolleys.

  Once books have been purchased, we should code them for level and genre so that students can easily identify what kind of books they are. We should make the students aware of what the library contains and explain our classification system to them.

  We need to devise some way of keeping track of the books in the library. A simple signing-out system should ensure that our collection does not disappear over time.

  All of these setting-up procedures take time. But we can use students to help us administer the scheme. We can, if we are lucky, persuade the school administration to help us.

  If our students take part in extensive reading programmes, all the time we have spent on setting up a library will not have been wasted.

- **The role of the teacher in extensive reading programmes:** most students will not do a lot of extensive reading by themselves unless they are encouraged to do so by their teachers. Clearly, then, our role is crucial. We need to promote reading and by our own espousal of reading as a valid occupation, persuade students of its benefits. Perhaps, for example, we can occasionally read aloud from books we like and show, by our manner of reading, how exciting books can be.

Having persuaded our students about the benefits of extensive reading, we can organise reading programmes where we indicate to students how many books we expect them to read over a given period. We can explain how they can make their choice of what to read, making it clear that the choice is theirs, but that they can consult other students' reviews and comments to help them make that choice. We can suggest that they look for books in a genre (be it crime fiction, romantic novels, science fiction, etc.) that they enjoy, and that they make appropriate level choices. We will act throughout as part organiser, part tutor (see Chapter 4B).

- **Extensive reading tasks:** because students should be allowed to choose their own reading texts, following their own likes and interests, they will not all be reading the same texts at once. For this reason – and because we want to prompt students to keep reading – we should encourage them to report back on their reading in a number of ways.

  One approach is to set aside a time at various points in a course – say every two weeks – at which students can ask questions and/or tell their classmates about books they have found particularly enjoyable, or noticeably awful. However, if this is inappropriate because not all students read at the same speed – or because they often do not have much to say about the book in front of their colleagues – we can ask them each to keep a weekly reading diary either on its own, or as part of any learning journal they may be writing (see Chapter 24, A1). Students can also write short book reviews for the class noticeboard. At the end of a month, a semester, or a year, they can vote on the most popular book in the library.

  We can also put comment sheets into the books for students to write in, as the following example for a book called *The Earthquake* shows:

Rating	Your comment and Your Name
5	I'm afraid earthquake happens to us. Shoko
5	Great! Gabriel is nice. He is cool. TOMOKO
4	"Who is really taking care of me," I think after reading this book. YOKO
4	I had a chance to think what's the most important thing by reading this book. Hisako

From *Extensive Reading in the Second Language Classroom* by R Day and J Bamford
(Cambridge University Press)

It does not really matter which of these tasks students are asked to perform provided that what they are asked to do helps to keep them reading as much and as often as possible.

A2 Intensive reading: the roles of the teacher

In order to get students to read enthusiastically in class, we need to work to create interest in the topic and tasks (see Chapter 14, B2). However, there are further roles we need to adopt when asking students to read intensively:

- **Organiser:** we need to tell students exactly what their reading purpose is (see Chapter 14, B4), and give them clear instructions about how to achieve it, and how long they have to do this. Once we have said 'You have four minutes for this' we should not change that time unless observation (see below) suggests that it is necessary.

- **Observer:** when we ask students to read on their own we need to give them space to do so. This means restraining ourselves from interrupting that reading, even though the temptation may be to add more information or instructions.

  While students are reading we can observe their progress since this will give us valuable information about how well they are doing individually and collectively, and will tell us whether to give them some extra time or, instead, move to organising feedback more quickly than we had anticipated.

- **Feedback organiser:** when our students have completed the task, we can lead a feedback session to check that they have completed the task successfully. We may start by having them compare their answers in pairs and then ask for answers from the class in general or from pairs in particular. Students often appreciate giving paired answers like this since, by sharing their knowledge, they are also sharing their responsibility for the answers.

  When we ask students to give answers we should always ask them to say where in the text they found the information for their answers. This provokes a detailed study of the text which will help them the next time they come to a similar reading passage. It also tells us exactly what comprehension problems they have if and when they get answers wrong.

  It is important to be supportive when organising feedback after reading if we are to counter any negative feelings students might have about the process (see Chapter 14, B4), and if we wish to sustain their motivation (see Chapter 3, C3).

- **Prompter:** when students have read a text we can prompt them to notice language features in that text (see Chapter 5C). We may also, as controllers, direct them to certain features of text construction, clarifying ambiguities, and making them aware of issues of text structure which they had not come across previously.

A3 Intensive reading: the vocabulary question

A common paradox in reading lessons is that while teachers are encouraging students to read for general understanding, without worrying about the meaning of every single word, the students, on the other hand, are desperate to know what each individual word means. Given half a chance, many of them would rather tackle a reading passage with a dictionary (electronic or otherwise) in one hand and a pen in the other to write translations all over the page!

It is easy to be dismissive of such student preferences, yet as Carol Walker points out, 'It seems contradictory to insist that students "read for meaning" while simultaneously discouraging them from trying to understand the text at a deeper level than merely gist' (1998: 172). Clearly we need to find some accommodation between our desire to have students develop particular reading skills (such as the ability to understand the general message without understanding every detail) and their natural urge to understand the meaning of every single word.

One way of reaching a compromise is to strike some kind of a bargain with a class (see Chapter 6, B1) whereby they will do more or less what we ask of them provided that we do more or less what they ask of us. Thus we may encourage students to read for general understanding without understanding every word on a first or second read-through. But then, depending on what else is going to be done, we can give them a chance to ask questions about individual words and/or give them a chance to look them up. That way both parties in the teaching–learning transaction have their needs met.

A word of caution needs to be added here. If students ask for the meaning of all the words they do not know – and given some of the problems inherent in the explaining of different word meanings – the majority of a lesson may be taken up in this way. We need, therefore, to limit the amount of time spent on vocabulary checking in the following ways:

- **Time limit:** we can give a time limit of, say, five minutes for vocabulary enquiry, whether this involves dictionary use, language corpus searches, or questions to the teacher.

- **Word/phrase limit:** we can say that we will only answer questions about five or eight words or phrases.

- **Meaning consensus:** we can get students to work together to search for and find word meanings. To start the procedure individual students write down three to five words from the text they most want to know the meaning of. When they have each done this, they share their list with another student and come up with a new joint list of only five words. This means they will probably have to discuss which words to leave out. Two pairs join to make new groups of four and once again they have to pool their lists and end up with only five words. Finally (perhaps after new groups of eight have been formed – it depends on the atmosphere in the class) students can look for meanings of their words in dictionaries and/or we can answer questions about the words which the groups have decided on.

  This process works for two reasons. In the first place students may well be able to tell each other about some of the words which individual students did not know. More importantly, perhaps, is the fact that by the time we are asked for meanings, the students really do want to know them because the intervening process has encouraged them to invest some time in the meaning search. 'Understanding every word' has been changed into a cooperative learning task in its own right.

In responding to a natural hunger for vocabulary meaning both teachers and students will have to compromise. It is unrealistic to expect only one-sided change, but there are ways of dealing with the problem which make a virtue out of what seems – to many teachers – a frustrating necessity.

B Reading lesson sequences

We use intensive reading sequences in class for a number of reasons. We may want to have students practise specific skills such as reading to extract specific information, or reading for general understanding (gist) (see Chapter 14, A4). We may, on the other hand, get students to read texts for communicative purposes, as part of other activities, as sources of information, or in order to identify specific uses of language. Reading is often a prelude to a speaking or writing activity (see Chapter 17, B1).

Most reading sequences involve more than one reading skill. We may start by having students read for gist and then get them to read the text again for detailed comprehension. They may start by identifying the topic of a text before scanning it quickly to recover specific information; they may read for specific information before going back to the text to identify features of text construction.

B1 Examples of reading sequences

In the following examples the reading activity is specified. The skills which are involved are detailed, and the way that the text can be used within a lesson is explained.

Example 1: AKA Diaz	Activity: reading to confirm expectations
	Skills: predicting, reading for gist, reading for detailed comprehension
	Age: adult
	Level: upper intermediate

In this example students predict the content of a text not from a picture, but from a few tantalising clues they are given (in the form of phrases from the passage they will read).

The teacher gives each student in the class a letter from A to E. She then tells all the students to close their eyes. She then asks all the students with the letter A to open their eyes and shows them the word: *lion*, written large so that they can see it. Then she makes them close their eyes again and this time shows the B students the phrase *racial groups*. She shows the C students the phrase *paper aeroplanes*, the D students the word *tattoos*, and the E students the word *guard*.

She now puts the students in five-person groups composed of students A–E. By discussing their words and phrases, each group has to try and predict what the text is all about. The teacher can go round the groups encouraging them and, perhaps, feeding them with new words like *cage*, *the tensest man*, or *moral authority*, etc.

Finally, when the groups have made some predictions, the teacher asks them whether they would like to hear the text that all the words came from before reading the following text aloud, investing it with humour and making the reading dramatic and enjoyable.

'This is it,' Rick said, in a cheerful voice. Through the windows of the classroom I could see the men. They were not in their seats; instead they were circling the room restlessly, like lions in a cage.

'Is there going to be a guard in the room while I teach?' I asked. I realized that this was something that should have been straightened out earlier.

Rick looked at me with deep concern. 'I'll come by a bit later, see that you're OK,' he said.

I walked through the door into the classroom. My students barely looked human. The desks were arranged in no special order, except that some of the men had got into racial groups. Many of them were smoking, and under the glare of the lights I could see their tattoos. One man with a pointed beard and a long mane of black hair circled behind me and around the other side of the desk. He was easily the tensest man I had ever seen. I thought of telling him to sit down but wondered what I would do if he refused so I kept the suggestion to myself. I placed my leather bag on the desk and faced the class. Nobody paid any attention to me. The conversation grew louder. I wanted to cut out and run. I had volunteered for this.

Every teacher has these moments of panic. We worry about rebellion: our moral authority lost, the students taking over. I had a teacher in high school, a Miss Hutchinson, who after taking roll would turn towards the board and be followed by an avalanche of paper aeroplanes and spitballs, sometimes even the bodies of students flying forward, an impromptu riot.

I unpacked my bag and began the roll. A few names down, I called out 'Diaz.' No answer. 'Diaz,' I said again.

'Ain't my name,' a man in the front row volunteered.

'Why did you answer?' I asked.

'I'm here under another name,' he said. 'An alias. I could tell you my real name, but then I'd have to kill you.'

'We'll count that as "present",' I said. Several members of the class laughed: at least that slowed down the conversation. I finished the roll and handed out the syllabus for the class. I read it aloud and when I got to the end I looked up. 'So any questions?' I asked. The paper trembled in my hand.

'Yeah, I got a question.' AKA Diaz raised his hand. 'I want to know what the *&!* it means.'

From *Maximum Security* by R O'Connor in the literary magazine *Granta* (no. 54, 1996)

The students now read the text for themselves to answer the following detailed comprehension questions:

1 True, false, or probably (not)?
  a The class is in a prison.
  b There's a guard in the classroom.
  c Robert O'Connor had offered to teach the class.
  d There are white, black, Hispanic and Asian students in the class.
  e The class has both sexes.
  f Robert O'Connor was frightened.
  g The men threw paper aeroplanes at the teacher.
  h The men wanted to take the class.
  i Diaz is the man's real name.
  j AKA means 'also known as'.
  k The class was going to be a great success.

Before moving on to work with the content of the text the teacher may well take advantage of the language in it to study some aspects that are of interest. For example, how is the meaning of *would* different in the sentences *I wondered what I would do if he refused* and *a teacher … who … would turn towards the board …*? Can students make sentences using the same construction as *He was easily the tensest man I had ever seen* (e.g. *He/she was easily the* (superlative adjective + noun) *I had ever* (past participle)) or *I could tell you my real name, but then I'd have to kill you* (e.g. *I could … but then I'd have to …*)?

The discussion possibilities for this text are endless. How many differences are there between Robert O'Connor's class and the students' own class? How many similarities are there? How would they (the students) handle working in a prison? Should prisoners be given classes anyway, and if so, of what kind? What would the students themselves do if they were giving their first English class in a prison or in a more ordinary school environment?

Part of this sequence has involved the teacher reading aloud. This can be very powerful if it is not overdone (see Chapter 4, D2). By mixing the skills of speaking, listening, and reading the students have had a rich language experience, and because they have had a chance to predict content, listen, read and then discuss the text, they are likely to be very involved with the procedure.

Example 2: Going home	Activity: general reading
	Skills: reading for gist, reading for detailed comprehension
	Age: any
	Level: upper intermediate

Many years ago Michael Scott and his colleagues working at university level with ESP students in Brazil designed a 'standard exercise' which could be used by their students with any reading text (Scott et al. 1984). In their version the questions were detailed and were in Portuguese. The usefulness of the questions was assured because any students, even if they were having trouble with their spoken English, could read a text with the help of this broad-based reading 'kit'.

For general English we can use the same principle, and design questions which can be given to students in English or in their own language, and which can be used for any reading text they meet. Consider the following general questions:

> 1 What is the text about?
> 2 Who was it written by?
> 3 Who was it written for?
> 4 What is the writer's intention?
> 5 Do you like the text?

These can be used with any text such as the one opposite (page 219), where, when students have discussed their answers to the reading kit questions, they can then go back to the text to answer more detailed questions (e.g. *Who went for a picnic? Who has to pay rupees?*). The teacher may then want to draw their attention to certain items of vocabulary in the text with a task such as:

> **Match the words from the text with their definitions.**
> **a** gesturing   **i**   move eyes in order to see something
> **b** glance   **ii**   give a short quick look
> **c** grins   **iii** looking at something for a period of time, often
> **d** look   when it is moving/doing something
> **e** smile   **iv** look for a long time with eyes wide open because of
> **f** stare   interest, surprise, etc. Can be rude.
> **g** watching   **v**   moving hands, arms, head, etc. to express an idea or
>   feeling
>   **vi** smile widely
>   **vii** use the position of the mouth to show pleasure

The students can now make sentences with these words using the pronouns *I* or *we*, e.g. *I like it when people smile at me.* They could discuss why Penny has written her story in the present tense, and they could then go on to talk about journeys they have made, or discuss how they feel if they spend a long time away from home. Or perhaps they could work on an exercise like the following:

> **You are going home after six months in the jungle or on a desert island. Copy and complete the chart with things you are looking forward to most when you get home.**
>
> | | |
> |---|---|
> | food | |
> | drink | |
> | object(s) | |
> | activity | |

In whatever ways the text is exploited, the use of the general questions ensures that students will approach it – for the first read anyway – in a general way.

19-year-old Penny Elvey and her project partner Anna are going home after six months as volunteers in a school in Nepal. But then the rain starts, and the roads are flooded. This is part of their story.

At the village of Meestal there is a huge river blocking our path. We came here a few weeks ago with some students for a picnic but the innocent little stream that we sat by had now become a raging torrent.

Across the water we can see a truck. On our side a man approaches us.

'That is my friend,' he says gesturing to a man standing by the vehicle. 'You go with truck.'

Anna and I smile enthusiastically. But our guide steps forward.

'It is too dangerous. We must wait. The river will become smaller.'

Anna and I glance at each other. It is a curious philosophy since the rain is still falling steadily.

The truck driver's friend grins at me.

'We help. You give me 600 rupees.'

600 rupees is far too much but we are desperate. He knows. He knows I know he knows. Our eyes lock.

People are watching us curiously to see how we are going to react. I fold my arms and force a laugh.

'Then we will stay the night here.'

For a terrible moment I think he is going to walk away, but then he smiles nervously.

'I mean 300 for you; 300 for your friend.'

He calls two of his friends and they hold our luggage above their heads as they step into the water. Slowly and steadily they cross the river and reach the other side safely.

Suddenly a man taps my shoulder.

'For you too dangerous. You must stay here.'

My rucksack and walking boots are now sitting on a rock across the water. In the pocket of my rucksack are all my papers and money. Where my passport goes I follow. Maybe the current is not that strong.

'You can swim?'

A small crowd of people gathers on the other side. Anna goes first. Four men take hold of her and lead her safely across. Now it is my turn. I step forward gingerly but catch my ankle on a rock. The water pulls my legs away from under me. But the men drag me to the safety of the far side.

Anna and I pick up our things and climb into the old truck. The people there stare at us in amusement. We are wet through, covered in mud, our clothes in tatters. But as the truck shudders to life, we look at each other and smile. We are going to make it to Kathmandu in time for breakfast!

Adapted from *Network*, the *GAP Activity Projects* annual newsletter

Of course many texts can be used in this way, whether for beginners or advanced students.

Example 3: Village of snakes	Activity: modified cloze text
	Skills: reading for gist, reading for detailed comprehension
	Age: teenage
	Level: elementary

A popular test of comprehension is the 'modified' cloze procedure (see Chapter 23, B2) where every *n*th word is replaced by a blank. Although there may be some doubts about this as a testing technique, when used with students for fun it can be a good way to help them arrive at a general understanding of a piece of text and a detailed understanding of the sentences in it. It may be necessary, however, for the teacher to choose some of the words that will be replaced by blanks – because some of them which happen, say, every seventh word, may cause too much trouble and should therefore be avoided.

In this example, teenage students are going to read about snakes and snake charmers in an Indian village. The teacher starts by asking students if they know any words about snakes and the people who play music to snakes. Words like *poison*, *poisonous*, and *snake charmer* will then be elicited.

Students are now given the following text and asked to work with a colleague to see if they can fill in the blanks as they read:

VILLAGE OF SNAKES

by Sohan Devu

Saperagaon isn't an ordinary Indian village – (1) _____ a village of snake charmers. In (2) _____ house in the village there are (3) _____ lot of poisonous snakes; vipers, kraits (4) _____ cobras. Each one of these snakes (5) _____ poisonous enough to kill you, but (6) _____ children love playing with them.

It (7) _____ the beginning of a new day (8) _____ Saperagaon. The sun is coming up. Twelve-(9) _____ -old Ravi is happy because it (10) _____ warm enough to wake the cobras. (11) _____ opens the basket and a king cobra (12) _____ its head. It hisses and then (13) _____ to bite. 'It doesn't like waking (14) _____ !' says Ravi, laughing.

The villagers use (15) _____ snakes to earn money for food. '(16) _____ day we walk 15 or 20 (17) _____ to the nearest town,' says Ravi. '(18) _____ play music on the pipes and (19) _____ snakes dance. People enjoy the show, (20) _____ they don't like paying. Each day (21) _____ earn only 25 or 30 rupees.' ((22) _____ not enough for an ice cream (23) _____ the UK).

'There aren't many snake charmers (24) _____ India now,' says Sanjay Nath, (25) _____ father.

'Do many snake charmers die (26) _____ snake bites?' I ask.

'No, not (27) _____ ,' says Sanjay, 'but that isn't the (28) _____ . We haven't got much money or (29) _____ . It's too difficult to earn money. (30) _____ is not a good enough life (31) _____ children. They go to school now. (32) _____ learning a different way to live.'

The text is taken from *Go Students Book 2* by S Elsworth and J Rose (Pearson Education Ltd)

When the teacher and students have checked the answers to the blanks, they can read the complete text again for answers to more detailed questions such as *How many types of poisonous snakes are there?*, *Why does Ravi like the sun?* Students can then be directed to look at the text again for any language points which are interesting and/or to make sure they have understood the text as fully as is necessary. They may then say if they would like to be a snake charmer, or talk about animals they like/dislike. They might listen to an interview with Ravi about his daily life and then talk about their own.

Example 4: The right film	Activity: researching a topic
	Skills: scanning, reading for gist
	Age: any
	Level: elementary plus

The following example (especially appropriate for students in the UK) shows how computers and the Internet can be used in class (or in a self-access or computer centre) to get students searching for information in an entirely realistic and enjoyable way.

Students are told that they are going to the cinema in Cambridge, England. They have to find a film that is suitable for themselves and a fourteen-year-old, and which is on in the evening. They will have to check reviews to make sure the film is a good one. Before they do this they have the British rating system explained to them (U = anyone can go, PG = parental guidance (children can go with their parents or alone if their parents say they can), 12 = suitable for twelve-year-olds upwards, 15 = suitable for fifteen-year-olds upwards, and 18 = anyone eighteen or older).

Students are directed to *Guardian Unlimited*, the web site for one of Britain's most widely-read quality newspapers – http://www.guardian.co.uk/ – and then to the 'Films' pages within the web site. The teacher tells them to enter a Cambridge postcode in the space provided. When they hit the 'Go' button, they will find something like the following on the screen:

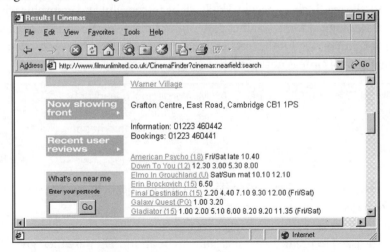

They now have to click on the U, PG, and 12 films to read summaries and short film reviews (which are also available at this site). If they choose *Down To You* they find the following:

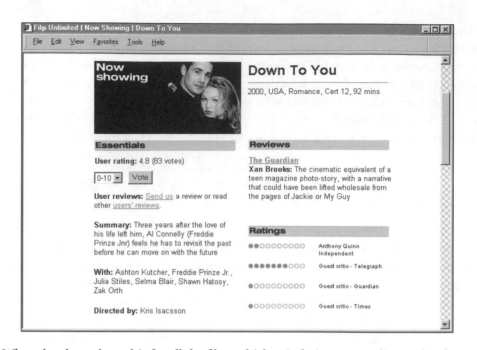

When they have done this for all the films which suit their target audience, they have to make a choice based on the summaries and the review information. But they have to do this as quickly as possible.

When choices have been made the students have to explain which film they are going to see and why. They can also tell their classmates which films they would have preferred to go and see – if they did not have to worry about the fourteen-year-old and/or they could go at different times of the day.

The Internet (see Chapter 10F) is the ideal resource tool for this kind of reading. Provided that the teacher has researched the topic (and the appropriate web sites) beforehand, the reading for specific detail will be purposeful and enjoyable whether students are looking at films, weather patterns, or holiday destinations, for example. However, it is important for the teacher to have done some of the work in locating sites so that a lot of time is not spent searching uselessly.

Example 5: The neighbours' cat	Activity: ordering paragraphs
	Skills: reading for gist, reading for detailed information
	Age: any
	Level: intermediate plus

In this example students first have to do a reading puzzle, before going on to use the reading for a discussion and/or a role-playing task.

The students are told they are going to read a story called 'The neighbours' cat' and they are asked to predict what it is going to be about. They are then given the following jumbled paragraphs where, apart from the first two, they are in the wrong order for the story. In pairs they are told to number the paragraphs to show how they can be reconstructed to make a coherent narrative.

[1] The Moriarty family moved into a house two doors down the road one sunny Wednesday in July. They seemed like nice people. We invited them for a drink for the following Friday.

[2] Our next-door neighbour (Jane) loves animals. She has a pet rat and two budgerigars. She knocked on our door on Thursday morning. 'Is this your cat?' she asked. She was holding an old, thin ginger cat with a little green collar. 'No,' we replied. 'We've never seen it before. Why?'

[3] 'How are you getting on in your new home?' one of us asked.

[4] 'I don't think it's very well,' Jane said. 'I'm going to take it to the vet.' We agreed with her idea. She cares about animals a lot. But when we saw her again that evening she was looking sad.

[5] 'Oh fine,' said Mrs Moriarty looking happily at her husband and her two young children. 'But there's just one problem. Our cat's gone missing.'

[6] 'You know that cat?' she said, 'the ginger one with the green collar? Well the vet said it was very old and very sick. So he gave it an injection. Put it to sleep. It's in cat heaven now. Well, what else could he do? We didn't know whose cat it was.'

[7] On Friday evening the Moriartys came for a drink. So did Jane and two other friends from across the street.

When they have done this the teacher checks to see that their orders are correct (e.g. 1, 2, 4, 6, 7, 3 and 5).

The class now decide exactly who is at the small neighbours' party, and in groups they decide how the story continues. Does the next-door neighbour explain what has happened? Do they brush the conversation aside and tell the Moriartys quietly the next day? How will Mr Moriarty react? What will the children feel?

The point here is that one reading puzzle leads into an imaginative task. The students have to take the text further, extending the original story and meaning. It should be enjoyable, and it gives the reading a real purpose.

Example 6: The other Bruce	Activity: picturing from a text
	Skills: reading for gist, interpreting text
	Age: adult
	Level: upper intermediate

In this example students read a text and use the information in it to build up a picture of one of the characters, even though there is not a lot of physical description on the page.

Students are asked to read the following text. All they have to do is find out how many people there are in it and what their names are (if this information is given).

Back at the motel, I was half asleep when there was a knock on my door.
'Bru?'

'Yes.'

'It's Bru.'

'I know.'

'Oh!'

This other Bru had sat next to me on the bus from Katherine. He was travelling down Darwin, where he had just broken up with his wife. He had a big pot belly and was not very bright.

At Tenant Creek he had said, 'You and me could be mates, Bru. I could teach you to drive a "dozer".' Another time, with greater warmth, he said, 'You're not a whingeing Pom, Bru.' Now long after midnight, he was outside my door calling.

'Bru?'

'What is it?'

'Want to come and get pissed?'

'No.'

'Oh!'

'We could find some sheilas,' he said.

'That a fact?' I said. 'This time of night?'

'You're right, Bru.'

'Go to bed,' I said.

'Well, goo' night, Bru.'

'Good night!'

'Bru?'

'What do you want now?'

'Nothing,' he said and shuffled off, dragging his rubber thongs *shlip ... shlip* along the corridor.

From *The Songlines* by Bruce Chatwin (Jonathan Cape)

Students and the teacher agree that there are two main characters in the text (the narrator 'Bru' and the other 'Bru'), and that the other Bru's unnamed wife is also briefly mentioned. The teacher then asks them to agree – first in pairs, and then in groups – on five words or phrases that they want to know the meaning of, and then allows them to find these words in a dictionary or discuss them with classmates (see A3 above).

The students are then asked to say whether there is any physical description in the text. When they have identified and understood *pot belly* and *rubber thongs*, they are then asked to build up a complete physical picture of 'this other Bru'. What is he wearing? What colour is his hair? What are his eyes like? His arms? It is interesting to see how clearly a physical picture has formed in their minds as a result of reading only this short text.

Now that the students have their physical picture they can discuss the question of what they think the narrator's attitude is to the man who is knocking on the door. Why is he telling this story? Does he admire the other Bru or pity him? Does he find him repulsive or amusing? What can they find out by 'reading between the lines'?

As a follow-up students can be asked to write the conversation the two Brus had on the bus from Katherine, or they can write conversations where people they only vaguely know suddenly turn up on their doorstep.

The point of this kind of activity is that when we ask students to make these kinds of imaginative leaps (picturing a character in a text, or trying to think their way into a character's head) we are asking them to relate to a reading passage in a completely different, personal way, allowing the words to create pictures for them. Such reading is a powerful alternative to some of the more utilitarian tasks we have described so far in this chapter.

Example 7: Fire hero	Activity:	identifying text construction
	Skills:	identifying topic, prediction, reading for gist, reading for detailed comprehension
	Age:	young adult and above
	Level:	intermediate plus

In the following example, students will study a reading text to identify facets of its construction which make it typical of the genre it is written in. The text has potential for student motivation since it is entirely authentic (see Chapter 14, B1).

The class starts with the teacher asking the students to look at the text – that is glance at the pictures, and scan the text without properly reading it – and say where they think it comes from. When they have agreed that it comes from a newspaper, they are asked whether they think it is local or national.

HERO PULLS NEIGHBOUR FROM BLAZE

By DAN GRIMMER

A **COURAGEOUS** villager battled through a burning bungalow to carry his neighbour to safety.

Hero Laurence Broderick rescued Jean Buiter after a fire tore through her home in High Street, Waresly, destroying much of the roof.

Around 30 firefighters tackled the blaze, which broke out at about 10am on Saturday.

While crews using breathing equipment were fighting the flames, the roof caved in and one firefighter needed hospital treatment after being injured.

Mr Broderick of Vicarage Road, said he realised something was amiss in the normally quiet village when he heard a car beeping its horn.

The driver was his son Graeham, who had spotted smoke billowing from the bungalow on his way to visit his father.

Mr Broderick, a sculptor, rushed to the bungalow because he knew Ms Buiter, who is in her 50s, had been ill.

He said: 'The whole place was smoking. At first I ran around like a headless chicken. But once I had calmed down I rushed in and there she was in her nightdress with no shoes.

'My first reaction was to get her out. I got her out of the door and it was a gravel drive so I picked her up and carried her clear of the house. I felt remarkably in control.'

A passing motorist took care of Ms Buiter while Mr Broderick returned to the house in case anyone else was there. He found the smoke so dense he could not get in.

After the dramatic rescue, fire crews from St Neots, Gamlingay and Potton, along with the command vehicle from Huntingdon, spent an hour bringing the fire under control and then making the building safe.

Station officer Mike Church said: 'The flames were through the roof. It was a very serious house fire. The middle section of the roof is gone so we have had to make it stable.'

John Archer, of Manor Close, a cousin of Mrs Buiter, said she had moved into the house just before Christmas.

He said: 'We got a call saying the house was on fire and came down here. The house is in a terrible state but at least she is all right.'

Ms Buiter is being kept in Hinchinbrook hospital for observation after treatment for smoke inhalation.

The injured firefighter received stitches after cutting his hand.

Hero ... Laurence Broderick, who carried Jean Buiter to safety and above left, firemen at the scene.
Pictures: Matthew Power 1721399

Thousands gather for Duxford Air Show – Page 5

INSIDE: TV 2 18 & 19, WEATHER 2, LETTERS, WHAT'S ON, STARS 22, CLASSIFIEDS 23, CROSSWORD 35

From *The Cambridge Evening News*, Monday 3rd May 1999

The class then discusses what the headline is designed for (impact, topic identification) and what is special about its construction (it is written in the present simple for dramatic effect, and misses out linguistic items such as possessive pronouns and articles). They are then asked to predict the content of the text before reading it in full.

Students can now answer general questions about the text: *Who rescued whom? Where was the fire? Who controlled the fire? Where is the rescued person now?*

When they have all agreed on the answers, the teacher can ask them for more detailed information, for example:

Name of hero: ....
Address: ....
Occupation: ....
Number of firefighters: ....
Number of injured people: ....
Damage to the house: ....

Students will now want to study the text to assess certain features of its construction. In the first place the text is a collection of short sentences and paragraphs. It does not use many of the linking devices nor the paragraph construction that we might expect from more literary writing, or from more carefully constructed reports. As with many newspaper articles the whole story is told in the first sentence/ paragraph, which acts as a summary.

In this newspaper article both reported and direct speech are used, the latter being more immediate (and easier to write) than the former. The article concludes with a statement of where the main protagonists are now.

The teacher can use the text for any number of other activities such as role-playing interviews with the various people concerned, writing the information in a short radio news broadcast, using the information as the basis for a discussion about how heroic people are, and what students would be prepared to risk their lives for. The text can also be used as a model for writing despite its 'journalistic' construction.

Chapter notes and further reading

- **Reading**

  On reading in general, see C Nuttall (1996), C Wallace (1992), and F Grellet (1981).

  On encouraging students to analyse the language of texts in detail, see R Gower (1999). As a learner he found 'explication de texte' (e.g. describing features of a text in detail after reading/listening to it) extremely useful, however 'old-fashioned' it was (see also C Walker (1998: 172)).

  On reading for reaction to content, see A Kennedy (2000).

- **Testing reading**

  On the testing of reading, see J C Alderson in Nuttall (1996).

- **Extensive reading**

  The Edinburgh Project on extensive reading (EPER) run by David Hill maintains a complete bibliography of all readers currently in print. Many publishers (Pearson Education, Cambridge University Press, Oxford University Press, and Macmillan Heinemann) publish a variety of simplified readers.

  C Nuttall (1996: 127) talks about 'vicious' and 'virtuous' reading circles. The former occur when weak readers read less and less and so read slower and less effectively, whereas a virtuous circle occurs when students read faster and therefore more effectively. Day and Bamford use the term 'book strapping' to describe how the effects of an action (extensive reading) are fed back into the process to achieve greater results with less effort (1998: 30).

16 | Listening

A Extensive and intensive listening

Students can improve their listening skills – and gain valuable language input – through a combination of extensive and intensive listening material and procedures. Listening of both kinds is especially important since it provides the perfect opportunity to hear voices other than the teacher's, enables students to acquire good speaking habits as a result of the spoken English they absorb, and helps to improve their own pronunciation.

A1 Extensive listening

Just as we can claim that extensive reading helps students to acquire vocabulary and grammar and that, furthermore, it make students better readers (see Chapter 15, A1), so extensive listening (where a teacher encourages students to choose for themselves what they listen to and to do so for pleasure and general language improvement) can also have a dramatic effect on a student's language learning.

Extensive listening will usually take place outside the classroom, in the students' home, car, or on personal stereos as they travel from one place to another. The motivational power of such an activity increases dramatically when students make their own choices about what they are going to listen to.

Material for extensive listening can be found from a number of sources. A lot of simplified readers are now published with an audio version on tape. These provide ideal listening material. Many students will enjoy reading and listening at the same time using both the reader and tape. Students can also have their own copies of coursebook tapes, or tapes which accompany other books written especially at their level. They can also listen to tapes of authentic material (see Chapter 14, B1), provided that it is comprehensible (see Chapter 5B).

In order for extensive listening to work effectively with a group of students – or with groups of students – we will need to make a collection of appropriate tapes clearly marked for level, topic, and genre. These can be kept – like simplified readers – in a permanent collection (such as in a self-access centre, or in some other location), or be kept in a box or some other container which can be taken into classrooms. We will then want to keep a record of which students have borrowed which tapes; where possible we should involve students in the tasks of record-keeping.

The keenest students will want to listen to English tapes outside the classroom anyway, and will need little encouragement to do so. Many others, however, will profit from having the teacher give them reasons to make use of the resources available. We need to explain the benefits of listening extensively, and come to some kind of agreement (see Chapter 9, B1) about how much and what kind of listening they should do. We can recommend certain tapes, and get other students to talk about the ones which they have enjoyed the most.

In order to encourage extensive listening we can have students perform a number of tasks. They can record their responses to what they have heard in a personal journal (see Chapter 24, A1), or fill in report forms which we have prepared asking them to list the topic, assess the level of difficulty, and summarise the contents of a tape. We can have them write comments on cards which are kept in a separate 'comments' box, add their responses to a large class 'listening' poster, or write comments on a student web site. The purpose of these or any other tasks is to give students more and more reasons to listen. If they can then share their information with colleagues they will feel they have contributed to the progress of the whole group. The motivational power of such feelings should not be underestimated.

A2 Intensive listening: using taped material

Many teachers use taped materials, and increasingly material on disk, when they want their students to practise listening skills. This has a number of advantages and disadvantages:

- **Advantages:** taped material allows students to hear a variety of different voices apart from just their own teacher's. It gives them an opportunity to 'meet' a range of different characters, especially where real people are talking. But even when tapes contain written dialogues or extracts from plays, they offer a wide variety of situations and voices.

   Taped material is extremely portable and readily available. Tapes are extremely cheap, and machines to play them are relatively inexpensive.

   For all these reasons most coursebooks include tapes, and many teachers rely on tapes to provide a significant source of language input.

- **Disadvantages:** in big classrooms with poor acoustics, the audibility of taped and disk material often gives cause for concern. It is often difficult to ensure that all students in a room can hear equally well.

   Another problem with classroom tapes is that everyone has to listen at the same speed, a speed dictated by the tape, not by the listeners. Although this replicates the situation of radio, it is less satisfactory when students have to take information from the tape. This is because they cannot, themselves, interact with the taped speakers in any way. Nor can they see the speaking taking place.

   Finally, having a group of people sit around listening to a tape recorder or disk player is not an entirely natural occupation.

Despite the disadvantages, however, we still want to use taped material at various stages in a sequence of lessons for the advantages mentioned above. In order to counteract some of the potential problems described above, we need to check tape and machine quality before we take them into class. Where possible we need to change the position of the playback machine or the students to offset poor acoustics or, if this is feasible, take other measures such as using materials to deaden echoes which interfere with good sound quality.

If it is possible we can have a number of machines for students to listen to tapes or disks at their own speed, or we can take the group into the language laboratory (see Chapter 10E). In order to show students what speaking looks like we can use videotapes (see Chapter 20). As an alternative to tapes we can also encourage interaction by providing 'live' listening (see below).

An issue that also needs to be addressed is how often we are going to play the tapes or disks we ask students to listen to. The methodologist Penny Ur points out that in real-life discourse is rarely 'replayed' and suggests, therefore, that one of our tasks is to encourage students to get as much information as is necessary/appropriate from a single hearing (Ur 1996: 108).

It is certainly true that extracting general or specific information from one listening is an important skill, so that the kind of task we give students for the first time they hear a tape is absolutely critical in gradually training them to listen effectively. However, we may also want to consider the fact that in face-to-face conversation we do frequently have a chance to ask for clarification and repetition. More importantly perhaps, as Penny Ur herself acknowledges, this 'one listening' scenario conflicts with our wish to satisfy our students' desire to hear things over and over again (see Chapter 6, B1).

If students are to get the maximum benefit from a listening then we should replay the tape two or more times, since with each listening they may feel more secure, and with each listening (where we are helping appropriately) they will understand more than they did previously. As the researcher John Field suggests, students get far more benefit from a lot of listening than they do from a long pre-listening phase followed by only one or two exposures to the listening text (Field 1998a). So even when we set prediction and gist tasks for first listenings, we can return to the tape again for detailed comprehension, text interpretation, or language analysis. Or we might play the tape again simply because our students want us to. Whatever the reason, however, we do not want to bore our students by playing them the same extract again and again, nor do we want to waste time on useless repetition.

A3 Intensive listening: 'live' listening

A popular way of ensuring genuine communication is live listening where the teacher and/or visitors to the class talk to the students. This has obvious advantages since students can interrupt speakers and ask for clarification (see Chapter 19, A1). They can, by their expressions and demeanour, indicate if the speaker is going too slowly or too fast. Above all they can see who they are listening to.

Live listening can take the following forms:

- **Reading aloud:** an enjoyable activity, when done with conviction and style, is the teacher reading aloud to a class (see Chapter 4, D2 and Example 1 in Chapter

15, B1). This allows them to hear a clear spoken version of written text, and can be extremely enjoyable if the teacher is prepared to make a big thing of it.

The teacher can also read/act out dialogues either by playing two parts or by inviting a colleague into the classroom.

- **Story-telling:** teachers are ideally placed to tell stories which, in turn, provide excellent listening material. At any stage of the story, the students can be asked to predict what is coming next, or be asked to describe people in the story or pass comment on it in some other way.

- **Interviews:** one of the most motivating listening activities is the live interview, especially where students themselves dream up the questions (see Example 1 in B1 below). In such situations, students really listen for answers they themselves have asked for, rather than adopting other people's questions. Where possible we should have strangers visit our class to be interviewed, but we can also be the subject of interviews ourselves. In such circumstances we might want, though, to set the subject and/or take on a different persona for the activity.

- **Conversations:** if we can persuade a colleague to come to our class we can hold conversations with them – about English or any other subject. Students then have the chance to watch the interaction as well as listen to it. We can also extend story-telling possibilities by role-playing.

Live listening is not a substitute for audiotapes or disks – either in the classroom, language laboratory, or self-access centre – but it does offer an extra dimension to the listening experience over a series of lessons.

A4 Intensive listening: the roles of the teacher

As with all activities, for listening we need to be active in creating student engagement through the way we set up tasks. We need to build up students' confidence by helping them listen better rather than by testing their listening abilities (see Chapter 14, B3). In particular we need to focus on the following roles:

- **Organiser:** we need to tell students exactly what their listening purpose is (see Chapter 14, B4), and give them clear instructions about how to achieve it. One of our chief responsibilities will be to build their confidence through offering tasks that are achievable and texts that are comprehensible.

- **Machine operator:** when we use tape or disk material we need to be as efficient as possible in the way we use the tape player. This means knowing where the segment we wish to use is on the tape or disk, and knowing, through the use of the playback machine counter, how to get back there. Above all it means trying the material out before taking it into class so that we do not waste time making things work when we get there. We should take decisions about where we can stop the extract for particular questions and exercises, but, once in class, we should be prepared to respond to the students' needs in the way we stop and start the machine.

If we involve our students in live listening we need to observe them with great care to see how easily they can understand us. We can then adjust the way we use the 'machine' (in this case ourselves or a visitor) accordingly.

- **Feedback organiser:** when our students have completed the task, we should lead a feedback session to check that they have completed the task successfully. We may start by having them compare their answers in pairs (see Chapter 8, A3) and then ask for answers from the class in general or from pairs in particular. Students often appreciate giving paired answers like this since, by sharing their knowledge, they are also sharing their responsibility for the answers. Because listening can be a tense experience, encouraging this kind of cooperation is highly desirable.

  It is important to be supportive when organising feedback after listening if we are to counter any negative expectations students might have (see Chapter 14, B4) and if we wish to sustain their motivation (see Chapter 3, C3).

- **Prompter:** when students have listened to a tape or disk for comprehension purposes we can have them listen to it again for them to notice a variety of language and spoken features. Sometimes we can offer them script dictations (where some words in a transcript are blanked out) to provoke their awareness of certain language items.

B Listening lesson sequences

Listening can occur at a number of points in a teaching sequence. Sometimes it forms the jumping-off point for the activities which follow. Sometimes it may be the first stage of a 'listening and acting out' sequence where students role-play the situation they have heard on the tape. Sometimes live listening may be a prelude to a piece of writing which is the main focus of a lesson. Other lessons, however, have listening training as their central focus.

However much we have planned a lesson, we need to be flexible in what we do (see Chapter 22, C1). Nowhere is this more acute than in the provision of live listening, where we may, on the spur of the moment, feel the need to tell a story, or act out some role. Sometimes this will be for content reasons – because a topic comes up – and sometimes it may be a way of refocusing our students' attention.

Most listening sequences involve a mixture of language skills – though one, in particular, is often the main focus of the sequence. Frequently students listen for gist on first hearing before moving on to different task skills; at other times they may listen for specific information straight away.

In general we should aim to use listening material for as many purposes as possible – both for practising a variety of skills and as source material for other activities – before students finally become tired with it.

B1 Examples of listening sequences

In the following examples the listening activity is specified. The skills which are involved are detailed, and the way that the listening text can be used within a lesson is explained.

Example 1: Interviewing a stranger	Activity: live listening
	Skills: predicting, listening for specific information, listening for detailed information
	Age: any
	Level: beginner and above

Where possible, teachers can bring strangers into the class to talk to the students or be interviewed by them (see A3 above). Although students will be especially interested in them if they are native speakers of the language, there is no reason why they should not include any competent English speakers.

The teacher briefs the visitor about the students' language level, pointing out that they should be sensitive about the level of language they use, but not speak to the students in a very unnatural way. They should probably not go off into lengthy explanations, and they may want to consider speaking especially clearly.

The teacher takes the visitor into the classroom without telling the students who or what the visitor is. In pairs and groups they try to guess as much as they can about the visitor. Based on their guesses about who has come into the room, they write questions that they wish to ask.

The visitor is now interviewed with the questions the students have written. As the interview proceeds, the teacher encourages them to seek clarification where things are said that they do not understand (see Chapter 19, A1). The teacher will also prompt the students to ask 'follow-up' questions, so that if a student asks *Where are you from?* and the visitor says *Scotland* he or she is then asked *Where in Scotland?* or *What's Scotland like?*

During the interview the students make notes. When the interviewee has gone these notes form the basis of a written follow-up. The students can write a short biographical piece about the person, or write the encounter up as a profile page from a magazine. They can discuss the interview with their teacher, asking for help with any points they are still unclear about. They can role-play similar interviews amongst themselves.

Pre-recorded interviews in coursebooks and other materials are also extremely useful for giving students the chance to hear different voices talking about a variety of subjects. It is often useful to give students the interviewer's questions first so that they can predict what the interviewee will say.

Example 2: Sorry I'm late	Activity: getting events in the right order
	Skills: predicting, listening for gist
	Age: young adult and above
	Level: lower intermediate

A popular technique for having students understand the gist of a story – but which also incorporates prediction and the creation of expectations – involves the students in listening so that they can put pictures in the order in which they hear them.

In this example, students look at the following four pictures:

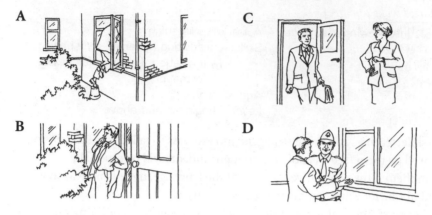

A

C

B

D

They are given a chance, in pairs or groups, to say what they think is happening in each picture. The teacher will not confirm or deny their predictions.

Students are then told that they are going to listen to a tape and that they should put the pictures in the correct chronological order (which is not the same as the order of what they hear). This is what is on the tape:

Anna: Good morning Stuart. What time do you call this?
Stuart: Oh dear. Yes, sorry I'm late.
Anna: Well? What happened to you?
Stuart: I woke up late, I'm afraid. I didn't hear the alarm.
Anna: Were you out late last night?
Stuart: Yes. I'm afraid I was.
Anna: So what happened?
Stuart: Well, when I saw the time I jumped out of bed, had a quick shower, and ran out of the house. But then, when I got to the car I realised I'd forgotten my keys.
Anna: Oh really!
Stuart: But the door to my house was shut.
Anna: What did you do?
Stuart: I ran round to the garden at the back and climbed in through the window.
Anna: And?
Stuart: Well someone saw me and called the police.
Anna: What happened then?
Stuart: Well, I told them it was my house and at first they wouldn't believe me. It took a long time!
Anna: I can imagine.
Stuart: And you see that's why I'm late!

The students check their answers with each other and then, if necessary, listen again to ensure that they have the sequence correct (B, A, D, C).

The teacher can now get students to listen/look at the tapescript again, noting phrases of interest – such as those that Stuart uses to express regret and apology (*sorry I'm late; I woke up late, I'm afraid; I'm afraid I was*), Anna's insistent questioning (*What time do you call this? Well? What happened to you? And?*), and her reactions (*Oh really!; I can imagine*). The class can then go on to role-play similar scenes in which they have to come up with stories and excuses for being late at school or work.

Example 3: Telephone messages	Activity: taking messages
	Skills: predicting, listening for specific information
	Age: teenager
	Level: elementary

Although most textbooks have taped material to accompany their various lessons, there is no reason why teachers should not record their own tapes with the help of colleagues and other competent speakers of the language provided that they take care to use a decent microphone and to record the voices as naturally as possible. This will allow them freedom to create material which is relevant to their own students' special needs.

This sequence shows the kind of thing that teachers might have their colleagues help them with – they can get them to play the parts of the occupant of the house and the three callers.

The sequence starts when the teacher asks students the kind of short messages people might leave for members of their family if and when they take phone calls while they are out. The messages are often quite simple, for example:

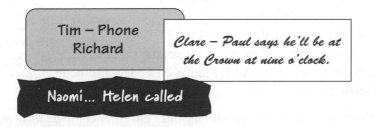

Students are told that they are going to hear three phone conversations in which the callers leave messages for people who are not in. They are told that Mrs Galloway has three daughters, Lyn (19), Eryn (17), and Kate (13). They are all out at the cinema, but three of their friends ring up and leave messages. All the students have to do is to write the messages which Mrs Galloway leaves for her daughters.

This is what the students hear:

Mrs Galloway: Hello.
Adam: Hello. Is Lyn there?

Mrs Galloway:	No, she's out at the moment. Who's that?
Adam:	This is Adam. Do you know when she'll be back?
Mrs Galloway:	About ten, I think. Can I give her a message?
Adam:	No ... er yes. Can you tell her Adam rang?
Mrs Galloway:	Sure, Adam.
Adam:	Thanks. Bye.

Mrs Galloway:	Hello.
Ruth:	Can I speak to Eryn?
Mrs Galloway:	Is that Ruth?
Ruth:	Yes. Hello Mrs Galloway. Is Eryn there?
Mrs Galloway:	No, Ruth, sorry. She's at the cinema with her sisters.
Ruth:	Oh. Well could you ask her to bring my copy of *Romeo and Juliet* to college tomorrow?
Mrs Galloway:	Your copy?
Ruth:	Yes. She borrowed it.
Mrs Galloway:	So you want her to take it in tomorrow? To college?
Ruth:	Yes. That's it. Thanks. Bye.
Mrs Galloway:	Oh ... bye.

Mrs Galloway:	Hello.
Jane Metcalfe:	Can I speak to Kate?
Mrs Galloway:	I'm afraid she's not here. Can I take a message?
Jane Metcalfe:	Yes please. This is Jane Metcalfe, the drama teacher. Can you tell Kate that the next rehearsal is at three-thirty on Friday?
Mrs Galloway:	The next rehearsal?
Jane Metcalfe:	Yes, for the school play.
Mrs Galloway:	Kate's in a play?
Jane Metcalfe:	Yes. Didn't she tell you?
Mrs Galloway:	No ... I mean yes, of course she did.
Jane Metcalfe:	OK, then. We'll see her on Friday afternoon.
Mrs Galloway:	Er ... yes.

When they have written messages for the three girls they compare their versions with each other to see if they have written the same thing. They listen to the tape again to clear up any problems they might have had.

This sequence naturally lends itself to a progression where students 'ring' each other to leave messages. Perhaps they do this after they look at the language of the three phone calls so that they can use phrases like *I'm afraid she's not here/Can I take a message?*

Message taking from phone calls is a genuinely communicative act. Where possible students will be involved in the phone calls themselves, if possible taking messages from someone speaking from another room, or from another booth in a language laboratory (see Chapter 10E), or at least working in pairs to role-play calls.

Example 4: UFO	Activity: jigsaw listening
	Skills: listening for detailed information
	Age: adult
	Level: upper intermediate

This listening sequence also involves filling in a form, but it has a jigsaw element built into it, so that to complete the task, students who have listened to one tape have to share their information with students who have listened to another.

The effect of having to gather and share detailed information to complete the forms is that the students in different groups end up with a good general understanding of the whole text.

The students have been working on a unit in their textbook called 'Anyone out there?' about space. In this class they are given the following 'UFO report form':

UFO REPORT FORM

1	Name and address:		
2	Place:	Date:	Time:
3	Other witnesses (names and addresses):		
4	Weather conditions:		
5	Description of sighting (where seen and for how long):		
6	Appearance (indicate size, shape, colour, distinguishing features – draw a sketch):		
7	Sound and movement:		
8	Description of any aliens (appearance, manner, behaviour, speech, purpose for being here):		
9	Conclusions:		

From *Upper Intermediate Matters* by J Bell and R Gower (Pearson Education Ltd)

One group (group A) listen to the following taped extract and fill in all the information they can on the form:

Extract A: Whitley Strieber and the aliens

And then there was the story of the home-loving dad who claims he was experimented on by space alien scientists. Human guinea pig Whitley Strieber suffered a terrifying brain examination as he lay naked inside the hi-tech surgery of the cruel creatures' spacecraft. The writer of the best-selling book *Communion* wants the world to know extraterrestrials are out there – and they're not friendly. Whitley trembled as he recalled his operation millions of light years from Earth.

'I had been captured like a wild animal and it was like they were trying to tame me,' said the 41-year-old.

'They performed bizarre medical procedures on me and inserted a thin metal instrument into my brain.'

Whitley claims his outer space tormentors were like giant-sized insects.

They were bald, with massive liquid-like narrow eyes, yellowish-brown skin that felt like leather, two holes for nostrils and big, floppy lips.

And to prove his chilling time with the beings actually took place, he agreed to take a lie detector test – and passed!

The New Yorker says his nightmare began when an army of aliens invaded his home while he slept.

He was unable to move as they ripped off his pyjamas, poked him with their wrinkled hands, then took him off to their waiting craft.

'They told me they were going to do an operation…'

The other group (group B) fill in as much of the form as they can based on the particular tape extract that they listen to:

Extract B: Mrs Coe and the aliens

Yes, the aliens have landed. Only yesterday they stepped out of their spaceship and went for a walk in the park. Three giant creatures twelve feet tall with tiny heads and wearing bluish metallic clothing chose Russia for a very close encounter with the human race.

Their arrival was heralded by a shining ball seen hovering over the local park by residents of Voronezh, 300 miles east of Moscow.

The UFO landed and out came the giants, similar to humans and accompanied by a small robot.

'They went for a walk near their spaceship,' said the official news agency Tass. 'Then they disappeared back inside. Onlookers were overwhelmed with fear that lasted several days.'

The landing was authenticated by staff from the Voronezh Geophysical Laboratory, whose head, Genrikh Silanov, is a respected scientist.

Tass said: 'Scientists confirmed that a UFO landed in the park. They also identified the landing site and found traces of aliens.'

Silanov's men discovered a twenty-yard depression in the park with four deep dents and two pieces of rock.

'They looked like deep red sandstone. But analysis showed that the substance cannot be found on Earth.'

There was speculation among UFO experts in Britain that the aliens could have been those that Mrs Coe said landed in her garden last month in a spacecraft which was surrounded by bubbles of light. According to her amazing story the aliens grabbed her by the arms and lifted her up a beam of light into a kind of room. Mrs Coe was reported as saying she felt they meant her no harm and that when she came round she was in her garden and not hurt in any way.

Now students from group A interview students from group B (and vice versa) using the form as a basis for making notes about their partner's story.

All students now have both UFO stories. They discuss which one they found the most believable, and say why they think this. The sequence ends when the students either write a diary entry by Whitley Strieber for the day he saw the aliens, or as Mrs Coe, write a letter to the newspaper about her experiences.

Using jigsaw techniques in listening presents greater logistical difficulties than it does in reading. It requires different tape machines in different places. However, if these difficulties can be overcome such tasks are well worth doing since they involve both listening and speaking in a thoroughly attractive way.

Example 5: We had a nice time, but …	Activity: analysing conversations
	Skills: predicting, listening for detailed information, listening for text construction
	Age: young adult and above
	Level: intermediate

In the following sequence, students are working on a unit called 'Regrets'. The lesson starts with the teacher leading a discussion about the kinds of things that can go wrong on holiday, and helps the students to come up with sentences like *You might be ill* or *Perhaps you'll miss your flight*, etc. If any of the students have a holiday 'horror story' they can tell it to their partner, their group, or to the class.

The students are told that they are going to listen to three people talking about things going wrong on holiday. They look at the photographs on the next page and try to predict what the problem is likely to be in each case. They can discuss this in pairs and groups to think of all the possibilities they can.

From *Lifelines Intermediate* by T Hutchinson (Oxford University Press)

They now listen to the tape to see if they were right. This is what they hear:

1 A Hello. Did you have a good holiday?
 B Well, yes and no.
 A Why? What was the problem?
 B My wallet was stolen.
 A No! That's a bit rough. How did that happen?
 B Oh, we stopped at this market and I was just sitting in the car when some people – a man and a woman, it was – came up. I thought they were selling things. Well, like a fool, I'd put my wallet on the dashboard. Anyway, these people came up to the car, and while I was talking to the man, the woman put her hand in and grabbed the wallet.
 A Goodness me! What did you do?
 B There wasn't much I could do. I was stunned. They just ran off into the crowd. Well, I reported it to the police, but they weren't much help.
 A Was there much money in it?
 B Yes, quite a bit, and my credit cards. But it was my own fault. I shouldn't have put it on the dashboard where people could see it. If I'd left it in my pocket, as I usually do, it wouldn't have happened.
 A Well, I hope it didn't spoil your holiday too much. Actually it reminds me of when we were on holiday a couple of years ago and …

2 A Hello, I haven't seen you around for a while. Have you been away?
 B Yes, we've been skiing in the States.
 A Oh yes, I remember you telling me you were going. Was it good?
 B Well, it was until the last few days.
 A Why? What happened?
 B Well, Tina decided that she wanted to have a go at snowboarding. You know this thing where you stand on, like a board.
 A Yes, I know.
 B Well, I thought it was a bit dodgy, but she wanted to do it. You know what kids are like. So she did. Well, anyway, she fell off and broke her arm.
 A Oh no. Poor Tina. Was she all right?
 B Yes, she was OK. The ambulance took her to the hospital and they dealt with it. But then when I came to pay, I found that our insurance didn't cover us for snowboarding – only for skiing.
 A Blimey! So what did you do?
 B Well, what could I do? I had to pay for everything myself. It cost me an arm and a leg! You know what medical costs are like in the States.
 A I hear they're rather expensive.
 B You're telling me! Well, I suppose I should have checked the insurance policy before she went snowboarding, but I blame the insurance company. I mean lots of people go snowboarding these days.
 A Well, funnily enough, something similar happened to a friend of mine. His son wanted to go snowboarding and …

3 A Hi. Welcome back. Have you had a good time?
 B Well, we did when we finally got there.
 A What do you mean?
 B Well, we only missed the flight, didn't we?
 A No! How did you manage that?
 B We got stuck in a traffic jam on the way to the airport and by the time we got there the flight had already left.
 A Oh dear.
 B It was all John's fault. We should have set off earlier. But you know what he's like – everything at the last minute. I mean, it would have been all right if the road had been clear, but it wasn't, so …
 A So what happened?
 B Well, the tour company got us on another flight later in the day. So we had to wait for 12 hours at the airport and then when we arrived it was too late to get to our hotel, so we had to book into another hotel at the airport for the night.
 A But you got there in the end?
 B Yes, but I was not in too good a mood by then, I can tell you.
 A I'm not surprised. We missed a flight once, but it wasn't because of the traffic. We …

and then in a subsequent listening (or listenings), they fill in the following chart:

	1	2	3
Problem Cause Result(s) Whose fault? Why?			

Students now listen to the extracts again, but this time they are listening out for exactly how the speakers construct their discourse, as the following exercise shows:

Talking about a holiday

a Listen to the conversations again. How do people
- ask about holidays?
- indicate that there was a problem?
- ask what happened?
- show sympathy?
- relate the story back to their own experience?

b Look at tapescript 13.3 and check your answers.

When they have done this exercise in pairs or groups they check through the language with the teacher before moving on to use the results of their enquiries in a 'making conversations' activity which encourages them to try out the language for themselves.

Make more conversations about holiday disasters.

a Work with a partner and make conversations about the situations below, following the diagram.

A	**B**
Greet and ask about the holiday	
	Indicate a problem
Ask what happened	
	Describe what happened
Sympathize	
	Express blame or regrets
Ask about results	
	Describe results
Compare the problem to your own experience	

1 lose passports/leave bag on beach/have to get new ones at the embassy/wife's fault/didn't leave passports at hotel
2 injured/walk into glass door/go to hospital/hotel's fault/couldn't see door
3 get lost/car runs out of petrol/spend night in car/own fault/didn't check the petrol gauge
4 holiday cancelled/tour company goes bust/have to go home/husband's fault/choose cheap holiday
5 house burgled while away/door not locked/TV and video stolen/neighbour's fault/came in to feed pets and forgot to lock door
6 arrested/smuggling money out of the country/taken to police station/own fault/didn't declare it on immigration form

b Think of a similar experience that might have happened to you. Make more conversations with your partner.

From *Lifelines Intermediate* by T Hutchinson (Oxford University Press)

This sequence shows how listening extracts can be used for a variety of different purposes – from training in (and practice of) language skills, to language analysis and as a stimulus for language production (see Chapter 17).

Example 6: At the post office	Activity: analysing language exchanges
	Age: adult
	Level: upper intermediate/advamced

Any spoken language can be studied for information about how the text is constructed and in what order certain functions can occur within an exchange. This can be useful at any level – with both simplified and authentic text. To collect the latter type speakers can wear voice-activated microphones as they go about their normal lives so that the recordings which are obtained are a record of everyday spoken reality.

The following extract was collected in just such a way. A male customer <S 01> has gone to the post office and is talking to a female post office clerk <S 02>:

<S 01>	Right, send that first class please.	1
<S 02>	That one wants to go first class, right we'll see if it is,	2
	it's not it's not 41, it's a 60, I thought it would be, I'd	3
	be in the … 60 pence [6 secs] there we are	4
<S 01>	Lovely thank you	5
<S 02>	Okay 70 80 whoops 90 100	6
<S 01>	Thanks very much	7
<S 02>	Thank you	8

From *Exploring Spoken English* by R Carter and M McCarthy (Cambridge University Press)

Students looking at this transcript will notice how apparently messy and arbitrary real language is. However, closer inspection – taking into account the false starts, thinking aloud, etc. – shows that the extract above contains the bare essentials of what the customer needs to complete his business. The pattern, according to the authors of the book, seems to be: 1 a request for service (line 1), 2 an acknowledgement of the request and a statement of the price (lines 2–3), 3 the handing over of the goods (line 4), 4 the giving of money and receiving the change (lines 5–6), and 5 a closure of the encounter (lines 7–8) (Carter and McCarthy 1997: 93).

There is much more to notice here, too. For example, *Right* is a common way of opening transactions. *Send that first class* may be an imperative, but because it is almost certainly an ellipsis of a sentence like *I'd like to send that first class* or *Can I send that first class?* it is not considered rude; the clerk almost certainly understands it to be a request, not an order.

In their commentary on the extract Ronald Carter and Michael McCarthy note how *That one wants to go first class* only makes sense when we realise that *wants* is here used to mean *needs* or *should* – a common use of the verb in spoken English. And so on.

Examination of real informal spoken exchanges like the one above yields a fantastic amount about the way we speak to each other, yet it is problematic too. It is extremely culture-bound, for one thing, and while it may make us aware of exactly how conversations are constructed it is difficult to see how we might translate that into active use. Do we teach students to hesitate and change their minds for example? Should we promote ellipsis and the use of informal conversation markers which might sound strange coming from a foreign language student's lips when used to a native language speaker? What level is this kind of study suitable for? These questions have formed the focus for a lively debate so that it is still unclear what teachers and students might do with such extracts beyond having students 'notice' certain features of speech.

However, for anyone interested in how native speakers really communicate, such close attention to the construction of informal encounters of this kind gives invaluable insights into the way the language works.

C The sound of music

Music is a powerful stimulus for student engagement precisely because it speaks directly to our emotions while still allowing us to use our brains to analyse it and its effects if we so wish. A piece of music can change the atmosphere in a classroom or prepare students for a new activity. It can amuse and entertain, and it can make a satisfactory connection between the world of leisure and the world of learning. Because the appreciation of music is not a complex skill, and because many different patterns of music from a variety of cultures have become popular all over the globe through satellite television and the Internet, most students have little trouble perceiving clear changes of mood and style. In class, therefore, we can play film music and get students to say what kind of film they think it comes from. We can get them to listen to music which describes people and say what kind of people they are. They can write stories based on the mood of the music they hear, or listen to more than one piece of music and discuss with each other what mood the music describes, what 'colour' it is, where they would like to hear it, and who with.

Even those who are sceptical about their ability to respond to music often end up being convinced despite themselves; as one of David Cranmer and Clement Laroy's students wrote after hearing Honegger's 'Pacific 231':

> I am really puzzled by people's ability to see things in music. I can't. Take this music for example ... if you ask me, I would visualise a train steaming through the prairie and Indians attacking it ... while some people are desperately trying to defend it.
>
> From D Cranmer and C Laroy (1992: 57)

Example 7: Ironic		
	Activity:	understanding song lyrics
	Skills:	listening, reading for general and detailed comprehension
	Age:	young adult and above
	Level:	intermediate

One of the most useful kinds of text for students to work with is song lyrics, especially where the song in question is one which the students are very keen on. However, songs can present a problem, particularly with teenage students, precisely because it is often difficult to know exactly which songs the students like at a particular time and which songs, very popular last week, have suddenly gone out of favour!

There are two ways of dealing with this problem: the first is to have students bring their own favourite songs to class. If they do this, however, the teacher may want to have time (a day or two) to listen to the song and try and understand the lyrics. Some of the songs may deal with issues and language which the teacher is not keen to work with. Another solution is to use older songs, and to ask students whether they think they still have merit – whether they like them, despite their antiquity. Teachers can then choose songs which they like, or which are appropriate in terms of topic and subject matter, and which they themselves think pass the test of time.

The following example takes a song released in the mid-1990s. Students are told that they are going to hear the singer Alanis Morrissette perform her track 'Ironic'. Do any of them know it? What do they think it is going to be about?

They are then given the following worksheet and told that when they listen to the song, all they have to do is put the verses in the correct order – even if they do not understand all of the words.

Listen to 'Ironic'. Match the numbers on the left with the verses on the right.

1 _ _ _ _ _ _ _ _ _ _ _ _ _ _ _ _ _ _

CHORUS
It's like rain on your wedding day
It's a free ride when you've already paid.
It's the good advice that you just didn't take
And who would have thought it? … it figures.

2 _ _ _ _ _ _ _ _ _ _ _ _ _ _ _ _ _

CHORUS

3 _ _ _ _ _ _ _ _ _ _ _ _ _ _ _ _ _

4 _ _ _ _ _ _ _ _ _ _ _ _ _ _ _ _

a A traffic jam when you're already late
A no-smoking sign on your cigarette break
It's like 10,000 spoons when all you need is a knife
It's meeting the man of my dreams and then meeting his beautiful wife
And isn't it ironic, don't you think?
A little too ironic, yeah, I really do think.

b Mr Play-It-Safe, was afraid to fly
He packed a suitcase and kissed his kids goodbye
He waited his whole damn life to take that flight
And as the plane crashed down he thought 'well, isn't this nice!'
And isn't it ironic, don't you think?

CHORUS

Life has a funny way of sneaking up
   on you
Life has a funny way of helping
   you out.

c An old man turned ninety-eight
   He won the lottery and died the next
      day
   It's a black fly on your Chardonnay
   It's a death row pardon two minutes
      too late
   And isn't it ironic, don't you think?

d Life has a funny way of sneaking up
   on you
   When you think everything is OK and
      everything's going right.
   And life has a funny way of helping
      you out
   When you think you've gone wrong
      and everything blows up in your
      face.

Students compare their answers and the teacher checks that they have the verses in the right place. They can now listen to the song again, and this time they should read each verse as it is sung. At the end of this procedure the teacher asks them what the song is about, and what the tone of it is, to elicit the information that it is about things always turning out the opposite to what you want. It is half bitter, half jokey.

The teacher can then take the students through the lyrics, explaining phrases they did not understand, asking questions to check their comprehension of various words and expressions (e.g. *It figures, sneaking up on you, everything blows up in your face*). Although this kind of text study is somewhat cumbersome, a detailed look at song lyrics, if the students are interested in them, will really help some of them to remember some of the expressions, especially when they are combined with catchy music.

There are many other ways of using songs lyrics, of course. Teachers can give students lyrics with various words blanked out; the teacher can give students a list of words and ask them to listen to the song to see which of the words are used. The teacher can ask students to put lines in order, or complete half-finished lines. Or the teacher can simply have students listen to a song and say what they think the title might be – or say where they would most like to hear it.

Chapter notes and further reading

- **Listening**

  On listening in general, see M Underwood (1989), A Anderson and T Lynch (1988), M Rost (1990), and J Field (1998a). T Ridgeway (2000) and J Field (2000) argue about the relative merits of listening strategy training.

- **Authentic text**

  On the advantages of using authentic listening texts in class, see J Field (1998b: 13).

- **Using authentic transcripts**

  On using transcripts of conversations in teaching, see R Carter (1998a), and G Cook (1998) who questions the use of such samples of 'authentic' speech, and a reply to his criticisms in R Carter (1998b). L Prodromou (1997a) strongly questioned the work of Carter and McCarthy, and their reply is most instructive – see M McCarthy and R Carter (1997) to which Prodromou himself replied (Prodromou 1997b).

- **Using music and songs in the classroom**

  On using music generally, see D Cranmer and C Laroy (1992). On songs see, T Murphey (1992), L Domoney and S Harris (1993), and S Coffrey (2000).

17 | Teaching productive skills

A Productive skills

The productive skills of writing and speaking are different in many ways. However, there are a number of language production processes which have to be gone through whichever medium we are working in.

A1 Structuring discourse

In order for communication to be successful we have to structure our discourse in such a way that it will be understood by our listeners or readers. In speech this often involves following conversational patterns and the use of lexical phrases, the pre-fixed or semi-fixed word strings that have led methodologists to look carefully at lexical approaches (see Chapters 2, B4 and 6, A8). In general, fewer formulaic phrases are found in writing than in speech (Wray 1999: 227–228), and this is why writing in particular has to be both coherent and cohesive. Coherent writing makes sense because you can follow the sequence of ideas and points. Cohesion is a more technical matter since it is here that we concentrate on the various linguistic ways of connecting ideas across phrases and sentences. These may be 'chains of reference' (Biber et al. 1999: 42) where we use language features such as pronouns, lexical repetition, and synonymy to refer to ideas that have already been expressed. We can use various linkers as well, such as for addition (*also, moreover*), contrast (*although, however, still*), cause and effect (*therefore, so*), and time (*then, afterwards*).

Although spontaneous speech may appear considerably more chaotic and disorganised than a lot of writing, speakers nevertheless employ a number of structuring devices, from language designed to 'buy time', to turn-taking language (see A2 below), and quite specific organising markers such as *firstly, secondly,* or even *and as if that wasn't enough,* as in *and as if that wasn't enough he lost my money on a horse!*

A2 Following the rules

When people with similar cultural and linguistic backgrounds get together they speak to each other easily because they know the rules of conversation in their language and their shared culture. When they write to each other they obey certain conventions. Such rules and conventions are not written down anywhere, nor are they easy to define. But at some cultural level our shared schemata (see Chapter 14, A1) help us to communicate with each other successfully.

There are three areas of rules which we should consider:

- **Sociocultural rules:** speakers from similar cultural backgrounds know how to speak to each other in terms of how formal to be, what kind of language they can use, how loud to speak, or how close to stand to each other. Such sociocultural rules – or shared cultural habits – determine how women and men speak to each other in different societies, how conversations are framed when the participants are of different social or professional status, and guide our behaviour in a number of well recognised speech events such as invitation conversations, socialising moves, and typical negotiations.

  Sociocultural rules and habits change over time, but at any given moment they exist in the public consciousness so that obeying them or purposefully flouting them become acts of belonging or rejection.

- **Turn-taking:** in any conversation decisions have to be taken about when each person should speak. This is 'turn-taking', a term which refers to the way in which participants in conversations get their chance to speak. They do this by knowing how to signal verbally or visually that they want a turn or, conversely, by recognising when other speakers are signalling that they want to finish and are therefore giving them space to take a speaking turn.

- **Rules for writing:** writing has rules too, which we need to recognise and either follow or purposefully flout. These range from the 'netiquette' (Teeler 2000: 9–10) of computer users, who chat to each other on the Internet, to the accepted and successful patterns of a letter supporting an application or the conventions followed in journalism or fiction. When we produce language in these genres (see A3 below), part of our skill lies in negotiating these rules successfully.

A3 Different styles, different genres

One of the reasons that people can operate within sociocultural rules is because they know about different styles, and recognise different written and spoken genres.

In Chapter 2C we saw how our language use is determined by a number of factors. First among these is the purpose of our communication, what we want to achieve. But the form in which we try to achieve that purpose is determined by other parameters such as the setting, the channel we are using to communicate by, and the type of communication (genre) which we are involved with. If we want to give people facts (our purpose) in a lecture theatre (setting) through a microphone (channel) we will probably use a lecture genre with its typical patterns of rhetoric and organisation, and this genre will determine the style of the language we use. The whole event will be different from how we might transmit the same information to a friend in an informal conversation. This in turn would be different from the kind of language we might use when writing the same information in a particular magazine genre: when exchanging e-mails on the subject with a close colleague our use of language will almost certainly be very different again.

In each of the above cases, the writer or speaker will operate at a different level of formality. We can characterise this as a level of intimacy, where the more distant a speaker or writer feels themselves to be from their audience, or the more tentative they feel about their message, the greater will be their use of formal grammar and lexis. When people talk about spoken and written grammar, therefore (see Chapter 2, A1), one of the differences they are sometimes describing is between 'distance' and 'closeness'.

A feeling of distance will make the use of well-formed sentences in writing a priority. It will suggest the use of full forms and written equivalencies in spoken communication. Closeness, on the other hand, leads to spontaneity so that in conversation the occurrence of ellipsis, non-clausal sentences, tags, hesitators etc. is more common.

Distance and closeness are not the same as writing and speaking, however. People sometimes write 'closely' in media such as postcards, e-mails, and notes left around the house. They can speak more 'distantly' in speeches, formal interviews, and prescribed ceremonies. It may, therefore, be useful to think of language production as being more 'writing-like' or more 'speaking-like' (Tribble 1997: 21). Thus essays, formal articles, reports, and some novels are very distant and 'writing-like' whereas some writing such as particular magazine articles, fiction, advertising and, especially, e-mail writing is much closer and more 'speaking-like'.

In order to speak and write at different levels of intimacy students need practice in different genres (see Chapter 18, B2) and different styles so that as their level increases they can vary the grammar, functions, and lexis that they use. It is vital, therefore, that if the coursebook does not offer a satisfactory range of such genre-based activities, we should supply it ourselves (see Chapter 21, C2).

A4 Interacting with an audience

Part of our speaking proficiency depends upon our ability to speak differentially, depending upon our audience, and upon the way we absorb their reaction and respond to it in some way or other. Part of our writing ability depends upon our ability to change our style and structure to suit the person or people we are writing for.

Where people are giving formal 'writing-like' lectures, they are likely to adapt the way they are speaking and the words they are using on the basis of audience reaction; just as good actors, for example, are expert at riding a laugh, or changing their pace to suit public conditions, so good presenters, salespeople, and politicians keep their ears and eyes open to see how their words are going down and speak accordingly. Writers engaged in an e-mail correspondence modify subsequent communications on the basis of the reaction of the people they are communicating with. Novelists and playwrights at a conscious or subconscious level identify a prototypical audience to write for. In informal spontaneous conversations we are constantly alert for the reactions of the people we are interacting with so that we make our communication as informative as required, amending it depending on how the other participants in the interaction behave.

A5 Dealing with difficulty

When speakers or writers of their own or of a foreign language do not know a word or just cannot remember it, they may employ some or all of the following strategies to resolve the difficulty they are encountering:

- **Improvising:** speakers sometimes try any word or phrase that they can come up with in the hope that it is about right. Such improvisations sometimes work, but they can also obscure meaning.

- **Discarding:** when speakers simply cannot find words for what they want to say, they may discard the thought that they cannot put into words.

- **Foreignising:** when operating in a foreign language, speakers (and writers) sometimes choose a word in a language they know well (such as their first language) and 'foreignise' it in the hope that it will be equivalent to the meaning they wish to express in the foreign language.

- **Paraphrasing:** speakers sometimes paraphrase, talking about something *for cleaning the teeth* if they do not know the word *toothbrush*, or saying that they are *not happy with* somebody when they want to say that they are really fed up. Such lexical substitution or circumlocution gets many speakers out of trouble, though it can make communication longer and more convoluted.

Clearly some of these 'difficulty strategies' are more appropriate than others. As teachers we should encourage paraphrasing and improvising as more useful techniques than discarding thoughts or foreignising words blindly.

B Productive skills in the classroom

When students write or speak in lessons they have a chance to rehearse language production in safety, experimenting with different language in different genres that they will use on some future occasion away from the classroom.

When students are working on their language production, they should be operating towards the communicative end of the communication continuum (see Chapter 6, A4). Activities at the non-communicative end of the continuum – such as language drills – are excluded from the category of productive skills even though they may be done orally. Similarly, the writing of sentences to practise a grammar point may be very useful for a number of reasons, but such exercises are not writing skill activities. This is because language production means that students should use all and any language at their disposal to achieve a communicative purpose rather than be restricted to specific practice points.

However, skill training is not always communicative in itself, since teaching people to take turns or use correct punctuation, for example, is often fairly controlled – and may involve quite a lot of teacher intervention.

One of the chief advantages of production activities is that they provide evidence for students and their teachers to assess how well things are going (see Chapter 7B).

The freer the task the greater the chance of seeing how successful a language learning programme has been.

B1   Reception and production

The teaching of productive skills is closely bound up with receptive skill work. The two feed off each other in a number of ways.

- **Output and input:** when a student produces a piece of language and sees how it turns out, that information is fed back into the acquisition process. Output becomes input.

   Such input or feedback can take various forms. Some of it comes from ourselves, whether or not we are language learners. We modify what we write or say as we go along based on how effective we think we are being. Feedback also comes from the people we are communicating with. In face-to-face spoken interaction our listeners tell us in a number of ways whether we are managing to get our message across. On the telephone listeners can question us and/or show through their intonation, tone of voice, or lack of response that they have not understood us.

   Teachers can of course provide feedback too, not just when a student finishes a piece of work but also during the writing process for example (see Chapter 18, B1), or when as prompters or as a resource teachers offer ongoing support (see Chapter 4B).

   Figure 22 shows the relationship between input and output:

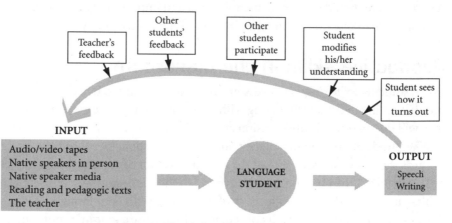

FIGURE 22: The circle of input and output

- **Texts as models:** especially where students are working with genre-focused tasks, written and spoken texts are a vital way of providing models for them to follow. One of the best ways of having students write certain kinds of report, for example, is to show them some actual reports and help them to analyse their structure and style; to get students to give spoken directions they will benefit from hearing other people doing it first.

Productive work need not always be imitative. But students are greatly helped by being exposed to examples of writing and speaking which show certain conventions for them to draw upon.

- **Texts as stimuli:** a lot of language production work grows out of texts that students see or hear. A controversial reading passage may be the springboard for discussion, or for a written riposte in letter form. Listening to a tape or disk in which a speaker tells a dramatic story may provide the necessary stimulus for students to tell their own stories, or it may be the basis for a written account of the narrative.

- **Reception as part of production:** in many situations production can only continue in combination with the practice of receptive skills. Thus conversation between two or more people is a blend of listening and speaking; comprehension of what has been said is necessary for what the participant says next. In writing too what we write often depends upon what we read. Letters are often written in reply to other letters, and e-mail conversation proceeds much like spoken dialogues. Indeed, in the case of chat rooms and MOOs (permanent spaces on the Internet where a number of users can meet in real time in virtual rooms), the computer discourse takes place, like spoken conversation, in real time (see Teeler 2000: 31–35).

  The fact that reception and production are so bound up together suggests strongly that we should not have students practise skills in isolation even if such a thing were possible. That is why many of the examples in this book show integrated skill sequences, where the practice of one skill leads naturally on to other linked activities.

- **Production enables reception:** productive skill work is a way of helping students with their receptive skills. Students can apply the insights they gain from their writing work to their reading. When they have tried to speak within certain genres, they are better attuned to understanding other people speaking in the same context.

C Problems and solutions

There are a number of reasons why students find language production difficult, especially with tasks at the communicative end of the communication continuum. However there are a number of ways in which teachers can help students get as much out of such activities as possible. In the first place, we need to match the tasks we ask students to perform with their language level. This means ensuring that they have the minimum language they would need to perform such a task. Secondly, we need to ensure that there is a purpose to the task (that it has some outcome) and that students are aware of this. We should also remember that students who are not used to speaking or writing spontaneously need to be helped to cultivate such habits. Teachers should not expect instant fluency and creativity; instead they should build up students' confidence 'bit by bit' (see Chapter 6, B1), giving them restricted tasks first before prompting them to be more and more spontaneous later. Finally, teachers need to assess the problems caused by the language they need, and the difficulties which the topic or the genre might create.

C1 Language

Learners engaged in a productive task can become very frustrated when they just do not have the words or the grammar they need to express themselves. Sometimes, of course, they can research language they would like to use (see Chapter 12), but this can make writing a very cumbersome process, and in speaking such an option is anyway not available, at least not in spontaneous speech.

There are a number of steps we can take which will help students achieve success:

- **Supply key language:** before we ask students to take part in a spoken or written activity we may check their knowledge of key vocabulary, and help them with phrases or questions that will be helpful for the task – e.g. an interview situation or the writing of a particular kind of letter. However, where speaking is concerned, we should remember that language which students have only just met for the first time (whether grammatical, lexical, or phrasal) is often not available for instant use in spontaneous conversation; more exposure and practice is usually necessary before people can use new language fluently. We should not expect, therefore, that we can introduce new language and have students use it instantly in communicative activities.

- **Plan activities in advance:** because of the time-lag between our students meeting new language and their ability to use it fluently, we need to plan production activities that will provoke the use of language which they have had a chance to absorb at an earlier stage.

Language production activities which fall at the communicative end of the communication continuum are not just practice activities, however. One of the strategies which speakers need to develop is the art of getting round language problems in communication; writers, too, will have to find ways of saying things even though a lack of language makes this difficult.

C2 Topic and genre

If students are not interested in the topics we are asking them to write or speak about, they are unlikely to invest their language production with the same amount of effort as they would if they were excited by the subject matter. If they are completely unfamiliar with the genre we are asking them to write in, for example, they may find it difficult to engage with the task we have given them.

In order to write or speak successfully it helps if we 'know what we are talking about'. Yet the variety in a general English classroom sometimes means that students are at times expected to write or speak about topics they have little knowledge of.

When students with language limitations are asked to work with topics that do not interest them, perhaps in unfamiliar genres, and without the necessary information, then language production activities suffer. We need to have ways of avoiding such a scenario:

- **Choose interesting topics:** although there is no magical way of ensuring that our students will be engaged with the topics we offer them, it is nevertheless important to try and find the type of tasks (and the topic material) which will involve the members of our classes.

  One way of doing this is to use our instinct, but this is unreliable. It may be better to find out from students what their favourite topics are through interviews and questionnaires – or, by observing them (see Chapter 4, B8) – and then come to conclusions about what kinds of topics seem to produce the best results.

  However, it is worth reminding ourselves that even unpromising tasks and topics can be invested with success if teachers can think of ways of engaging their students with them.

- **Create interest in the topic:** because we want students to be engaged in the task we are asking them to become involved in, we will want to create interest in the topic which the activity explores.

  We can create interest by talking about the topic and communicating enthusiasm. We can have students discuss the topic in 'buzz groups' (see Chapter 19, B3) to get them involved in it, or we can ask the group if anyone knows anything about the topic and can therefore tell the others about it. We can ask students to think about what they might say or write and give them opportunities to come up with opinions about the topic before the activity starts.

- **Activate schemata:** even though students are now interested in a topic, they may find it difficult to take part with any enthusiasm if they are unfamiliar with the genre the task asks them to work in. For this reason, we should give them time to do things such as discuss what happens in interviews if they are going to role-play an interview, or show them examples of typical letters written to newspapers before we ask them to write one themselves.

- **Vary topics and genre:** variety, as a cornerstone of good planning (see Chapter 22, A and B) does not just apply to the activities we ask students to be involved in. It is also important to vary the topics we offer them so that we cater for the variety of interests within the class. Our chances of organising successful language production activities over a period of time will be greatly enhanced if we provide a varied diet of topic and activity.

  It is also vitally important to vary the genres we ask our students to work with if we want them to gain confidence in writing and speaking in different situations.

- **Provide necessary information:** when we plan a writing or speaking task we need to ask ourselves which bits of information are absolutely essential for the task to be a success and then give that information to our students before they start. We cannot expect them to role-play if they do not know who they are supposed to be and what they are supposed to achieve. We cannot ask them to write a report if they do not have the necessary facts at their disposal.

Chapter notes and further reading

- **Interacting with an audience**

  Making communication as informative as required and amending it on the basis of participant reaction were major features of the 'cooperative principle' (H Grice 1975).

- **Dealing with difficulties when speaking**

  See M Bygate (1987: Chapter 5).

18 | Writing

A Writing conventions

Written text has a number of conventions which separate it out from speaking. Apart from differences in grammar (see Chapter 2, A1) and vocabulary, there are issues of letter, word, and text formation, manifested by handwriting, spelling, and layout and punctuation.

A1 Handwriting

Many students whose native-language orthography is very different from English have difficulty forming English letters. Such students should get special training. This might involve practice in the formation of individual letters as the following example demonstrates:

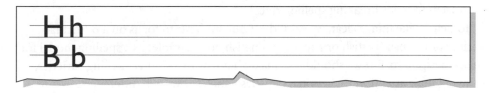

Sometimes the teacher can write sentences out neatly with spaces underneath for the student to imitate that writing:

Handwriting is a personal issue. Students should not all be expected to use exactly the same style, despite copying exercises like the one above. Nevertheless badly-formed letters may influence the reader against the writer, something which is undesirable whether the work is the product of some creative task or, more seriously, work that is going to be assessed in a test or exam. We should encourage students with problematic handwriting to improve it.

Though more and more written communication takes place from a computer keyboard, handwriting is still important for personal letters, written assignments, and most (but not all) exams (see the Chapter notes on pages 333–334).

A2 Spelling

Although incorrect spelling does not often prevent the understanding of a written message, it can adversely affect the reader's judgement. All too often bad spelling is perceived as a lack of education or care.

One of the reasons that spelling is difficult for students of English is that the correspondence between the sound of a word and the way it is spelt is not always obvious (see Chapter 2, D4). A single sound (or more correctly, a single phoneme) may have many different spellings (*paw, poor, pore, pour, daughter, Sean*), and the same spelling may have many different sounds (*or, word, information, worry, correspond*). When students work on different phonemes, we need to draw their attention to the common spellings of those phonemes. We should also get them to look at different ways of pronouncing the same letters (or combinations of letters) or have them do exercises to discover spelling rules (see Chapter 13, B4). When students come across new words we can ask them what other words they know with the same kinds of spelling or sounds. When they listen to tapes they can study transcripts and/or copy down sections of the tape.

An issue that makes spelling difficult for some students is the fact that not all varieties of English spell the same words in the same way. Which is correct: *color* or *colour*, and *theater* or *theatre*? How do we decide between the use of *s* and *z* in words like *apologise* and *customize*. What position can we take about those Internet users who seem to enjoy breaking spelling rules?

To help make things clear, we should get our students to focus on a particular variety of English (British or American English, for example) as a spelling model for them to aspire to. But we should also make them aware of other spelling varieties, drawing their attention to dictionary entries which show such differences.

One of the best ways to help students improve their spelling is through reading, especially extensively (see Chapter 15, A1). We can also draw their attention to spelling problems and explain why they occur. Copying from written models is one way to do this; when students see and reflect on their copying mistakes, their spelling 'consciousness' is raised (Porte 1995).

A3 Layout and punctuation

Different writing communities (both between and within cultures) obey different punctuation and layout conventions in communications such as letters, reports, and publicity. These are frequently non-transferable from one community or language to another. Such differences are easily seen in the different punctuation conventions for the quotation of direct speech which different languages use, or the way in which commas are used instead of/as much as full stops in certain languages, while comma 'overuse' is frowned on by many writers and editors of English. Some punctuation conventions, such as the capitalisation of names, months, and the pronoun *I*, are specific to only one or a few languages. Though punctuation is frequently a matter of personal style, violation of well-established customs makes a piece of writing look awkward to many readers.

Different genres of writing are laid out differently; business and personal letters are different from each other, and e-mails have conventions all of their own. Newspaper articles are laid out in quite specific ways, and certain kinds of 'small ads' in magazines follow conventional formats (see Chapter 2, C4). To be successful as writers in our own or another language, we need to be aware of these layouts and use/modify them when appropriate to get our message across as clearly as we can.

B Approaches to student writing

There are a number of different approaches to the practice of writing skills both in and outside the classroom. We need to choose between them, deciding whether we want students to focus more on the process of writing than its product, whether we want them to study different written genres, whether we want to encourage creative writing – either individually or cooperatively – and how the computer can be a useful writing tool. We need to be aware of the different roles we can and should assume for writing activities.

B1 Process and product

In the teaching of writing we can focus on the product of that writing or on the writing process itself. When concentrating on the product we are only interested in the aim of a task and in the end product. Those who advocate a process approach to writing, however, pay attention to the various stages that any piece of writing goes through. By spending time with learners on pre-writing phases, editing, redrafting, and finally 'publishing' their work, a process approach aims to get to the heart of the various skills that should be employed when writing.

In its simplest form a process approach asks students to consider the procedure of putting together a good piece of work. We might, for example, discuss the concept of first and final drafts with our students and then ask them to say whether the following activities take place at first or final stages, and to put them in the best order:

a   Check language use (grammar, vocabulary, linkers).
b   Check punctuation (and layout).
c   Check your spelling.
d   Check your writing for unnecessary repetition of words and/or information.
e   Decide on the information for each paragraph, and the order the paragraphs should go in.
f   Note down various ideas.
g   Select the best ideas for inclusion.
h   Write a clean copy of the corrected version.
i   Write out a rough version.

First draft	Final draft
f,	

In reality, the writing process is more complex than this of course, and the various stages of drafting, reviewing, redrafting and writing, etc. are done in a recursive way: we loop backwards and move forwards between these various stages (Tribble 1997: 37–39). Thus at the editing stage we may feel the need to go back to a pre-writing phase and think again; we may edit bits of our writing as we draft it.

Ron White and Valerie Arndt are keen to stress that 'writing is *re*-writing; that *re*-vision – seeing with new eyes – has a central role to play in the act of creating text' (White and Arndt 1991: 5). In their model, process writing is an interrelated set of recursive stages which include:

- drafting
- structuring (ordering information, experimenting with arrangements, etc.)
- reviewing (checking context, connections, assessing impact, editing)
- focusing (that is making sure you are getting the message across you want to get across)
- generating ideas and evaluation (assessing the draft and/or subsequent drafts)

White and Arndt's model can be represented diagramatically, as in Figure 23:

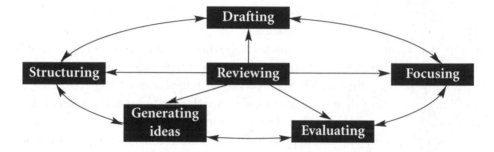

FIGURE 23: White and Arndt's process writing model

One of the disadvantages of getting students to concentrate on the process of writing is that it takes time: time to brainstorm ideas or collect them in some other way; time to draft a piece of writing and then, with the teacher's help perhaps, review it and edit it in various ways before, perhaps, changing the focus, generating more ideas, redrafting, re-editing and so on. This cannot be done in fifteen minutes. However, the various stages may well involve discussion, research, language study, and a considerable amount of interaction between teacher and students and between the students themselves so that when process writing is handled appropriately it stretches across the whole curriculum.

There are times when process writing is simply not appropriate, either because classroom time is limited, or because we want students to write quickly as part of a communication game, or when working alone, we want them to compose a letter or brief story on the spot.

B2 Writing and genre

In a genre approach to writing students study texts in the genre they are going to be writing before they embark on their own writing. Thus, if we want them to write business letters of various kinds we let them look at typical models of such letters before starting to compose their own. If we want them to write newspaper articles we have them study real examples to discover facts about construction and specific language use which is common in that genre. This forms part of the pre-writing phase.

Chris Tribble (1997: 148–150) suggests the following 'data collection' procedure as a prelude to the writing of letters to newspapers. Students are asked to spend some time every day, for a week, looking at letters to the newspapers. They are asked to make notes of particular vocabulary and/or grammar constructions in the letters. For example we might tell them to find any language which expresses approval or disapproval, or to note down any *if*-sentences they come across. They can use dictionaries or any other resources they need to check understanding. At the end of a week they bring the results of their research to the class and make a list of commonly occurring lexis or grammar patterns.

The teacher now gets the students to read controversial articles in today's paper and plan letters (using language they have come across in the data collection phase) in response to those articles. Where possible they should actually send their letters in the hope that they will be published.

A genre approach is especially appropriate for students of English for Specific Purposes (see Chapter 1, B3). But it is also highly useful for general English students if we want them, even at low levels, to produce written work they can be proud of.

Students who are writing within a certain genre need to consider a number of different factors. They need to have knowledge of the topic, the conventions and style of the genre, and the context in which their writing will be read, and by whom. Many of our students' writing tasks do not have an audience other than the teacher, of course, but that does not stop us and them working as if they did.

Asking students to imitate a given style could be seen as extremely prescriptive, encouraging them to see writing as a form of 'reproduction' rather than as a creative act. Imitation is only a first stage, however, designed as much to inform as to enforce adherence to strict genre rules. In the end it is up to them to decide what to do with the data they have collected (however this has been done).

B3 Creative writing

The term 'creative writing' suggests imaginative tasks such as writing poetry, stories, and plays. Such activities have a number of features to recommend them. Chief amongst these is that the end result is often felt to be some kind of achievement, and that 'most people feel pride in their work and want it to be read' (Ur 1996: 169). This is significantly more marked for creative writing than for other more standard written products.

Creative writing is 'a journey of self-discovery, and self-discovery promotes effective learning' (Gaffield-Vile 1998: 31). When teachers set up imaginative writing tasks so that their students are thoroughly engaged, those students frequently strive harder than usual to produce a greater variety of correct and appropriate language than they might for more routine assignments. While students are writing a simple poem about someone they care about, or while they are trying to construct a narrative or tell stories of their childhood, for example, they are tapping into their own experiences. This provides powerful motivation to find the right words to express such experience. Creative writing also provokes the kind of input–output relationship we described in Chapter 17, B1.

In order to bolster the 'product pride' that students may feel when they have written creatively, we need to provide an appropriate reader audience. Apart from ourselves as teachers, the whole class can also be such an audience. We can put students' writing up on a class noticeboard, or copy it and include it in class magazines. We can make anthologies and distribute them to friends, parents, and other teachers; we can, if we want, set up web sites for our classes on the Internet (see Chapter 10F).

There is always a danger that students may find writing imaginatively difficult. Having 'nothing to say' they may find creative writing a painful and de-motivating experience, associated in their minds with a sense of frustration and failure. A lot will depend upon how we encourage them (see B6 below). It is also important not to expect whole compositions from the very first. We need to build up creative writing bit by bit (see Chapter 6, B1), starting with phrases and sentences before expecting whole compositions.

B4 Writing as a cooperative activity

Although many people in their personal lives write on their own, whether at home or at work, in language classes teachers and students can take advantage of the presence of others to make writing a cooperative activity, with great benefit to all those involved. In one example of such an approach, group writing allowed the lecturer to give more detailed and constructive feedback since she was dealing with a small number of groups rather than many individual students (Boughey 1997). Individual students also found themselves saying and writing things they might not have come up with on their own, and the group's research was broader than an individual's normally was.

Cooperative writing works well with both process and genre-based approaches. In the first case, reviewing and evaluation are greatly enhanced by having more than one person working on it, and the generation of ideas is frequently more lively with two or more people involved than it is when writers work on their own. In genre-based writing, two heads analyse genre-specific texts as well as, if not better than, one head would do, and often create genre-specific texts more successfully as a result.

Writing in groups, whether as part of a long process or as part of a short game-like communicative activity, can be greatly motivating for students, including as it does, not only writing, but research, discussion, peer evaluation and group pride in a group accomplishment.

B5 Using the computer

Where schools have computers which students have access to, there are many good reasons for using them for writing, as the following list shows:

- A word-processing package removes the problem of poor handwriting that some students suffer from.
- A word-processing package allows the competent user to edit his or her material at great speed and with great facility.
- Spellcheckers can ease the task of achieving correct spelling.
- If students are working in groups, a computer screen can sometimes be far more visible to the whole group than a piece of paper might be.

A computer screen frequently allows students to see their writing more objectively. It also has the advantage of greatly enhancing the participation of individuals when they are working with their colleagues in pairs or groups.

An important use of the computer is as the means of creating 'mouse-pals', the e-mail equivalent of pen-pals. Getting students to write e-mails in English to others around the world can be extremely motivating. The communication is immediate and exciting, and may well stimulate and motivate students where other letter writing does not.

Teachers can have students e-mail each other within a school provided that they can set up the requisite number of individual addresses. If teachers can make contact with another school, they can then get lists of those students' addresses and have their own students write to individuals at the other school.

E-mails represent a genre all of their own where linguistic accuracy is not so formally important. But despite this, we can still encourage students to 'sit back' and consider the results of their efforts before clicking on the 'send' icon.

B6 The roles of the teacher

Although the teacher needs to deploy some or all of the usual roles (see Chapter 4B) when students are asked to write, the ones that are especially important are as follows:

- **Motivator:** one of our principal roles in writing tasks will be to motivate the students, creating the right conditions for the generation of ideas, persuading them of the usefulness of the activity, and encouraging them to make as much effort as possible for maximum benefit. This may require special and prolonged effort on our part for longer process-writing sequences.

  Where students are involved in a creative writing activity it is usually the case that some find it easier to generate ideas than others. During poem-writing activities, for example, we may need to suggest lines to those who cannot think of anything, or at least prompt them with our own ideas.

- **Resource:** especially during more extended writing tasks, we should be ready to supply information and language where necessary. We need to tell students that we are available and be prepared to look at their work as it progresses, offering advice and suggestions in a constructive and tactful way. Because writing takes longer than conversation, for example, there is usually time for discussion with individual students, or students working in pairs or groups.

- **Feedback provider:** giving feedback on writing tasks demands special care (see Chapter 7D). Teachers should respond positively and encouragingly to the content of what the students have written. When offering correction teachers should choose what and how much to focus on based on what students need at this particular stage of their studies, and on the tasks they have undertaken.

C Writing lesson sequences

In the following examples the writing activity is specified, together with its particular focus. The way that the text can be used within a lesson is explained.

Example 1: Paul's business trip	Activity: punctuating a text
	Focus: writing conventions
	Age: young adult and above
	Level: elementary

In this task students practise basic punctuation such as capital letters, commas, apostrophes and full stops. To complete the task, they need to be aware of where a speaker would pause to breathe when reading the text out loud, as this will help them punctuate the task correctly.

Students are told to look at the pictures and listen to the story. While and after they listen, they have to change the unpunctuated text by using capital letters, commas, apostrophes and full stops (the ends of the first two sentences are given):

it was friday and it was pauls big business trip to new york in america / he got up at 5 am got dressed had a cup of coffee and read the newspaper / at 6 am a taxi arrived to take him to london airport paul locked the door and put his bags in the taxi but he left his briefcase in the house his business papers his money his credit cards his plane ticket and his passport were all in his briefcase luckily the taxi driver asked paul if he had his ticket paul ran back into the house and got his briefcase but this time he ran out of the house and left his keys inside

From *Elementary Matters Workbook* by G Cunningham (Pearson Education Ltd)

If the unpunctuated text can be displayed on computer screens, students can discuss as a whole group how to punctuate it, helping each other to understand how punctuation works.

Example 2: The genre analyser	Activity: writing a review
	Focus: identifying genre features
	Age: young adult and above
	Level: upper intermediate and above

In this sequence we want our students to write reviews of plays, concerts, or films they have seen, and to do this in a way which is appropriate for the kind of audience (either real or imaginary) they are writing for.

First we ask our students to look at a collection of reviews of plays and films, from newspapers, magazines, and/or on the Internet. For each one they have to use the following reviewers' 'genre-analysing' kit:

REVIEWERS' GENRE-ANALYSING KIT

Answer the following questions about the review you are reading:

MEANING
What is being reviewed?
Does the reviewer like it?
What, if anything, was especially good about the thing/event being reviewed?
What, if anything, was especially bad about the thing/event being reviewed?
Who, if anybody, deserves credit for their part in it?
Who, if anybody, should be criticised for their part in it?
What, if anything, does the thing/event remind the reviewer of?

CONSTRUCTION
How is the headline/caption constructed?
What does each paragraph contain, and how are the paragraphs sequenced?
What grammar and lexis is used to show approval?
What grammar and lexis is used to show disapproval?

By studying the reviews and answering the questions above about them, students build up a picture of how they are usually written.

We can now show them a video or get them to go to a play or a film. While watching it they make notes about such items as the plot, the characters, the performances, the music, the cinematography and the special effects.

Afterwards students draft their reviews, using language – if appropriate – from the reviews they read previously. The teacher can go round, encouraging and helping. If there is time he or she can read the full drafts and give constructive feedback on each one. Students then write their final version, and later, when all the reviews have been read, the class can vote on the best one.

Writing reviews can be greatly enhanced by having students write in pairs or groups, keying their opinions directly into a word processor. The discussion and focus which the computer screen provides will add to the creative nature of the activity in many ways.

Studying different writing genres – whether through a 'genre-analysing kit', data collection, or even putting a variety of texts into a corpus to run with concordancing packages (see Chapter 12 C) – is a vital first stage in having students do their own writing in specific genres.

Example 3: A poem	Activity: 'running dictation'
	Focus: writing for fun, concentrating on writing correctly
	Age: any
	Level: pre-intermediate and above

In the following example (adapted from Davis and Rinvolucri 1988) the basic idea of a dictation has been subverted somewhat so that students dictate to each other, making the writing that happens as a result of this enjoyable and perplexing in turns.

Students are put into groups. The teacher puts an A4 copy of the following poem on a table at the front of the classroom:

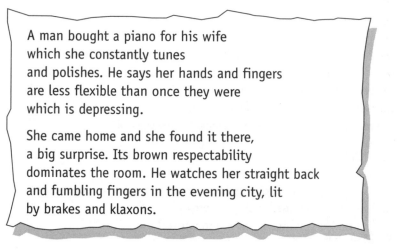

A man bought a piano for his wife
which she constantly tunes
and polishes. He says her hands and fingers
are less flexible than once they were
which is depressing.

She came home and she found it there,
a big surprise. Its brown respectability
dominates the room. He watches her straight back
and fumbling fingers in the evening city, lit
by brakes and klaxons.

Each group sends a representative to the front of the class to read only the first line of the poem, memorise it, and then run back to their group and dictate the line. When this has happened, groups send a second (and then a third) representative to read the second (and third) line(s) and take that back to their groups and dictate it.

The activity goes on in this way until one group has the whole poem. The teacher can then give that group a further task while the others finish, or stop the class and show everyone a complete version of the poem for them to check their own version against. They are then asked to decide on their own title for the poem (originally called 'Piano Piece').

An alternative procedure at this point is to ask all the students to write down, in complete silence, what the poem means for them – however flippant or profound their response is. They can, for example, write 'nothing' if they feel like it. When they have done this they stand up, still in silence, and go round reading what other people have written. The effect of writing and silence in this way can be dramatic and enjoyable.

Example 4: Julia's story	Activity: story circle
	Focus: cooperative narrative writing
	Age: any
	Level: elementary and above

In this activity students join together to write a story. But there is an element of fun built into the activity and the results are not intended to be taken too seriously.

Students are put into groups of about five, sitting in circles. The teacher then dictates a sentence such as:

> That day, when Julia came back from work, she knew something was different.

Each student writes the sentence at the top of their piece of paper. They are then asked to write the next sentence in Julia's story; all they have to do is write one sentence which follows on from this introduction.

When all the students have done this the teacher tells them to pass their pieces of paper to the person on their left. They all now have to write the next sentence of the story which has just been passed to them. When they have finished, the teacher asks everyone to pass their papers to the person on their left. They all now have to write the next sentence of the story on the piece of paper in front of them.

The procedure continues until the pieces of paper return to their original owners. At this point the teacher tells everyone to write a sentence to finish the story off – however ridiculous!

The students are then encouraged to read out the stories they have just finished. The results are often highly amusing, and because many hands have collaborated in the process, nobody has to suffer individual responsibility for the final versions. The teacher should make sure that quite a few of the stories are heard by the class, and that the rest are available for everyone else to read.

This kind of group writing is enjoyable and useful for developing writing fluency. However, it should be used sparingly, otherwise it will lose its main attraction of spontaneity.

Example 5: Lady Margaret Beaufort	Activity: looking at notes
	Focus: abbreviations and other note-taking conventions
	Age: adult
	Level: advanced

If students are to write complex compositions they will need to make notes when they plan their work. In this example at the advanced level students are first asked to think of at least three situations when they might need or want to take notes. They are then asked to say when abbreviations, punctuation, initials, numbered points and drawings might help them. They are then asked if they have any special methods that they personally find useful.

Students are then asked to say what the following signs and symbols mean and to write examples of each in an appropriate context:

a	e.g.	**e**	c. 500 people	**i**	=
b	etc.	**f**	Shakespeare et al.	**j**	<
c	N.B.	**g**	→	**k**	>
d	15th c.	**h**	∴	**l**	&

From *English Panorama 1* by F O'Dell (Cambridge University Press)

They are now given the following text and task:

Lady Margaret Beaufort. b. 1443

= d. of Sir John Beaufort, 1st Duke of Somerset

= m. of Henry VII (b. 1457)

1455 (!) married Edmund Tudor

During part of Wars of Roses (1455–85, betw.

Houses of Lancaster & York) MB imprisoned at

Pembroke by Yorkists.

Lancastrian claim to Eng. throne passed to MB

as grand-d. of John of Gaunt (after extinction

of male line)

Henry ascended throne after defeat Richard III

1485 (Battle of Bosworth Field)

1464 m. 2 Henry Stafford (s. of Duke of

Buckingham)

1475 m. 3 Thomas Stanley (1st Earl of Derby)

Founded Christ's and St John's Colls., Camb.

Endowed 2 divinity professorships at Oxford

& Cambridge

Patron of Will Caxton (1st Eng. printer)

d. 1509

Subsequently students read and listen to additional information related to the topic which they have to make notes on.

The whole sequence has allowed students to consider the business of note-taking and the symbols we use. We could also show students three or four different note-taking methods (numbered points, a spidergram, or points recorded in no particular style or order) and ask which they would find most useful (see page 338).

Example 6: Women in the US	Activity: report writing
	Focus: coherence
	Age: adult
	Level: advanced

In this sequence students write a report based on the following statistics about women in the USA:

Women in the U.S. – *A New Look*

NUMBER:
More than half of the population

The nation's 119.1 million females comprise 51.3 percent of the total population. Ten years from now, they will number 130.3 million, but their proportion of the total population will be about the same as today. Now, there are 88.4 million women age 18 and up.

RACE:
6 of 7 are white

Of all females – 101.6 million or 85 percent, are whites, 14.6 million, or 12 percent, are blacks, 2.9 million are of other races.

AGE:
Older than men on the average

The median age of females is 31.9 years, compared with 29.3 years for males. And females are getting older, in 10 years, their median age will be 34.5 years, and by the year 2000, 36.8 years.

LIFE SPAN:
Women live longer than men

The average female lives to a little more than 78 years, or nearly eight years longer than the average male. The gap in life expectancy is widening – it was little more than seven years two decades ago.

EDUCATION:
More likely to attend college

Among persons age 18 to 24, 35 percent of women are enroled in college, compared with 34 percent of men. At last count, 23.4 percent of graduating medical doctors were women, as were 30.2 percent of lawyers.

MARRIAGE:
More women are putting It off

Just over half of the women age 20–34 have never been married, compared with 35.8 percent in 1970 and 28.4 percent in 1960. But 83 percent of women ultimately do marry.

FAMILIES:
Those headed by women rise sharply

More than 1 in 7 families – 9.1 million – are headed by women. The number has risen by 65 percent since 1970, largely because of the climbing divorce rate.

CHILDREN:
Women want fewer offspring

Of childless married women age 18–34, 23 percent expect to have one child or none, while 72 percent expect to bear two or three children. Only 5 percent expect four or more. If fulfilled, these plans mean little population growth.

POLITICAL POWER:
Edge in numbers at the top

Women of voting age are 52.2 percent of all Americans age 18 and up. With women living longer than men, the proportion is growing.

From *Language Issues* by G Porter-Ladousse (Pearson Education Ltd)

They start, in groups of three, by deciding which topics go together to make a coherent paragraph (as an example they are told that the topic of children probably goes well with the topic of families).

Each person in the group chooses one of the paragraphs they have planned and writes it up. They are told to link the information together with cohesive devices they have studied, especially contrasting two pieces of information with words such as *whereas, but, in spite of*, etc.

In their groups students now study their three paragraphs and work out what order they should go in and how to join them together. If they have access to computer screens, each group has a chance to make immediate changes of sequence and language.

When the complete reports have been finished, they can be put up on the board or included in a web site so that they can be compared with other groups' versions. A discussion can now develop about which versions are more coherent or easy to read.

This sequence shows how planning the order of ideas in a text, coupled with the use of previously studied cohesive language, can produce well thought out reports which can then provide good material for comparison and discussion.

Chapter notes and further reading

- **Spelling and pronunciation correspondence**

    See J O'Connor and C Fletcher (1989), G Kelly (2000: Appendix C), and R Shemesh and S Waller (2000).

- **Genre writing**

    C Tribble (1997: Chapters 5 and 6) makes a strong case for a genre-based approach. R Badger and G White (2000) advocate a 'process genre' approach!

- **Computers**

    An early but still extremely useful article on word processing for students is A Piper (1987).

- **Pen-pals/mouse-pals**

    See H Hennigan (1999) on how pen-pals became, in his words, 'keypals'. See also D Teeler (2000: 175–176).

    There are many pen-pal sites on the Internet as any search will show. Typical of what is on offer at the time of writing are:

    http://www.penpalgarden.com/ – a large free pen-pal site where you fill in details about yourself and indicate whether you want pen-pals of the same or opposite gender.

    http://www.penpal.net – one of the largest free pen-pal sites on the Internet, you can select contacts by age and country.

    http://www.nationalgeographic.com/kids/ngo/penpal/index.html – where children are matched to similar pen-pals around the world. There is a small charge per person.

- **Dictation**

    The renaissance of various forms of dictation (such as the poetry dictation in this chapter) can be chiefly ascribed to P Davis and M Rinvolucri (1988).

19 | Speaking

A Elements of speaking

The ability to speak fluently presupposes not only a knowledge of language features, but also the ability to process information and language 'on the spot'.

A1 Language features

Among the elements necessary for spoken production (as opposed to the production of practice examples in language drills, for example), are the following:

- **Connected speech:** effective speakers of English need to be able not only to produce the individual phonemes of English (as in saying *I would have gone*) but also to use fluent 'connected speech' (as in *I'd've gone*). In connected speech sounds are modified (assimilation), omitted (elision), added (linking *r*), or weakened (through contractions and stress patterning) (see Chapter 2, D4 and D5). It is for this reason that we should involve students in activities designed specifically to improve their connected speech (see Chapter 13, B5).

- **Expressive devices:** native speakers of English change the pitch and stress of particular parts of utterances, vary volume and speed, and show by other physical and non-verbal (paralinguistic) means how they are feeling (especially in face-to-face interaction). The use of these devices contributes to the ability to convey meanings. They allow the extra expression of emotion and intensity. Students should be able to deploy at least some of such suprasegmental features and devices in the same way if they are to be fully effective communicators.

- **Lexis and grammar:** spontaneous speech is marked by the use of a number of common lexical phrases, especially in the performance of certain language functions (see Chapter 2, C1). Teachers should therefore supply a variety of phrases for different functions such as agreeing or disagreeing, expressing surprise, shock, or approval. Where students are involved in specific speaking contexts such as a job interview, we can prime them, in the same way, with certain useful phrases which they can produce at various stages of an interaction.

- **Negotiation language:** effective speaking benefits from the negotiatory language we use to seek clarification and to show the structure of what we are saying.

We often need to 'ask for clarification' when we are listening to someone else talk. For students this is especially crucial. A useful thing teachers can do, therefore, is to offer them phrases such as the following:

> (I'm sorry) I didn't quite catch that.
> (I'm sorry) I don't understand.
> What exactly does X mean?
> Could you explain that again, please?

A way of getting students to practise this language is to give individuals cards which each have one of these phrases written on them. We can then start to explain something but insert words or explanations that are purposefully incomprehensible or obscure. Students then have to use the language forms written on their cards to interrupt and ask what we mean.

Speakers also need to 'structure their discourse' if they want to be understood, especially in more 'writing-like' speech such as giving presentations. They need to use certain phrases to highlight the content structure of their discourse. They use negotiation language to show the structure of their thoughts, or reformulate what they are saying in order to be clearer, especially when they can see that they are not being understood.

We can help our students to structure discourse by giving them language such as the following:

> The important thing to grasp is that ...
> To begin with/And finally ...
> What I am trying to say is that ...
> What I mean is ...
> The point I am trying to make is that ...
> ... or, to put it another way ...,
> etc.

If students are going to give a presentation they can be told to include this kind of structuring/reformulating language. We can provoke its use, too, by giving those who are listening role cards like the following:

> Without speaking, show that you do not understand what the speaker is saying, by looking confused, scratching your head in confusion, etc. However, only do this once.

> Without speaking, show that you do not agree with something the speaker is saying, by looking angry, shaking your head, etc. However, only do this once.

Mental/social processing

If part of a speaker's productive ability involves the knowledge of language skills such as those discussed above, success is also dependent upon the rapid processing skills that talking necessitates.

- **Language processing:** effective speakers need to able to process language in their own heads and put it into coherent order so that it comes out in forms that are not only comprehensible, but also convey the meanings that are intended. Language processing involves the retrieval of words and phrases from memory and their assembly into syntactically and propositionally appropriate sequences. One of the main reasons for including speaking activities in language lessons is to help students develop habits of rapid language processing in English.

- **Interacting with others:** most speaking involves interaction with one or more participants. This means that effective speaking also involves a good deal of listening, an understanding of how the other participants are feeling, and a knowledge of how linguistically to take turns or allow others to do so (see Chapter 17, A2).

- **(On-the-spot) information processing:** quite apart from our response to others' feelings, we also need to be able to process the information they tell us the moment we get it. The longer it takes for 'the penny to drop' the less effective we are as instant communicators. However, it should be remembered that this instant response is very culture-specific, and is not prized by speakers in many other language communities.

B Classroom speaking activities

Many of the classroom speaking activities which are currently in use fall at or near the communicative end of the communication continuum (see Chapter 6, A4). In this section we will look at some of the most widely-used.

B1 Acting from a script

We can ask our students to act out scenes from plays and/or their coursebooks, sometimes filming the results (see Example 5 in Chapter 20, D2). Students will often act out dialogues they have written themselves. This frequently involves them in coming out to the front of the class.

When choosing who should come out to the front of the class we need to be careful not to choose the shyest students first, and we need to work to create the right kind of supportive atmosphere in the class. We need to give students time to rehearse their dialogues before they are asked to perform them. Where the whole class is working on the same dialogue or play extract, we can go through the script as if we were theatre directors, drawing attention to appropriate stress, intonation, and speed. By giving students practice in these things before they give their final performances, we ensure that acting out is both a learning and a language producing activity.

B2 Communication games

Games which are designed to provoke communication between students frequently depend on an information gap (see Chapter 6, A4) so that one student has to talk to a partner in order to solve a puzzle, draw a picture (describe and draw), put things in the right order (describe and arrange), or find similarities and differences between pictures.

Television and radio games, imported into the classroom, often provide good fluency activities, as the following examples demonstrate. In 'Twenty Questions' the chairperson thinks of an object and tells a team that the object is either *animal, vegetable,* or *mineral* – or a combination of two or three of these. The team has to find out what the object is asking only 'yes/no' questions such as *Can you use it in the kitchen?* or *Is it bigger than a person?* They get points if they guess the answer in twenty questions or less.

'Just a Minute' is a long running comedy contest where each participant has to speak for sixty seconds on a subject they are given by the chairperson/teacher without hesitation, repetition, or deviation – or, in the case of language students, language mistakes. If another contestant hears any of these he or she interrupts, gets a point and carries on with the subject. The person who is speaking at the end of sixty seconds gets two points.

'Call My Bluff' involves two teams. Team A is given a word that members of the other team are unlikely to know. Team A finds a correct dictionary definition of the word and then makes up two false ones of their own. They read out their definitions and team B has to guess which is the correct one. Now team B reads out three definitions of their word (one correct and two false) and team A has to guess.

In other games, different tricks or devices are used to make fluent speaking amusing. In 'Fishbowl', for example, two students speak but at a prearranged signal one of the participants has to reach into the fishbowl and take out one of the many pieces of paper on which students have previously written phrases, questions, and sentences. They have to incorporate these into the conversation straight away.

B3 Discussion

One of the reasons that discussions fail (when they do) is that students are reluctant to give an opinion in front of the whole class, particularly if they cannot think of anything to say and are not, anyway, confident of the language they might use to say it. Many students feel extremely exposed in discussion situations.

The 'buzz group' is one way in which a teacher can avoid such difficulties. All it means is that students have a chance for quick discussions in small groups before any of them are asked to speak in public. Because they have a chance to think of ideas and the language to express them with before being asked to talk in front of the whole class, the stress level of that eventual whole-class performance is reduced.

Buzz groups can be used for a whole range of discussions. For example, we might want students to predict the content of a reading text, or we may want them to talk about their reactions to it after they have read it. We might want them to discuss what should be included in a news broadcast or have a quick conversation about the right kind of music for a wedding or party.

Another way in which we can train students to respond fluently and immediately is to insert 'instant comment' mini-activities into lessons. This involves showing them photographs or introducing topics at any stage of a lesson and nominating students to say the first thing that comes into their head.

The opposite extreme to informal buzz groups is the formal debate, where students prepare arguments in favour or against various propositions, so that, when the debate starts, the panel speakers produce well-rehearsed 'writing-like arguments', whereas others in the 'audience' pitch in with their own (less scripted) thoughts on the subject as the debate progresses.

A popular debating game which has survived many decades of use is the 'balloon debate', so called because it is based on a scenario in which a group of people are travelling in the basket of a balloon. Unfortunately, however, the balloon cannot take their weight. There is a leak, and unless someone leaves the balloon, they will all die. Students take on the role of a real-life person, either living or historical – from Confucius to Shakespeare, from Cleopatra to Marie Curie. They think up arguments about why they should be the survivors either individually, or in pairs or groups. After a first round of argument, everyone votes on who should be the first to jump. As more air escapes a second round means that one more person has to go, until, some rounds later, the eventual sole survivor is chosen.

Participants in a balloon debate can represent occupations rather than specific characters; they can take on the roles of different age groups, hobby enthusiasts, or societies.

Some discussions just happen in the middle of lessons; they are unprepared for by the teacher, but, if encouraged, can provide some of the most enjoyable and productive speaking in language classes. Their success will depend upon our ability to prompt and encourage and, perhaps, to change our attitude to errors and mistakes (see Chapter 7C) from one minute to the next. Pre-planned discussions, on the other hand, depend for their success upon the way we ask students to approach the task in hand.

One of the best ways of encouraging discussion is to provide activities which force students to reach a decision or a consensus, often as a result of choosing between specific alternatives. An example of this kind of activity (with particular relevance to schools) is where students consider a scenario in which an invigilator during a public exam catches a student copying from hidden notes. The class has to decide between a range of options, such as:

> The invigilator should ignore it.
> She should give the student a sign to show that she's seen (so that the student will stop).
> She should call the family and tell them the student was cheating.
> She should inform the examining board so that the student will not be able to take that exam again.

The fact of having to make such an awkward choice gives the discussion a clear purpose, and an obvious outcome to aim for.

B4 Prepared talks

A popular kind of activity is the prepared talk where a student (or students) makes a presentation on a topic of their own choice. Such talks are not designed for informal spontaneous conversation; because they are prepared, they are more 'writing-like' than this (see Chapter 17, A3). However, if possible, students should speak from notes rather than from a script.

Prepared talks represent a defined and useful speaking genre, and if properly organised, can be extremely interesting for both speaker and listeners. Just as in process writing (see Chapter 18, B1) the development of the talk, from original ideas to finished work, will be of vital importance.

B5 Questionnaires

Questionnaires are useful because, by being pre-planned, they ensure that both questioner and respondent have something to say to each other. Depending upon how tightly designed they are, they may well encourage the natural use of certain repetitive language patterns – and thus be situated in the middle of our communication continuum (see Chapter 6, A4).

Students can design questionnaires on any topic that is appropriate. As they do so the teacher can act as a resource, helping them in the design process. The results obtained from questionnaires can then form the basis for written work, discussions, or prepared talks.

B6 Simulation and role-play

Many students derive great benefit from simulation and role-play. Students 'simulate' a real-life encounter (such as a business meeting, an encounter in an aeroplane cabin, or an interview) as if they were doing so in the real world, either as themselves in that meeting or aeroplane, or taking on the role of a character different from themselves or with thoughts and feelings they do not necessarily share. Simulation and role-play can be used to encourage general oral fluency, or to train students for specific situations especially where they are studying ESP (see Chapter 1, B3).

For a simulation to work it must, according to Ken Jones, have the following characteristics:

- **reality of function:** the students must not think of themselves as students, but as real participants in the situation.

- **a simulated environment:** the teacher says that the classroom is an airport check-in area, for example.

- **structure:** students must see how the activity is constructed and they must be given the necessary information to carry out the simulation effectively.

From K Jones (1982: 4–7)

In a role-play we add the element of giving the participants information about who they are, and what they think and feel. Thus we might tell a student that they are *a motorist who thinks that parking restrictions are unnecessary* or *You are Michelle and you want Robin to notice you, but you don't want him to know about your brother*, etc.

Role-plays are effective when they are open-ended, so that different people have different views of what the outcome should be, and a consensus has to be reached. That way there is a dynamic movement as the role-play progresses, with people clearly motivated to say as much or as little as they need to achieve their aims. In one such intermediate level activity ('Knife in the school') a boy has brought a large hunting knife into a school and the boy, his parents, the head teacher, and class teacher have a meeting to decide what must be done about it. The students take the role of one of these characters based on a role card which tells them how they feel (e.g. *Jo Glassman, teacher: Two of your pupils, Sean and Cathy, told you that they had seen the knife, but are afraid to confront Brian about it. You believe them absolutely even though you didn't actually see the knife yourself. However, you don't want Brian to know that Sean and Cathy are responsible for this meeting. You want to see Brian suspended from the school.*). In groups of five the students role-play the meeting, and at the end different groups discuss the decisions they have come to.

Clearly 'Knife in the school' might be inappropriate in some situations, but other role-plays such as planning meetings, television 'issue' shows, and public protest meetings are fairly easy to replicate in the classroom.

In a different kind of role-playing activity, students write the kind of questions they might ask anybody when they meet them first. Students are then given paintings by Goya, for example, and are asked to answer those questions as if they were characters from the painting (Cranmer 1996: 68–72). The same kind of imaginative interview role-play could be based around people in dramatic photographs.

Simulation and role-play went through a period of relative unpopularity, yet this is a pity since they have three distinct advantages. In the first place they can be good fun and thus motivating. Second, they allow hesitant students to be more forthright in their opinions and behaviour than they might be when speaking for themselves, since they do not have to take the same responsibility for what they are saying. Third, by broadening the world of the classroom to include the world outside, they allow students to use a much wider range of language than some more task-centred activities may do (see Chapter 6, A5).

B7 The roles of the teacher

As with any other type of classroom procedure, teachers need to play a number of different roles (see Chapter 4B) during the speaking activities described above. However, three have particular relevance if we are trying to get students to speak fluently:

- **Prompter:** students sometimes get lost, cannot think of what to say next, or in some other way lose the fluency we expect of them. We can leave them to · struggle out of such situations on their own, and indeed sometimes this may be the best option (see Chapter 7, C1). However, we may be able to help them and the activity to progress by offering discrete suggestions. If this can be done supportively – without disrupting the discussion, or forcing students out of role – it will stop the sense of frustration that some students feel when they come to a 'dead end' of language or ideas.

- **Participant:** teachers should be good animators when asking students to produce language. Sometimes this can be achieved by setting up an activity clearly and with enthusiasm. At other times, however, teachers may want to participate in discussions or role-plays themselves. That way they can prompt covertly, introduce new information to help the activity along, ensure continuing student engagement, and generally maintain a creative atmosphere. However, in such circumstances they have to be careful that they do not participate too much, thus dominating the speaking and drawing all the attention to themselves.

- **Feedback provider:** the vexed question of when and how to give feedback in speaking activities is answered by considering carefully the effect of possible different approaches.

  When students are in the middle of a speaking activity, over-correction may inhibit them and take the communicativeness out of the activity. On the other hand, helpful and gentle correction may get students out of difficult misunderstandings and hesitations. Everything depends upon our tact and the appropriacy of the feedback we give in particular situations.

  When students have completed an activity it is vital that we allow them to assess what they have done and that we tell them what, in our opinion, went well. We will respond to the content of the activity as well as the language used. Feedback for oral fluency work is described in detail in Chapter 7, C3.

C Speaking lesson sequences

In the following examples the speaking activity is specified, together with its particular focus.

Example 1: Experts	Activity: communication game
	Focus: controlled language processing
	Age: any
	Level: elementary and above

The following game-like activity based on a London 'Comedy Store' routine is used by the writer Ken Wilson (Wilson 1997) for getting students to think and speak quickly.

The class chooses four or five students to be a panel of 'experts'. They come and sit in a row facing the class. The class then chooses a subject that these students are going to have to be experts on. This can be anything, from transport policy to film music, from fish to football. In pairs or groups, the class write down the questions they want to ask the experts about this particular subject. The teacher can go round the class checking the questions as they do this. Finally, once the questions have been written, they are put to the experts.

The element of this activity that makes it amusing is that each expert only says one word at a time, so the sentence is only gradually built up. Because the experts often cannot think of how to continue it, it can ramble on in ever more extreme contortions until someone is lucky enough or clever enough to be in a position to finish it (with just one word). The following example shows how it might begin:

Question: How do fish breathe?
Expert 1: The
Expert 2: answer
Expert 3: to
Expert 4: this
Expert 1: question
Expert 2: is
Expert 3: an
Expert 4: answer
Expert 1: that ...
etc.

'Experts' encourages even reluctant speakers on the panel to speak, even if (or perhaps because) they only have to produce one word at a time. It keeps both experts and questioners engaged in the construction of utterances in a controlled but often surreal environment.

Example 2: Films	Activity: questionnaire
	Focus: lexis and grammar, interacting with others
	Age: young adult and above
	Level: lower intermediate and above

In this sequence the class have recently been working on the contrasting uses of the present perfect and the past simple.

The activity starts when the teacher talks to the students about the five or six most popular films that are currently on show or which have been extremely popular in the last six months or a year. They are then told that they are going to find out which of these films is the most popular one in the class.

The teacher hands out the following questionnaire form – or writes it on the board and has the students copy it. They put the names of the films they have discussed in the left-hand column.

Name of film	Tick if seen	Good (✔✔), satisfactory (✔), bad (✗) or very bad (✗✗)

The class now discuss the kinds of questions they can use, e.g. *Have you seen X? What did you think of it?* In pairs students now interview each other and ask if they have seen any of the films and what they thought of them. They complete the charts about their partner.

The teacher now gets a student up to the board and asks them to fill in the chart based on what students have found out, e.g. *How many people have seen X?* and *How many people thought that X was very good?* This can then lead on to a discussion of the films in question. Students can be encouraged to say which was the best bit of one of the films, who their favourite actors are, etc. The results of the questionnaires can be put on the board.

Questionnaires are often the first stage in much longer sequences, leading on to written reports and discussions. In this case, for example, students can use the questionnaire results for discussion or to write their own 'film page' for a real or imagined magazine.

Example 3: Whose line is it anyway?	Activity: improvisation game
	Focus: language processing, interacting with others
	Age: upper intermediate and above
	Level: young adult and above

'Whose Line is it Anyway?', taken from a British Channel 4 television game, is a challenging exercise for students. Two students come to the front of the class. The teacher asks the rest of the class to say <u>who</u> each of the students is (e.g. *policeman, nurse, teacher, president*) and chooses the most interesting and communicatively generative suggestions. The pair of students might now represent a policeman and a midwife – or any other combination of occupations.

The teacher then asks the students <u>where</u> a conversation between these two is taking place; they might suggest a café, the street, a cinema, or a beach. Finally, the teacher asks the students <u>what</u> they are talking about. It could be speeding, nuclear physics, childcare, a film they have both seen, or football. The pair at the front might now be a policeman and a midwife on a beach talking about speeding.

The two students playing the game have to improvise a conversation straight away. They win points based on how well they manage. As an added twist the teacher can give one of the participants a card with a word describing how they speak, e.g. *politely, angrily, ingratiatingly*, and when the conversation is over the rest of the class has to guess what word that participant was given.

The game does not have to be quite so brutal, however. Students can practise the conversations in pairs before coming up to the front. Everything depends upon the teacher–student relationship.

Example 4: Rooms in a house	Activity: discussion
	Focus: interacting with others
	Age: adult
	Level: upper intermediate

The following sequence is designed to train students for the speaking component of the Cambridge First Certificate exam (FCE – see page 333 for details).

Students are shown the following information about a family who are going to move into a house:

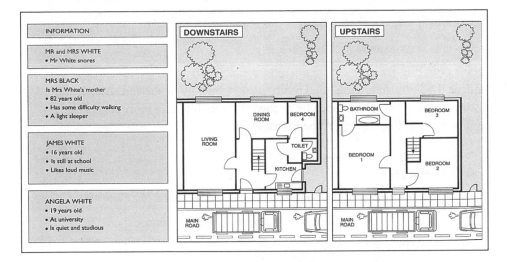

From *New First Certificate Masterclass* by S Haines and B Stewart (Oxford University Press)

They then have to decide which bedroom would be the most suitable for each member of the family. Subsequently, they have to choose any two members of the family and say how they might decorate and furnish their rooms.

Though the task is, in itself, fairly easy, the ability to discuss issues like this in a foreign language is not, especially when (as in an FCE exam situation) they have to talk to each other with an examiner listening and assessing their performance. A lot will depend on how we have approached discussion, in general, in the class (see B3 above).

Example 5: Travel agent	Activity: role-play
	Focus: interacting with others, information processing
	Age: any
	Level: intermediate and above

In this example, an information gap is created which means that the role-play has a genuinely communicative dimension built into it. The students have been working in the area of tourism. They are told that in pairs they are going to act out a scene in a travel agency, where one student is a customer and the other is a travel agent. Student A is given the following information:

A Customer

You want:
- a double room
- to go to a hotel in Miami for 7 nights (You can spend up to $1400 on a hotel.)
- to be as near as possible to the city centre
- to go to a hotel with a good discotheque
- a children's swimming pool for your small son
- someone to be available to look after your son at the hotel
- the hotel to serve good food
- a comfortable room (with a good view)

Student B gets the following hotel information which he or she can show to the customer if necessary, but which he or she will probably have more success explaining by telling student A the information:

B Travel agent

Study the following information carefully so that you can answer **A** (the customer).

	Sun Inn	Regency Park	Paradiso	Oasis
Cost (double) per night	$180	$175	$210	$130
View	☺	☺☺	☺☺☺	☺☺
Distance from centre	10 miles	12 miles	20 miles	3 miles
Disco	☺	☺☺	☺☺☺	—
Restaurant	☺☺	☺☺☺	☺☺☺	
Adults' swimming pool	☺☺☺	☺	☺☺	☺
Children's swimming pool	☺	☺☺	☺☺☺	—
Childcare facilities	—	☺☺	☺	—

Note: Various features (e.g. view, discos, restaurants, etc.) have been given different 'smile' ratings to indicate quality.

☺☺☺ = excellent, ☺☺ = very good, and ☺ = good

As an example we can say that you get a better view if you're staying at the Paradiso than you do if you are staying at the Regency Park.

Students are given time to study their information. The teacher points out that the customer needs to select the hotel based, as far as possible, on the six qualities they want.

While students act out the scene in pairs we can go round listening, prompting if necessary, recording examples of especially good or not very successful language use.

When the pairs have completed their role-plays we can have them compare what happened. Did all the customers choose the Regency Park (the hotel with the nearest set of qualities to the customer's needs)? What did they find difficult/easy? We can then discuss things we heard which went well – and not so well.

Chapter notes and further reading

- **Discussion**

  P Ur (1981) is still a classic account of different discussion activities. On developing discussion skills, see C Green et al. (1997).

- **Debate**

  On 'democratic debates' (with the students choosing the topic) see P Capone and K Hayward (1996).

- **Prepared talks**

  On student lectures see M Geldicke (1997).

- **Teacher roles**

  On intervention during communication activities see T Lynch (1997).

- **Role-play and simulation**

  The best account of role-play and simulation is still K Jones (1982) (see B6 above) which includes a wonderful simulation about simulations for teachers. However, A Al-Arishi (1994) sees reasons why role-play should not be widely used.

20 | Teaching with video

A Using video in language learning

The use of videotapes has been a common feature in language teaching for many years. It is rare, these days, for a publisher to produce a major coursebook without a video component added in, and teachers frequently enliven their classes with off-air material or tapes produced for language learning.

A1 Why use video?

To some people videotape is merely a glorified version of audiotape, and the use of video in class is just listening 'with pictures'. But there are many reasons why video can add a special, extra dimension to the learning experience:

- **Seeing language-in-use:** one of the main advantages of video is that students do not just hear language, they see it too. This greatly aids comprehension, since for example, general meaning and moods are often conveyed through expression, gesture (see Chapter 2, E2), and other visual clues. Thus we can observe how intonation can match facial expression. All such paralinguistic features give valuable meaning clues and help viewers to see beyond what they are listening to, and thus interpret the text more deeply (see Chapter 14, A4).

- **Cross-cultural awareness:** video uniquely allows students a look at situations far beyond their classrooms. This is especially useful if they want to see, for example, typical British 'body language' when inviting someone out, or how Americans speak to waiters. Video is also of great value in giving students a chance to see such things as what kinds of food people eat in other countries, and what they wear.

- **The power of creation:** when students use video cameras themselves they are given the potential to create something memorable and enjoyable. The camera operators and directors suddenly have considerable power. The task of video-making can provoke genuinely creative and communicative uses of the language, with students finding themselves 'doing new things in English' (Cooper et al. 1991: 6).

- **Motivation:** for all of the reasons so far mentioned, most students show an increased level of interest when they have a chance to see language in use as well as hear it, and when this is coupled with interesting tasks.

A2 Video problems

If we wish to use video successfully in classes we need to be aware of a number of potential problems:

- **The 'nothing new' syndrome:** just switching on the monitor in a classroom is not especially exciting for a television (and Internet) viewing population. Both in our choice of video material and in the way we exploit it, we have to provide video activities that are unique learning experiences and do not just replicate home television viewing.

- **Poor quality tapes and disks:** poorly filmed and woodenly acted material will not engage students who are used to something better. When deciding whether to use a videotape or disk, we have to judge whether the quality is sufficiently good to attract our students' interest.

- **Poor viewing conditions:** we have to be sure that students can see and hear the video. The monitor must big enough for the people at the back of the class to see the screen clearly. We also need to see if we can dim the ambient light sufficiently for the picture to be clear.

- **Stop and start:** some students become frustrated when teachers constantly stop and start the video, only showing little bits at a time. It can also be extremely irritating if a teacher fails to show the class how the 'story' ends. Sometimes this is done on purpose – as a spur to creativity or prediction – but at other times some teachers fail to take students' natural curiosity into account.

    There is no hard and fast rule about this. We need to ask ourselves how many stops and starts we ourselves could cope with, and how much we would want to see the end of a sequence. The answers will guide the way we use video with others.

- **The length of extracts:** some people think that more than two or three minutes of video sends students to sleep. Others, however, like to show students whole programmes.

    Short video sequences of between one and four minutes can yield a number of exercises, demonstrate a satisfying range of language, are easier to manipulate, and can be highly motivating. Such short extracts are usually the best option; where we want to use longer ones – because of the topic, or because it is impossible to extract a good short extract – we will need to design activities to keep our students involved.

- **Fingers and thumbs:** students can be irritated by teachers who cannot find what they want or get back to where they have just been on the tape or disk. Teachers themselves become frustrated when the machine does not work the way they want it to. The only answer is for us to familiarise ourselves with the system we're using.

283

A3 Video types

There are three basic types of video which can readily be used in class: 'off-air' programmes, 'real-world' videos, and language learning videos.

- **Off-air programmes:** programmes recorded from a television channel should be engaging for our students, and of a sensible length. We have to consider their comprehensibility too. Apart from overall language level, some off-air video is also extremely difficult for students to understand, especially where particularly marked accents are used or where there is a high preponderance of slang or regional vernacular. The best programmes and excerpts are ones which we can use for a range of activities including prediction, cross-cultural awareness, teaching language, or as spurs for the students' own creativity.

   All television programmes have copyright restrictions which vary from country to country. It is important to know what that law is and realise that breaking it can have serious consequences.

- **Real-world video:** there is no reason why we and our students should not use separately published videotape material such as feature films, exercise 'manuals', wildlife documentaries or comedy provided that there are no copyright restrictions for doing this. Once again we need to make our choice based on how engaging and comprehensible the extract is likely to be, and whether it has multi-use potential. We need to judge the length of the extract in the same way too.

- **Language learning videos:** many publishers now produce free-standing language learning videos – or videos to accompany coursebooks. Frequently these have accompanying workbooks.

   The main advantage of specially made videos is that they have been designed with students at a particular level in mind. They are thus likely to be comprehensible, designed to appeal to students' topic interests, and multi-use since they can not only be used for language study, but also for a number of other activities as well.

   The danger of language learning videos, however, is that they fail the quality test either because the production is poor, the situations and the language are inauthentic, or the content is too unsophisticated. Our choice, therefore, has to be limited to those sequences which our students will accept and enjoy.

A4 Whole-lesson video

Where there are no copyright restrictions, teachers can record programmes off-air and base a whole-class sequence around them. For example, suppose that with an intermediate class we wish to show all or part of a thirty-minute documentary about young boys being sent to private boarding schools in Britain. We might start the sequence with a discussion about which of the following types of school students would prefer to go to/send their children to and why:

	Single sex	Co-educational
Privately owned		
State run		

We might then check our students' knowledge of certain key vocabulary, before giving them a prediction exercise based on what they are going to see. They then watch and listen for gist, and having checked that they have a general understanding of what they have seen, we can then ask them whether the programme has changed the views that they expressed in the initial discussion (above).

Students now watch excerpts from the video again to check on detailed aspects of the video sequence such as how a particular seven-year-old felt about being sent away from home, what his mother's reaction was, and what the head teacher of the school said about the system's advantages.

Before leaving the watching of the video, we can rewind and pick out particular uses of language, which we can ensure students understand and know how to use.

We can follow up this viewing with a number of possible activities: writing a review of the programme, role-playing an interview with the school's head teacher, a parent, or one of the children, discussing the pros and cons of sending children away to school, or writing letters to the programme makers.

This sequence shows a way of exploiting a documentary strand – whether about private schooling, slum living, medical progress, the environment or recent developments in pop music. The video programme has become the main text for a topic-focused lesson.

A5 Video as part of a lesson

We can use a short video extract as one component in a longer lesson sequence, whether to illustrate the topic we are working on, to highlight language points, or to settle a class after a noisy activity.

- **Topic:** we will often be able to introduce a short two- or three-minute video extract into a lesson devoted to a particular topic. If students are working on a reading text about genetically modified food and animals, for example, we might show a quick interview clip with a government minister, or a quick burst of a news bulletin about campaigners against genetic modification.

- **Language:** when a class is working on an area of language, whether grammatical, functional, or lexical – or a mixture of all three – the lesson can be greatly enhanced by a video extract which shows that language in operation.

  Video extracts can be used to introduce new language, practise already known items, or analyse the language used in certain typical exchanges and genres (see Chapter 14, B2).

• **Relaxation:** video can occasionally be used for relaxation, but this use must not be overdone since, as we have said, we usually need to make it an active process. But we might show/play a music video at the end of a long lesson or show a quick bit of video film about a place or a person as a bridge between, for example, a noisy activity and a quiet one.

A6 Self-access video

Students do not have to watch videos only in the classroom. They can also watch them at home, or in their school's self-access centres (see Chapter 24, A2). These will be especially useful where there are worksheets and related material for them to work with, and where teachers are on hand to offer guidance since both may encourage students to make the most of self-access viewing rather than just whiling away the time in non-focused watching.

Many modern language laboratories (see Chapter 10E) have video stations too, where students can watch and interact with specially designed sequences on film or disk.

B Common video teaching techniques

There are a number of teaching techniques which can be used in video-based lessons.

B1 Viewing techniques

All of the following viewing techniques are designed to awaken the students' curiosity, through prediction activities (see Chapter 14, A4), so that when they finally watch the video sequence in its entirety they will have some expectations about it.

• **Fast forward:** the teacher presses the 'play' button and then fast forwards the video so that the sequence shoots pass silently and at great speed, taking only a few seconds. When it is over the teacher can ask students what the extract was all about and whether they can guess what the characters are saying.

• **Silent viewing (for language):** the teacher plays the tape at normal speed, but without the sound. Students have to guess what the characters are saying. When they have done this, the teacher plays the tape with sound so that they can check to see if they guessed correctly.

• **Silent viewing (for music):** the same technique can be used with music. Teachers show a sequence without sound and ask students to say what kind of music they would put behind it and why. When the sequence is then shown again, with sound, students can judge whether they chose the same mood as the director/composer.

• **Freeze frame:** at any stage during a video sequence we can 'freeze' the picture, stopping the participants dead in their tracks. This is extremely useful for asking the students what they think will happen next or what the character will say next.

• **Partial viewing:** one way of provoking the students' curiosity is to allow them only a partial view of the pictures on the screen. We can use pieces of card to cover most of the screen, only leaving the edges on view; we can put little squares of paper all over the screen and remove them one-by-one so that what is happening is only gradually revealed.

A variation of partial viewing occurs when the teacher uses a large 'divider', placed at right angles to the screen so that half the class can only see one half of the screen, whilst the rest of the class can see the other half. They then have to say what they think the people on the other side saw.

B2 Listening (and mixed) techniques

Listening routines, based on the same principles as those for viewing, are similarly designed to provoke engagement and expectations.

- **Pictureless listening (language):** the teacher covers the screen, turns the monitor away from the students, or turns the brightness control right down. The students then listen to a dialogue and have to guess such things as where it is taking place and who the speakers are. Can they guess their age, for example? What do they think the speakers actually look like?

- **Pictureless listening (music):** where an excerpt has a prominent music track, students can listen to it and then say – based on the mood it appears to convey – what kind of scene they think it accompanies and where it is taking place.

- **Pictureless listening (sound effects):** in a scene without dialogue students can listen to the sounds to guess the scene. For example, they might hear the lighting of a gas stove, eggs being broken and fried, coffee being poured and the milk and sugar stirred in. They then tell 'the story' they think they have just heard.

- **Picture or speech:** we can divide the class in two so that half of the class faces the screen, and half faces away. The students who can see the screen have to describe what is happening to the students who cannot. This forces them into immediate fluency while the non-watching students struggle to understand what is going on, and is an effective way of mixing reception and production in spoken English (see Chapter 17, B1). Halfway through an excerpt the students can change round.

C Video watching activities

In this section we will look at a number of activities designed for specific video situations. They explore the range of options for use with both 'off-air' and language learning videos. The specific comprehension skills that each activity seeks to develop are specified; many of these are similar to the skills required in listening to purely audio materials (see Chapter 14, A4).

C1 General comprehension

The following activity is designed to have students watch a video in order to understand the gist of it, and then look back again for details.

Example 1: Witness statement	Activity: being observant
	Skills: watching, listening for detail
	Age: any
	Level: elementary and above

In this activity the students have to try and give as much information as they can about what they have seen – as if they were witnesses being questioned by the police. The best kind of video extract for this is a short one- or two-minute conversation in an interesting location.

After being told to remember as much as they can, they watch the sequence. In pairs they now have to agree on everything they heard and saw: *Who said what to who? Where did the action take place? Who was wearing what? How many people were there in the scene? What was the name of the shop? How many windows were there in the house? Was there anything in the distance? What exactly did the characters say (if anything)?*

When the pairs have finished their discussion the teacher reads out questions and the students have to write their answers. The questions might be something like the following:

1 How many people did you see in total in the excerpt?
2 How many of them were women? How many were men?
3 What did the man say first?
4 Were there any vehicles in the picture? If so what were they?
5 How many different buildings were there?
6 What colour was the old man's jacket?
etc.

When students have written the answers, they compare them with other pairs to see whether they all agree. Now they watch the excerpt again to see how good they are as witnesses.

Other general comprehension tasks include watching to confirm expectations, similar to reading and listening tasks of the same type, and using a genre analyser to scrutinise advertisements (see Example 2 in Chapter 18c).

C2 **Working with aspects of language**

The activity in this section shows language work unique to the medium of video.

Example 2: Subtitles	Activity: comparing languages
	Skills: watching for gist, watching for detailed comprehension, translation
	Age: adult
	Level: intermediate and above

A way of getting students in monolingual groups to focus on language is to get hold of English language films which have subtitles in the students' language. The way in which dialogue is subtitled can sometimes seem strange or funny, but even where this is true, the subtitler has tried to capture the meaning which the speakers wished to convey in the best way they can.

The teacher can start by discussing film subtitles in general. How accurate are they? Why do they sometimes miss out bits of dialogue – especially where there are many speakers talking rapidly? She now tells them that they are going to watch an extract with no sound, but that they will be able to read the subtitles. For the first viewing they should just concentrate on the 'story'.

After the first viewing the teacher and students discuss what they have seen. She then tells them that they are going to watch again, also without sound, but that this time she will stop the video every time a subtitle comes up. The students will then have to do their best to write down what they think the original English words were. When they have done this they can compare their attempts with a colleague. For the final viewing they watch the extract with the sound turned up, to compare their English with the words that were actually spoken.

C3 Video as a springboard to creativity

The activity in this section shows how a video excerpt can be used to spark students' creativity by encouraging interpretation, provoking thought, and asking for language use.

Example 3: Different season, different sex	Activity: making changes
	Skills: watching for gist, interpreting text
	Age: young adult and above
	Level: lower intermediate and above

In this activity students watch a video excerpt and the teacher makes sure that they understand it. They do any language work which may be appropriate.

The teacher now asks the students to watch the excerpt again. But this time they have to imagine how the scene would be different if, for example, instead of the summer which is clearly shown, the episode were taking place in an icy winter. Or, if the excerpt takes place in rain, how would it be different in bright sunshine? They can discuss the differences in pairs or groups, talking about everything from what the characters might wear to how they might speak, how they might behave.

An interesting variation on this is to ask students how the scene would be different if the participants were the opposite sex. Would the conversation between two women be different if the women were changed into men? How might the invitation dialogue they have just watched change if the sex of the participants were reversed? The responses to these questions are often revealing (and amusing). What students say will depend a lot upon their age and culture, of course, and there is always the danger of unnecessary sexism. But where teachers handle the activity with finesse and skill, the exercise can be very successful.

Having students think about video excerpts in this way not only helps them understand more about the language being used (and how it might change), but also directs them to insights about language and behaviour in general.

We can also get students to write captions (similar to the captions in early films) for videos which we play without sound.

D Video-making activities

The activities in this section suggest ways in which the camera can become a central learning aid, as a result of which students work cooperatively together using a wide variety of language both in the process and the product of video-making. Where sophisticated editing facilities are available, and there are trained video personnel on the premises, high production values can be achieved. But that is not the main point of these activities, since a lot can be achieved with just a hand-held camera and a playback monitor.

D1 Video simulations

Video can enhance simulations, not only because it can provide very telling feedback when students can watch themselves and evaluate their performance, but also because the presence of a video camera helps to make media simulations (such as TV programmes) more realistic.

Example 4: News bulletin	Activity: presenting information clearly
	Age: young adult and above
	Level: elementary and above

News bulletins are especially interesting for students of English not only because they will want to be able to understand the news in English, but also because news broadcasts have special formats and use recognisable language patterns. Recognition of such formats allows teachers to ask students to put their own bulletins together, based on the news from today's papers, or on stories which they have been studying. How would television news present the deaths of Romeo and Juliet, the Spanish conquest of Mexico, or the demise of Captain Ahab in his pursuit of the great white whale?

Students can first watch news bulletins and analyse the language that is particular to this genre (for example, passive usage, the use of present tenses to tell stories, and the way in which speech is reported). In small groups they then choose the stories they wish to tell and the order in which they wish to tell them. After writing the script – and editing it with the help of the teacher – they film their broadcasts; these are then watched by their classmates, and by the teacher who can lead the feedback session which ensues.

We can also have students record their own political broadcasts or advertisements.

D2 Creative ideas

The following activity expects the students to use their imagination and creativity to bring a fresh dimension to their learning.

Example 5: Put it on screen	Focus:	acting from a script, interpreting text
	Age:	any
	Level:	any

When students read a story, study an extract from a novel, or work with a coursebook dialogue, they form some kind of mental picture of what they are understanding. This ranges from a perception of the setting to an idea of what characters look and sound like.

A way of really 'getting inside the text' is to have students film the episode they have just read. If they are studying a textbook dialogue, for example, we might tell them that they should disregard the textbook illustration, and take the words and situation only. With these in mind they should plan and film their own versions of the text. On the other hand, we might encourage them to change aspects of the dialogue – the ending perhaps – that they do not like, so that even a textbook dialogue becomes their own.

Any text which involves human interaction can be exploited in this way. Would it be possible to film Robert O'Connor's first nerve-wracking class in the prison (see Example 1, Chapter 15, B1)?

Filming an episode involves discussion about acting and direction and a close focus on the text in question. However, despite possible problems of logistics and time, the results can be extremely satisfying, and the activity itself highly motivating.

D3 Working with language

We can ask students to make videos with a focus on particular language points.

Example 6: The grammar lecture	Focus:	language description
	Age:	young adult and above
	Level:	intermediate and above

For more advanced students the teacher can set a 'grammar lecture' task where the group makes their own grammar teaching video for their classmates or for students at lower levels.

Students select, or are given, a particular grammar topic. The teacher can give them ideas about sources of information for their research (see Chapter 12B and C). In groups they then do their research and then discuss how to explain the grammar to a different group of learners. They have to do this in the form of a filmed lecture, with acted out examples. More than one person should take part, giving examples or taking over the next point in the explanation, but the object is for a short video sequence to give the essential information about a language point.

Provided that we do not expect a superb finished product, this kind of grammar exploration, and the attempt to put such concepts into words, really does focus the students' attention on features of the language. It is not for the faint-hearted, however, since it demands time, patience, and doggedness. The focus does not have to be grammar of course; lectures can also concentrate on lexical areas, features of pronunciation, or ways of performing language functions.

Students can also conduct interviews with competent speakers and use what they say for language analysis. 'Vox pop' interviews (where members of the public are asked their opinions on a certain issue) are ideal for this.

D4 Getting everyone involved

Because filming usually involves one camera operator, and may be confined to one narrator and one overall director, there is a danger that some students may get left out of the video-making process. However, there are ways of avoiding this danger:

- **The group:** if more than one video camera is available we can divide a class into groups. That way each member of each group has a function.

- **Process:** we can ensure participation in the decision-making process by insisting that no roles (such as actor, camera operator, director) are chosen until the last moment.

- **Assigning roles:** we can assign a number of different roles as in a real film crew. This includes such jobs as clapperboard operators, script consultants, lighting and costumes.

D5 What to do with the videos

One of the main benefits of video-making for students is the chance to display what they have done and get feedback on it from classmates and teachers. This can be achieved in a number of ways:

- **Class feedback:** when students show their videos to the rest of the class, there are a number of ways in which those classmates can react. They can vote for the best video, or they can record the successful and less successful examples of what they hear and see (see Chapter 7, c3). This will be greatly enhanced if different students take charge of different areas such as effectiveness, clarity, grammar, vocabulary, production, and voice quality.

- **Teacher feedback:** one of the ways in which we can be sure that video-making is a learning process is by responding to the students' work with the same care that we give to written work (see Chapter 7D). This means responding to each video, saying either face-to-face or in writing what we liked about it, correcting mistakes, where appropriate, and making suggestions about how it might be improved.

- **Video installation:** we can organise a video day in which all of our students' videos are shown in an exhibition. If possible, we will have more than one machine running so that visitors to our exhibition can see all the videos that have been made while walking around. With the appropriate technological resources we can also put the video clips on to a student web site.

- **Individual and library copies:** if we have copying facilities we can make copies of our students' work. These can then be deposited in the school's video library or given to each student as a memento.

D6   Video and the teacher

We cannot leave the topic of video without mentioning the invaluable contribution that it can make to teacher development (see Chapter 24B). Having someone film you when you are teaching can be a challenging experience, but it can be extremely valuable.

Most teachers have an idea of how they appear as teachers – and about how effective certain mannerisms and techniques can be. Most of us have favourite activities, and cultivate particular classroom personae. We judge the success of what we do not only on the students' gradual acquisition of the language, but also on their minute-by-minute reactions to how we behave in class, and on the perceptions this gives us of how well and appropriately we are teaching. Watching a film of a lesson we have taught, however, may give us different perceptions altogether, since it offers us the opportunity to see our teaching as others see it.

Many teachers are alarmed at seeing themselves on video, just as many people dislike their voices on audiotape. It is very easy to perceive one's own faults in such a situation: favourite catchphrases sound hackneyed and repetitive; rapport seems over-strained or over-intimate, and the voice is too dramatic or too boring. But viewers should treat themselves charitably. The point of watching ourselves teach is not to engage in an orgy of self-criticism, but to evaluate our actions in terms of their effectiveness. Which bits of the lesson clearly work? How could we change the way we do this exercise so that next time it is more engaging, less confusing, more efficient?

One major caveat about classroom videoing is that the camera does not actually tell the truth. If the lens is focused on the teacher it automatically makes them the main player in the scene even if what they are actually doing is just listening to students. This is why it is a good idea for the camera to be pointed as much at the students as at the teacher. This means that the teacher can see the effect of what she does. Nor can a vision and sound medium entirely capture the atmosphere of a lesson. The classroom on the video screen is only a partial version of the real thing.

Chapter notes and further reading

- **Video and motivation**

  See S Stempleski and B Tomalin (1990: 3).

- **Video activities**

  A range of excellent video activities can be found in S Stempleski and B Tomalin (1990), R Cooper et al. (1991), and M Allen (1986).

- **Subtitles**

For the use of teletext subtitles, see R Vanderplank (1988 and 1996).

- **Videoing teachers**

See J Laycock and P Bunnag (1991) and R Cooper (1993).

- **Copyright**

Copyright regulations vary from country to country, and depending on the type of video involved. Under US law, fair use of videos includes education provided that off-air videos are not used for profit, and provided that they are not kept beyond a certain time. The same kind of law operates in the UK, though at the time of writing the European Union may be bringing in draconian new laws to prohibit this. Commercially produced videos have their own restrictions; teachers should carefully check the copyright notices that come with them. There are restrictions, too, on the copying of most specially made educational videos.

For more on copyright issues, see A Williams et al. (1999). University law faculties have sites which can be searched for copyright law, and for the USA it might be worth looking at 'multimedia law' at http://www.oikoumene.com/.

21 Syllabuses and coursebooks

Writers and course designers have to take a number of issues into account when designing their materials. Once they have a clear idea of how their theories and beliefs about learning can be translated into appropriate activities they will have to think about what topics to include. This will be based on perceptions of what students find engaging, what research shows in this area, and on the potential for interesting exploitation of the topics they might select. It will also be necessary to consider what kind of culture the material should reflect or encourage, and to ensure some kind of appropriate balance in terms of gender and the representation of different groups in society, racial, ethnic, and socioeconomic.

Writers and course designers also have to decide what language variety or varieties they wish to focus on or have represented (see Chapter 1B), and they need to adopt a position on how authentic the language should be, especially at beginner levels (see Chapter 14, B1).

Once these decisions have been taken, coursebook writers (and language program designers in general) can then turn their attention to the central organising strand of their materials, namely the syllabus.

A Syllabus design

Syllabus design concerns the selection of items to be learnt and the grading of those items into an appropriate sequence. It is different from curriculum design (Nunan 1988a: Chapter 1). In the latter, the designer is concerned not just with lists of what will be taught and in what order, but also with the planning, implementation, evaluation, management and administration of education programmes.

There are now a number of different types of language syllabus (see A2 below), all of which might be taken as a starting point in the planning of a new coursebook, or of a term's, or year's work. But, whatever type it is, every syllabus needs to be developed on the basis of certain criteria, such as 'learnability' and 'frequency', which can inform decisions about selection and ordering, as described below.

A1 Syllabus design criteria

When designers put syllabuses together they have to consider each item for inclusion on the basis of a number of criteria. This will not only help them to decide if they want to include the item in question, but also where to put it in the sequence. However, these different design criteria point, in many cases, to different conclusions. The syllabus designer has to balance such competing claims when making decisions about selection and grading.

- **Learnability:** some structural or lexical items are easier for students to learn than others. Thus we teach easier things first and then increase the level of difficulty as the students' language level rises. Learnability might tell us that, at beginner levels, it is easier to teach uses of *was* and *were* immediately after teaching uses of *is* and *are*, rather than follow *is* and *are* with the third conditional. Learnability might persuade us to teach *some* and *any* on their own rather than introduce a whole range of quantifiers (*much, many, few,* etc.) all at the same time.

- **Frequency:** it would make sense, especially at beginning levels, to include items which are more frequent in the language, than ones that are only used occasionally by native speakers. Now that corpus information can give us accurate frequency counts (see Chapter 2, B1), we are in a position to say with some authority, for example, that *see* is used more often to mean *understand* (e.g. *Oh, I see*) than it is to denote vision. It might make sense, therefore, to teach that meaning of *see* first – but that decision will also have to depend upon the other design criteria listed here, which might lead us to a different conclusion.

- **Coverage:** some words and structures have greater coverage (scope for use) than others. Thus we might decide, on the basis of coverage, to introduce the *going to* future before the present continuous with future reference, if we could show that *going to* could be used in more situations than the present continuous.

- **Usefulness:** the reason that words like *book* and *pen* figure so highly in classrooms (even though they might not be that frequent in real language use) is because they are useful words in that situation. In the same way, words for family members occur early on in a student's learning life because they are useful in the context of what students are linguistically able to talk about.

A2 Different syllabuses

- **The grammar syllabus:** this is the commonest type of syllabus, both traditionally and currently. A list of items is sequenced in such a way that the students gradually acquire a knowledge of grammatical structures, leading to an understanding of the grammatical system. Even in multi-syllabuses (see A3 below), it is the grammar syllabus which tends to be the main organising foundation, with units devoted to the verb *to be*, the present simple, the present continuous, countable and uncountable nouns, the present perfect, etc.

  Although grammar syllabuses have been used with success over a long period of time, many methodologists have come to see grammar as the wrong organising principle for a syllabus and have proposed a number of alternatives as frameworks to hang a language programme on (as we shall see below).

- **The lexical syllabus:** it is possible to organise a syllabus on the basis of vocabulary and lexis to create a lexical syllabus (see Chapter 6, A8).

  Applying syllabus design criteria to a lexical syllabus can be complex since there are so many facets to lexis, such as:

  - the vocabulary related to topics (e.g. art, clothes, crime)
  - issues of word formation (e.g. suffixes and other morphological changes)
  - word-grammar triggers (e.g. verbs which are followed by certain syntactic patterns)
  - compound lexical items (e.g. *walking-stick, multi-storey car park*)
  - connecting and linking words (e.g. *when, if, he/she*)
  - semi-fixed expressions (e.g. *Would you like to … ?, If I were you I'd …*)
  - connotation and the use of metaphor (see Chapter 2, B3)

  Another problem with lexical syllabuses is the relationship between lexis and grammar. Should phrasal verbs be taught as simple multi-word lexical items as they occur, or as a grammatical class? At what stage is the study of word formation appropriate, and when will it be useful to include fixed and semi-fixed expressions? What grammar should be included with new words, and how should that be selected and graded?

  Though syllabus designers may have little difficulty in applying design criteria to individual words, melding all the other concerns of lexis into a coherent order to make a truly lexical syllabus has not yet been shown to be feasible. A lexical syllabus produced by John Sinclair and Antoinette Renouf was 'several hundred pages long' (Sinclair and Renouf 1988: 156). Nevertheless, lexis in all its many forms does appear in wider syllabus plans (see A3 below).

- **The functional syllabus:** in his book *Notional Syllabuses* David Wilkins (1976) included categories of 'communicative function' (see Chapter 2, C1). These language functions are events which 'do things' such as *inviting, promising,* and *offering,* so that a functional syllabus might look like this:

  1 Requesting
  2 Offering
  3 Inviting
  4 Agreeing and disagreeing   etc.

The syllabus designer then chooses exponents for (ways of expressing) each function. For example, for *offering* she could choose from the following:

Would you like me to … ?
Do you want some help?
I'll help if you want.
Let me give you a hand.
Here, let me.
I'll do that … ,   etc.

But the syllabus designer can then run into problems of lexical and structural grading. If a syllabus is designed on the basis of the functions which students are most likely to have to perform (their 'usefulness'), the designer still needs to choose and order the exponents for each of those functions on the basis of 'learnability', 'coverage', and 'frequency' and may have trouble matching the functions with these criteria. It is possible to end up, too, with a series of phrases rather than a coherent system.

The modern consensus seems to be that functions may not be the best sole organising units for a syllabus, but that the teaching and learning of functions is an important part of a wider syllabus (see below).

- **The situational syllabus:** a situational syllabus offers the possibility of selecting and sequencing different real-life situations rather than different grammatical items, vocabulary topics, or functions. A situational syllabus might look something like this:

  1 At the bank
  2 At the supermarket
  3 At the travel agent
  4 At the restaurant
  etc.

Where students have specific communicative needs (see Chapter 1, B3), organising teaching material by the situations which students will need to operate in is attractive, since the syllabus designer will be able to define the situation, the likely participants, and communicative goals with some certainty. Material for business or tourism students, for example, can profitably be organised in this way. But situational syllabuses are less appropriate for students of general English largely because it is difficult to guarantee that language for one specific situation will necessarily be useful in another. Furthermore, choosing which situations are 'key' situations for a general class is problematic since it depends on who the students are (they are never all the same) and where they are learning. It is for these reasons that situations are rarely taken as the main organising principle in general syllabus design.

- **The topic-based syllabus:** another framework around which to organise language is that of different topics, e.g. *the weather, sport, survival, literature, music,* and so on. This list can then be refined, so that the weather topic is subdivided into items such as the way weather changes, weather forecasting, weather and mood, and the damage that weather can cause.

Topics provide a welcome organising principle in that they can be based on what students will be interested in. It may also be possible to identify what topics are most relevant to students' communicative needs (their usefulness) – though this may differ from what they want. Yet marrying topics to the concepts of learnability, frequency, and coverage is once again problematic since they will still have to be subdivided into the language and lexis which they generate.

Providing students with a sequence of topics which are relevant and engaging is an important part of a syllabus designer or coursebook writer's skill. But on its own such organisation is unlikely to be sufficient for syllabus organisation.

- **The task-based syllabus:** a task-based syllabus (see Chapter 6, A5) lists a series of tasks, and may later list some or all of the language to be used in those tasks. N S Prabhu, whose experiments in Bangalore, India did so much to advance the cause of task-based learning, organised a programme in just such a way, calling it a 'procedural syllabus' (Prabhu 1987). The only piece of 'deliberate language grading' occurred when teachers set oral before written tasks (Prabhu 1987: 26). Otherwise it was a question of putting one task before or after another.

  Prabhu's tasks are related to topics, as in this example:

  1 Clockface
     a Telling the time from a clockface; positioning the hands of a clock to show a given time.
     b Calculating durations from the movement of a clock's hands; working out intervals between given times.
     c Stating the time on a twelve hour clock and a twenty-four hour clock; relating times to phases of the day and night.

  From N S Prabhu (1987: 138)

Jane Willis lists six task types that can be used with almost any topics. These are: listing, ordering and sorting, comparing, problem solving, sharing personal experience, and creative tasks (Willis 1996: 26–27 and 149–154).

As with situations and topics, it is difficult to know how to grade tasks in terms of difficulty. Prabhu does suggest sequences of lessons where the same topic information is used in more than one lesson and where the tasks to go with that information become more complex with each subsequent lesson, but there is little to say how such complexity is measured. The focus is, in David Nunan's words, on 'learning process' rather than 'learning product', and there is 'little or no attempt to relate these processes to outcomes' (Nunan 1988a: 44). A variety of factors interact to determine the difficulty of a task, but as yet, no one has worked out a satisfactory system with which to combine them into any kind of decent measure of difficulty.

A task-based syllabus may well satisfy the desire to provide meaning-based learning but until there is a way of deciding which tasks should go where, such a syllabus remains tantalisingly 'ad hoc', and fails to command sufficiently widespread support amongst teachers and methodologists for it to become universally accepted.

A3 The multi-syllabus syllabus

A common solution to the competing claims of the different syllabus types we have looked at is the 'multi-syllabus'. Instead of a program based exclusively on grammatical or lexical categories, for example, the syllabus now shows any combination of items from grammar, lexis, language functions, situations, topics, tasks, different language skill tasks or pronunciation issues.

Where coursebook writers are not following a syllabus laid down by an education ministry, educational institution, or examination board, this is the approach that is most often followed. As the following example shows, authors often present their multi-syllabus in a 'map of the book':

Units	Grammar	Vocabulary/Pronunciation	Skills
(1) All work and no play... page 14	Present Simple: *I, you, we, they* Prepositions in time expressions	Jobs Leisure: activities and places Pron: word stress	Reading: people at work Listening and speaking: a job interview Writing and speaking: work and play
(2) Family, friends and neighbours page 19	Present Simple: *he, she, it* Frequency adverbs	People in your life Pron: does /dʌz/ and /dəz/; /s/, /z/ and /ɪz/	Reading: a letter home Speaking: *Do you ever ...? How often do you ...?*
Reading for pleasure 1, *page 24:* Exercises on *He-mail, she-mail* from *On the same wavelength and other stories*			
(3) Lifestyles page 25	Love / like / don't mind / hate + verb + -ing Can / can't for ability	Likes and dislikes Leisure activities and holidays Pron: word stress; *can* and *can't*	Listening: likes and dislikes; *The Real You!* questionnaire; working with *Mr Perfect* Speaking: *What can you do?*
(4) Secrets and lies page 30	Present Continuous: now; around now	Telephoning Little white lies	Speaking: *Are you a "phonaholic"?* questionnaire; *My wonderful life!* Listening: phone conversations Reading: a letter to a friend
Reading for pleasure 2, *page 35:* Exercises on *Lost opportunities* from *On the same wavelength and other stories*			
(5) You are what you wear page 36	Have got / has got and have / has	Clothes and shopping	Listening: clothes; in a shop Writing and speaking: clothes and fashion Reading: The Fashion Maze
(6) Have we got news for you! page 41	Past Simple of regular and irregular verbs Time expressions for the past	News stories Pron: /d/, /t/ and /ɪd/	Listening: a TV news programme; a radio news interview Reading: a newspaper article Speaking: *When did you last...?* questionnaire
Reading for pleasure 3, *page 46:* Exercises on *The red dress* from *On the same wavelength and other stories*			

Adapted from *Wavelength Elementary* by Kathy Burke and Julia Brooks (Pearson Education Ltd)

In practice, many multi-syllabuses of this type take a grammar syllabus as a starting point. The materials designers then start the long and often frustrating business of trying to match this list with all the other items they wish to include – the vocabulary and the skills, the tasks and the functions. As the process goes on, the original order of the grammar syllabus will have to change to accommodate some of the other claims; the list of functions will shift around to accommodate the grammar, and the tasks will have to take account of the language at the students' disposal for the performing of those tasks. No one element predominates; all have to shift to accommodate the others, and the end result is always a compromise between the competing claims of the different organising elements.

B Choosing coursebooks

The 'assessment' of a coursebook is an out-of-class judgement as to how well a new book will perform in class. Coursebook 'evaluation', on the other hand, is a judgement on how well a book has performed in fact.

One approach to the assessment of coursebooks is to use a checklist – or checklists prepared by others which analyse various components of the material whether linguistic, topic, or activity based (see Cunningsworth 1984 and 1995; Littlejohn 1998). However, a problem with such assessments is that however good they are, they may still fail to predict what actually happens when the material is used. And when we use a checklist prepared by other people we are accepting their view of what is appropriate in our particular situation. Nevertheless, we need some basis for choosing which books to use or pilot, whether we use checklists prepared by others or whether we make them ourselves (see B1 below). We can then see whether our out-of-class judgements are borne out in reality.

A potential difficulty for successful post-use 'evaluation' of a coursebook, on the other hand, is that 'teachers see no need for systematic and principled post-programme evaluation' (Ellis 1998: 221). In part this is because teachers tend to feel that they 'know' whether a coursebook worked or not, and they are reluctant to give time to a more formal evaluation once a course has finished. Yet we need to evaluate material in a reasonably structured way if we are to properly see if our pre-use assessment was accurate, and whether to continue to use the coursebook.

Whether assessing or evaluating coursebooks, we should do our best to include student opinion and comment. Their view of layout, design, content and feel should inform our pre-use assessment and our post-course evaluation.

B1 Criteria for assessment

The following three-stage procedure allows teachers to assess books on the basis of their own beliefs and their assessment of their students' needs and circumstances:

- **Selecting areas for assessment:** we first need to list the features we wish to look at in the coursebook(s) under consideration, as in the following example:

> Price (of coursebook components)
> Availability
> Layout and design
> Instructions
> Methodology
> Syllabus type, selection and grading
> Language study activities
> Language skill activities
> Topics
> Cultural acceptability
> Usability
> Teacher's guide

The list can be reduced or expanded, of course. We might separate language study activities into vocabulary, grammar, and pronunciation, for example; or, we might want to concentrate solely on topics and cultural acceptability. We can choose what we want to focus on in the light of our own teaching situation.

- **Stating beliefs:** we are now in a position to make 'belief statements' about any or all of the areas we have decided to concentrate on. This can be done by a group of teachers writing their individual beliefs and then combining them into an agreed set – such as the following statements about layout:

> The page should look clean and uncluttered.
> The lesson sequence should be easy to follow.
> The illustrations should be attractive and appropriate.
> The instructions should be easy to read.

- **Using statements for assessment:** we are now ready to use our statements of belief as assessment items. This means that for each of our areas we list our statements, and can then use a simple tick and cross system to compare different books, as in this layout and design checklist:

Area	Assessment statements	Coursebook 1	Coursebook 2	Coursebook 3
Layout and design	The page is uncluttered.	✓	✗	✓✓
	The lesson sequence is easy to follow.	✓	✓	✗
	The illustrations are attractive and appropriate for the age group.	✓✓	✓	✗
	The instructions are easy to read.	✓	✗	✓✓

B2 Evaluation measures

Evaluation of materials which we have been using is somewhat different from assessment. Once again, however, it can have three stages:

- **Teacher record:** in order to evaluate materials we need to keep a record of how successful different lessons and activities have been. One way of doing this is to keep a diary of what happens in each lesson (see Chapter 24, B1). A more formal version of the same thing might involve detailed comments on each activity, for example:

> Unit/lesson: _____
> General comments _____
> (include timing, effectiveness, _____
> ease, etc.): _____

Comment on the advantages/disadvantages of:

Exercise 1: _____

Exercise 2: _____

Exercise 3: _____

Exercise 4: _____

Exercise 5: _____

Exercise 6: _____

How did the students react to the lesson? _____

_____

_____

There are many other ways of keeping records: we could give each activity a score from 0–5; we could design a rating scale to measure student satisfaction with a lesson or parts of a lesson. We could write reports at the end of every week under headings such as *recycling, reading progress, vocabulary work,* or *teacher's guide.* Some teachers write comments in the coursebook itself. But in each case we will end up with something which is more useful than a mere feeling.

- **Teacher discussion:** when new books are being used it helps if the teachers who are using the same book get together and compare their experiences. This may involve going through lessons (and exercises) one by one, or it may centre round a discussion of the audio material and its related exercises. Someone in the group should circulate a record of what is said, so that teachers can review the discussions before coming to a conclusion.

- **Student response:** as with teachers' reactions, student responses can be collected in a number of ways. One way is to ask them if they enjoyed the material they have just been using. This kind of oral feedback can be unreliable, however, since some students can dominate the conversation and influence their colleagues.

    We may get better feedback by asking for a written response to the materials with questions such as the following:

    What was your favourite lesson in the book during the last week? Why?
    What was your least favourite lesson from the book during the last week? Why?
    What was your favourite activity during the last week?
    What was your least favourite activity during the last week? Why?
    etc.

Because students' perception of their own progress will influence their responses to the material they are using, it is important to encourage them to assess their own performance, in the ways we suggested in Chapter 7, B2, and to discuss the conclusions they come to. Alternatively, we could have them (in groups) talk about the lessons they have been studying and provide a short written summary of their group's joint conclusions.

The information gained through the evaluations we have been discussing now has to be set against other measures such as achievement test scores (see Chapter 23, A1), and durability. With all this information we can compare results with colleagues so that we reach confident decisions about whether the book has lived up to the original assessment we made of it.

C Using coursebooks

For years methodologist have been arguing about the usefulness of coursebooks, questioning their role (Allwright 1981), defending their use (O'Neill 1982), worrying that they act as methodological straitjackets (Tice 1991) or promoting their value as agents of methodological change (Hutchinson and Torres 1994).

C1 Coursebook or no coursebook?

The benefits and restrictions of coursebook use can be easily summarised:

- **Benefits:** good coursebooks are carefully prepared to offer a coherent syllabus, satisfactory language control, motivating texts, tapes and other accessories such as videotapes, CD-ROMs, extra resource material, and useful web links. They are often attractively presented. They provide teachers under pressure with the reassurance that, even when they are forced to plan at the last moment, they will be using material which they can have confidence in. They come with detailed teacher's guides which not only provide procedures for the lesson in the student's book, but also offer suggestions and alternatives, extra activities, and resources. The adoption of a new coursebook provides a powerful stimulus for methodological development (see Hutchinson and Torres 1994).

  Students like coursebooks too since they foster the perception of progress as units and then books are completed. Coursebooks also provide material which students can look back at for revision, and at their best their visual and topic appeal can have a powerfully engaging effect.

- **Restrictions:** coursebooks, used inappropriately, impose learning styles and content on classes and teachers alike appearing to be '*faits accomplis* over which they can have little control' (Littlejohn 1998: 205). Many of them rely on Presentation, Practice, and Production as their main methodological procedure (see Chapter 6, A2) despite recent enthusiasm for other teaching sequences. Units and lessons often follow an unrelenting format so that students and teachers eventually become de-motivated by the sameness of it all. And in their choice of topics coursebooks can sometimes be bland or culturally inappropriate.

One solution to the perceived disadvantages of coursebooks is to do without them altogether, to use a 'do-it-yourself' approach (Block 1991; Maley 1998). Such an approach is extremely attractive. It can offer students a dynamic and varied programme. If they can see its relevance to their own needs, it will greatly enhance their motivation and their trust in what they are being asked to do. It allows teachers to respond on a lesson-by-lesson basis to what is happening in the class. Finally, for the teacher, it means an exciting and creative involvement with texts and tasks.

In order for the DIY approach to be successful teachers need access to (and knowledge of) a wide range of materials, from coursebooks and videos to magazines, novels, encyclopedias, publicity brochures and the Internet. They will have to make (and make use of) a variety of homegrown materials (see Chapter 10G). They will also need the confidence to know when and what to choose, becoming, in effect, syllabus designers in their own right. This not only makes preparing lessons a very time-consuming business, but also runs the risk that students will end up with an incoherent collection of bits and pieces of material.. However, where there is time for the proper planning and organisation of DIY teaching, students may well get exceptional programmes of study which are responsive to their needs, and varied in a way that does not abandon coherence.

C2 Options for coursebook use

Where teachers reject a fully DIY approach because of time, a lack of resources, or a preference for published materials, they then have to decide how to use the coursebooks they have chosen. One way of doing this is to start at page 1 and keep going until you get to the end. But that will probably bore both the students and the teacher and has far less chance of answering the needs of a class than if teachers use the book more creatively, adapting it in various ways to suit the situation they and their students are in.

When we plan a lesson around our coursebook, we have a number of possible options:

- **Omit and replace:** the first decision we have to make is whether to use a particular coursebook lesson or not. If the answer is 'no', there are two possible courses of action. The first is just to omit the lesson altogether. In this case we suppose that the students will not miss it because it does not teach anything fundamentally necessary and it is not especially interesting. When, however, we think the language or topic area in question is important, we will have to replace the coursebook lesson with our own preferred alternative.

  Although there is nothing wrong with omitting or replacing coursebook material, it becomes irksome for many students if it happens too often, especially where they have had to buy the book themselves. It may also deny them the chance to revise (a major advantage of coursebooks), and their course may lose overall coherence.

- **To change or not to change?** When we decide to use a coursebook lesson we can, of course, do so without making any substantial changes to the way it is presented. However, we might decide to use the lesson, but to change it to make it more appropriate for our students. If the material is not very substantial we might add something to it – a role-play after a reading text, perhaps, or extra situations for language practice. We might rewrite an exercise we do not especially like or replace one activity or text with something else such as a download from the Internet, or any other homegrown items (see Chapter 10G). We could re-order the activities within a lesson, or even re-order lessons (within reason). Finally, we may wish to reduce a lesson by cutting out an exercise or an activity. In all our decisions, however, it is important to remember that students need to be able to see a coherent pattern to what we are doing and understand our reasons for changes.

Using coursebooks appropriately is an art which becomes clearer with experience. If the teacher approaches lesson planning (see Chapter 22B) in the right frame of mind, it happens almost as a matter of course. The options we have discussed for coursebook use are summarised in Figure 24:

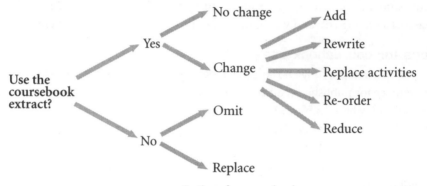

FIGURE 24: Options for coursebook use

Chapter notes and further reading

- **Choosing appropriate topics**
  On classroom needs (and 'wants') analysis, see P Seedhouse (1995) and L Kuc (1999).

- **Culture in language materials and teaching**
  See C Alptekin (1993) and M Zülkuf Altan (1995). A Pulverness (1995) argues for the importance of cross-cultural awareness.

- **Gender issues in coursebook design**
  See C Manheim (1994) and other articles in J Sunderland (ed.) (1994: Quadrant 11).

- **Syllabus and curriculum**
  See D Nunan (1988b) on the 'learner-centred curriculum'. The Council of Europe has commissioned detailed syllabuses. See, for example, J Van Ek and J Trim (1998, 1999, and 2001).

- **The lexical syllabus**
  On the lexical syllabus, see D Willis (1990) and also M Lewis (1993 and 1997) – though see S Thornbury (1998).

The only coursebook to have used a lexical syllabus as its main organising principle is D and J Willis (1988–1989).

- **Functional syllabuses**

  For functional syllabus design see K Johnson (1982: Chapter 8), K Johnson and K Morrow (1978), and C Brumfit (1980).

- **The situational syllabus**

  For an example of a situational syllabus approach absorbed into a multi-syllabus for tourism students, see M Jacob and P Strutt (1997).

- **Grading tasks**

  C Candlin (1987) attempts a complex task-grading system. On the evaluation of tasks see R Ellis (1998).

- **Coursebooks – to use or not to use**

  I Freebairn (2000) defends coursebook use, though S Thornbury (2000), using the example of 'Dogme' film makers, suggests (half seriously) material-free classrooms where communication between teacher and students is all that matters.

- **Coursebook evaluation**

  See A Cunningsworth (1984 and 1995) and A Littlejohn (1998).

- **The Internet in a non-coursebook programme**

  D Teeler (2000: Chapter 6) shows how the Internet can be used as an alternative to a coursebook, giving guidance about routines and planning.

  Internet-based courses for self-study are available on the Web. At the time of writing two of the best are the Surf2school site at /www.surf2school.com/ and Global English at /www.globalenglish.com/. However, many other organisations run, or are in the process of designing, online courses and learning systems (see Chapter 10F).

- **Using coursebooks**

  Neville Grant offered the options of 'omit, replace, add and adapt' for coursebook users – see N Grant (1987: Chapter 1). R Acklam (1994) suggested 'SARS', which stands for Select, Adapt, Replace, Supplement. A Maley says that materials use is a 'complex trade-off between the three major elements in the equation: the materials, the teachers and the learners' (1998: 279).

22 | Planning lessons

Lesson planning is the art of combining a number of different elements into a coherent whole so that a lesson has an identity which students can recognise, work within, and react to – whatever metaphor teachers may use to visualise and create that identity. But plans – which help teachers identify aims and anticipate potential problems – are proposals for action rather than scripts to be followed slavishly, whether they are detailed documents or hastily scribbled notes.

A Pre-planning

Before we start to make a lesson plan we need to consider a number of crucial factors such as the language level of our students, their educational and cultural background (see Chapter 6, B1), their likely levels of motivation (see Chapter 3C), and their different learning styles (Chapter 3, B3). Such knowledge is, of course, more easily available when we have spent time with a group than it is at the beginning of a course. When we are not yet familiar with the character of a group, we need to do our best to gain as much understanding of them as we can before starting to make decisions about what to teach.

We also need a knowledge of the content and organisation of the syllabus or curriculum we are working with (see Chapter 21A), and the requirements of any exams which the students are working towards (see Chapter 23).

Armed now with our knowledge of the students and of the syllabus we can go on to consider the four main planning elements:

- **Activities:** when planning, it is vital to consider what students will be doing in the classroom; we have to consider the way they will be grouped, whether they are to move around the class, whether they will work quietly side-by-side researching on the Internet or whether they will be involved in a boisterous group-writing activity.

  We should make decisions about activities almost independently of what language or skills we have to teach. Our first planning thought should centre round what kind of activity would be best for a particular group of students at a particular point in a lesson, or on a particular day. By deciding what kind of activity to offer them – in the most general sense – we have a chance to balance the exercises in our lessons in order to offer the best possible chance of engaging and motivating the class.

The best lessons offer a variety of activities within a class period. Students may find themselves standing up and working with each other for five minutes before returning to their seats and working for a time on their own. The same lesson may end with a whole-class discussion or with pairs writing dialogues to practise a language function or grammar point.

- **Skills:** we need to make a decision about which language skills we wish our students to develop. This choice is sometimes determined by the syllabus or the coursebook. However, we still need to plan exactly how students are going to work with the skill and what sub-skills we wish to practise.

    Planning decisions about language skills and sub-skills are co-dependent with the content of the lesson and with the activities which the teachers will get students to take part in.

- **Language:** we need to decide what language to introduce and have the students learn (see Chapter 11A), practise (see Chapter 11, B3), research (see Chapter 12) or use (see Chapters 18 and 19).

    One of the dangers of planning is that where language is the main focus it is the first and only planning decision that teachers make. Once the decision has been taken to teach the present continuous, for example, it is sometimes tempting to slip back into a drill-dominated teaching session which lacks variety and which may not be the best way to achieve our aims. But language is only one area that we need to consider when planning lessons.

- **Content:** lesson planners have to select content which has a good chance of provoking interest and involvement. Since they know their students personally they are well placed to select appropriate content.

    Even where the choice of subject and content is to some extent dependent on a coursebook, we can still judge when and if to use the coursebook's topics, or whether to replace them with something else. We can predict, with some accuracy, which topics will work and which will not.

    However, the most interesting content can be made bland if the activities and tasks that go with it are unimaginative. Similarly, subjects that are not especially fascinating can be used extremely successfully if the good planner takes time to think about how students can best work with them.

When thinking about the elements we have discussed above we carry with us not only the knowledge of the students, but also our belief in the need to create an appropriate balance between variety and coherence. With all of these features in mind we can finally pass all our thinking through the filter of practical reality, where our knowledge of the classrooms we work in, the equipment we can use, the time we have available, and the attitude of the institution we work in all combine to focus our planning on what we are actually going to do. Now, as Figure 25 on the next page shows, we are in a position to move from pre-planning to the plan itself.

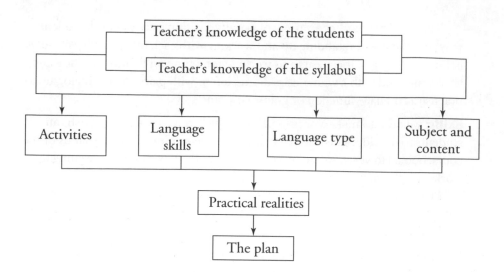

FIGURE 25: Pre-planning and the plan

B The plan

Having done some pre-planning and made decisions about the kind of lesson we want to teach, we can make the lesson plan. This may take a number of different forms, depending upon the circumstances of the lesson and depending also, on our attitude to planning in general.

B1 The planning continuum

The way that teachers plan lessons depends upon the circumstances in which the lesson is to take place and on the teacher's experience. Near one end of a 'planning continuum', teachers may do all the (vague) pre-planning in their head and make actual decisions about what to include in the lesson as they hurry along the corridor to the class. Those with experience can get away with this some of the time because they have a number of familiar routines to fall back on.

Another scenario near the same end of the continuum occurs when teachers are following a coursebook and they do exactly what the book says, letting the coursebook writers, in effect, do their planning for them. This is especially attractive for teachers under extreme time pressure, though if we do not spend time thinking about how to use the coursebook activities (and what happens when we do) we may run into difficulties later. Really effective coursebook use is more complex than this (see Chapter 21, C2).

At the very end of the planning continuum is the kind of lesson described by one writer as the 'jungle path', where teachers walk into class with no real idea of what they are going to do (Scrivener 1994b: 34–37); thus they might say *What did you do last weekend?* and base the class on what replies they get. They might ask the students what they want to do that day, or take in an activity to start the class with no real idea of where it will lead them and their students. Such an approach is favoured by Mario Rinvolucri, who has suggested that instead of working to a pre-arranged plan, a teacher should be more like a doctor, basing treatment upon accurate diagnosis. All classes and students are different, he argued, so to decide beforehand what they should learn on a given day (especially when this is done some days before) is to confine them to a mental structure and ignore the 'flesh-and-blood here-and-now learners' (Rinvolucri 1996).

Experienced teachers may well be able to run effective lessons in this way, without making a plan at all. When such lessons are successful they can be immensely rewarding for all concerned. But more often they run the risk of being muddled and aimless. There is a real danger that if teachers do not have a clear idea of their aims – and, crucially, if the students cannot or will not help to give the lesson shape, 'then nothing useful or meaningful can be achieved at all' (Malamah-Thomas 1987: 3). And though some students may enjoy the adventure of the jungle path, the majority will benefit both linguistically and psychologically from the forethought the teacher has given to the lesson.

At the other end of the continuum teachers write formal plans for their classes which detail what they are going to do and why (see B3 below), perhaps because they are about to be observed or because they are required to do so by some authority.

The vast majority of lesson planning probably takes place between these two extremes. Teachers may scribble things in their notebooks, sometimes only noting the page of a book or the name of an activity. Other teachers may write something more complex. Perhaps they list the words they are going to need, or write down questions they wish to ask. They may make a list of the web sites they want students to visit together with the information they have to look for online (see Chapter 10F).

We can represent this planning continuum diagrammatically in the following way:

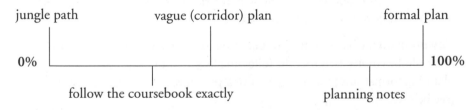

FIGURE 26: The planning continuum

The actual form a plan takes is less important than the thought that has gone into it; the overriding principle is that we should have an idea of what we hope our students will achieve in the class, and that this should guide our decisions about how to bring it about. However, written plans (both sketchy and more detailed) do have a secondary function as a record of what has gone on (see C2 below), and in the lesson itself they help to remind teachers of what they had decided to do, what materials they need, and how long they had planned to spend on certain activities.

B2 **Making a plan**

The following example of making a plan exemplifies how a teacher might proceed from pre-planning to a final plan.

- **Pre-planning background:** for this lesson, some of the facts that feed into pre-planning decisions are as follows:

  1 The class is at intermediate level. There are 31 students. They are between the ages of 18 and 31. They are enthusiastic and participate well when not overtired.
  2 The students need 'waking up' at the beginning of a lesson.
  3 They are quite prepared to 'have a go' with creative activities.
  4 Lessons take place in a light classroom equipped with a whiteboard and an overhead projector.
  5 The overall topic thread into which the lesson fits involves forms of transport and different travelling environments. In the coursebook this will change next week to the topic of 'avoidable disasters'.
  6 The next item on the grammar syllabus is the construction *should have + DONE.*
  7 The students have not had any reading skills work recently.
  8 The students need more oral fluency work.

- **Pre-planning decisions:** as a result of the background information listed above the teacher takes the following decisions:

  1 The lesson should include an oral fluency activity.
  2 The lesson should include the introduction of *should have + DONE.*
  3 It would be nice to have some reading in the lesson.
  4 The lesson should continue with the transport theme – but make it significantly different in some way.

- **The plan:** on the basis of our pre-planning decisions we now make our plan. It should be emphasised that the following lists are not examples of any planning format since that is a matter of style unless we are planning formally (see below).

  The teacher has taken the decision to have the students read the text about a space station (see Example 1 in Chapter 11), and build activities around this. The text does not come from their coursebook, but is one the teacher has used before.

  The probable sequence of the lesson will be:

  1 An oral fluency activity with 'changing groups' (see Chapter 8, B2) in which students have to reach a decision about what five personal possessions they would take into space.
  2 Reading for prediction and then gist, in which students are asked to say what they expect to be in a text about a space station, before reading to check their predictions and then reading again for detailed understanding.

3 Ending the story, in which students quickly devise an ending for the story.

4 New language introduction in which the teacher elicits 'should have' sentences and has students say them successfully.

5 Language practice in which students talk about things they did or did not do, and which they should not or should have done.

6 A space job interview in which students plan and role-play an interview for a job in a space station.

However, the teacher makes (or thinks of) a list of additional task possibilities, for example:

1 Interview Cathy years later to find out what happened to her.
2 Students write a 'newsflash' programme based on what happened.
3 A short extract from a video on future space exploration.
4 Students discuss the three things they would miss most if they were on a space station.

B3 The formal plan

Formal plans are sometimes required, especially when, for example, teachers are to be observed and/or assessed as part of a training scheme or for reasons of internal quality control. A formal plan should contain some or all of the following elements:

- **Class description and timetable fit:** a class description tells us who the students are, and what can be expected of them. It can give information about how the group and how the individuals in it behave, as in the following example:

CLASS DESCRIPTION

The students in this upper intermediate class are between the ages of 18–31. There are 21 women and 9 men. There are PAs/secretaries, 5 housewives, 10 university students (3 of these are postgraduates), teachers, 2 businessmen, a musician, a scientist, a chef, a shop assistant and a waiter.

Because the class starts at 7.45 in the evening, students are often quite tired after a long day at work (or at their studies). They can switch off quite easily, especially if they are involved in a long and not especially interesting piece of reading, for example. However, if they get involved they can be noisy and enthusiastic. Sometimes this enthusiasm gets a little out of control and they start using their first language a lot.

Depending on the circumstances of the plan, the teacher may want to detail more information about individual students, e.g. *Hiromi has a sound knowledge of English and is very confident in her reading and writing abilities. However, she tends to be rather too quiet in groupwork, since she is not especially comfortable at 'putting herself forward'. This tends to get in the way of the development of her oral fluency.* Such detailed description will be especially appropriate with smaller groups, but becomes increasingly difficult to do accurately with larger classes.

However, a record of knowledge of individual students gained through such means as observation, homework, and test scores is invaluable if we are to meet individual needs.

We also need to say where the lesson fits in a sequence of classes (the before and after) as in the following example:

> **TIMETABLE FIT**
>
> The lesson takes place from 7.45 to 9 pm on Tuesday and Thursday evenings. In the past three lessons the students have been discussing the issues of journeys and travelling — how people adapt to different travelling environments. They have listened to an interview with someone who lives in a bus and travels around the country looking for places to park it. They have been looking at vocabulary and expressions related to travelling. They have revisited a number of past tenses, including hypothetical past (third) conditionals ('If he hadn't lost his job, he wouldn't have sold his house'). Next week the class will start working on a 'crime and punishment' unit which includes a courtroom role-play, with work on crime-related lexis, and passive constructions.

We will also include information about how the class have been feeling and what kind of activities they have been involved in (e.g. controlled or communicative, pairwork, or groupwork). All these factors should have influenced our planning choices for this lesson.

- **Lesson aims:** the best classroom aims are specific and directed towards an outcome which can be measured. If we say *My aim is that my students should/can … by the end of the class*, we will be able to tell, after the lesson, whether that aim has been met or not. Aims should reflect what we hope the students will be able to do, not what the teacher is going to do. An aim such as *to teach the present perfect* is not really an aim at all – except for the teacher.

  A lesson will often have more than one aim. We might well say, for example, that our overall objective is to improve our students' reading ability, but that our specific aims are to encourage them to predict content, to use guessing strategies to overcome lexical problems, and to develop an imaginative response to what they encounter.

  Aims can be written in plans as in the following example:

> **AIMS**
>
> 1 To allow students to practise speaking spontaneously and fluently about something that may provoke the use of words and phrases they have been learning recently.
> 2 To give students practice in reading both for gist and for detail.
> 3 To enable students to talk about what people have 'done wrong' in the past, using the 'should (not) have' + 'done' construction.
> 4 To have students think of the interview genre and list the kinds of questions which are asked in such a situation.

- **Activities, procedures, and timing:** the main body of a formal plan lists the activities and procedures in that lesson, together with the times we expect each of them to take. We will include the aids we are going to use, and show the different interactions which will take place in the class.

  When detailing procedure, 'symbol' shorthand is an efficient tool to describe the interactions that are taking place: *T = teacher; S = an individual student; T→C = the teacher working with the whole class; S,S,S = students working on their own; S←→S = students working in pairs; SS←→SS = pairs of students in discussion with other pairs; GG = students working in groups,* and so on. The following example shows how the procedure of an activity can be described:

	Activity/Aids	Interaction	Procedure	Time
1	Group decision-making Pen and paper	a T→C	T tells students to list five things they would take into space with them (apart from essentials).	1'
		b S,S,S	SS make their lists individually.	2'
		c S←→S	In pairs students have to negotiate their items to come up with a shared list of only five items to take to a space station.	3'
		d SS←→SS (GG)	Pairs join with other pairs. The new groups have to negotiate their items to come up with a shared list of only five items to take to a space station.	4'
		e T←→GG	The T encourages the groups to compare their lists.	3'

Specific language that is to be focused on should also be included, as in this example:

	Activity/Aids	Interaction	Procedure	Time
4	Language study Space station text/board	a T←→C	T elicits sentences based on the previous 'problem identification' session e.g. 'She shouldn't have been rude to Cathy.' 'She should have looked at the record book.' 'She should have told the others where she was going.'	10'
		b T←→S,S,S	T has students say the sentences, and may do individual/class work on the pronunciation of the shortened form e.g. /ʃədəv/ — should've, and /ʃədntəv/shouldn't have.	

- **Problems and possibilities:** a good plan tries to predict potential pitfalls and suggests ways of dealing with them. It also includes alternative activities in case we find it necessary to divert from the lesson sequence we had hoped to follow (see c1 below).

When listing anticipated problems it is a good idea to think ahead to possible solutions we might adopt to resolve them, as in the following example:

Anticipated problems	Possible solutions
Students may not be able to think of items to take to a space station with them for activity 1.	I will keep my eyes open and go to prompt any individuals who look 'vacant' or puzzled with questions about what music, books, pictures, etc. they might want to take.
Students may have trouble contracting 'should not have' in Activity 4.	I will do some isolation and distortion work until they can say /ʃədntəv/.

Where we need to modify our lesson dramatically, we may choose to abandon what we are doing and use different activities altogether. If our lesson proceeds faster than we had anticipated, on the other hand, we may need additional material anyway. It is therefore sensible, especially in formal planning, to list additional possibilities, as in the following example:

ADDITIONAL POSSIBILITIES

Extra speaking:	If some groups finish first they can quickly discuss what three things from home they would most miss if they were on a space station.
News broadcast:	Students could write an earth 'newsflash' giving news of what happened at the space station starting 'We interrupt this programme to bring you news of . . .'
Video clip:	If there's time I can show the class an extract from the 'Future of Space Exploration' programme.
Interview plus:	Interview Cathy years later to find out what happened to her.

B4 Planning a sequence of lessons

Planning a sequence of lessons is based on the same principles as planning a single lesson, but there are number of additional issues which we need to pay special attention to:

- **Before and during:** however carefully we plan, in practice unforeseen things are likely to happen during the course of a lesson (as we shall see in C1 below), and so our plans are continually modified in the light of these. Even more than a plan for an individual lesson, a scheme of work for weeks or months of lessons is only a proposal of what we hope to achieve in that time. We will need to revisit this scheme constantly to update it.

- **Short and long-term goals:** however motivated a student may be at the beginning of a course, the level of that motivation may fall dramatically if the student is not engaged or if they cannot see where they are going – or know when they have got there.

  In order for students to stay motivated, they need goals (see Chapter 3, C3) and rewards. While a satisfactory long-term goal may be 'to master the English language', it can seem only a dim and distant possibility at various stages of the learning cycle. In such circumstances students need short-term goals too, such as the completion of some piece of work (or some part of the programme), and rewards such as success on small, staged lesson tests, or taking part in activities designed to recycle knowledge and demonstrate acquisition.

  When we plan a sequence of lessons, we need to build in goals for both students and ourselves to aim at, whether they are end-of-week tests, or major revision lessons. That way we can hope to give our students a staged progression of successfully met challenges.

- **Thematic strands:** one way to approach a sequence of lessons is to focus on different content in each individual lesson. This will certainly provide variety. It might be better, however, for themes to carry over for more than one lesson, or at least to reappear, so that students perceive some coherent topic strands as the course progresses. With such thematic threads we and our students can refer backwards and forwards both in terms of language – especially the vocabulary that certain topics generate – and also in terms of the topics we ask them to invest time in considering.

- **Language planning:** when we plan language input over a sequence of lessons we want to propose a sensible progression of syllabus elements such as grammar, lexis, and functions (see Chapter 21, A2 and A3). We also want to build in sufficient opportunities for recycling or remembering language, and for using language in productive skill work. If we are following a coursebook closely, many of these decisions may already have been taken, but even in such circumstances we need to keep a constant eye on how things are going, and with the knowledge of 'before and after' modify the programme we are working from when necessary.

    Language does not exist in a vacuum, however. Our decisions about how to weave it through the lesson sequence will be heavily influenced by the need for a balance of activities.

- **Activity balance:** the balance of activities over a sequence of lessons is one of the features which will determine the overall level of student involvement in the course. If we get it right, it will also provide the widest range of experience to meet the different learning styles of the students in the class (see Chapter 3, B3).

    Over a period of weeks or months we would expect students to have received a varied diet of activities; they should not have to role-play every day, nor would we expect every lesson to be devoted exclusively to language study (in the ways we described it in Chapter 11). There is a danger, too, that they might become bored if every Friday was the reading class, every Monday the presentation class, every Wednesday was speaking and writing. In such a scenario the level of predictability may have gone beyond the sufficient to the exaggerated. What we are looking for, instead, is a blend of the familiar and the new.

Planning a successful sequence of lessons means taking all these factors into consideration and weaving them together into a colourful but coherent tapestry.

C Using lesson plans

However carefully we plan, and whatever form our plan takes, we will still have to use that plan in the classroom, and use our plans as records of learning for reference.

C1 Action and reaction

Planning a lesson is not the same as scripting a lesson. Wherever our preparations fit on the planning continuum, what we take into the lesson is a proposal for action, rather than a lesson blueprint to be followed slavishly. And our proposal for action, transformed into action in the classroom, is bound to 'evoke some sort of student reaction' (Malamah-Thomas 1987: 5). We then have to decide how to cope with that reaction and whether, in the light of it, we can continue with our plan or whether we need to modify it as we go along.

There are a number of reasons why we may need to modify our proposal for action once a lesson is taking place:

- **Magic moments:** some of the most affecting moments in language lessons happen when a conversation develops unexpectedly, or when a topic produces a level of interest in our students which we had not predicted. The occurrence of such magic moments helps to provide and sustain a group's motivation. We have to recognise them when they come along and then take a judgement about whether to allow them to develop, rather than denying them life because they do not fit into our plan.

- **Sensible diversion:** another reason for diversion from our original plan is when something happens which we simply cannot ignore, whether this is a surprising student reaction to a reading text, or the sudden announcement that someone is getting married! In the case of opportunistic teaching (see Chapter 11, A2), we take the opportunity to teach language that has suddenly come up. Similarly, something might occur to us in terms of topic or in terms of a language connection which we suddenly want to develop on the spot.

- **Unforeseen problems:** however well we plan, unforeseen problems often crop up. Some students may find an activity that we thought interesting incredibly boring; an activity may take more or less time than we anticipated. It is possible that something we thought would be fairly simple for our students turns out to be very difficult (or vice versa). We may have planned an activity based on the number of students we expected to turn up, only to find that some of them are absent. Occasionally we find that students have already come across material or topics we take into class, and our common sense tells us that it would be unwise to carry on.

  In any of the above scenarios it would be almost impossible to carry on with our plan as if nothing had happened; if an activity finishes quickly we have to find something else to fill the time. If students cannot do what we are asking of them, we will have to modify what we are asking of them. If some students (but not all) have already finished an activity we cannot just leave those students to get bored.

  It is possible to anticipate potential problems in the class (see c2 below) and to plan strategies to deal with them. But however well we do this, things will still happen that surprise us, and which, therefore, cause us to move away from our plan, whether this is a temporary or permanent state of affairs.

However well we plan, our plan is just a suggestion of what we might do in class. Everything depends upon how our students respond and relate to it. In Jim Scrivener's words, 'prepare thoroughly. But in class, teach the learners – not the plan' (Scrivener 1994b: 44).

C2 **Plans as records and research tools**

Written plans are not just proposals for future action; they are also records of what has taken place. Thus, when we are in the middle of a sequence of lessons, we can look back at what we have done in order to decide what to do next.

Since we may have to modify our lessons depending on student reactions we need to keep a record of how successful certain activities were to aid our memory. A record of lessons can also help colleagues if and when they have to teach for us when we are absent.

Our original written plans will, therefore, have to be modified in the light of what actually happened in the classes we taught. This may simply mean crossing out the original activity title or coursebook page number, and replacing it with what we used in reality. However, if we have time to record how we and the students experienced the lesson, reflecting carefully on successful and less successful activities, not only will this help us to make changes if and when we want to use the same activities again, but it will also lead us to think about how we teach and consider changes in both activities and approach. Lesson planning in this way allows us to act as our own observers and aids us in our own development (see Chapter 24, B1).

Chapter notes and further reading

- **Lesson metaphors**

  Penny Ur (1996: 213) and Scott Thornbury (1999b) both suggest seeing lessons as, for example, a show, a menu, a story, a film. Thornbury stresses the importance of the 'sense of an ending' for lessons.

- **To plan or not to plan?**

  When Craig Thaine wrote an article about getting teacher trainees to plan a sequence of lessons (Thaine 1996a), Mario Rinvolucri replied with a letter attacking the whole principle of lesson planning (Rinvolucri 1996). Thaine's reply (Thaine 1996b) defending the need for (and benefits of) planning helps to make the three contributions into a fascinating discussion about the purpose and value of planning.

- **Unforeseen problems**

  See R Gower et al. (1995: 178).

Testing students

A1 Different types of test

There are four main reasons for testing which give rise to four categories of test:

- **Placement tests:** placing new students in the right class in a school is facilitated with the use of placement tests. Usually based on syllabuses and materials the students will follow and use once their level has been decided on, these test grammar and vocabulary knowledge and assess students' productive and receptive skills.

  Some schools ask students to assess themselves as part of the placement process, adding this self-analysis into the final placing decision.

- **Diagnostic tests:** while placement tests are designed to show how good a student's English is in relation to a previously agreed system of levels, diagnostic tests can be used to expose learner difficulties, gaps in their knowledge, and skill deficiencies during a course. Thus, when we know what the problems are, we can do something about them.

- **Progress or achievement tests:** these tests are designed to measure learners' language and skill progress in relation to the syllabus they have been following.

  Achievement tests only work if they contain item types which the students are familiar with. This does not mean that in a reading test, for example, we give them texts they have seen before, but it does mean providing them with similar texts and familiar task types. If students are faced with completely new material, the test will not measure the learning that has been taking place, even though it can still measure general language proficiency.

  Achievement tests at the end of a term (like progress tests at the end of a unit, a fortnight, etc.) should reflect progress, not failure. They should reinforce the learning that has taken place, not go out of their way to expose weaknesses. They can also help us to decide on changes to future teaching programmes where students do significantly worse in (parts of) the test than we might have expected.

- **Proficiency tests:** proficiency tests give a general picture of a student's knowledge and ability (rather than measure progress). They are frequently used as stages people have to reach if they want to be admitted to a foreign university, get a job, or obtain some kind of certificate.

Proficiency tests have a profound backwash effect since, where they are external exams, students obviously want to pass them, and teachers' reputations sometimes depend (probably unfairly) upon how many of them succeed.

A2 Characteristics of a good test

In order to judge the effectiveness of any test it is sensible to lay down criteria against which the test can be measured, as follows:

- **Validity:** a test is valid if it tests what it is supposed to test. Thus it is not valid, for example, to test writing ability with an essay question that requires specialist knowledge of history or biology – unless it is known that all students share this knowledge before they do the test.

  A particular kind of 'validity' that concerns most test designers is face validity. This means that the test should look, on the 'face' of it, as if it is valid. A test which consisted of only three multiple choice items would not convince students of its face validity however reliable or practical teachers thought it to be.

- **Reliability:** a good test should give consistent results. For example, if the same group of students took the same test twice within two days – without reflecting on the first test before they sat it again – they should get the same results on each occasion. If they took another similar test, the results should be consistent. If two groups who were demonstrably alike took the test, the marking range would be the same.

  In practice, 'reliability' is enhanced by making the test instructions absolutely clear, restricting the scope for variety in the answers, and making sure that test conditions remain constant.

  Reliability also depends on the people who mark the tests – the scorers. Clearly a test is unreliable if the result depends to any large extent on who is marking it. Much thought has gone into making the scoring of tests as reliable as possible (see c2 below).

B Types of test item

Whatever purpose a test or exam has, a major factor in its success or failure as a good measuring instrument will be determined by the item types that it contains.

B1 Direct and indirect test items

A test item is **direct** if it asks candidates to perform the communicative skill which is being tested. **Indirect** test items, on the other hand, try to measure a student's knowledge and ability by getting at what lies beneath their receptive and productive skills. Whereas direct test items try to be as much like real-life language use as possible, indirect items try to find out about a student's language knowledge through more controlled items, such as multiple choice questions or grammar transformation items. These are often quicker to design and, crucially, easier to mark, and produce greater scorer reliability.

Another distinction needs to be made between **discrete-point** testing and **integrative** testing. Whereas discrete-point testing only tests one thing at a time (such as asking students to choose the correct tense of a verb), integrative test items expect students to use a variety of language at any one given time – as they will have to do when writing a composition or doing a conversational oral test.

In many proficiency tests where students sit a number of different papers, there is a mixture of direct and indirect, discrete-point and integrative testing. Test designers find that this combination gives a good overall picture of student ability. Placement tests often use discrete-point testing to measure students against an existing language syllabus, but may then compare this with more direct and integrative tasks to get a fuller picture.

B2   Indirect test item types

Although there is a wide range of indirect test possibilities, certain types are in common use:

- **Multiple choice questions (MCQs):** a traditional vocabulary multiple choice question looks like this:

> The journalist was _____ by enemy fire as he tried to send a story by radio.
>
> **a** wronged   **b** wounded   **c** injured   **d** damaged

For many years MCQs were considered to be ideal test instruments for measuring students' knowledge of grammar and vocabulary. Above all this was because they were easy to mark, and since the advent of computers the answer books for these tests can be read by machines, not people, thereby cutting out the possibility of scorer error.

However, there are a number of problems with multiple choice questions. In the first place, they are extremely difficult to write well, especially in the design of the incorrect choices. These 'distractors' may actually put ideas into students' heads that they did not have before they read them. Second, while it is possible to train students so that their MCQ abilities are enhanced, this may not actually improve their English. The difference between two student scores may be between the person who has been trained in the technique and a person who has not, rather than being a difference of language knowledge and ability.

MCQs are still widely used, but though they score highly in terms of practicality and scorer reliability, their 'validity' and overall 'reliability' are suspect.

- **Cloze procedures:** cloze procedures seem to offer us the ideal indirect but integrative testing item. They can be prepared quickly and if the claims made for them are true, they are an extremely cost-effective way of finding out about a testee's overall knowledge.

Cloze, in its purest form, is the deletion of every nth word in a text (somewhere between every fifth or tenth word). Because the procedure is random, it avoids test designer failings. It produces test items like this:

> They sat on a bench attached 1 _____ a picnic table. Below them
> they 2 _____ see the river gurgling between overgrown
> 3 _____. The sky was diamond blue, with 4 _____ white clouds
> dancing in the freshening 5 _____. They could hear the call of
> 6 _____ and the buzzing of countless insects. 7 _____ were
> completely alone.

Cloze testing seems, on the face of it, like a perfect test instrument, since, because of the randomness of the deleted words, anything may be tested (e.g. grammar, collocation, fixed phrases, reading comprehension), and therefore it becomes more integrative in its reach. However, it turns out that the actual score a student gets depends on the particular words that are deleted, rather than on any general English knowledge. Some are more difficult to supply than others, and in some cases there are several possible answers. Even in the short sample text above it is clear that whilst there is no doubt about items such as 1 and 8, for example, item 4 is less predictable. Different passages produce different results.

Despite such problems of 'reliability', cloze is too useful a technique to abandon altogether, however, because it is clear that supplying the correct word for a blank does imply an understanding of context and a knowledge of that word and how it operates. Perhaps it would be better, therefore, to use 'rational' or 'modified' cloze procedures (Alderson 1996: 222) where the test designer can be sure that the deleted words are recoverable from the context. This means abandoning the completely random nature of traditional cloze procedure. Instead, every eighth or tenth word is deleted, but the teacher has the option to delete a word to the left or right if the context makes this more sensible.

Modified cloze is useful for placement tests since students can be given texts that they would be expected to cope with at certain levels – thus allowing us to judge their suitability for those levels. They are useful, too, as part of a test battery in either achievement or proficiency tests.

- **Transformation and paraphrase:** a common test item asks candidates to rewrite sentences in a slightly different form, retaining the exact meaning of the original. For example, the following item tests the candidates' knowledge of verb and clause patterns that are triggered by the use of *I wish*:

> I'm sorry that I didn't get her an anniversary present.
> I wish _____

In order to complete the item successfully the student has to understand the first sentence, and then know how to construct an equivalent which is grammatically possible. As such they do tell us something about the candidates' knowledge of the language system.

- **Sentence re-ordering:** getting students to put words in the right order to make appropriate sentences tells us quite a lot about their underlying knowledge of syntax and lexico-grammatical elements. The following example is typical:

> **Put the words in order to make correct sentences.**
>
> called / I / I'm / in / sorry / wasn't / when / you
>
> _____

Re-ordering exercises are fairly easy to write, though it is not always possible to ensure only one correct order.

There are many other indirect techniques too, including sentence fill-ins (*Jan _____ to the gym every Tuesday morning*), choosing the correct tense of verbs in sentences and passages (*I have arrived/arrived yesterday*), finding errors in sentences (*She noticed about his new jacket*), and choosing the correct form of a word (*He didn't enjoy being on the (lose) _____ side*). All of these offer items which are quick and efficient to score and which aim to tell us something about a student's underlying knowledge.

B3 Direct test item types

For direct test items to achieve 'validity' and to be 'reliable', test designers need to do the following:

- **Create a 'level playing field':** in the case of a written test, teachers and candidates would almost certainly complain about the following essay question:

  > *Why was the discovery of DNA so important for the science of the twentieth century?*

  since it unfairly favours candidates who have sound scientific knowledge and presupposes a knowledge of twentieth-century scientific history.

  However, the following topic comes close to ensuring that all candidates have the same chance of success:

  > Some businesses now say that no one can smoke cigarettes in or even near any of their offices. Some governments have banned smoking in all public places – whether outside or inside.
  >   This is a good idea but it also takes away some of our freedom.
  >   Do you agree or disagree?
  >   Give reasons for your answer.

  General writing question from *The IELTS Handbook* (see notes at the end of this chapter)

Receptive skill testing also needs to avoid making excessive demands on the student's general or specialist knowledge. Receptive ability testing can also be undermined if the means of testing requires students to perform well in writing or speaking (when it is a test of reading or listening). In such a situation we can no longer be sure that it is the receptive skill we are measuring.

- **Replicate real-life interaction:** in real life when people speak or write they generally do so with some real purpose. Yet traditional writing tests have often been based exclusively on general essay questions, and speaking tests often included hypothetical questions about what candidates might say if they happened to be in a certain situation. More modern test writers now include tasks which attempt to replicate features of real life (Weir 1993: 167). They will often look similar to the kind of speaking activities described in Chapter 19.

  Tests of reading and listening should also, as far as possible, reflect real life. This means that texts should be as realistic as possible, even where they are not authentic (see Chapter 14, B1). Although there are ways of assessing student understanding (using matching tasks or multiple choice questions) which do not necessarily satisfy these criteria, test items should be as much like real reading and listening as possible.

The following direct test item types are a few of the many which attempt to meet the criteria we have mentioned above:

SPEAKING

- an interviewer questioning a candidate about themselves
- 'information gap' activities where a candidate has to find out information either from an interlocutor or a fellow candidate. (The role-play on page 279, Example 5, would not need much modification to serve as a test item.)
- 'decision-making' activities, such as showing paired candidates ten photos of people and asking them to put them in order of the best and worst dressed
- using pictures for candidates to compare and contrast, whether they can both see them or whether (as in many communication games) they have found similarities and differences without being able to look at each other's material
- role-play activities where candidates perform tasks such as introducing themselves, or ringing a theatre to book tickets

WRITING

- writing compositions and stories
- 'transactional letters' where candidates reply to a job advertisement, or pen a complaint to a hotel based on information given in the exam paper
- information leaflets about their school or a place in their town
- a set of instructions for some common task
- newspaper articles about a recent event

READING

- multiple choice questions to test comprehension of a text
- matching written descriptions with pictures of the items, or procedure, they describe

- transferring written information to charts, graphs, maps, etc. (though special care has to be taken not to disadvantage non-mathematically minded candidates)
- choosing the best summary of a paragraph or a whole text
- matching jumbled headings with paragraphs
- inserting sentences provided by the examiner in the correct place in the text

LISTENING

- completing charts with facts and figures from a listening text
- identifying which of a number of objects (pictures on the test paper) is being described
- identifying which (out of two or three speakers) says what
- identifying whether speakers are enthusiastic, encouraging, in disagreement, or amused
- following directions on a map and identifying the correct house or place

In the interests of 'reliability', listening tests are most often supplied on tape to ensure that all candidates have the same opportunities, irrespective of the speakers' voices, speeds, or expressions. Sometimes, as in the computerised TOEFL test (see the notes at the end of this chapter) candidates work with headphones from an individual computer. Where a group of students listen to the same tape or disk, however, we need to be sure that the material is clearly and easily audible (see Chapter 16, A2).

C Writing and marking tests

At various times during our teaching careers we may have to write tests for the students we are teaching, and mark the tests they have completed for us. These may range from a lesson test at the end of the week to an achievement test at the end of a term or a year.

C1 Writing tests

Before designing a test and then giving it to a group of students, there are a number of things we need to do:

- **Assess the test situation:** before we start to write the test we need to remind ourselves of the context in which the test takes place. We have to decide how much time should be given to the test-taking, when and where it will take place, and how much time there is for marking.

- **Decide what to test:** we have to list what we want to include in our test. This means taking a conscious decision to include or exclude skills such as reading comprehension or speaking (if speaking tests are impractical). It means knowing what syllabus items can be legitimately included (in an achievement test), and what kinds of topics and situations are appropriate for our students.

  Just because we have a list of all the vocabulary items or grammar points the students have studied over the term, this does not mean we have to test every single item. If we include a representative sample from across the whole list, the students' success or failure with those items will be a good indicator of how well they have learnt all of the language they have studied.

- **Balance the elements:** if we are to include direct and indirect test items we have to make a decision about how many of each we should put in our test. A 200-item multiple choice test with a short real-life writing task tacked onto the end suggests that we think that MCQs are a better way of finding out about students than more integrative writing tasks would be.

   Balancing elements involves estimating how long we want each section of the test to take and then writing test items within those time constraints. The amount of space and time we give to the various elements should also reflect their importance in our teaching.

- **Weight the scores:** however well we have balanced the elements in our test, our perception of our students' success or failure will depend upon how many marks are given to each section or sections of the test. If we give two marks for each of our ten MCQs, but only one mark for each of our ten transformation items, it means that it is more important for students to do well in the former than in the latter.

- **Making the test work:** it is absolutely vital that we try out individual items and/or whole tests on colleagues and students alike before administering them to real candidates.

   When we write test items the first thing to do is to get fellow teachers to try them out. Frequently they spot problems which we are not aware of and/or come up with possible answers and alternatives that we had not anticipated.

   Later, having made changes based on our colleagues' reactions, we will want to try out the test on students. We will not do this with the students who are going to take the test, of course, but if we can find a class that is roughly similar – or a class one level above the proposed test – then we will soon find out what items cause unnecessary problems. We can also discover how long the test takes.

   Such trialling is designed to avoid disaster, and to yield a whole range of possible answers/responses to the various test items. This means that when other people finally mark the test we can give them a list of possible alternatives and thus ensure reliable scoring.

C2 Marking tests

When Cyril Weir gave copies of the same eight exam scripts to his postgraduate students they marked them first on the basis of 'impressionistic' marking out of a possible total of 20 marks. The results were alarming. Some scorers gave higher marks overall than others. But for some of the EFL student scripts, the range of marks was excessive. For one script the lowest mark awarded was 5, whereas another scorer gave it 20. For another the range was 1–15. As Cyril Weir writes 'the worst scripts … if they had been marked by certain markers, might have been given higher marks than the best scripts!' (1993: 157).

There are a number of solutions to this kind of scorer subjectivity:

- **Training:** if scorers have seen examples of scripts at various different levels and discussed what marks they should be given, then their marking is likely to be less erratic than if they come to the task fresh. If scorers are allowed to watch and discuss videoed oral tests, they can be trained to 'rate the samples of spoken English accurately and consistently in terms of the pre-defined descriptions of performance' (Saville and Hargreaves 1999: 49).

- **More than one scorer:** reliability can be greatly enhanced by having more than one scorer. The more people who look at a script, the greater the chance that its true worth will be located somewhere between the various scores it is given. Two examiners watching an oral test are likely to agree a more reliable score than one.

  Many public examination boards use **moderators** whose job it is to check samples of individual scorers' work to see that it conforms with the general standards laid down for the exam.

- **Global assessment scales:** a way of specifying scores that can be given to productive skill work is to create 'pre-defined descriptions of performance'. Such descriptions say what students need to be capable of in order to gain the required marks, as in the following assessment (or rating) scale for oral ability:

Score	Description
0	The candidate is almost unintelligible, uses words wrongly, and shows no sign of any grammatical understanding.
1	The candidate is able to transmit only very basic ideas using individual words rather than phrases or fuller patterns of discourse. Speech is very hesitant and the pronunciation makes intelligibility difficult.
2	The candidate transmits basic ideas in a fairly stilted way. Pronunciation is sometimes problematic and there are examples of grammatical and lexical misuse and gaps which impede communication on occasions.
3	The candidate transmits ideas moderately clearly. Speech is somewhat hesitant and there are frequent lapses in grammar and vocabulary use. Nevertheless, the candidate makes him/herself understood.
4	The candidate speaks fairly fluently, showing an ability to communicate ideas with not too much trouble. There are some problems of grammatical accuracy and some words are inappropriately used.
5	The candidate speaks fluently with few obvious mistakes and a wide variety of lexis and expression. Pronunciation is almost always intelligible, and there is little difficulty in communicating ideas.

Global assessment scales are not without problems, however: perhaps the description does not exactly match the student who is speaking as in a case (for the scale above) where he or she had very poor pronunciation but was nevertheless grammatically accurate. There is also the danger that different teachers 'will not agree on the meaning of scale descriptors' (Upshur and Turner 1995: 5). Global assessment, on its own, still falls short of the kind of reliability we wish to achieve.

- **Analytic profiles:** marking gets more reliable when a student's performance is analysed in much greater detail. Instead of just a general assessment, marks are awarded for different elements.

  For oral assessment we can judge a student's speaking in a number of different ways such as pronunciation, fluency, use of lexis and grammar, and intelligibility. We may want to rate their ability to get themselves out of trouble (repair skills) and how well they successfully completed the task which we set them.

  The resulting analytic profile might end up looking like this:

Criteria	Score (see analytic scales)
Pronunciation	
Fluency	
Use of vocabulary	
Use of grammar	
Intelligibility	
Repair skills	
Task completion	

For each separate criterion, we can now provide a separate 'analytic scale', as in the following example for fluency:

Score	Description
0	The candidate cannot get words or phrases out at all.
1	The candidate speaks hesitatingly in short, interrupted bursts.
2	The candidate speaks slowly with frequent pauses.
3	The candidate speaks at a comfortable speed with quite a lot of pauses and hesitations.
4	The candidate speaks at a comfortable speed with only an occasional pause or upset.
5	The candidate speaks quickly with few hesitations.

A combination of global and analytic scoring gives us the best chance of reliable marking. However, a profusion of criteria may make the marking of a test extremely lengthy and cumbersome; test designers and administrators will have to decide how to accommodate the competing claims of reliability and practicality.

- **Scoring and interacting during oral tests:** scorer reliability in oral tests is helped not only by global assessment scores and analytic profiles but also by separating the role of scorer (or examiner) from the role of **interlocutor** (the examiner who guides and provokes conversation). This may cause practical problems, but it will allow the scorer to observe and assess, free from the responsibility of keeping the interaction with the candidate or candidates going.

   In many tests of speaking, students are now put in pairs or groups for certain tasks since it is felt that this will ensure genuine interaction, and will help to relax students in a way that interlocutor–candidate interaction might fail to do on its own. However, at least one commentator worries that pairing students in this way leads candidates to perform below their level of proficiency, and that when students with the same mother tongue are paired together their intelligibility to the examiner may suffer (Foot 1999: 52).

D Teaching the test

When students are preparing for a public exam or school test it is the teacher's responsibility not only to help them get their English to the level required, but also familiarise them with the kinds of exam items they are likely to encounter, and give them training in how to succeed.

Students can be prepared for future tests and exams in a variety of ways:

- **Training for test types:** we can show the various test types and ask them what the item is testing so that they are clear about what is required. We can help them to understand what the test or exam designer is aiming for; by showing them the kind of marking scales that are used, we can make them aware of what constitutes success. We can then give them training to help them approach such items more effectively. After they have completed a test item type we can tell them what score an examiner might give and why. We will also equip students with appropriate negotiating language (see Chapter 19, A1) to help them get over awkward moments in such tasks.

   When training students to handle reading test items we will discuss with them the best way to approach a first reading of the text, and how that can be modified on second reading to allow them to answer the questions provided.

   If the test or exam is likely to contain multiple choice questions, we can help students to appreciate the advantages of finding the obvious distractor(s) first. They can then work out what similarities and differences the other distractors have so that they can identify the area of meaning or grammar that is being targeted.

- **Discussing general exam skills:** most students benefit from being reminded about general test and exam skills, without which much of the work they do will be wasted. Such general skills for written tests include studying questions properly, and then reading them again so that they are absolutely sure what they should do. Students need to check their work over thoroughly before considering that they have finished. They need to pace themselves so that they do not spend a disproportionate amount of time on only one part of an exam.

- **Doing practice tests:** students need a chance to practise taking the test or exam so that they get a feel for the experience, especially with regard to issues such as pacing. At various points in a course students can sit practice papers, or whole practice tests, but this should not be done too often since not only will it give teachers horrific marking schedules, but it will also be less productive than other test and exam preparation procedures are.

- **Promoting autonomy:** although we can do a lot of exam preparation in class, we need to impress on students that their chances of success are far greater if they study and revise on their own. We will want them to read more, listen more, work on self-study exercises, and use dictionaries and other means to build up their language store. All of these activities are desirable for any student (see Chapter 24, A1), but are especially appropriate when an exam is approaching.

- **Having fun:** just because students need to practise certain test types does not mean this has to be done in a boring or tense manner. There are a number of ways of having fun with tests and exams.

  If a typical test item asks candidates to put words in order to make sentences (see B2 above), the teacher might prepare the class for this kind of item by giving students a number of words on cards which they have to physically assemble into sentences. They can hold them above their heads (so that they cannot see the words on them) and their classmates have to tell them where to stand to make a 'human sentence'. Students can play 'transformation tennis' where one student 'serves' a sentence, e.g. *India is the country I would like to visit more than any other* and the receiving student has to reply with a transformation starting with *The country*, e.g. *The country I would most like to visit is India* (Prodromou 1995: 22–23). They can change the sex of all the people in direct and indirect test items to see if the items still work and if not, why not.

  Students can be encouraged to write their own test items, based on language they have been working on and the examples they have seen so far. The new test items can now be given to other students to see how well they have been written and how difficult they are. This helps students to get into the minds of their test and exam writers.

- **Ignoring the test:** if students who are studying for an exam only ever look at test types, discuss exam technique, and take practice tests, lessons may become monotonous. There is also the possibility that general English improvement will be compromised at the expense of exam preparation.

When we are preparing students for an exam, we need to ignore the exam from time to time so that we have opportunities to work on general language issues, and so that students can take part in the kind of motivating activities that are appropriate for all English lessons.

Chapter notes and further reading

- **Public exams**

  Among the international exams which students can take are the following:

  – Cambridge exams are offered by the University of Cambridge Local Examinations Syndicate (UCLES), Cambridge, UK (http://www.cambridge-efl.org.uk). These are exams in general English. There are five main levels:

    Key English Test (KET) for elementary candidates
    Preliminary English Test (PET) for lower intermediate candidates
    First Certificate in English (FCE) for upper intermediate candidates
    Certificate of Advanced English (CAE) for upper intermediate/advanced candidates
    Certificate of Proficiency in English (CPE) for very advanced candidates

  – City and Guilds Pitman qualifications offered by City and Guilds, London (http://www.city-and-guilds.co.uk/Pitman/default.htm). Exams are offered in:

    Communication in Technical English
    English for Business Communication
    English for Office Skills
    ESOL (English for Speakers of Other Languages)
    ESOL for Young Learners
    Spoken ESOL
    Spoken ESOL for Young Learners

  – IELTS (International English Language Testing System), administered jointly by UCLES (see above), the British Council, and IDP Education, Australia (http://www.ielts.org).
    IELTS scores (on a 0–9 band) are used especially by British and Australian universities to gauge the level of would-be students or trainers/teachers. There are papers in listening and speaking. Candidates then choose general or academic writing, and general or academic reading.

  – Diploma in English for International Communication is offered by the Institute of Linguists, London (http://www.iol.org.uk) for anyone who has reached a degree-equivalent level of attainment and does not have English as their first language.

  – SESOL (Spoken English for Speakers of Other Languages) offered by Trinity College London (www.trinitycollege.co.uk). These are one-to-one interviews with an examiner at a level to suit the candidate.

- TOEFL (Test of English as a Foreign Language) is offered by Educational Testing Services, New Jersey, USA (http://www.toefl.org).
  TOEFL scores are used by colleges and universities in North America and elsewhere to measure English proficiency for would-be students. The tests are now computer-administered in parts of the world where this is possible.

- TOEIC (Test of English for International Communication) is offered by TOEIC Service International, Princeton, New Jersey, USA (http://www.toeic.com). TOEIC scores are used by a number of companies in the USA and elsewhere to judge the level of English of potential employees.

- Exams for Business are offered by the University of Cambridge Local Examinations Syndicate (see above) and by the London Chamber of Commerce and Industry (LCCI) (http://www.lccieb.org.uk/qualifications.htm).

● **Testing in general**

The best and most accessible books on testing are still A Hughes (1989) and C Weir (1993). See also J C Alderson et al. (1995).

● **Cloze procedures**

A Hughes (1989: 67–70) repeats his earlier claims that cloze passages taken from real conversation transcripts can be good predictors of oral ability.

● **Oral testing**

B Knight (1992) describes a fascinating workshop in which teachers investigate how to measure students' speaking skills.

● **Using rating scales**

J Upshur and C Turner (1995) suggest replacing descriptive rating scales with scales where test markers have to answer a series of binary (yes/no) questions about student performance.

24 | Learner automony, teacher development

A The autonomous learner

However good a teacher may be, students will never learn a language – or anything else – unless they aim to learn outside as well as during class time. This is because language is too complex and varied for there to be enough time for students to learn all they need to in a classroom. Even if students have three English lessons a week, it will take a great number of weeks before they have had the kind of exposure and opportunities for use which are necessary for real progress. As David Nunan suggests, not everything can be taught in class (Nunan 1988a: 3), but even if it could a teacher will not always be around if and when students wish to use the language in real life (Cotterall 1995: 220).

To compensate for the limits of classroom time and to counter the passivity that is an enemy of true learning, students need to develop their own learning strategies, so that as far as possible they become autonomous learners. This does not always happen automatically. Attitudes to self-directed learning are frequently conditioned by the educational culture in which students have studied or are studying (see Chapter 6, B1, and A2 below); autonomy of action is not always considered a desirable characteristic in such contexts. Teachers sometimes, as a result, encounter either passive or active resistance if they attempt to impose self-directed learning inappropriately.

Even where there is no resistance to self-directed learning, some students will be more successful than others as autonomous learners because of their learning style(s) (see Chapter 3, B3). Icy Lee points out that some of her students responded well to work in this area after they had signed a 'learner contract' with their teacher, but that others were not nearly so successful (Lee 1998). The more enthusiastic of her learners spent more time learning 'on their own', and felt more positive about themselves and about learning both during and after a term in which self-directed learning had been actively promoted by their teacher. They were confident that they would continue learning on their own after the course. The less enthusiastic learners, however, suffered from low self-esteem, had an ambivalent attitude to learner autonomy and spent less time in self study than their peers. They were unlikely to continue studying on their own after the course had finished.

Despite such variation, however, there are various ways that we can help students to become autonomous learners, both during language courses and then for continuing learning when such courses have finished.

Routes to autonomy

Teachers can promote autonomous learning in a number of ways:

- **Learner training:** in the classroom we can help students to reflect on the way they learn, give them strategies for dealing with different kinds of activities and problems and offer them different learning-style alternatives to choose from.

  Reflection helps students to think about their own strengths and weaknesses with a view to making a plan for future action. Thus, for example, we might ask students to complete a questionnaire in which they profile their feelings about aspects of language:

How difficult do you think each of these language areas are?
Give a score from 0 (= very easy) to 5 (= very difficult). Say why you have given each score.

Language area	Score (0–5)	Comment
Grammar		
Words and phrases		
Pronunciation		
Listening		
Reading		
Writing		
Speaking		

Personal language reflection

We can then probe the student's self-analysis in more detail, discussing with them issues such as why listening is difficult and what strategies they might adopt to deal with this (see Chapter 14, A4 and Chapter 16B). We can refer them to practice exercises for grammar or vocabulary and tell them where to find pronunciation practice or extra reading (see Chapter 15, A1).

Having students reflect privately on how they learn can be enhanced by frequent discussion of the learning experience. At certain times (such as at the end of every two weeks) students can be asked to describe their favourite lessons, and say which lessons or parts of lessons they found easiest or most difficult and why. They can discuss how and why they remember certain words and not others (they often remember ones they love or hate, or ones that they notice often and in different contexts) and what they might do to help them with the less memorable or difficult words (writing their own sentences, looking for them in anything they read, reading more, memorising lists). They can also be encouraged to evaluate their own progress (see Chapter 7, B2) by answering questions about how well they think they have learnt the material in the last few lessons.

We can have students reflect on the language itself: they can list the most difficult grammar they came across, or say what their favourite ten new words have been in the last fourteen days. We can give them opportunities to ask us specific questions about things they are having difficulty with.

Students can be given specific strategies for better learning. This may be given in the form of 'learning hints', such as these:

> • Make your own vocabulary notebook.
> • List the words in the notebook alphabetically.
> • For each word write an example sentence showing how the word is used, for example:
>
> library   I went to the library and borrowed a book for two weeks.

Vocabulary 'learning hints'

When training students to be better readers (see Chapter 15), we can encourage them not to worry about the meaning of every single word when they are reading for gist (see Chapter 14, A4). When training students in speaking, we can give them exponents for turn-taking (see Chapter 17, A2); for listening we can show them how to recognise the meaning of various intonation patterns.

When training students in writing skills (see Chapter 18B) we may want to train them in effective note-taking or composition planning. However, we need to be cautious about the way we do this. Rather than attempting to impose our own habits on students, we might instead offer them three alternatives (as in the example below) as a stimulus for discussion and as prompts for their own future note-taking methods:

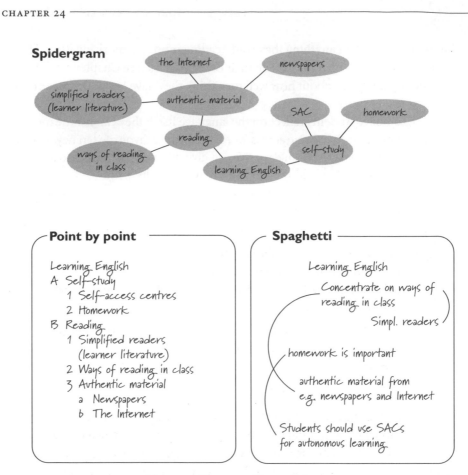

Spidergram

Point by point

Learning English
A Self-study
 1 Self-access centres
 2 Homework
B Reading
 1 Simplified readers
  (learner literature)
 2 Ways of reading in class
 3 Authentic material
  a Newspapers
  b The Internet

Spaghetti

Learning English
 Concentrate on ways of
 reading in class
  Simpl. readers
homework is important
authentic material from
e.g. newspapers and Internet
Students should use SACs
for autonomous learning

Three possible note-taking techniques

- **Homework:** learner autonomy gets a powerful boost the first time that homework is set for students to do out of class. They will now have to study without the help of a teacher.

  Homework is not easy for teacher or students to get right. In the first place a decision has to be made about how much homework to set. Many school and college students have a number of different subjects to contend with, and English homework sometimes gets put to the bottom of the pile. When students are adults working in full-time jobs, the demands of self study may have to fight it out with work, family responsibilities, and other pursuits and hobbies.

  In order to get the level just right, teachers need to discuss with students how much homework they can cope with, given the other commitments they have. If there is class agreement between students and teacher about what is reasonable, there is a much greater chance of compliance (see Chapter 9, B1 for agreement on a general code of conduct).

  Homework is frequently seen as a necessary evil rather than as an important contribution to learner autonomy. The teacher Lesley Painter noticed that when she set homework tasks she looked at her students and noticed their 'glazed expressions' (Painter 1999: 42). Her students did the homework, but it bored them. They were not engaged by it and neither was she. Her response was to think how she might make homework 'more relevant to their personal and language-learning needs'. She constructed a homework questionnaire which students could administer to each other and to students in other classes. In the questionnaire respondents were asked what type of homework they were normally given, whether they ever skipped homework and why, and what homework they would find most useful. They were then asked to dream up a fun activity which both they and their classmates would find useful.

The result of this questionnaire was that the nature of homework tasks started to change dramatically. They now included scanning English language newspapers to report back on stories they found, writing film reviews, collecting real-life language examples, presenting English language songs to their classmates, or researching a topic for a future written or spoken performance.

None of these activities are particularly new, but, as Painter suggests, they are student-driven and, as a result, command much greater student engagement. As with all successful moves to encourage greater student autonomy, teacher and students together arrived at techniques and exercises which best suited the students themselves. Homework tasks become more like personal schemes of study, relevant, interesting, and useful.

- **Keeping 'learning journals':** many teachers ask students to keep journals or diaries of their learning experiences, in the hope that their students will then reflect on their lessons, explore their successes and difficulties, and come to a greater understanding about learning and language.

    Journal writing can be entirely voluntary or the teacher can set aside time for writing (ten minutes at the end of every Friday). Students can be directed to either write about anything they want, to write about what they have learnt in their lessons (and how they feel about it) or to write entries using recently studied language.

    Once students have started keeping journals, the way we respond to them may determine whether or not they keep them up. We might first discuss with the students exactly what responses they can expect from us. For example, we might decide to comment on content only. This would have the advantage of opening up a dialogue about learning and related issues without worrying overmuch about correct language use. But we might also agree to offer language comment or make suggestions about how to improve.

    Some teachers write letters rather than have students keep journals. Mario Rinvolucri started a course by writing the same letter to all his students inviting them to write back to him about anything they wanted (Rinvolucri 1983, 1995). He then entered into a correspondence with some of the class, and because the communication was written and personal, he was able to address learning problems in a way that was easier than in face-to-face interactions, especially during a whole-class discussion.

There are some dangers to letter writing of this kind – and to journal keeping in general. We may want to keep a greater distance between ourselves and our students than letter writing, especially, seems designed to encourage. Responding to letters and journals also takes time. Yet the advantages of having students think about what they are doing outweighs the disadvantages in the eyes of many teachers.

A2 The self-access centre (SAC)

A useful adjunct to classroom learning – or indeed alternative to it – is the **self-access** or **open learning centre**. In SACs students can work on their own (or in pairs and groups) with a range of material, from grammar reference and workbook-type tasks to cassette tapes and video excerpts. SACs may have large collections of learner literature (see Chapter 15, A1), dictionaries (see Chapter 12A), reading texts and listening materials. Increasingly, SACs are equipped with computers for reference and language activities, together with access to the Internet and the rich possibilities it provides (see Chapter 10F). Where possible, SACs are rooms divided into sections for different kinds of material, though it is also possible to put large amounts of self-access materials on a trolley that can be wheeled from class to class.

The idea of a self-access centre is that students should drop into it either as a regular part of the timetable or in their own spare time. Some students may not actually be following a regular course, but may have signed up to be allowed to use the SAC even though they are not in any English class. Once inside the room, learners will decide what work to do, find the right kind of material, and settle down to complete the learning task. However, in order for this procedure to work effectively, a number of things have to take place.

- **Classification systems:** nothing will de-motivate a student more than trying to work on something that is too easy or way outside their reach. Yet this is a distinct possibility unless there is a clear system of classification which details the type of material and the level it is designed for. Thus when students come into a SAC they should find it easy to know where listening material is kept, what kind of listening material there is, and what levels are available. Such classification information should be visually prominent, using colour coding and/or clear labelling. Students should also be able to consult a card index or database. Guidance will also be needed for students who wish to access the Internet so that they do not waste their time on fruitless searches and inappropriate web sites (see Chapter 10F).

- **Pathways:** once students have completed an exercise, they can be given suggestions about where to go next. The material they have been using can list other items on the same topic or comment that, for example, *Now you have done this scanning exercise, you might want to try R/6/2 which asks you to skim a text – another important reading skill.* The activity thus becomes the jumping-off point for students to follow pathways suggested by SAC designers (and written into the material itself).

SAC assistants and teachers have a major role to play in helping students to use the centres successfully and follow appropriate pathways. Students can be shown where things are, be helped with hardware and software problems, and directed down new pathways. In order to help students in this way teachers need to be fully aware of a centre's contents and benefits, and trained – through induction materials, specially designed SAC lessons, and staff seminars – to help students appropriately (O'Dell 1992).

Although the materials and/or the teacher may suggest pathways for users to follow, our eventual aim is that students should be able to design their own routes for maximum personal benefit.

- **Training students:** most students, left to their own devices in a self-access centre, will not know how to use the facility to its best advantage, however good the classification system is. A self-access centre is likely to look either boring or intimidating. To prevent this situation students need to be trained to use centres appropriately.

  Some teachers provide training in class, giving students clear tasks and then taking them directly to the SAC to have them complete these tasks. This can happen on a regular basis over a period of weeks, at the end of which time the students are thoroughly familiar with what is in the centre and how best to use it. Many teachers design quizzes to get students hunting around the centre, in the process finding out what it has to offer. Guy Aston took a slightly different approach; he told his students to explore the centre, trying out the machines and rummaging through the shelves, with a view to producing leaflets and notices to show other students how to use them. Thus one group wrote about a concordancing package and other computer-based programmes with advice on which items were the best; another group gave advice on the video material (Aston 1993). The need to make things clear for their colleagues meant that students spent more time than they might otherwise have done investigating the contents of the centre.

  Even though students have been trained to use a self-access centre, they will still benefit from the help that assistants and teachers can give them in the centre itself.

- **Making self-access centres appropriate for students:** one view of a SAC has a group of individual students sitting apart from each other in silence, working profitably and autonomously. Yet as Jeremy Jones points out: 'To make autonomy an undiluted educational objective in a culture where it has no traditional place is to be guilty at least of cultural insensitivity' (Jones 1995: 229). Working at Phnom Penh University in Cambodia, he was concerned to make SAC use appropriate to the styles of learning which his students found most comfortable. Clear evidence suggested that students enjoyed working collaboratively and so, instead of the usual individual seating spaces in many SACs, students could choose more 'coffee-table' places, designed specifically to have groups working together. There was a higher tolerance of noise than might be expected in some other places, and tasks were designed which specifically encouraged pair and group interaction.

Anyone setting up a SAC or designing material and tasks for use in it should think carefully about who is likely to use it and what patterns of use will be most culturally appropriate. One way of doing this is to set up a student advisory panel who take part in planning and evaluating the centre. Apart from guaranteeing the involvement of those particular students, this has the potential for a SAC design which really meets the needs of its users.

- **Keeping interest going:** SACs really come into their own when students take the decision to go and study there by themselves – and continue to do so over a period of time. For this reason, administrators and teachers have to devise methods to keep users involved and interested.

  One way of doing this is to give students a feedback sheet to fill in after every activity. Though such forms are ostensibly for the centre's use the process of reflecting on an activity helps to maintain the user's engagement and prepares them for the next task.

  Another means of maintaining student involvement is through a SAC-users' committee which students can apply to become members of. With monthly meetings which bring about change and improvement, they have a genuine part to play in directing the centre's present and future course.

  An ideal way of keeping users 'on board' is for the centre to provide a monthly or quarterly newsletter and/or web site in which students and centre administrators list new material, and new ways of using things. Different pathways can be explored, and different users can be profiled. The newsletter/web site can run competitions and include the kind of news and gossip that newsletters in other fields use to keep their members involved.

A3 After the course

At some stage in any student's learning life, they will find themselves studying on their own, either out of choice or because they cannot attend lessons or use a self-access centre. We need, therefore, to give them help and advice about how to continue with their learning when they have stopped attending our lessons.

- **Staying in touch with the language:** for those students who wish to continue learning the most important thing we can tell them is that they should stay in contact with English. They can do this by finding an English language TV or radio channel, by watching English language films, especially those with subtitles (see Chapter 20, c2), by listening to pop songs (especially if they can get hold of the lyrics), or by reading English language newspapers, magazines, and novels. Students should also use the various sources of learner literature (see Chapter 15, A1), reading and rereading as many books at their level of proficiency as possible. Students can also be encouraged to use the Internet for learner sites (see Chapter 10F) or as a varied general English language resource. They can also sign up for Internet-based courses (see, for example, the sites listed at the end of Chapter 21).

- **Training students to continue learning:** much of the advice that students are given about continued learning is not taken up (Braymen 1995). It is too general and though students know it is all sound counsel, they cannot follow the advice because the whole idea is too 'big', too amorphous. We need, therefore, to offer specific guidance which will allow them to focus on exactly what suits them best.

  The first thing we need to do is to include 'continuing learning' as a topic in the syllabus. We can involve students in awareness-raising activities; together we can list all available sources of English before discussing which are most appropriate for their individual needs and how and where to get hold of them. We can consider the various skills that the students might want to work on (see Chapters 14–19), and revisit various styles of language study (Chapter 11) and language research (Chapter 12) which they can usefully carry out on their own.

  To train students in ways of using resources at their disposal, we can organise 'self-study' projects. We might direct them to watch an English language news channel (or video) and note down the main story headlines before following up those stories in newspapers or on the Internet under our guidance. At the beginning we can provide the material on tape, but later students can start accessing news material on their own, using the techniques we have practised earlier.

  We can get students to use classroom techniques on their own, encouraging them to predict the content of texts before they read in detail, and then decide on a maximum of ten unknown words to look up in their dictionaries after they have read (see Chapter 15, A3). We can train them to be their own language researchers by looking for new words and patterns that they have come across in subsequent texts.

- **Personal plans:** we can negotiate personal study plans for future use based on our students' individual needs. Thus we might have them complete 'work cards'. The following example is for a learner at intermediate level who works in an office where the British magazine *The Economist* is available, who has their own learner dictionary (see Chapter 12A), and who has a copy of the vocabulary book *English Vocabulary in Use* (McCarthy and O'Dell 1994):

> Aim: to improve my vocabulary
>
> Tasks:
>
> 1. Read at least three magazine articles from 'The Economist' every week. For each article note down three words I want to know the meaning of. Look the word up in my dictionary. Find the words again in next week's articles and check (with the dictionary) that they mean the same in the new articles.
> 2. Do one unit from 'English Vocabulary in Use' every week and check with the answer key and my dictionary.

If we do not have time for this, we can offer general work plans for anybody and everybody in which we list, for example, three good techniques for maintaining listening ability (and where to find listening material), or give details of Internet sites for language learners.

- **Staying in touch:** we can encourage students to stay in touch with each other after the course either by letter, e-mail, or through meeting up with each other from time to time. That way they can consult each other about problems, talk about the best magazines or books to read, share the most enjoyable web sites, or tell each other the best places to find English speakers to talk to.

B The developing teacher

A potential danger for many teachers is that though each year or term brings us new groups of students with challenging individual personalities and distinct group dynamics, it is sometimes difficult to maintain a sense of excitement and engagement with the business of teaching. The constant repetition of lesson routines, the revisiting of texts and activities with student reactions that become increasingly predictable, can – if we do not take steps to prevent it – dent even the most ardent initial enthusiasm.

Perhaps what we are talking about is the difference between teachers 'with twenty years' experience and those with one year's experience repeated twenty times' (Ur 1996: 317). Teachers who seek to develop themselves and their practice – despite, or because of, their 'twenty years' experience' – will benefit both their students and themselves far more than those who, by constant and unthinking repetition, gradually become less and less engaged with the task of language teaching. Development may be a move from 'unconscious incompetence' (where we are unaware that we are doing something badly) to 'unconscious competence' (where we do something well without having to think about it). In order for this to happen we have to become aware of our incompetence (conscious incompetence) and know that we have made it better (conscious competence) (Underhill 1992: 76).

Development may be brought about by breaking our own teaching rules or norms as a way of challenging what we have taken for granted (Fanselow 1987). It may involve trying out new ideas or changing the ways we use old ones. It may involve investigating something that puzzles us or that we do not know about. But in all these cases our intention is not only to improve our own performance, but also to learn more about teaching and about ourselves.

Many teachers transform their professional lives by entering in-service training programmes, by studying for higher teaching qualifications, or by getting a place on a postgraduate course such as an MA in Applied Linguistics or TESOL. Such training not only offers chances for promotion, but also adds to our knowledge of issues which a heavy teaching timetable often makes it difficult to consider. Apart from such formal training, however, there is a great deal we can do to ensure that we continue to develop and grow.

B1 Action research

Action research is the name given to a series of procedures teachers can engage in, either because they wish to improve aspects of their teaching, or because they wish to evaluate the success and/or appropriacy of certain activities and procedures. Julian Edge describes a process where a teacher, feeling unhappy about what she is doing, sets out on her own course of action to see how she might change things for the better (Edge 1999). The teacher is worried about the kind of feedback she gives in distance-learning courses. She feels her criticisms often seem very negative. She does some reading on the subject of feedback and then sends out her conclusions to students and colleagues for their opinions on her conclusions. Once she has synthesised all these opinions she issues her criteria for giving feedback. Her students are then asked to grade her feedback according to these criteria. She tries giving spoken feedback on cassette and finds that student response is very favourable. However, one student points out that written notes were much easier to refer back to later. The teacher then talks to her colleagues about what has happened so far. Some of them decide to try taped oral feedback; some decide to remain with written feedback. The teacher then writes up the whole process as an article for a teachers' magazine. The point of this description is that, like much action research, theory comes out of experience rather than experience being dependent upon theory.

The teacher described by Julian Edge is following a version of the classic action research sequence in which teachers first consider problems or issues in their teaching which lead them to design questions (or use other methods) in order to collect data. Having collected the data they analyse the results, and it is on the basis of these results that they decide what to do next. They may then subject this new decision to the same examination that the original issue generated (this possibility is reflected by the broken line in Figure 27). Alternatively, having resolved one issue they may focus on a different problem and start the process afresh for that issue.

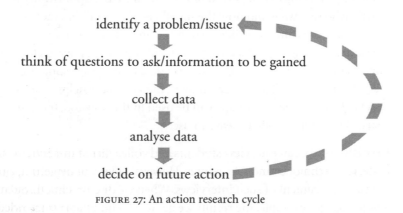

identify a problem/issue

think of questions to ask/information to be gained

collect data

analyse data

decide on future action

FIGURE 27: An action research cycle

- **Aims:** there are many possible reasons for conducting our own action research. We may want to know more about our learners and what they find motivating and challenging. We might want to learn more about ourselves as teachers – how effective we are, how we look to our students, how we would look to ourselves if we were observing our own teaching. We might want to gauge the interest generated by certain topics, or judge the effectiveness of certain activity types. We might want to see if an activity would work better done in groups rather than pairs, or investigate whether reading is more effective with or without pre-teaching vocabulary.

It is a good idea to think carefully about what our aim is before we embark upon research. Although general observation on its own often yields results, identifying a specific aim is far more effective in terms of deciding how to collect the data we need.

- **Methods:** there are a number of different methods for collecting the data we need:

KEEPING A JOURNAL: many teachers keep a record of what they and their students do in the form of a journal or diary. This encourages them to reflect upon their practice, and allows them to compare different reactions and re-evaluate the predictions that were made based on what actually happened.

OBSERVATION TASKS: we can record who speaks when in class, how many times each individual student asks for the teacher's help over a week's study, who chooses to sit with whom in freely-chosen pairs, or count how many times certain specific items of language are used. We can watch and make written records of student language production in general.

If we set ourselves tasks such as these, the data we collect will often be more reliable than more general reflection such as journal keeping. Everything will depend on identifying our aims and choosing the most appropriate methods for the data we think we need.

Videotape and audiotape are especially useful for precise observation tasks since they allow us to watch and/or listen to events repeatedly. If we have taped one group working over a period of time, we have the opportunity to identify exactly who says what and how the members of a group interact with each other. If a class is filmed as they respond to an activity we have a chance to measure their reactions objectively. Video filming also allows us to watch ourselves (see Chapter 20, D6); where we decide to change something for the sake of variety (see Chapter 22A and B4), the videotape helps us to gauge the effects of the change. Audiotape can be used in this way too, though without the visual element it is often less easy to use.

INTERVIEWS: we can interview students and colleagues about activities, materials, techniques and procedures. However, a lot will depend upon the manner and content of such interviews. When we discuss something with the whole class, for example, the results we get will be unreliable since not all students are prepared to offer an opinion, especially if it runs counter to a perceived majority opinion. Even with one-to-one interviews (if there is enough time for this), a lot will depend upon the questions we ask and how well we listen to the answers we are given.

An alternative to whole-class interviews is for teachers to ask students to discuss certain issues in small groups and then have group reporters give their conclusions back to the whole class.

WRITTEN QUESTIONNAIRES: these are often more effective than interviews, especially when administered to individual students. Questionnaires can get respondents to answer **open questions** such as *How did you feel about activity X?*, 'yes/no' questions such as *Did you find activity X easy?*, or questions which ask for some kind of rating response, for example:

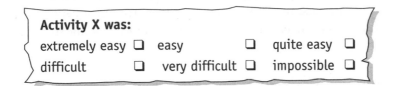

Activity X was:

extremely easy ❑   easy   ❑   quite easy ❑

difficult   ❑   very difficult ❑   impossible ❑

We can also ask students to rate the qualities of an activity in order of importance or write a short paragraph about an activity, some material, or a unit.

LANGUAGE PROGRESS: we can measure the students' language progress as a result of our new and different activities through homework assignments and test results.

Data collection frequently involves more than one method. Indeed the more methods we use, the more reliable our analysis is likely to be. By weighing up our journal entries, our observations, and our students' written responses, we will be in a good position to decide on future action.

B2 Professional literature

There is much to be learnt from the various methodology books, journals, and magazines produced for teachers of English. Books and articles written by teachers and theorists will often open our eyes to new possibilities. They may also form part of the action research or 'search' and 'research' cycles discussed above, either by raising an issue which we want to focus on, or by helping us to formulate the kinds of questions we wish to ask.

There are a number of different journals which cater for different tastes (see the list at the end of this chapter); whereas some report on academic research, others prefer to describe classroom activities in detail, often with personal comment from the writer. Some journals impose a formal style on their contributors, whereas others allow for a variety of approaches, including letters and short reports. Some journals are now published exclusively on the Internet, while others have Internet archives of past articles.

B3 Developing with colleagues

Not all reflection, action research, or reading needs to be done by teachers working alone. There are many ways teachers can confer with each other.

- **Cooperative/collaborative development:** teachers need chances to discuss what they are doing and what happens to them in class, so that they can examine their beliefs and feelings. However much we have reflected on our own experiences and practice, most of us find discussing our situation with others helps us to sort things out in our own mind. This has given rise to the concept of **cooperative development** (Edge 1992a, 1992b), where the role of the listener is crucial since 'the queen of facilitative skills is listening in a non-judgemental, respectful and empathetic way' (Underhill 1992: 79).

In cooperative development, **speakers** interact with **understanders**; a teacher, in this case, talks to an empathetic colleague. The empathetic colleague (the understander) makes every effort to understand the speaker but crucially, in Edge's realisation, does not interpret, explain, or judge what he or she is hearing. All that is necessary is for the understander to say 'this is what I'm hearing. This is what I've understood. Have I got it right?' (Edge 1992a: 65).

This style of empathising is similar to 'co-counselling', where two people agree to meet, and divide the allotted time in half so that each is a speaker and listener for an equal time period (Head and Taylor 1996: 143–144).

Charles Lansley, while sympathetic to the idea of empathetic colleagues, suggests that just listening does not change anything (Lansley 1994) and that 'phatic communion' may even reinforce the opinions that the speaker started with. People do not progress, he suggests, just by having good listeners agree with them all the time. What is needed is collaborative development, a sympathetic but critical discourse where colleagues challenge what each other says, tease out exactly what they mean, and subject their beliefs to careful scrutiny.

- **Peer teaching, peer observation:** in our teaching lives we are frequently observed by others. It starts on teacher training courses and goes on when academic coordinators, directors of study, or inspectors come into our class as part of some quality control exercise. In all these situations the observed teacher is at a disadvantage since the observers – however sympathetically they carry out their function – have power over the teacher's future career.

  Peer observation and peer teaching, on the other hand, involve colleagues – who are equal – watching and teaching together so that both may be helped in their understanding and practice.

  There are various forms of peer teaching. In the first, two teachers hold a dialogue in front of the class about a language point, a text, or an aspect of culture. Students gain from hearing different views on the same topic, and the participating teachers learn through their public interaction with each other. Sometimes two teachers can take different parts of the same lesson so that at one stage one might be acting as organiser and then observer, while the other plays the roles of prompter, and resource (see Chapter 4B). At other points in the lesson one teacher could explain a grammar point before the other takes over to run a short controlled practice session.

  A more formal way of organising peer teaching and observation is for two teachers to plan a lesson which one of them then teaches. After the lesson they both describe what happened to their joint plan and detail their experiences of the lesson. They can then discuss how it could be improved. For the next class the position is reversed.

As teachers most of us are understandably nervous about having other people observing our lessons. However, when we work with peers this nervousness is dissipated, and the result of our collaboration helps each participant to develop as teachers and as people.

- **The teachers' group:** one of the most supportive environments for teachers, where real teacher development can take place, is the small teachers' group. In this situation colleagues, usually working in the same school, meet together to discuss any issues and problems which may arise in the course of their teaching.

  Some teacher development meetings of this kind are organised by principals and directors of study. Outside speakers and animators are occasionally brought in to facilitate discussions. The director of studies may select a topic – in conjunction with the teachers – and then ask a member of staff to lead a session. What emerges is something halfway between bottom–up teacher development and top–down in-service teacher training (INSETT). At their best, such regular meetings are extremely stimulating and insightful. In many schools an INSETT coordinator is appointed to arrange a teacher development programme. Where this is done effectively, he or she will consult widely with colleagues to see what they would most like to work on and with.

  A popular alternative is where a group of teachers takes the decision to meet once a week and runs what is, in effect, its own support group (Plumb 1994). Any member of the group can suggest topics for future meetings; topics can range far and wide, from new ideas for pronunciation teaching to how to react when students make complaints, from the most appropriate kind of clothes to wear for teaching to five new uses for the video camera. The point of this kind of peer development is that teachers themselves are in charge of it, and as such are best placed to identify areas for development which are most relevant to them.

- **Teachers' associations:** there are many teachers' associations around the world. Some of them are international such as IATEFL based in Britain and TESOL, based in the USA; some are country-based such as JALT (in Japan), FAAPI (in Argentina), ELICOS (in Australia) or ATECR (in the Czech Republic); still others are smaller and regional such as APIGA (in Galicia, Spain), or BELTA (in Bournemouth, England).

  Teachers' associations provide two possible development opportunities:

  CONFERENCES: attending conferences, meetings, and workshops allows us to hear about the latest developments in the field, take part in investigative workshops, and enter into debates about current issues in theory and practice. We can 'network' with other members of the TEFL community, and best of all we learn that other people from different places, different countries and systems even, share similar problems and are themselves searching for solutions.

PRESENTING: submitting a paper or a workshop for a teachers' association meeting, whether regional, national, or international, is one of the most powerful catalysts for reflecting upon our practice. When we try and work out exactly what we want to say and the best way of doing it we are forcing ourselves to assess what we do. The challenge of a future audience sharpens our perceptions.

Some teachers get very nervous about presenting, yet audiences of their peers are on the whole overwhelmingly supportive and friendly. Teachers who present to them, work with them, or lead discussions usually find their self-esteem enhanced, their beliefs challenged and expanded, and their possibilities for the future expanded.

- **The virtual community:** there are now a large number of channels on the Internet by which teachers can 'talk' to each other, exchanging ideas and opinions, and asking for help. Some of these, like TESL-L are extremely large, with daily postings of anywhere between fifteen and thirty submissions. Some of them, on various more or less formal sites, are smaller. Many language departments, institutes, and schools operate their own teacher-talk sites for people to visit and exchange information.

Teachers who work on their own or feel isolated can enter into interesting discussions on these sites. In particular, they can post questions (asking for information about books, places, techniques, etc.) which someone will probably be able to answer.

Communication via the Internet will, hopefully, never replace face-to-face encounters; it cannot really emulate cooperative and/or collaborative development or peer teaching, for example. But in subscribing to some teachers' mailing lists, we can keep ourselves in touch with a larger teacher community, so that the information we find there, and the 'discussions' we enter into, can all feed into our continuing development.

B4 A broader view of development

In order to enhance professional and personal growth, teachers sometimes need to step outside the world of the classroom where the concentration, all too frequently, is on knowledge and skill alone. There are other issues and practices which can be of immense help in making their professional understanding more profound and their working reality more rewarding, such as:

- **Learning by learning:** one of the best ways of reflecting upon our teaching practice is to become learners ourselves so that our view of the learning–teaching process is not always influenced from one side of that relationship. By voluntarily submitting ourselves to a new learning experience especially (but not only) if this involves us in learning a new language, our view of our students' experience can be changed. We might suddenly find out how frightening it is to speak in class (Lowe 1987); perhaps we will realise that many 'communicative' activities are mundane, or realise how difficult it is to speak when we have nothing much to say (Ahrens 1993a); we might be surprised by how much we want to go through texts word for word (Gower 1999). It can be eye-opening to find out how important our teacher's approval is for us, how susceptible we are to teacher criticism, or to realise how important it is for the teacher to set us clear goals and guide us in other ways.

Those who teach a language which they themselves learnt as a foreign or second language will, of course, have highly relevant memories of the experience. Teachers who teach their first language will not have the same history. However, in both cases, continuing (or restarting) as a learner will offer significant insights into the whole business in which we are engaged as professionals.

- **Mind and body:** in his article 'Finding the centre' Alan Maley suggested that because teachers have stressful jobs, they need to pay attention to their physical well-being, not only so that they can teach better but also so that they can survive, learn, and grow as people (1993: 14).

  Teachers need to care for their bodies to counteract stress and fatigue. Katie Head and Pauline Taylor (1996: Chapter 6) suggest techniques for breathing and progressive relaxation. They advocate the use of disciplines such as Tai Chi, yoga, and the Alexander technique to achieve greater physical ease and counteract possible burnout.

  One of a teacher's chief physical attributes is the voice. Roz Comins observes that at least one in ten long-serving teachers need clinical help at some time in their career (1999: 8) to counteract vocal damage. Yet voice is part of the whole person, both physically and emotionally. When we misuse it, it will let us down. But when we care for it, it will help to keep us healthy and build our confidence. We can do this by breathing correctly, and resting our voice and ourselves when necessary. We can drink water or herbal tea rather than ordinary tea, coffee or cola if and when we suffer from laryngitis; we can adjust our pitch and volume, and avoid shouting and whispering.

- **Supplementing teaching:** one way of countering the potential sameness of a teacher's life is to increase our range of occupations and interests, so that teaching becomes the fixed centre in a more varied and interesting professional life.

  There are many tasks that make a valuable contribution to the teaching and learning of English. First among these is writing materials – whether these are one-off activities, longer units, or whole books. Materials writing can be challenging and stimulating, and when done in tandem with teaching can provide us with powerful insights, so that both the writing and the teaching become significantly more involving and enjoyable.

  It is not just materials writing that matters here, however. There are other things of equal potential interest. Some people write items for public exams. Some make tapes or set up web sites. Some help to organise entertainments for their students or run drama groups, sports teams, or conversation get-togethers. But whatever the tasks are, the positive effects of them can be felt in all aspects of our professional lives.

Chapter notes and further reading

- **Learner training and learner autonomy**

  See A Scharle and A Szabo (2000). The most often cited work in this area – and still one of the best – is G Ellis and B Sinclair (1989) which expounds a theory of learner training and then provides a range of activities for preparation and skills training. See also K Bertoldi et al. (1988) which describes a three-stage process from awareness to action, and L Dickinson (1987). M Geldicke (2000) describes how she gives learners 'action plans' to guide their learning and S Cotterall (1995) discusses course design principles for promoting learner autonomy.

- **Student journal writing**

  See L Lonon Blanton (1987) and K Richards (1992).

- **Classification systems in self-access centres**

  See L Barnett and G Jordan (1991) for a description an early database.

- **Pathways in self-access centres**

  See C Gierse (1993) and L Barnett and G Jordan (1991).

- **Learning outside the classroom**

  Two articles which are well worth reading are N Braymen (1995) and N Pickard (1996).

- **The developing teacher**

  On teacher development see especially the excellent K Head and P Taylor (1996), S Bax (1995), J Edge and K Richards (1993), D Nunan (1989b) and A Underhill (1991). IATEFL (see below) has a special interest group (SIG) devoted to teacher development which publishes its own newsletter.

- **Reflective teaching**

  The best all-round book on the subject that I know is M Wallace (1998).

- **Keeping journals**

  The most impressive published teacher journal is J Appel (1995) – a whole book of reflections on his teaching experiences.

  On journals as training tools, see J McDonough (1994). S Hundelby and S Breet (1988) used journals as a kind of self-generated methodology book when giving Chinese teachers language improvement courses. See also J Jarvis (1992), S Thornbury (1991b), H Woodfield and E Lazarus (1998).

- **Observation tasks**

  D Kurtoglu Eken (1999) suggests having students themselves perform observation tasks as a way of collecting lesson data.

- **Peer teaching**

  See W Assinder (1991) and D Britten (1991).

- **Teacher development groups**

  K Head and P Taylor (1996: Chapter 5) describe different kinds of/experiences with teacher development groups.

- **Voice**

  See A Maley (2000), R Comins (1999), and R Whitehead in K Head and P Taylor (1996: 137–139).

- **Teachers' associations**

  Two of the major international teachers' associations (whose web sites have links to other associations) are:

  – (IATEFL) The International Association of Teachers of English as a foreign language, 3 Kingsdown Chambers, Kingsdown Park, Tankerton, Whitstable, Kent CT5 2DJ, UK (http://www.iatefl.org/)

  – (TESOL) Teachers of English to Speakers of Other Languages, 1600 Cameron Street, Suite 300, Alexandria, Virginia 22314, USA (http://www.tesol.edu/)

- **Journals for teachers** Some of the more useful journals for teachers are:

  – *English Language Teaching Journal (ELTJ)*, published jointly by the British Council and Oxford University Press. (http://www.eltj.oupjournals.org/) – articles are both practical and research-based and cover the full range of topics to do with language, methodology, class management, and theory. Niche Publications (http://www.niche-publications.co.uk/) supply a CD-ROM with all the articles from 1981–1998.

  – *Modern English Teacher (MET)* published by Pearson Education Ltd – a variety of articles with classroom ideas, current issues, 'about language', tips and hints for individual activities, and book reviews (http://www.onlineMET.com/).

  – *English Teaching Professional (ETP)* published by First Person Publishing – a practical magazine with articles on background theory, classroom activities, teacher development, etc. (http://www.etprofessional.com/)

- **Online journals, newsletters, ELT mailing lists and other teacher sites**

  There are too many teacher sites on the Internet to list here. Instead, teachers may want to go to some of the 'gateway' sites which offer links of all sorts for teachers. At the time of writing two of the best links sites are:

  – David Eastment's links page at http://www.eastment.com/links.html/

  – The Internet TESL Journal's links page – one of the biggest around – at http://www.aitech.ac.jp/%7Eiteslj/links/

Follow-up tasks

Chapter 1

1 Pick a common language function, such as inviting someone, thanking them, or acknowledging thanks. How many different variations can you think of for this function in the English used in different countries or different language communities within a country?
2 What effects has the introduction or learning of English had upon other languages (or a particular language you know about) which it has come into contact with?
3 Profile a student (or group of students) of English as a foreign or second language. What variety or varieties of English should that student or group be exposed to and why?

Chapter 2

1 Is the following piece of language an example of speech or writing? How would it look different if it was the other variety?

    A: Cold?
    B: Yes. I'm freezing.
    A: Coffee?
    B: Sure. Two sugars.

2 Animal species, noises, and movement are often used for metaphorical purposes. What examples of animal words that operate in this way can you think of?
Take any of the examples you have come up with.

  a How many different meanings does the word have?
  b What part of speech (word class) is it?
  c Can you change it into another part of speech?
  d What words can your word combine with?
  e Does it commonly occur in lexical phrases?

3 Record some conversation either of an informal nature and/or from the radio/television. Take no more than two minutes of the conversation, transcribe it, and say as much as you can about exactly how it takes place and how it is structured. What situational factors affect the use of language?
4 Look at the following sentence and answer the questions about it.

    She talked to Peter at the club.

  a What would be the difference between starting the sentence at a low or a high pitch?
  b How many phonemes are there in *Peter*, *club*, and *talked to*?
  c How can you make the sentence sound like a question?
  d How many different meanings can you give the sentence by varying the main stress?

Chapter 3

1 Choose a classroom activity for a particular age group that you are familiar with. What changes would you make to it for use with other age groups?
2 Take any three classroom activities that you are familiar with – or that you have been told about. In each case, describe the kind of students who would benefit most from the activity.

3 You are teaching a group of young adults on a Friday evening. Their motivation is not strong, and after a long week of studying and/or work they are a bit tired. What kind of topic/activity/material can you think of which would make the class 'interesting' enough to keep them engaged?

Chapter 4

1 Choose a classroom activity and then say how you would organise it, including the lead-in and instructions. How would you finish it?
2 How would you answer students if they asked (a) *What's the difference between 'ironic' and 'sarcastic'?* or (b) *When can we use the phrase 'You must be joking!'?*
3 What performance adverbs would you use for appropriate teaching behaviour when (a) giving a lecture, (b) observing students having a discussion, (c) offering help to a group of students working at a computer screen, or (d) getting students to sing a song?

Chapter 5

1 Design a language drill which follows a basic Stimulus–Response–Reinforcement model.
2 Think of opportunities which your students might have for receiving comprehensible input. How can you be sure that it is not incomprehensible input?
3 Take any newspaper article and say what language you would ask students to notice in it.

Chapter 6

1 What invented situation can you think of with which to use the PPP procedure to teach *can* and *can't* to express ability? What six sentences (three affirmative, three negative) can you get out of your situation?
2 Which of the following tasks would be appropriate for elementary students? How would you use Willis' task cycle with them?
   – a radio commercial
   – inviting friends for dinner
   – buying a railway ticket at the station
   – writing a play
3 Which of the following topics would you be happy to ask students to talk about and why?
   – films they have enjoyed
   – girlfriends and boyfriends they have had
   – the death of a close relative
   – holidays they have enjoyed
   – how they feel about their own appearance
   – hopes and ambitions for the future
4 List five lexical phrases in English (see Chapter 2, B4). How might you teach them to students?

Chapter 7

1 Transcribe a minute's worth of student speech. How many mistakes can you hear? What kind of mistakes are they, do you think?
2 Would you correct in the following two situations and if so, how would you do it?

   a Discussion
   > *Student 1:*   Look, I don't think that people should be let smoking in public places.
   > *Student 2:*   But that's not fair. Some people like to smoking.
   > *Student 1:*   Perhaps they do, but ...

   b Accuracy work
   > *Teacher:*   Give me a sentence with 'like', Sergio.
   > *Student:*   Okay. He like watching television.

3 You are going to observe your students in a formal debate, where opposing points of view are discussed. Design a form which you could use to record more and less successful language use.

Chapter 8

1 Think of two activities which would be appropriate for whole-class teaching, and which would be difficult to do with any other grouping.
2 Choose three different activities and say whether individual study, pairwork, or groupwork would be the best grouping to use with them.
3 Choose an activity (or activities) where you would definitely want to group students according to ability (streaming).

Chapter 9

1 List ten examples of problem behaviour and put them in order of seriousness.
2 What solutions would you employ for these situations: (a) two students are always chattering and giggling together, (b) a student never does any homework, (c) a student always shouts out answers before anyone else has a chance?
3 Think of two activities where it would be inappropriate for students to use their mother tongue and two where you would not be too concerned.

Chapter 10

1 Design or find a selection of pictures that you could use to present the vocabulary of jobs and occupations to a beginners' class.
2 Design a gapped text activity for use with an overhead projector. Outline the procedure you would use with it in a lesson.
3 Think of a topic which your students would find interesting. See what you can find out about it on the Internet. On the basis of what you find, plan an Internet-based lesson.

Chapter 11

1 List at least three language points that it might be appropriate to 'introduce' to elementary language students.
2 What kind of discovery activity could you use to help students work out either (a) how adjectives become adverbs, or (b) how passive sentences work.
3 Think of an activity to help students 'remember' the contrasting uses of the past simple and the past continuous.

Chapter 12

1 Design three activities for intermediate students in which you introduce them to different aspects of dictionary use.
2 Consult more than three grammar books on the use of either reported speech or adverbs. Which grammar is most useful for you? Which would be most useful for your students?
3 Which is more common: the pattern *like to* + infinitive or *like* + verb *-ing*? Use a language corpus and concordancing software to find out.
4 If you found the following sentence in a student's homework, what 'research' suggestions would you write in the margin: *I am not interesting by that opinions of yours*?

Chapter 13

1 Design an activity to teach the difference between /æ/ (hat), /ɒ/ (hot), and /ʌ/ (hut).
2 Design an activity to show contrastive stress in a sentence or question.
3 How would you include intonation teaching in a lesson about ways of expressing agreement and disagreement? Give examples.
4 Design an exercise to make students aware of the different spellings of the sound /iː/.
5 Make a list of utterances you could use to help students improve their connected speech at a lower intermediate level.

Chapter 14

1 Find a text designed for competent language users. What schemata are necessary for readers to understand it without difficulty?
2 List examples of the kind of texts you might want to read or listen to for (a) gist, (b) specific information, and (c) detailed information.
3 Find a written or spoken text. What level can you use it with? Will you pre-teach any vocabulary? Could you rewrite it to make it more suitable for a lower level whilst at the same time maintaining its realism?
4 Find a written or spoken text for students at an intermediate level. What will you do to try and ensure their interest in it?
5 Take any article from a newspaper and/or record an extract from the radio. Write appropriate comprehension tasks for students at different levels.

Chapter 15

1 Take any of the reading texts from Section B1 of Chapter 15. Design completely different lesson sequences for them from the ones detailed there.
2 Choose a topic that might be of interest to a young intermediate learner. Find a text in that topic area and design a lesson sequence around it.
3 Write your own text for adult beginners and design questions and activities to go with it.

Chapter 16

1 Take a listening extract from Chapter 16 – or from a coursebook you know. What different ways can you think of for exploiting it?
2 Make your own taped extract for use in class. Say what level it is for and design the exploitation to go with it.
3 Find two contrasting pieces of music which you could use in class. What would you ask students to do while they listened to them?

Chapter 17

1 Take any transcript of speaking (or a written text) and analyse how the speaker or writer has organised their ideas, and the cohesive devices they have used.
2 Describe a group of students and then say what topics for production activities they might be interested in. How would you try and find out which those topics are?
3 Consider any spoken interaction type your are familiar with in your own working or social life. How culturally specific is the behaviour of the people involved in the interaction type? What would someone from another culture find difficult to understand in it?

Chapter 18

1 Write an unpunctuated text which would be appropriate for elementary students to practise their punctuation on.
2 Find a poem that would be suitable for a running dictation. What level could you use it with, and why?
3 Write the questions for a 'newspaper article analysing kit'.
4 Write a first sentence which you could use to start off a story circle.
5 Find a text or listening extract that will be useful for practising note-taking. Design the lesson sequence you would use with it.

Chapter 19

1 Design a situation with a number of alternatives which could be used for a consensus-reaching discussion (see Chapter 19, B3).
2 What games from the radio or any other source which you know could be adapted for use in language classes?

3 Find a dialogue from a coursebook or a play extract. Say what level you would use it for, and what suprasegmental elements you would concentrate on when coaching students to perform it.

4 What typical work situation could you use for a simulation? What functional or other language will it be helpful for your students to have at their command?

Chapter 20

1 Find a video sequence which could be used for prediction using typical video-watching techniques. What activities would follow a second and third viewing?

2 Video your favourite programme from the television. How much of it could you use for what level of student? How would you exploit it?

3 Choose a dialogue from a coursebook you know that would be appropriate for filming. How could you help students film it successfully?

Chapter 21

1 Find three coursebooks – if possible published at different times over the last thirty years – and say what kind of syllabus they are based on.

2 Select an area for coursebook assessment (apart from layout and design). Write down four 'belief statements' and use them to assess two or more coursebooks.

3 Design a questionnaire to find out if/how much a group of students have enjoyed using their coursebook.

4 Take a lesson from a coursebook. What different options are there for using or not using it? How might you add to it, rewrite it, replace parts of it, re-order it, or reduce it?

Chapter 22

1 Design a lesson for a group of students you know and/or can describe.

2 Find a group of learners and describe them as you might in a formal lesson plan.

3 With a particular group in mind, plan a sequence of four classes. What thematic and linguistic links will you build into the sequence? How can you ensure a suitable balance between variety and coherence?

Chapter 23

1 Choose a vocabulary or grammar area, and write indirect discrete-point items to test it.

2 Find a text for a particular test level and adapt it using a 'rational' or 'modified' cloze procedure.

3 Design a choice of writing topics which constitute a 'level playing field' for candidates at a specified level to choose from.

4 Find a reading or listening text and write questions designed to test students' comprehension of it.

5 Design a speaking task for the assessment of oral performance. Write global assessment scales and analytic profiles for scorers to use.

Chapter 24

1 Write 'learning hints' (see Chapter 24, A1) for intermediate students about either reading techniques or fluent speaking.

2 Design or find a reading activity and a grammar practice activity for use in a self-access centre. What instructions would you include? How (if at all) would you provide answers? What future pathway hints would you include? How would you label the activity?

3 Choose a specific class and write a general work plan to give to them at the end of the course.

4 Choose an area of doubt or interest in your teaching. How would you set about gathering data on the topic as part of an action research plan?

5 If you were part of an informal teachers' group, what three topics related to any aspect of teaching and learning would you most like to discuss?

6 If you had to present a paper or workshop at a teachers' conference what would your topic be, and how would you structure your presentation?

Bibliography

Acklam, R 1994 The role of the coursebook. *Practical English Teaching* 14/3.

Adrian-Vallance, D 1986 Oral practice activities. In *Meridian Teacher's Guide 2* Pearson Education Ltd.

Ahrens, P 1993a Diary of a language learner/teacher. *Modern English Teacher* 2/2.

Ahrens, P 1993b Displaying visuals. *Modern English Teacher* 2/4.

Aitchison, J 1994 *Words in The Mind* 2nd edn Blackwell.

Al-Arishi, A 1994 Role-play, real-play, and surreal play in the ESOL classroom. *ELT Journal* 48/4.

Alderson, J 1996 The testing of reading. In Nuttall, C.

Alderson, J, Clapham, C, and Wall, D 1995 *Language Test Construction and Evaluation* Cambridge University Press.

Alderson, J and Wall, D 1993 Does washback exist? *Applied Linguistics* 14/2.

Alexander, L 1988 The three best kept secrets about grammar. *Practical English Teaching* 9/2.

Allen, M 1986 *Teaching English with Video* Pearson Education Ltd.

Allwright, R 1977 Motivation – the teacher's responsibility? *ELT Journal* 31/4.

Allwright, R 1979 Language learning through communication practice. In Brumfit, C and Johnson, K (eds) *The Communicative Approach to Language Teaching* Oxford University Press.

Allwright, R 1981 What do we want teaching materials for? *ELT Journal* 36/1 and in Rossner and Bolitho (eds).

Alptekin, C 1993 Target-language culture in EFL materials. *ELT Journal* 47/2.

Amer, A 1997 The effect of the teacher's reading aloud on the reading comprehension of EFL students. *ELT Journal* 51/1.

Anderson, A and Lynch, T 1988 *Listening* Oxford University Press.

Appel, J 1995 *Diary of a Language Teacher* Macmillan Heinemann.

Arnold, J 1998 Point and counterpoint. Towards more humanistic English teaching. *ELT Journal* 52/3.

Arnold, J (ed) 1999 *Affect in Language Teaching* Cambridge University Press.

Asher, J 1977 *Learning Another Language Through Actions: The Complete Teacher's Guidebook* Sky Oaks Productions.

Assinder, W 1991 Peer teaching, peer learning: one model. *ELT Journal* 45/3.

Aston, G 1993 The learner's contribution to the self-access centre. *ELT Journal* 47/3

Atkinson, D 1987 The mother tongue in the classroom: a neglected resource? *ELT Journal* 41/4.

Atkinson, D 1989 'Humanistic' approaches in the language classroom: an affective reaction. *ELT Journal* 43/4.

Austin, J 1982 *How to do Things with Words* 2nd edn Clarendon Press.

Badger, R and White, G 2000 A process genre approach to teaching writing. *ELT Journal* 54/2.

Baigent, M 1999 Teaching in chunks: integrating a lexical approach. *Modern English Teacher* 8/2.

Bandler, R 1985 *Using your brains for a change* Real People Press.

Bandler, R and Grinder, J 1979 *Frogs into Princes* Real People Press.

Barnett, L and Jordan, G 1991 Self-access facilities: what are they for? *ELT Journal* 45/4.

Batstone, R 1994 *Grammar* Oxford University Press.

Bax, S 1995 Principles for evaluating teacher development activities. *ELT Journal* 49/3.

Bertoldi, E, Kollar, J, and Ricard, E 1988 Learning how to learn English: from awareness to action. *ELT Journal* 42/3.

Biber, D, Johansson, S, Leech, G, Conrad, S and Finegan, E 1999 *Longman Grammar of Spoken and Written English* Pearson Education Ltd.

Bisong, J 1995 Language choice and cultural imperialism: a Nigerian perspective. *ELT Journal* 49/2.

Block, D 1991 Some thoughts on DIY materials design. *ELT Journal* 45/3.

Bolitho, R, Granescu, and Adam, E 1994 Current issues: error correction. *Modern English Teacher* 3/4.

Bolitho, R and Tomlinson, B 1995 *Discover English: New Edition* Macmillan Heinemann.

Boughey, C 1997 Learning to write by writing to learn: a group-work approach. *ELT Journal* 51/2.

Bowler, B and Parminter, S 1997 Mixed-level teaching: tiered tasks and bias tasks. *English Teaching Professional* 5.

Bowler, B and Parminter, S 2000 Mixed-level tasks. *English Teaching Professional* 15.

Braymen, D 1995 Training students for continued learning. *Modern English Teacher* 4/2.

Brewster, G, Ellis, G and Girard, D 1993 *The Primary English Teacher's Guide* Penguin.

Britten, D 1991 Peer teaching – the Argentine method. *The Teacher Trainer* 5/2.

Brown, H D 2000 *Principles of Language Learning and Teaching* 4th edn Pearson Education Ltd.

Brown, S and McIntyre, D 1993 *Making Sense of Teaching* Open University Press.

Brumfit, C 1980 *Problems and Principles in Language Teaching* Pergamon Institute of English.

Brumfit, C and Johnson, K (eds) 1979 *The Communicative Approach to Language Teaching* Oxford University Press.

Bruton, A 1998 PPP, CLT, NA, TBI, ARC, ESA, CFPU: for what? *IATEFL Teacher Training* SIG 21.

Burbidge, N, Gray, P, Levy, S and Rinvolucri, M 1996 *Letters* Oxford University Press.

Bygate, M 1987 *Speaking* Oxford University Press.

Bygate M, Tonkyn, A, and Williams, E (eds) 1994 *Grammar and the Language Teacher* Prentice Hall.

Byrne, D 1986 *Teaching Oral English* Pearson Education Ltd.

Byrne D 1988 *Teaching Writing Skills* Pearson Education Ltd.

Caffyn, R 1984 Rewards and punishments in schools. A study of their effectiveness as perceived by secondary school pupils and their teacher. MEd dissertation (unpublished), University of Exeter.

Canagarajah, A 1999 On EFL teachers, awareness, and agency *ELT Journal* 53/3.

Candlin, C 1987 Towards task-based language learning. In Candlin, C and Murphy, D (eds) *Language Learning Tasks* Prentice Hall.

Capone, P and Hayward, K 1996 Democratic debates. *Modern English Teacher* 5/4.

Carroll, J and Sapon, S 1958 *Modern Language Aptitude Test* The Psychological Corporation.

Carter, R 1998a Orders of reality: CANCODE, communication, and culture. *ELT Journal* 52/1.

Carter, R 1998b. Reply to Guy Cook. *ELT Journal* 52/1.

Carter, R, Hughes, R, and McCarthy, M 1998 Telling tails: grammar, the spoken language and materials development. In Tomlinson, B (ed).

Carter, R and McCarthy, M (eds) 1988 *Vocabulary and Language Teaching* Pearson Education Ltd.

Carter, R and McCarthy, M 1995 Grammar and the spoken language. *Applied Linguistics* 16/2.

Carter, R and McCarthy, M 1997 E*xploring Spoken English* Cambridge University Press.

Celce-Murcia, M 1981 New methods in perspective. *Practical English Teaching* 2/1.

Chomsky, N 1959 Review of verbal behaviour. *Language* 35.

Christison, M 1996 Teaching and learning languages through multiple intelligences. *TESOL Journal* 6/1.

Coffrey, S 2000 'Turn, turn, turn'. Alternative ways of presenting songs. *Modern English Teacher* 9/1.

Comins, R 1999 Voice, the neglected imperative. *Modern English Teacher* 8/2.

Cook, G 1989 *Discourse* Oxford University Press.

Cook, G 1994 Repetition and learning by heart: an aspect of intimate discourse and its implications. *ELT Journal* 48/2.

Cook, G 1998 The uses of reality: a reply to Ronald Carter *ELT Journal* 52/1.

Cook, G 2000 Repetition and learning by heart: an aspect of intimate discourse, and its implications. *ELT Journal* 48/2.

Cooper, R 1993 Video, fear and loathing: self-viewing in teacher training. *The Teacher Trainer* 7/3.

Cooper, R, Lavery, M, and Rinvolucri, M 1991 *Video* Oxford University Press.

Cotterall, S 1995 Developing a course strategy for learner autonomy. *ELT Journal* 49/3 .

Coulthard, M 1985 *An Introduction to Discourse Analysis* Pearson Education Ltd.

Courtney, M 1996 Talking to learn: selecting and using peer group oral tasks. *ELT Journal* 50/4.

Cox, K and Eyre, J 1999 A question of correction. *English Teaching Professional* 12.

Cranmer, D 1996 *Motivating High-Level Learners* Pearson Education Ltd.

Cranmer, D and Laroy, C 1992 *Musical Openings* Pearson Education Ltd.

Crookes, G and Gass, S 1993a *Tasks in a Pedagogical Context* Multilingual Matters.

Crookes, G and Gass, S 1993b *Tasks and Language Learning* Multilingual Matters.

Crookes, G and Schmidt, R 1991 Motivation: reopening the research agenda. *Language Learning* 41.

Crouch, C 1989 Performance teaching in ELT. *ELT Journal* 43/2.

Crystal, D 1995 *The Cambridge Encyclopaedia of the English Language* Cambridge University Press.

Crystal, D 1997 *English as a Global Language* Cambridge University Press.

Crystal, D 2000a Emerging Englishes. *English Teaching Professional* 14.

Crystal, D 2000b On Trying to be Crystal-clear: a Response to Phillipson. *Applied Linguistics* 21/3.

Cundale, N 1999 Picture this! *Modern English Teacher* 8/2.

Cunningham, S and Moor, P 1998 *Cutting Edge Intermediate* Pearson Education Ltd.

Cunningsworth, A 1984 *Evaluating and Selecting EFL Materials* Heinemann Educational.

Cunningsworth, A 1995 *Choosing your Coursebook* Macmillan Heinemann.

Cureau, J 1982 Harnessing the power of suggestion. *Practical English Teaching* 2/3.

Curran, C 1976 Counselling-learning in *Second Language* Apple River Press.

Dalton, C and Seidlhofer, B 1995 *Pronunciation* Oxford University Press.

Davis, C 1995 Extensive reading: an expensive extravagance? *ELT Journal* 49/4.

Davis, P and Rinvolucri, M 1988 *Dictation* Cambridge University Press.

Day, R and Bamford, J 1998 *Extensive Reading in the Second Language Classroom* Cambridge University Press.

Dickinson, L 1987 *Self-instruction in Language Learning* Cambridge University Press.

Doff, A and Jones, C 1991 *Language in Use* Cambridge University Press.

Domoney, L and Harris, S 1993 Justified and ancient: pop music in EFL classrooms. *ELT Journal* 47/3.

Dörnyei, Z 1998 Motivation in second and foreign language learning. *Language Teaching* 31.

Dudeney, G 2000 *The Internet and the Language Classroom* Cambridge University Press.

Dudley-Evans, T and St John, M 1998 *Developments in English for Specific Purposes* Cambridge University Press.

Early, M 1991 Using wordless picture books to promote second language learning. *ELT Journal* 45/3.

Edge, J 1989 *Mistakes and Correction* Addison Wesley Longman.

Edge J 1992a Co-operative development. *ELT Journal* 46/1.

Edge, J 1992b *Co-operative Development: Professional Self-Development through Co-operation with Colleagues* Pearson Education Ltd.

Edge, J 1999 In place of strife: theorising our practice. Paper given at the International House Teacher Training Conference.

Edge, J and Richards, K (eds) 1993 *Teachers Develop Teachers Research* Whitstable: IATEL.

Eldridge, J 1996 Code-switching in a Turkish secondary school. *ELT Journal* 50/4.

Ellis, G 1996 How culturally appropriate is the communicative approach? *ELT Journal* 50/3.

Ellis, G and Sinclair, B 1989 *Learning to Learn English* Cambridge University Press.

Ellis, R 1982 Informal and formal approaches to communicative language teaching. *ELT Journal* 36/2.

Ellis, R 1983 Review of Krashen, S 'Principles and Practice in Second Language Acquisition'. *ELT Journal* 37/3.

Ellis, R 1988 The role of practice in language learning. *AILA Review* 5.

Ellis, R 1994 *The Study of Second Language Acquisition* Oxford University Press.

Ellis, R 1998 The evaluation of communicative tasks. In Tomlinson, B (ed).

Ely, P 1984 *Bringing the Lab Back to Life* Pergamon.

Erikson, E 1963 *Childhood and Society* Norton.

Fanselow, J 1987 *Breaking Rules. Generating and Explaining Alternatives in Language Teaching* Longman.

Farrell, T 1998 Using TV 'soaps' for listening comprehension. *Modern English Teacher* 7/2.

Field, J 1998a Skills and strategies: towards a new methodology for listening. *ELT Journal* 52/2.

Field, J 1998b The changing face of listening. *English Teaching Professional* 6.

Field, J 2000 Not waving but drowning: a reply to Tony Ridgway. *ELT Journal* 54/2.

Flowerdew, L 1998 A cultural perspective on groupwork. *ELT Journal* 52/4.

Foot, M 1999 Relaxing in pairs. *ELT Journal* 53/1.

Fortune, A 1992 Self-study grammar practice: learners' views and preferences. *ELT Journal* 46/2.

Fox, G 1998 *Using corpus data in the classroom* in Tomlinson, B (ed).

Francis, G and Sinclair, J 1994 'I bet he drinks Carling Black Label': a riposte to Owen on Corpus grammar. *Applied Linguistics* 15/2.

Freebairn, I 2000 The coursebook – future continuous or past? *English Teaching Professional* 15.

Gadd, N 1998 Point and counterpoint. Towards less humanistic English teaching. *ELT Journal* 52/3.

Gaffield-Vile, N 1998 Creative writing in the ELT classroom. *Modern English Teacher* 7/3.

Gairns, R and Redman, S (1986) *Working with Words* Cambridge University Press.

Gardner, H 1983 *Frames of Mind: The Theory of Multiple Intelligences* Basic Books.

Gardner, H 1993 *Multiple Intelligences: The Theory of Practice* Basic Books.

Gattegno, C 1976 *The Common Sense of Teaching Foreign Languages* Educational Solutions.

Geldicke, M 1997 Lectures in the classroom. *English Teaching Professional* 4.

Geldicke, M 2000 Action plans. *English Teaching Professional* 14.

Gibran, K 1991 *The Prophet* Pan Books.

Gierse, C 1993 Ideas on how to motivate learner independence. *Modern English Teacher* 2/4.

Goleman, D 1996 *Emotional Intelligence. Why Can it Matter More than IQ?* Bloomsbury.

Gower, R 1999 Doing as we would be done by. *Modern English Teacher* 8/4.

Gower, R, Phillips, D, and Walters, S 1995 *Teaching Practice Handbook* Macmillan Heinemann.

Graddol, D 1997 *The Future of English* The British Council.

Grant, N 1987 *Making the Most of your Textbook* Pearson Education Ltd.

Green, C, Christopher, E, and Lam, J 1997 Developing discussion skills in the ESL classroom. *ELT Journal* 51/2.

Gregg, K 1984 Krashen's monitor and Occam's razor. *Applied Linguistics* 5/2.

Grellet, F 1981 *Developing Reading Skills* Cambridge University Press.

Grice, H 1975 Logic and conversation. In Cole, P and Morgan, J (eds): *Syntax and Semantics*, vol. 3 speech acts: Academic Press.

Grundy, P 2000 *Doing Pragmatics* 2nd edn Edward Arnold.

Hadfield, J 1984 *Elementary Communication Games* Pearson Education Ltd.

Hadfield, J 1987 *Advanced Communication Games* Pearson Education Ltd.

Hadfield, J 1990 *Intermediate Communication Games* Pearson Education Ltd.

Hadfield, J 1992 *Classroom Dynamics* Oxford University Press.

Haines, S 1995 For and against: pairwork. *Modern English Teacher* 4/1.

Hall, N and Shepheard, J 1991 *The Anti-grammar Grammar Book* Pearson Education Ltd.

Halliwell, S 1992 *Teaching English in the Primary Classroom* Pearson Education Ltd.

Hancock, M 1995 *Pronunciation Games* Cambridge University Press.

Harbord, J 1992 The use of the mother tongue in the classroom. *ELT Journal* 46/4.

Harmer, J 1982 What is communicative? *ELT Journal* 36/3.

Harmer, J 1983 Krashen's input hypothesis and the teaching of EFL. *World Language English* 3/1.

Harmer, J 1995 Taming the big 'I': teacher performance and student satisfaction. *ELT Journal* 49/4.

Harmer, J 1996 Is PPP dead? *Modern English Teacher* 5/2.

Harmer, J 1998 *How to Teach English* Pearson Education Ltd.

Harris, M 1997 Self-assessment of language learning in formal settings. *ELT Journal* 51/1.

Head, K and Taylor, P 1996 *Readings in Teacher Development* Macmillan Heinemann.

Hennigan, H 1999 Penpals to keypals. *Modern English Teacher* 8/2.

Hoey, M 1983 *On the Surface of Discourse* George Allen and Unwin.

Hopkins, A 1995 Revolutions in ELT materials? *Modern English Teacher* 4/3.

Horner, D 1987 Rehabilitating the language laboratory. *Practical English Teaching* 7/4.

Hughes, A 1989 *Testing for Language Teachers* Cambridge University Press.

Hundleby, S and Breet, F 1988 Using methodology notebooks on in-service teacher-training courses. *ELT Journal* 42/1.

Hutchinson, T 1998 *Lifelines Intermediate* Oxford University Press.

Hutchinson, T and Torres, E 1994 The textbook as agent of change. *ELT Journal* 48/4.

Illich, I 1972 *De-schooling Society* Harrow Books.

Jacob, M and Strutt, P 1997 *English for International Tourism* Pearson Education Ltd.

Jarvis, H 2000 The changing role of computers in language teaching and the case for 'study skills'. *Modern English Teacher* 9/1.

Jarvis, J 1992 Using diaries for teacher reflection on in-service courses. *ELT Journal* 46/2

Jenkins, J 1998 Which pronunciation norms and models for English as an International Language? *ELT Journal* 52/2.

Johnson, K 1982 *Communicative Syllabus Design and Methodology* Pergamon Institute of English.

Johnson, K and Morrow, K 1978 *Functional materials and the classroom teacher* Centre for Applied Language Studies, University of Reading.

Jones, J 1995 Self-access and culture: retreating from autonomy. *ELT Journal* 49/3.

Jones, K 1982 *Simulation and Role-play* Cambridge University Press.

Kachru, B 1983 Introduction: the other side of English. In Kachru, B (ed) *The Other Tongue – English Across Cultures* Pergamon.

Kachru, B 1985 Standards, codification and sociolinguistic realism: the English language in the outer circle. In Quirk and Widdowson (eds).

Kelly, G 2000 *How to Teach Pronunciation* Pearson Education Ltd.

Kennedy, A 2000 'Did you like the text?' *Modern English Teacher* 9/1.

Kenworthy, J 1987 *Teaching English Pronunciation* Pearson Education Ltd.

Kerr, J 1988 Changing focus of resonance. Paper presented at the 11th ELICOS Conference, Melbourne, Australia.

Knight, B 1992 Assessing speaking skills: a workshop for teacher development. *ELT Journal* 46/3.

Kramsch, C and Sullivan, P 1996 Appropriate pedagogy. *ELT Journal* 50/3.

Krashen, S 1985 *The Input Hypothesis: Issues and Implications* Longman.

Krashen, S and Terrell, 1982 *The Natural Approach* Pearson Education Ltd.

Kuc, L 1999 Do you know what your students want, what they really really want? *Modern English Teacher* 8/2.

Kumaravadivelu, B 1991 Language-learning tasks: teacher intention and learner interpretation. *ELT Journal* 45/2.

Kurtoglu Eken, D 1999 Through the eyes of the learner: learner observations of teaching and learning. *ELT Journal* 53/4.

Kyriacou, C 1992 *Effective Teaching in Schools* Simon and Schuster Education.

La Forge, L 1983 *Counselling and Culture in Second Language Acquisition* Pergamon.

Lansley, C 1994 'Collaborative development': an alternative to phatic discourse and the art of co-operative development. *ELT Journal* 48/1.

Lavezzo, M and Dunford, H 1993 To correct or not to correct? *MET* 2/3.

Lawlor, M 1986 The inner track method as successful teaching. *Practical English Teaching* 6/3.

Laycock, J and Bunnag, P 1991 Developing teacher self-awareness: feedback and the use of video. *ELT Journal* 45/1.

Lazar, D 1994 *Seven Ways of Learning* Zephyr Press.

Lee, I 1998 Supporting greater autonomy in language learning. *ELT Journal* 52/4.

Lewis, M 1986 *The English Verb* Language Teaching Publications.

Lewis, M 1993 *The Lexical Approach* Language Teaching Publications.

Lewis, M 1996 Implications of a lexical view of language. In Willis D and Willis J (eds) *Challenge and Change in Language Teaching*.

Lewis, M 1997 *Implementing the Lexical Approach* Language Teaching Publications.

Littlejohn, A 1998 The analysis of language teaching materials: inside the Trojan horse. In Tomlinson, B (ed).

Littlewood, W 2000 Do Asian students really want to listen and obey? *ELT Journal* 54/1.

Long, M 1977 Groupwork in the teaching and learning of English as a foreign language – problems and potential. *ELT Journal* 31/4.

Lonon Blanton, L 1987 Reshaping ESL students' perceptions of writing. *ELT Journal* 41/2.

Lowe, T 1985 Making teacher-talking time worthwhile. *Modern English Teacher* old edition 12/1.

Lowe, T 1987 An experiment in role reversal: teachers as language learners. *ELT Journal* 41/2.

Lozanov, G 1978 *Suggestology and the Outlines of Suggestopody* Gordon and Breach.

Lynch, T 1997 Nudge, nudge: teacher interventions in task-based learner talk. *ELT Journal* 51/4.

Mace, S 1998 Designing world wide web tasks for interactive learning. *IATEFL Issues* 144.

Malamah-Thomas, A 1987 *Classroom Interaction* Oxford University Press.

Maley, A 1993 Finding the centre. *The Teacher Trainer* 7/3.

Maley, A 1998 Squaring the circle – reconciling materials as constraint with materials as empowerment. In Tomlinson, B (ed).

Maley, A 2000 *The Language Teacher's Voice* Macmillan Heinemann

Manheim, C 1994 'The boss was called Mr Power': learners' perspectives on sexism in EFL materials. In Sunderland, J (ed).

Maslow, A 1987 *Motivation and Personality* 3rd edn Harper and Row.

Maule, D 1988 'Sorry, but if he comes, I go' – teaching conditionals. *ELT Journal* 42/2.

McCarthy, M 1990 *Vocabulary* Oxford University Press.

McCarthy, M and Carter, R 1995 Spoken grammar: what is it and how can we teach it? *ELT Journal* 49/3.

McCarthy, M and Carter, R 1997 Octopus or hydra? *IATEFL Newsletter* 137.

McCarthy, M and O'Dell, F 1994 *English Vocabulary in Use* Cambridge University Press.

McDonough, J 1994 A teacher looks at teachers' diaries. *ELT Journal* 48/1.

McEnery, T and Wilson, A 1999 *Corpus Linguistics* 2nd edn Edinburgh University Press.

McKay, H and Tom, A 2000 *Teaching Adult Second Language Learners* Cambridge University Press.

Medgyes, P 1986 Queries from a communicative teacher. *ELT Journal* 40/2 and in Rossner and Bolitho (eds).

Morgan, J and Rinvolucri, M 1986 *Vocabulary* Oxford University Press.

Morris, D 1977 *Manwatching: A Field Guide to Human Behaviour* Jonathan Cape Ltd.

Morris, D 1985 *Bodywatching: A Field Guide to the Human Species* Jonathan Cape Ltd.

Moscowitz, G 1978 *Caring and Sharing in the Foreign Language Classroom* Newbury House.

Muncie, J 2000 Using written teacher feedback in EFL composition classes. *ELT Journal* 54/1.

Murphey, T 1992 *Music and Song* Oxford University Press.

Murphy, R 1994 *English Grammar in Use* 2nd edn Cambridge University Press.

Naiman, N, Froelich, M, Stern, H and Todesco, A 1978 The good language learner. *Research in Education* series, no. 7, Ontario Institute for Studies in Education.

Nattinger, J 1988 Some current trends in vocabulary teaching. In Carter and McCarthy (eds).

Nattinger, J and DeCarrico, J 1992 *Lexical Phrases and Language Teaching* Oxford University Press.

Newton, C 1999 Phonemic script – the pros and cons. *English Teaching Professional* 12.

Nunan, D 1988a *Syllabus* Design Oxford University Press.

Nunan, D 1988b *The Learner-Centred Curriculum* Cambridge University Press.

Nunan, D 1989a *Designing Tasks for the Communicative Classroom* Cambridge University Press.

Nunan, D 1989b A client-centred approach to teacher development. *ELT Journal* 43/2.

Nuttall, C 1996 *Teaching Reading Skills in a Foreign Language* Macmillan Heinemann.

O'Connor, J and Fletcher, C 1989 *Sounds English* Pearson Education Ltd.

O'Dell, F 1992 Helping teachers to use a self-access centre to its full potential. *ELT Journal* 46/2.

O'Neill, R 1972 *English in Situations* Oxford University Press.

O'Neill, R 1982 Why use textbooks? *ELT Journal* 36/2 and in Rossner and Bolitho (eds).

O'Neill, R 1991 The plausible myth of learner-centredness: or the importance of doing ordinary things well. *ELT Journal* 45/4.

Owen, C 1993 Corpus-based grammar and the Heineken effect: lexico-grammatical description for language learners. *Applied Linguistics* 14/2.

Owen, C 1996 Do concordances require to be consulted? *ELT Journal* 50/3.

Painter, L 1999 Homework. *English Teaching Professional* 10.

Paran, A 1996 Reading in EFL: facts and fictions. *ELT Journal* 50/1.

Parrott, M 2000 *Grammar for English Language Teachers* Cambridge University Press.

Pearce, L 1998 Introducing a narrative essay: a painless way to start an academic writing programme. *Modern English Teacher* 7/1.

Pennycook, A 1994 *The Cultural Politics of English as an International Language* Pearson Education Ltd.

Pennycook, A 1998 *English and the Discourse of Colonialism* Routledge.

Phillipson, R 1992 *Linguistic Imperialism* Oxford University Press.

Phillipson, R 1996 Linguistic imperialism: African perspectives. *ELT Journal* 50/2.

Phillipson, R 1999 Voice in global English: unheard chords on Crystal loud and clear. *Applied Linguistics* 20/2.

Pickard, N 1996 Out-of-class language learning strategies. *ELT Journal* 50/2.

Pilger, J 1998 *Hidden Agendas* Vintage.

Pimsleur, P 1966 *Pimsleur Aptitude Test Battery* Harcourt, Brace and World.

Pinker, S 1994 *The Language Instinct* Penguin.

Pinker, S 1999 *Words and Rules* Weidenfeld and Nicolson.

Piper, A 1987 Helping learners to write: a role for the word processor. *ELT Journal* 41/2.

Plumb, K 1994 Teacher development: the experience of developing within a peer-group. *IATEFL Teacher Development SIG Newsletter* 25.

Porte, G 1995 Writing wrongs: copying as a strategy for underachieving EFL writers. *ELT Journal* 49/2.

Prabhu, N 1987 *Second Language Pedagogy* Oxford University Press.

Prodromou, L 1992 *Mixed Ability Classes* Prentice Hall.

Prodromou, L 1995 The backwash effect: from testing to teaching. *ELT Journal* 49/1.

Prodromou, L 1997a Global English and the octopus. *IATEFL Newsletter* 135.

Prodromou, L 1997b From Corpus to octopus. *IATEFL Newsletter* 137.

Puchta, H and Schratz, M 1993 *Teaching Teenagers* Pearson Education Ltd.

Pulverness, A 1995 Cultural studies, British studies and EFL. *Modern English Teacher* 4/2.

Quirk, R and Widdowson, H 1985 *English in the World. Teaching and Learning the Language and Literatures* Cambridge University Press in association with the British Council.

Rajagopalan, K 1999 Of EFL teachers, conscience, and cowardice. *ELT Journal* 53/3.

Rampton, M 1990 Displacing the native speaker: expertise, affiliation and inheritance. *ELT Journal* 44/2.

Reid, J 1987 The learning style preferences of ESL students. *TESOL Quarterly* 21/1.

Reilly, V and Ward, S 1997 *Very Young Learners* Oxford University Press.

Revell, J and Norman, S 1997 *In Your Hands: NLP in ELT* Saffire Press.

Richards, J and Rodgers, T 1986 *Approaches and Methods in Language Teaching* Cambridge University Press.

Richards, K 1992 Pepys into a TEFL course. *ELT Journal* 46/2.

Ridgeway, T 2000 Listening strategies – I beg your pardon? *ELT Journal* 54/2.

Rinvolucri, M 1983 Writing to your students *ELT Journal* 37/1.

Rinvolucri, M 1995 Language students as letter writers. *ELT Journal* 49/2.

Rinvolucri, M 1996 Letter to Craig Thaine. *The Teacher Trainer* 10/2.

Rinvolucri, M 1998 Mistakes. *Modern English Teacher* 7/3.

Rinvolucri, M and Davies, P 1995 *More Grammar Games* Cambridge University Press.

Roach, P 1991 *English Phonetics and Phonology* Cambridge University Press.

Rogers, A 1996 *Teaching Adults* Open University Press.

Rogers, C 1994 *Freedom to Learn* 3rd edn Merrill.

Rogers, J 1977 *Adults Learning* 2nd edn The Open University Press.

Rose, J 1997 Mixed ability – an 'inclusive' classroom. *English Teaching Professional* 3.

Rossner, R 1982 Talking shop: a conversation with Caleb Gattegno. *ELT Journal* 36/4.

Rossner, R and Bolitho, R (eds) 1990 *Currents of Change in English Language Teaching* Oxford University Press.

Rost, M 1990 *Listening in Language Learning* Pearson Education Ltd.

Roszak, T 1996 Dumbing us down. *The New Internationalist* 286.

Rubin, J and Thompson, I 1982 *How to be a More Successful Language Learner* Heinle and Heinle.

Rundell, M 1995 The word on the street. *English Today* 11/3.

Rundell, M 1998 Recent trends in English pedagogical lexicography. *International Journal of Lexicography* 11/4.

Saville, N and Hargreaves, P 1999 Assessing speaking in the revised FCE. *ELT Journal* 53/1.

Scharle, A and Szabo, A 2000 *Learner Autonomy* Cambridge University Press.

Schmidt, R 1990 The role of consciousness in second language learning. *Applied Linguistics* 11/2.

Scott, A and Ytreborg, L 1990 *Teaching English to Children* Pearson Education Ltd.

Scott, M, Carioni, L, Zanatta, M, Bayer, E and Quintilhana, T 1984 Using a 'standard exercise' in teaching reading comprehension. *ELT Journal* 38/2.

Scrivener, J 1994a PPP and after. *The Teacher Trainer* 8/1.

Scrivener, J 1994b *Learning Teaching* Macmillan Heinemann.

Scrivener, J 1996 ARC: a descriptive model for classroom work on language. In Willis, D and Willis, J (eds).

Seedhouse, P 1995 Needs analysis and the general English classroom. *ELT Journal* 49/1.

Seedhouse, P 1999 Task-based interaction. *ELT Journal* 53/3.

Sharwood-Smith, M 1981 Consciousness-raising and the second language learner. *Applied Linguistics* 2/2.

Shemesh, R and Waller, S 2000 *Teaching English Spelling.* Cambridge University Press.

Sinclair, J 1991 *Corpus, Concordance, Collocation* Oxford University Press.

Sinclair, J and Renouf, A 1988 A lexical syllabus for language learning. In Carter, R and McCarthy, M (eds).

Skehan, P 1998 *A Cognitive Approach to Language Learning* Oxford University Press.

Skinner, B 1957 *Verbal Behaviour* Appleton.

Skinner, B and Austin, R 1999 Computer conferencing – does it motivate EFL students? *ELT Journal* 53/4.

Sperling, D 1998 *Dave Sperling's Internet Guide* 2nd edn Pearson Education Ltd.

Stempleski, S and Tomalin, B 1989 *Video in Action* Pearson Education Ltd.

Stevick, E 1996 *Memory, Meaning and Method. Some Psychological Perspectives on Language Learning* Heinle and Heinle.

Sunderland, J (ed) 1994 *Exploring Gender: Questions and Implications for English Language Teaching* 2nd edn Prentice Hall.

Swain, M 1985 Communicative competence: some roles of comprehensible input and comprehensible output in development. In Gass, S and Madde, C (eds) *Input in SLA* Newbury House.

Swan, M 1985 A critical look at the communicative approach (1). *ELT Journal* 39/1 and in Rossner and Bolitho (eds).

Swan, M 1994 Design criteria for pedagogic language rules. In Bygate, Tonkyn and Williams (ed).

Swan, M 1995 *Practical English Usage* 2nd edn Oxford University Press.

Sweeney, P 1998 Multimedia madness. *IATEFL Issues* 144.

Tannen, D 1990 *You Just Don't Understand: Women and Men in Conversation* Virago.

Tanner, R 1992 Errorplay. *The Teacher Trainer* 6/2.

Teeler, D 2000 *How to use the Internet in ELT* Pearson Education Ltd.

Thaine, C 1996a Dealing with timetabling on second language teacher training courses. *The Teacher Trainer* 10/1.

Thaine, C 1996b Letter to Mario Rinvolucri. *The Teacher Trainer* 10/3.

Thornbury, S 1991a Metaphors we work by: EFL and its metaphors. *ELT Journal* 45/3.

Thornbury, S 1991b Watching the whites of their eyes: the use of teaching-practice logs. *ELT Journal* 45/2.

Thornbury, S 1998 The lexical approach: a journey without maps? *Modern English Teacher* 7/4.

Thornbury, S 1999a *How to Teach Grammar* Pearson Education Ltd.

Thornbury, S 1999b Lesson art and design. *ELT Journal* 53/1.

Thornbury S 2000 A Dogma for ELT. *IATEFL Issues* 153.

Thorp, D 1991 Confused encounters: differing expectations in the EAP classroom. *ELT Journal* 45/2.

Tice, J 1991 The textbook straitjacket. *Practical English Teaching* 11/3.

Toledo, P 1998 'Howl' - posting on the N & V-L Listerv (N & V-L Digest no 423), reprinted as *A modest proposal revised* in ELT News and Views 6/1 1999 – information at www.eayrs.com.

Tomlinson, B (ed) 1998 *Materials Development in Language Teaching* Cambridge University Press.

Tomlinson, B 1999 Developing criteria for materials evaluation. *IATEFL Issues* 147.

Tribble, C 1997 *Writing* Oxford University Press.

Tribble, C and Jones, G 1997 *Concordances in the classroom* Athelstan Publications.

Tudor, I 1993 Teacher roles in the learner-centred classroom. *ELT Journal* 47/1.

Underhill, A 1989 Process in humanistic education. *ELT Journal* 43/4.

Underhill, A 1991 Teacher development. *IATEFL Teacher Development SIG* Newsletter 17.

Underhill, A 1992 The role of groups in developing teacher self-awareness. *ELT Journal* 46/1.

Underhill, A 1994 *Sound Foundations* Macmillan Heinemann.

Underwood, M 1989 *Teaching Listening* Pearson Education Ltd.

Upshur, J and Turner, C 1995 Constructing rating scales for second language tests. *ELT Journal* 49/1.

Ur, P 1981 *Discussions that Work* Cambridge University Press.

Ur, P 1996 *A Course in Language Teaching* Cambridge University Press.

Van Ek, J and Trim, J 1998 *Threshold 1990* Cambridge University Press.

Van Ek, J and Trim, J 1999 *Waystage 1990* Cambridge University Press.

Van Ek, J and Trim, J 2000 *Vantage* Cambridge University Press.

Vanderplank, R 1988 The value of teletext sub-titles in language learning. *ELT Journal* 42/4.

Vanderplank, R 1996 Really active viewing with teletext subtitles and closed captions. *Modern English Teacher* 5/2.

Wadden, P and McGovern, S 1991 The quandary of negative class participation: coming to terms with misbehaviour in the language classroom. *ELT Journal* 45/2.

Walker, C 1998 Books on reading. *ELT Journal* 52/2.

Wallace, C 1992 *Reading* Oxford University Press.

Wallace, M 1998 *Action Research for Language Teachers* Cambridge University Press.

Warschauer, M and Healey, D 1998 Computers and language learning: an overview. *Language Teaching* 31.

Watcyn Jones, P 1997 *Top-class Activities* Penguin.

Watson, J and Raynor, R 1920 Conditioned emotional reactions. *Journal of Experimental Psychology* 3/1.

Weir, C 1993 *Understanding and Developing Language Tests* Prentice Hall.

Wells, J 2000 *Longman Pronunciation Dictionary* Pearson Education Ltd.

West 1953 *A General Service List of English Words* Longman.

Wharton, S 1998 Teaching language testing on a pre-service TEFL course. *ELT Journal* 52/2.

White, R and Arndt, V 1991 *Process Writing* Pearson Education Ltd.

Wicksteed, K 1998 Where next for the National Curriculum? *The Linguist.*

Widdowson, H 1985 Against dogma: a reply to Michael Swan. *ELT Journal* 39/3 and in Rossner and Bolitho (eds).

Wilkins, D 1976 *Notional Syllabuses* Oxford University Press.

Williams, A, Calow, D, and Higham N 1999 *Digital Media, Rights and Licences* (2nd edn) Sweet & Maxwell.

Williams, M and Burden, R 1997 *Psychology for Language Teachers* Cambridge University Press.

Willing, K 1987 *Learning Styles in Adult Migrant Education* Adult Migrant Education Programme: Adelaide.

Willis, D 1990 *The Lexical Syllabus* Collins.

Willis, D 1996 Accuracy, fluency and conformity. In Willis, J and Willis, D (eds).

Willis, D and Willis, J 1988–1989 *The Collins COBUILD English Course* Collins.

Willis, J 1994 Task-based language learning as an alternative to PPP. *The Teacher Trainer* 8/1.

Willis, J 1996 *A Framework for Task-Based Learning* Pearson Education Ltd.

Willis, J and Willis, D (eds) 1996 *Challenge and Change in Language Teaching* Macmillan Heinemann.

Wilson, K 1997 *Fastlane Teacher's Book 1* Pearson Education Ltd.

Windeatt S, Hardisty, D, and Eastment D 1999 *The Internet.* Oxford University Press.

Woodfield, H and Lazarus, E 1998 Diaries: a reflective tool on an INSET language course. *ELT Journal* 52/4.

Woodward, T 1993 Changing the basis of pre-service TEFL training in the UK. *IATEFL Teacher Training SIG* Newsletter 13.

Woodward, T 1995 Pair and groupwork – confessions of ignorance. *The Teacher Trainer* 9/1.

Wray, A 1999 Formulaic language in learners and native speakers. *Language Teaching* 32/4.

Wright, A 1984 *1000+ Pictures for Teachers to Copy* Pearson Education Ltd.

Wright, A and Haleem, S 1991 *Visuals for the Language Classroom* Longman.

Wright, T 1987 *Roles of Teachers and Learners* Oxford University Press.

Yule, G, Mathis, T, and Hopkins, M 1992 On reporting what was said. *ELT Journal* 46/3.

Zülküf Altan, M 1995 Culture in EFL contexts – classroom and coursebooks. *Modern English Teacher* 4/2.

Subject index

Note: references to figures are indicated as, for example, 85f.

accent 7
accuracy 104–7
acquisition 37, 69, 71, 72, 76
action research 344–7, 345f, 352
adjectives 22
adolescent learners 37, 38–9, 54 (*see also* learners)
adult learners 37, 40–1, 54 (*see also* learners)
adverbs 22
affective filter 74–5, 88, 89, 90, 96
alveolar plosives 30
ambiguity 42
American English 6–7, 32
anaphoric reference 26
antonyms 18
appropriacy 24–5, 36, 133, 136, 341–2
aptitude 41, 54
ARC (Authentic use, Restricted use, Clarification, and focus) 83 (*see also* methodology)
archetypal utterances 21
aspiration 30
assessing student performance (*see also* feedback; testing)
    comments 101
    global assessment scales 329–30
    marks and grades 101–2, 330–1
    production activities 249–50
    records of achievement(ROAs) 104
    reports 102
    student self-assessment 102–4, 113
    teachers assessing students 59–60, 100–2
assimilation 32, 197–8
atmosphere 89, 133, 242
audio tapes 228–30, 231–2, 235–7, 238–41, 245 (*see also* listening)
Audio-lingualism 79–80, 97 (*see also* methodology)
Australian English 7

BBC English 7
behaviour (*see* problem behaviour)
Behaviourism 68–70, 76
boards (black/white) 137–9, 138f, 139f
boredom 124, 127, 208
Business English 10

cataphoric reference 26
channel 25
child learners 37, 38, 54, 72 (*see also* learners)
chunking 21, 26, 91–2

classrooms
    anglicised names 89, 133
    atmosphere 89, 133, 242
    and motivation 53
    for young children 38
clichés 20
CLL *see* Community Language Learning
cloze procedures 220–1, 323–4, 334
CLT *see* Communicative Language Teaching
code of conduct 127–8, 132, 133 (*see also* problem behaviour)
collocations 20–1
communication continuum 85f
Communicative Language Teaching (CLT) 84–6, 96, 98, 135 (*see also* methodology)
Community Language Learning (CLL) 88, 98 (*see also* methodology)
competence 13
comprehension tasks 207–8, 213, 215–26, 233–42
computers 145, 150, 153 (*see also* Internet)
    as reference tool 146–7, 146f, 153, 171, 175–7, 182
    teaching and testing programs 147–8, 147f
    word processors 110, 150, 260–1, 268
concordancing packages 175–7, 182
conditioning 68–70, 76
connotations 19
consonants 30, 31f
corpus *see* language corpora
correction *see* errors; feedback; marks and grades
coursebooks 295 (*see also* syllabuses)
    assessment criteria 301–2, 306
    choosing 301–4
    evaluation 301, 302–4, 307
    pictures and images 135
    using or not 304–6, 306f, 307
Cuisenaire rods 89, 141, 141f, 152, 194
cultural issues
    coursebooks 306
    gesture 34, 34f, 178
    groupwork 125
    learner autonomy 341–2
    learning behaviour 42
    methodology 93–6, 98
    sociocultural rules 247
    visual aids 136, 282
curriculum design 295, 306

debates 273, 281

dictionaries
    bilingual 168, 171–2, 182
    CD-ROM 146, 153
    monolingual (MLDs) 168–9, 171, 172–3, 182
    on-line 146
    phonemic symbols 185–6
    production 170–1
    pronunciation 36
    reference 169–70, 171
    training to use 171–3
discourse 25–7, 36, 246
discourse markers 14–15
discovery learning 75–6, 77, 96
discussion 272–4, 278–9, 281
displacement activities 34
drills 134–5, 143–4

EAP (English for Academic Purposes) 10
echoing 35
elision 32, 197–8
ellipsis 14, 241–2
e-mail 148, 153, 247–8, 261, 268 (*see also* Internet)
English for Academic Purposes (EAP) 10
English for Science and Technology (EST) 10
English for Specific Purposes (ESP) 10, 11, 259
English language
    accent 7
    American 6–7, 32
    appropriate models 8–9, 11
    Australian 7
    future of 5–6
    general and specific 9–10
    as lingua franca 1, 2–4
    numbers of speakers 1–2, 10
    position in the world 4–5, 10
    three circles 8, 8f
    varieties of 6–8
enthusiasm 128
errors 99, 133 (*see also* accuracy; feedback; fluency)
    developmental 100
    L1 interference 99–100
    recording 108–9
ESA (Engage, Study, Activate) 84 (*see also* methodology)
ESP (English for Specific Purposes) 10, 11, 259
EST (English for Science and Technology) 10
examinations *see* testing
exophoric reference 26

facial expression 33–4
feedback 59–60, 99, 112, 113 (*see also* assessing student performance)

365

Author index